Samuel Colt

Samuel Colt Arms, Art, and Invention

Edited by **Elizabeth Mankin Kornhauser**

Herbert G. Houze

With essays and entries by
**Carolyn C. Cooper and
Elizabeth Mankin Kornhauser**

Yale University Press, New Haven and London

in association with the

Wadsworth Atheneum Museum of Art

Published in conjunction with the exhibition *Samuel Colt: Arms, Art, and Invention*, organized by the Wadsworth Atheneum Museum of Art, Hartford, Conn.

Wadsworth Atheneum Museum of Art
May 6, 2006–January 7, 2007

Designed by Wynne Patterson
Set in TheMix and TheSans type by Aardvark Type
Printed in China by Oceanic Graphic Printing, Inc.
Digital photography by Allen Phillips

Library of Congress Cataloging-in-Publication Data
Houze, Herbert G.
  Samuel Colt : arms, art, and invention / Herbert G. Houze ; edited by Elizabeth Mankin Kornhauser, with essays and entries by Carolyn C. Cooper and Elizabeth Mankin Kornhauser.
      p. cm.
  Includes bibliographical references and index.
  ISBN-13: 978-0-300-11133-0 (hardcover : alk. paper)
  ISBN-10: 0-300-11133-9 (hardcover : alk. paper)
  ISBN-13: 978-0-918333-22-3 (pbk. : alk. paper)
  ISBN-10: 0-918333-22-9 (pbk. : alk. paper)
  1. Colt firearms—Exhibitions. 2. Colt, Samuel, 1814–1862. I. Title: Arms, art, and invention. II. Cooper, Carolyn C., 1934– III. Kornhauser, Elizabeth Mankin, 1950– IV. Wadsworth Atheneum Museum of Art. V. Title.
TS532.2.U62H35 2006
683.40092—dc22   2005024430

10 9 8 7 6 5 4 3 2 1

Cover illustrations: *(front)* New Model Pocket Pistol, 1863 (cat. 113); *(back)* George Catlin, *Catlin the Artist Shooting Buffalos with Colt's Revolving Pistol*, 1855 (detail, cat. 146)

Frontispiece: Royal Porcelain Manufactury, Berlin, Prussia. *Portrait of Samuel Colt*, 1855. Lithopane. Wadsworth Atheneum Museum of Art, Bequest of Elizabeth Hart Jarvis Colt, 1905

Page x: Unknown artist, *View of the Colt Factory from Dutch Point or Little River*, 1857 (detail, cat. 158)

Page 16: Unknown photographer, *Samuel Colt*, ca. 1854–56. Daguerreotype, 4 ¾ x 3 ½ in. Wadsworth Atheneum Museum of Art, Gift of Mrs. Henry K. W. Welch, 1944.13

Page 202: George Catlin, *Mid-Day Halt on the Rio Trombutas, Brazil*, 1854 (detail, cat. 144)

Contents

Willard Holmes   vi

Foreword

Herbert G. Houze   viii

Elizabeth Mankin Kornhauser   ix

Acknowledgments

Carolyn C. Cooper   1

A Connecticut Yankee Courts the World

Herbert G. Houze   17

Samuel Colt: Arms, Art, and Invention

Note for the Reader   19

Samuel Colt: Arms, Art, and Invention   20

The Development of Firearms up to Samuel Colt's Time   22

From Navigator to Arms Designer, 1814–1836   37

The Paterson Era, 1836–1841   54

Samuel Colt in New York, 1841–1846   65

Hartford and Success   78

The Emergence of the Metallic Cartridge Era   115

Counterfeits, Infringements, and Competitors   123

The Memorial Collection Assembled by Elizabeth Hart Jarvis Colt   157

Samuel Colt's South Meadows Armory   171

Samuel Colt and the World   183

Epilogue: No New Thing Under the Sun   200

Elizabeth Mankin Kornhauser   203

George Catlin and the Colt Firearms Series

Appendix One   246

Colt Family Tree

Appendix Two   248

Patents, Patent Reissues, and Caveats Issued to Samuel Colt and Elisha K. Root

Glossary of Commonly Used Descriptive or Technical Words   251

Selected Bibliography   252

Index   254

Foreword

Of all those associated with the long history of the Wadsworth Atheneum, Samuel Colt is surely the most widely known, not only in America but around the world. This publication, like the exhibition that accompanies it, offers the public the opportunity to gain new insights into Colt's astounding success as an inventor, industrialist, and self-promoter in the America of the nineteenth century. It also illuminates the nature of the Atheneum's collection of firearms, consisting of Samuel Colt's personal collection and the memorial collection assembled immediately after his death by his widow, Elizabeth Hart Jarvis Colt. Elizabeth Colt bequeathed this combined collection, the finest of its kind in existence, along with more than six hundred works of art, to the museum in 1905. Also included in this exhibition and publication are nearly fifty additional firearms originally belonging to Samuel Colt and now in the Museum of Connecticut History, Hartford. We are extremely grateful to that institution for its generous participation in this project.

Herbert G. Houze, the principal author of the catalogue, has devoted decades to the study of Samuel Colt's life and the precision manufacturing company that transformed American industry. He presents an authoritative study of Colt's evolution as an inventor and industrialist, along with a brief history of firearms and meticulously detailed entries devoted to the pieces themselves.

Elizabeth Mankin Kornhauser, the Krieble Curator of American Painting and Sculpture at the Wadsworth Atheneum, provides a revealing essay on the innovative marketing techniques developed by Samuel Colt. She focuses on the close personal relationship between Colt and the celebrated painter of Native Americans, George Catlin, as much a showman as the arms manufacturer himself. Dr. Kornhauser demonstrates how a series of paintings Colt commissioned from Catlin—four of them recently acquired by the Wadsworth Atheneum—formed the basis of an advertising campaign that promoted a romantic and heroic view of Colt firearms in use.

Carolyn C. Cooper, a research affiliate and lecturer in the Department of Economics at Yale University, offers the reader an insightful perspective on Samuel Colt as a path-breaking industrialist and entrepreneur within the context of nineteenth-century industrial history.

Samuel Colt's personal connection to the Wadsworth Atheneum was tangential but not insignificant. In 1858, four years before his death, he was the largest donor to a subscription fund to purchase marbles and plaster casts from the Rome studio of Hartford sculptor Edward Sheffield Bartholomew. Subsequently Colt's name headed the list of subscribers to the museum's "Statuary Room" to house this collection.

Elizabeth Colt's role at the Atheneum was much greater. She became one of the first American women to patronize leading American artists and assembled a notable private paintings gallery at Armsmear, the Colt mansion. She was also a leader of the Art Society of Hartford, forerunner of the Hartford Art School, which helped to revive the Atheneum in 1886 after the museum's gallery had been forced to close for lack of funds. Elizabeth Colt joined others in the society to pay for opening the museum two days a week, free of charge, and then contributed to a capital campaign that raised over $400,000 to renovate and expand the Atheneum and its associated institutions, which reopened in 1893.

At her death, in addition to the fine art and firearms, Mrs. Colt bequeathed $50,000 to the Atheneum to build a new wing to the museum, the Colt Memorial, where her collections could be exhibited. Two years later, in 1907, the building was designed by the New York architect Benjamin Wistar Morris in conjunction with the much larger Junius Spencer Morgan Memorial, a gift of the Hartford-born financier J. Pierpont Morgan in memory of his father. The Colt Memorial, a granite and marble structure in the Tudor Revival style, opened in November 1910. There Mrs. Colt's collection of American landscape paintings—among them works by Thomas Cole, Frederic Church, Sanford R. Gifford, and John Frederick Kensett—furniture, sculpture, glass, ceramics, jewelry, metalwork, and the firearms could be seen by the public for the first time.

It was not until 1961 that the museum presented a major exhibition devoted to Colt firearms, *Samuel Colt Presents: A Loan Exhibition of Presentation Percussion Colt Firearms,* organized by Larry Wilson, who also wrote the catalogue. This show consisted of Colt presentation pieces borrowed from collections in the United States and abroad. The Atheneum's collection, which had not been seen for a number of years, was displayed separately in the Armsmear library, which was at that time installed in the Colt Memorial. With the opening of the reconstructed Wadsworth and Colt buildings in 1969, a portion of the firearms collection was on view for a decade in the Colt Memorial until plans for another renovation of the space sent them back to long-term storage. In 1996 the Atheneum produced a comprehensive exhibition devoted to the lives and collecting of the Colts in all spheres, *Sam and Elizabeth: Legend and Legacy of Colt's Empire,* organized by William N. Hosley, Jr., the museum's Richard Koopman Curator of American Decorative Arts. Selected firearms were again on display, supplemented with pieces from the Museum of Connecticut History and other lenders. The present exhibition and publication mark the first time that the Wadsworth Atheneum has thoroughly documented its world-famous collection of Colt firearms.

We are extremely grateful to the sponsors of the publication and the show, including Bonhams & Butterfields, David Grunberg and the Colt Collectors Association, Inc., and Sovereign Bank. As in the past, Yale University Press has been an invaluable partner in making this handsome publication possible.

We hope that all those who see the exhibition and read this publication will gain a new insight into the life of the brilliant and flamboyant inventor who became a giant in America's industrial revolution.

Willard Holmes
Director
Wadsworth Atheneum Museum of Art

Acknowledgments

I wish to express my sincerest thanks to Willard Holmes, director of the Wadsworth Atheneum Museum of Art, for the opportunity to work on this project. His faith in my abilities is very much appreciated.

During the course of preparing this catalogue numerous members of the Wadsworth Atheneum's staff were of assistance. Among them, Linda Roth, Maura Heffner, Mary Schroeder, Edd Russo, and Steve Winot were particularly helpful in providing information as well as encouragement.

The project would not have progressed so easily had it not been for four other members of the museum's staff. Elizabeth Mankin Kornhauser not only shepherded the preparation of this catalogue but also contributed an important essay discussing Samuel Colt's involvement in the arts. Adria Patterson carefully supplied me with a steady flow of data from the museum that enabled checklists and other documents to be updated regularly. Allen Phillips, assisted by Tim Phillips, designed a system for photographing the objects to their best advantage and then produced a truly stunning series of images that are reproduced on the pages of this volume. Jack Tracz was absolutely indispensable in locating objects and other materials in the museum's Colt Collection. Had it not been for his efforts, this catalogue would be far less comprehensive.

The participation of the Museum of Connecticut History would not have been possible without the enthusiastic support of its director, Dean Nelson, whose willingness to share material from his collections has made a valuable contribution to the exhibition.

The assistance of the Buffalo Bill Historical Center in Cody, Wyoming, and of Derek Povah and Ronald C. Romanella in loaning items from their collections is also gratefully acknowledged.

As is the case with any project of this kind, considerable research was necessary in preparing the essays and catalogue entries. The staff of the Connecticut Historical Society generously gave time and services to provide this information. Special thanks must be extended to Barbara Austen, as well as to Judy Johnson and Christie Moraza, who photocopied the seemingly endless stream of documents I laid out for them. Carol Ganze, Claire Murphy, and Jeannie Sherman at the Connecticut State Library are to be commended for their cheerful professionalism.

Thanks must also be extended to Alexander Russell Malcolm, who was instrumental in securing copies of all the relevant letters to and from Samuel Colt that are preserved in the archives of the University of Rhode Island Libraries.

Likewise, the contributions of Morihiro Ogawa of the Arms and Armor Department of the Metropolitan Museum of Art, New York, in translating the tang inscriptions found on the katana blades (cats. 136 and 137), as well as providing the biographical information concerning their makers, are gratefully acknowledged.

The exhibition itself reflects the vision of the Wadsworth Atheneum's designer, Cecil Adams.

Special thanks need to be given to Patricia Fidler, John Long, and Kate Zanzucchi at Yale University Press, who were responsible for the physical creation of this catalogue, and to Wynne Patterson for its superb design.

My extended visits to Hartford were made all the more pleasant by Robert J. Vitale and the staff of the Goodwin Hotel.

Finally, I would be remiss if I did not thank three others who helped make this catalogue possible. My wife, Christine, tolerated with gentle good humor my monopolizing of our computer and the stacks of photocopies spread out here and there. She also provided a dispassionate analysis of my initial drafts. The catalogue greatly benefited from the editorial review of Ann Brandwein, whose keen insights and suggestions are deeply appreciated. Likewise, manuscript editor Janet Wilson further refined the text.

Herbert G. Houze

The work for this book and exhibition has taken many years and, from its inception, has benefited from the generous support of countless individuals. We are indebted to the museum's director, Willard Holmes, who, along with our Board of Trustees, has provided constant support and encouragement. The assistance of the museum's staff over many years has made this project possible. In particular, we are grateful to our curatorial and conservation colleagues, who provided information and conservation treatment; to the Archive and Library staff, who answered endless questions; and to the Education, Exhibition, and Registrar departments.

We set out to produce a scholarly catalogue on the Colt arms collections at the Wadsworth Atheneum and were blessed to have an inspired team of contributors: Herbert Houze, the central author of the book, drew on a lifetime of research and scholarship to provide a detailed and intelligent assessment of Samuel Colt and of the Atheneum's arms collections. His use of primary research materials promises to make this book the most indispensable volume on Colt to date. Carolyn Cooper has drawn on her expertise in the field of nineteenth-century American industrial history to present a sweeping and insightful historical introduction to Samuel Colt and the era in which he lived. The very large manuscript for this book greatly benefited from the editorial work of Ann Brandwein and Mary Ellen Burd. Allen Phillips, head of the Imaging Department at the Atheneum, has provided high-quality digital images of the works in this catalogue.

The catalogue has also benefited from the assistance and generosity of many curators, dealers, librarians, and scholars. We particularly thank Ellen R. Cordes, head of Public Services, Todd P. Kennedy, Public Services assistant, and George A. Miles, Curator of Western Americana, at the Beinecke Rare Book and Manuscript Library, Yale University; Larry Martins, head librarian, Mudd Library, Yale University; Nancy Anderson, Curator of American and British Paintings, National Gallery of Art, Washington, D.C.; William H. Truettner, Senior Curator, Painting and Sculpture, Smithsonian American Art Museum, Washington, D.C.; Gerald Peters, Lily Downing Burke, and Julie Schimmel, Gerald Peters Gallery, Santa Fe and New York; William Reese, William Reese Company, New Haven, Conn.; W. Graham Arader III, Arader Gallery, New York; and Marjorie B. Searl, Chief Curator, Memorial Art Gallery, Rochester, N.Y.

At Yale University Press, thanks are due to Patricia Fidler, publisher, art and architecture books, who very ably guided us through the publication process; Kate Zanzucchi, senior production editor; Janet Wilson, freelance manuscript editor; and Wynne Patterson for her talented design work.

Elizabeth Mankin Kornhauser
Krieble Curator of American Painting and Sculpture

A Connecticut Yankee Courts the World

Carolyn C. Cooper

The good people of this world are very far from being satisfied with each other and my arms are the best peacemakers.
—Samuel Colt, 1852

In one larger-than-life person, Samuel Colt (1814–1862) was an inventor, patentee, entrepreneur, manufacturer, showman, and a supersalesman for his revolvers, working a worldwide market long before the globalization of today's economy. His success was partly due to dogged effort: he pursued his goals despite adversity in his personal life. National and overseas events also helped him by creating new demands for his revolvers frequently enough to reward him with worldly wealth in his short lifetime and lasting fame beyond it. His role in American and world history derives from the firearm he invented, the manufacturing system he adopted to produce it, and his ability to exploit "peacemaking" opportunities that came his way.

Colt energetically spread his revolvers and their manufacturing system in response to conflicts between various "good people" around the world. Conflicts and warfare in America had, of course, occurred earlier between Anglo-Americans and the peoples whose lands they variously bought, stole, and invaded while spreading north, south, and west from the eastern seaboard of the new American republic. Serious wars took place at several points during Samuel Colt's career. These were the Second Seminole Indian War in Florida of 1835–42, the Mexican War of 1846–48 in Texas, California, and Mexico, and the Civil War of 1861–65 throughout the nation. Colt seized the opportunities these wars offered for the production and sale of firearms.

Beginning with the Great Exhibition of the Industry of all Nations at the Crystal Palace in London in 1851, Colt expanded both his market and his production overseas, demonstrating the virtues of the "American system of manufactures" to visitors from "all nations." He opened a factory in London and supplied his "peacemakers" to participants in the Crimean War, 1853–56, and the Sepoy Mutiny in India, 1857–59.

"American System of Manufactures"

The manufacturing system that Colt vigorously expounded in London had begun in New England, where ingenious eighteenth- and nineteenth-century Yankees invented easier ways to make things by machine in an economy where skilled labor was scarce. It became obvious that standardization of shapes and sizes of particular objects made them still easier to make and also made it quicker to assemble the parts that were all precisely alike.

Yankee inventors like Eli Whitney (1765–1825) and Eli Terry (1772–1852) understood this concept, later called "interchangeability," and worked in the first decade of the nineteenth century toward putting it into practice in Connecticut at their respective manufactories for muskets at Whitneyville and clocks at Terryville. In 1815 interchangeability of muskets became an official goal of the U.S. Army Ordnance Department.[1] From then onward, the National Armory at Springfield, Massachusetts, strove to coordinate private arms contractors (including Whitney) in efficient systems for production of military muskets. Tasks in making a gun were divided and subdivided according to the machine processes involved, each worker becoming a specialist and gaining facility in a single process. To ensure uniformity, the Springfield Armory not only sent inspectors to check on the quality of arms produced but also developed and sent the contractors uniform sets of standard gauges for checking dimensions during production.[2]

The goal of interchangeability of parts among all the contractors and the Springfield Armory required much effort and several decades to accomplish, but judged retrospectively it was reached in the late 1840s.[3] That was also when Samuel Colt began, for the second time, to establish a factory to produce his revolver, this time adopting the American system and locating in Hartford, Connecticut. His first factory, in Paterson, New Jersey, had not panned out very well.

Paterson in Panic

Sam Colt's youthful ambition to become a sailor did not outlast his sea voyage to London and Calcutta in his sixteenth year. He shifted his life's goal to becoming a successful manufacturer of the "revolving pistol" he conceived while on board ship. By giving laughing-gas demonstrations on money-raising tours as "Dr. Coult," he was able to hire individual gunsmiths to make examples of his five-shot revolver, to obtain patents in France, England, and the United States (U.S. patent dated 25 February 1836), and to persuade relatives and their friends in New York City to invest enough money to set up a revolver manufactory in Paterson, New Jersey. National events, as well as interpersonal conflicts among the company's principals, militated against the survival of this enterprise. A serious economic "panic" began in 1837; banks failed, and money was very scarce for several years, while Colt's revolvers were both unusual and expensive. Colt attempted to prime the pump of earnings by presenting artistically engraved examples of his new-fangled firearm to influential political and military figures in Washington, D.C., hoping to gain a federal contract. Among the men he wined and dined, Col. William S. Harney became a lifelong friend. President Andrew Jackson accepted a revolver but declined to do more than write him a complimentary thank-you letter. However, Jackson's Indian policy had resulted in a conflict that provided an opportunity for military use of Colt's guns.

Warfare in Florida

A hero of the War of 1812, General Andrew Jackson had led troops in waging the first Seminole Indian War in 1817–18, which pushed the Seminoles in Florida southward to clear the way for white settlers from Georgia, Alabama, and Louisiana, and induced Spain to cede Florida to the United States for $5 million in 1819. As president from 1829 to 1837, Jackson continued to favor removing Indians from Florida for the sake of "development." Congress passed the Indian Removal Act in 1830, ordering all tribes to move west of the Mississippi River. Some Seminole Indian leaders signed a treaty to that effect in 1832, but few Seminoles actually moved from Florida until after long and bloody guerrilla warfare from 1835 to 1842, called the Second Seminole Indian War. It cost the federal forces $20 million and killed 1,500 soldiers. Osceola, a charismatic Seminole warrior of Creek and British parentage, led the fight from 1835 until he was captured by Quartermaster General Thomas S. Jesup, on active duty as commander-in-chief of the federal troops from 1836 to 1839, who tricked Osceola into a parley under a flag of truce in October 1837 (fig. 1).[4]

In February 1838 Colt showed up at Jesup's headquarters in Indian River, Florida, with a hundred revolving rifles and pistols. Colt knew that William Harney was second in command and thought highly of his revolver. Harney favored conciliation with Indians when possible but helped Colt convince General Jesup that revolvers would be advantageous in fighting Seminole guerrillas. Jesup bought fifty of the revolver-rifles for $6,250, and other officers individually bought about a dozen of his revolver-pistols. This was successful direct marketing, but the total output of the Paterson factory was only 5,000 firearms in six years, and sales in general were insufficient to keep it running, despite purchases of 360 revolving carbines and pistols by the Republic of Texas in 1839 and of 200 carbines by the U.S. Army and Navy in 1841 (see cat. 26).[5] The factory closed for good in September 1842, two months before the scheduled hanging of Sam's oldest brother, John, who had killed and dismembered the printer of a textbook that John was writing. He committed suicide in jail to forestall execution.

Seemingly little daunted by these misfortunes, Colt completed developing a waterproof ammunition cartridge made of tinfoil, which won contracts from the Navy and the Revenue Service. Borrowing from Samuel Morse's telegraph the idea of underwater electric transmission lines, he

Carolyn C. Cooper

also developed an electrically detonated mine to be used in a harbor protection system for blowing up enemy ships. He demonstrated it successfully in New York Harbor and on the Potomac River (see "George Catlin and the Colt Firearms Series," fig. 4). Military and congressional observers did not feel moved to adopt the system; John Quincy Adams called it "un-Christian." Colt also ventured into early telegraphy in the vicinity of New York City, with only limited success (see "Samuel Colt in New York, 1841–1846" for a discussion of these ventures). Meanwhile, his revolvers were making their way west.

Outward Bound

The hapless Seminoles and other eastern Native Americans who were variously induced or forced to leave their home territories and trek farther and farther west of the Mississippi were the reluctant front of an outward movement by the general American population. The number of Americans was growing by one-third every ten years, more than tripling from 7,239,881 in 1810 to 23,191,876 in 1850.[6] The vast lands of Thomas Jefferson's Louisiana Purchase, traversed by Lewis and Clark by 1806, beckoned fur-seeking trappers and traders, explorers and cartographers, surveyors and land speculators, miners, missionaries, artists, writers, cardsharps, ranchers, and farm families—adventurers all. "Out west," settlers met different sorts of Indians, some friendly, some hostile. Soldiers came to help them on their way by staving off unfriendly Indians and building forts that served as way stations. Settlers employed lawyers to help organize territories as preliminary to statehood; some became politicians. When they reached the farthest edges of the Purchase, they found Spanish in California and Mexico and British in the Pacific Northwest. This necessitated more action by politicians, lawyers, and sometimes soldiers. In all cases, it was a good idea to carry along a weapon. Thanks to the Paterson factory and Colt's trip to Florida in early 1838, that weapon was frequently a five-shooter revolver, sold and resold westward at escalating prices as its reputation grew.

Texas Troubles

The Mexican government, independent from Spain after 1821, initially welcomed American settlers, such as Stephen Austin and his colony, to its vast northern territory of Texas, where only a few thousand Mexican ranchers lived. It had second thoughts a decade later about the large numbers who came from southern American states, bringing their Protestant churches and their black slaves despite Mexico's restriction of citizenship to Catholics and its 1829 abolition of slavery. By 1835 the white Americans in Texas numbered 30,000, nearly ten times the number of Mexicans, and were chafing at their underrepresentation in the distant Mexican government and its attempts to enforce its laws in Texas. When dictator General Antonio López de Santa Anna arrived with troops in December to discipline the Texans, he met armed rebels, who on 2 March 1836 declared Texas an independent republic. Santa Anna's troops attacked and killed all 187 defenders of an old mission called the Alamo, but suffered 1,500 fatalities doing so. Colorful Tennessean Sam Houston organized the Americans into troops and captured Santa Anna at San Jacinto. Under threat of execution, Santa Anna signed treaties recognizing the Republic of Texas and setting its southern boundary at the Rio Grande. The Mexican government later repudiated these treaties, while successive American presidents, temporizing about the slavery issue, delayed granting Texans' wish to join the United States, leaving Texas as the Lone Star Republic for almost a decade. It attained U.S. statehood on 29 December 1845.

One former volunteer in the Seminole War, Samuel H. Walker (1817–1847), found his way to Texas in 1842, where he joined the continued fighting by Texas units against incursions by Mexican troops and depredations by unruly Indians. As one of the Texas Rangers, who had equipped themselves with unused Paterson revolvers purchased for the Texas Navy, Walker participated in 1844 in a mounted battle with eighty Comanche Indians along a tributary of the Pedernales River. Fifteen Rangers more than overcame the uneven odds, killing or wounding half of the Comanches and gaining fame for Rangers and the revolvers.[7]

Negotiations initiated by expansionist President James K. Polk to buy Mexican-claimed territory from Texas to the Pacific Ocean failed, and Congress declared war on Mexico in April 1846 after Polk sent troops south toward the Rio Grande, provoking Mexican troops to attack them. Americans in California immediately declared independence from Mexico.[8] Samuel Walker, who had enlisted in General Zachary Taylor's regular army in 1845, went with him into Mexico. When he returned to Washington, D.C., in late 1846 to recruit new men for his company, he detoured to advise

Samuel Colt on changes that would improve the revolver-pistol for military use and helped him obtain an order from the Army for a thousand of the redesigned guns—a bigger, more powerful six-shooter with a trigger guard. Walker wanted them in a hurry, as he had to return to the war. He told Colt to ship the revolvers to Veracruz. This order put Colt back into revolver production.

Lacking a factory, Colt looked for a subcontractor who could make the thousand Colt/Walker revolvers in three months. He turned to Eli Whitney, Jr., and his armory superintendent, Thomas Warner.

Whitneyville in 1847

Eli Whitney, Jr., only four years old when his famous father died in early 1825, had taken charge of the Whitney Armory in 1842. As a fresh Princeton graduate, Whitney recognized that he couldn't run the armory without substantial help, so he promptly hired Thomas Warner, the Springfield Armory's highly experienced master armorer, as his superintendent.[9] By late 1846 the Whitney Armory was operating so well that Whitney was able to boast to Colt, "I can make them … as soon as any establishment in the U. States except one of the public armories, and probably sooner since no Factory has machinery as complete as mine." He added, however, "The 1000 cannot be made in 3 months by Any Factory."[10] Nevertheless, he took on the contract, with Thomas Warner supervising, and succeeded in filling the order for the Walker model in six months.[11]

Samuel Walker's own pair of revolvers reached him in August 1847, but he was killed in combat (as was his faithful slave David) in the town of Huamantla on 9 October (see cat. 29).[12] After far-flung battles in California, New Mexico, Texas, and Mexico and the surrender of Mexico City in September 1847, the war officially ended on 2 February 1848 with the Treaty of Guadalupe Hidalgo. It had cost $97 million and 13,000 American deaths, mostly from disease.[13]

Taking Root in Hartford

Late in the summer of 1847, in expectation of a contract from the United States for another thousand of the Colt/Walker revolvers at twenty-five dollars each, Colt took his profit from the Whitneyville contract and the machines for producing the revolvers to Hartford, where he began pro-

Figure 2
Joseph Ropes
American, 1812–1898
View of Hartford to the South, ca. 1854 (detail showing
Colt's factory in downtown Hartford)
Daguerreotype
Museum of Connecticut History,
State Library, Hartford

duction in rented quarters on Pearl Street. The government contract arrived in November. Demand for revolvers also grew with the flow of forty-niners to California after the discovery of gold at Sutter's Mill in 1848, and Colt expanded his works into a larger building on Grove Lane (fig. 2). Like Whitney, he found a very competent mechanician to run his factory—Elisha K. Root. He had invented and built a series of machines at the Collins Company in Canton, Connecticut, that made axes much better and faster than blacksmiths could.[14] Root had turned down an offer to become master armorer at the Springfield Armory, but in late 1848, when Samuel Colt offered him twice his salary at Collins, he accepted the job.

Colt's well-placed confidence in Root's mechanical and supervisory capability meant that Colt could concentrate on marketing his revolvers. He toured Europe with Samuel Morse, making friends with potential customers in high positions. When Prince Albert and the Society of Arts in London held the first world's fair in 1851, Colt put up an exhibit, and the world came to see it.

Carolyn C. Cooper

The Crystal Palace

The bustling crowds at the Crystal Palace (fig. 3), built in Hyde Park for the Great Exhibition of all Nations in 1851, may have paused first at the American exhibit to look at Hiram Powers's marble sculpture *The Greek Slave* (fig. 4), but they stayed to notice more utilitarian American products. Gradually people came to realize that these items represented a mode of production that was much more reliant on labor-saving machines than were the usual English manufactured goods.[15] At Samuel Colt's display of his revolvers (fig. 5), a demonstrator showed how quickly the cylinder turned to bring another bullet into the firing chamber; the elderly Duke of Wellington, a frequent visitor, praised the revolvers to his friends.[16] Colt

Figure 3

H. Bibby

North Transept, Great Exhibition of 1851

Steel engraving

Frontispiece, *Tallis's History and Description of the Crystal Palace and the Exhibition of the World's Industry in 1851,* vol. 3 (London: John Tallis and Co., 1852)

Figure 4

Engraving showing the United States Section
of the Exhibition of the Works of Industry of all
Nations, with display of Hiram Powers's marble
sculpture *The Greek Slave*
Published in the *Illustrated London News,
Exhibition Supplement,* August 1851

Figure 5

Detail of engraving of Samuel Colt's
display at the Exhibition of the
Works of Industry of all Nations
Published in the *Illustrated London
News,* November 1851
Wadsworth Atheneum Museum
of Art

operating special-purpose machines arranged in sequence to shape large numbers of individual parts, checked during production against standardized gauges. Over time, producers of other consumer durables, such as watches, sewing machines, typewriters, bicycles, and automobiles, adopted the American system, which led to the mass production that we now take for granted.[18]

London Factory

Samuel Colt's display of revolvers at the Crystal Palace won such public acclaim and official favor that he was able to lease riverside government property in London and hire an unskilled English workforce—"butchers, clerks, servants, in fact anyone but a gunmaker"—to make revolvers (fig. 6).[19] Machines and mechanics from Hartford arrived to train the workers in machine operation, and the factory went into production in 1853. It employed boys and girls for two or three shillings and men for three to eight or even as much as twelve shillings a day and provided them with such unusual amenities as a bathroom and a reading room with newspapers.[20]

was invited to speak at the prestigious Institution of Civil Engineers, where he not only talked up his invention but also emphasized his reliance on machinery

> to the extent of about eight-tenths of the whole cost of construction of these firearms, [having found] that with hand labour it was not possible to obtain that amount of uniformity, or accuracy in the several parts, which is so desirable, and also because he could not otherwise get the number of arms made, at anything like the same cost as by machinery. Thus he obtains uniformity as well as cheapness in the production of the various parts, and when a new piece is required, a duplicate can be supplied with greater accuracy and less expense, than could be done by the most skilful manual labour.[17]

The way Colt and other American exhibitors at the Crystal Palace made things came to be called "the American system of manufactures," because it was different from the mode of production in other countries at that time. Instead of highly skilled craftsmen, it relied on ordinary workers

Figure 6

Letterhead of stationery for Colt's London factory, ca. 1853
Colt Collection, Connecticut Historical Society, Hartford

Carolyn C. Cooper

Figure 7
Armory of Colt's Patent Fire Arms
Manufacturing Company
Engraving
"A Day at the Armory of Colt's Patent
Fire Arms Manufacturing Company"
Published in *United States Magazine*
4, no. 3 (March, 1857)

Figure 9 (below)
Forging Shop
Engraving
"A Day at the Armory of Colt's Patent
Fire Arms Manufacturing Company"
Published in *United States Magazine*
4, no. 3 (March 1857)

Figure 8
Armory Proper—First Division
Engraving
"A Day at the Armory of Colt's Patent
Fire Arms Manufacturing Company"
Published in *United States Magazine*
4, no. 3 (March 1857)

Coltsville Factory

Meanwhile, Elisha Root helped build the American system into Colt's very large and final factory on riverside land that Colt had bought at the South Meadows in Hartford (fig. 7). Root designed machines for it, arranged them in efficient sequences, and powered them by large steam engines (figs. 8–9). Completed and running in 1855, the factory far outstripped Colt's other operations.[21] This was the "great arms factory" in which Mark

Twain's Connecticut Yankee said he learned how to "make everything ... all sorts of labor-saving machinery . . . as easy as rolling off a log."[22] Under Root, Colt's factory, in fact, did train later generations of "American system" mechanics, such as Francis A. Pratt and Amos Whitney, who formed the Pratt and Whitney Machine Tool Company in Hartford in 1860.[23]

Between the factory and the river, Colt had a dike built to prevent destruction by another flood like that of 1854. Behind it, besides the factory, a machine shop, and a separate cartridge works, he built worker housing and other social amenities. Charter Oak Hall provided a reading room and also functioned as a place for lectures, exhibitions, dances, and entertainments, as well as the company store selling provisions, medicines, and household items.[24] A brass band "formed among the workmen" gave concerts. Partly to upgrade the musical ability of the band, Colt imported whole families of German willowware workers and set them to work in yet another factory building, making items of furniture from the willow trees that grew on the dike. He housed them in their own "Potsdam Village." Although "Coltsville was first and foremost a place of work," it also included the Colt mansion, called "Armsmear," set in a park. This was a New England mill village with a difference and an international flavor.[25]

English Emulation of the American System

Colt's London venture not only served his own purpose of selling revolvers in Europe but also had far-reaching effects in spreading the American system of manufactures. As a result of the Crystal Palace exhibition and Colt's London factory, parliamentary commissioners visited the Springfield Armory in Massachusetts in 1853 and 1854 to learn about its production system.[26] After they reported, the British government bought complete sets of American metal- and woodworking machinery for manufacturing rifled longarms and established a Springfield-like system at the Royal Small Arms Factory at Enfield near London.[27] They hired Virginian James Burton, former master armorer at the Harpers Ferry National Armory, to run it. Like Colt, he found he needed Americans to help train English workers to run the machines. Since England had pioneered the use of machinery in the eighteenth century and had set the example for other countries of the Western world to follow, including her former colonies in America, this turnabout borrowing of American technology was remarkable.

Crimean War, 1853–56

Part of the British military's interest in upgrading firearms and adopting the American system for making them was due to growing uneasiness about the balance of power among European nations. Great Britain had leagued with Russia, Sweden, Prussia, and Austria-Hungary to fight Napoleon, but after he was finally immured at Saint Helena in 1815, the British had not fought a war for quite some time and were out of practice. While continental European monarchies were putting down internal rebellions, Great Britain was using its energy to industrialize, and getting rich in the process, as the Great Exhibition displayed to all comers. By the 1850s the British no longer assumed the French were enemies, and the Russians were not necessarily friends. In fact, they were suspected of bad intentions in the Balkans and the Middle East, in particular of wanting the Black Sea for themselves, as they had gone to war for it several times in previous centuries.

As sometimes happens, the Crimean War began with a seemingly small local issue: Russian Orthodox and French Catholic monks in Palestine (then part of the Ottoman Empire) quarreled, with violence, over who should have precedence at Christian shrines there. In response, Russia's Nicholas I and France's Napoleon III disputed which country had the right to protect Christians in the Ottoman Empire. Russian troops invaded Wallachia and Moldavia, Ottoman-controlled principalities bordering the Danube River and the Black Sea.[28] Attempts at diplomacy stopped at the end of November 1853, when a Russian fleet attacked and slaughtered a Turkish squadron at the Black Sea harbor of Sinop. Allied French and British forces, backed up by Austrian forces, helped the Turks drive the Russians out of the Danubian principalities by the end of summer in 1854, but then began preemptive action to forestall future Russian aggression in the area.[29]

Naval and land battles took place in the Baltic, Black, and White Seas, on the Danube, in the Caucasus, and even as far away as Kamchatka, but the war was primarily waged in the Crimea against the Russian naval base at Sevastopol. Hundreds of thousands of troops on both sides were involved, the Russians arriving over long distances by land with largely obsolete smooth-bore muskets, while the Allies arrived by sea with rifles that could shoot four times farther. Major battles took place at the River Alma, Inkerman, and Balaklava before the prolonged siege of Sevastopol finally overcame the Russians in September 1855. Military operations continued elsewhere around the Black Sea for a few months before a cease-fire, and a peace treaty was signed at the end of February 1856. By the end of the war, fighting and disease had killed 256,000 Russians and a total of 252,600 Allies, including (despite Florence Nightingale's heroic efforts) 45,000 English.[30]

Figure 10

Robert Gibb

English, 1845–1932

The Thin Red Line (93rd Highlanders
at Balaclava), 1881

Oil on canvas, 41¾ x 83½ in.

By Kind Permission of DIAGEO, on loan
to the National Museum of Scotland

The war was popular with the British public at first, but opinion changed when stories came home of their soldiers' suffering due to poor planning, tactical and strategic blunders, and confusions of communication, the most famous of which sent "the Charge of the Light Brigade" in the lethally wrong direction. The British press criticized, among other failings, the government's slowness to equip English forces with the Colt revolver. Military historians regard the Crimean War as Britain's most mismanaged war ever.

When the Crimean War broke out in 1853, the factory at Enfield was not yet American-systematized, but Colt's London factory was already under way and conveniently located for sales to the British War Office and to individual Army officers. Colt continually pressed for government contracts, and the British Board of Ordnance bought some 9,000 Colt Navy model revolvers for the Royal Navy, but in a "buy British" move chose the larger-caliber Beaumont-Adams revolver for general issue to the Army

instead of the equally powerful Colt Dragoon revolver. As the war wore on, however, in August 1855 the Board of Ordnance ordered 9,000 more Colt revolvers for the Army. All told, by the end of the war in February 1856 Colt had supplied British Ordnance with about 25,540 of his revolvers and had sold perhaps another 5,000 to 10,000 to individual officers.[31]

Colt also quietly arranged sales of revolvers to Czar Nicholas I through his agent in Belgium. In August 1855, 145 bales of cotton en route to Saint Petersburg from Antwerp were confiscated in neutral Germany because each bale contained twenty-four Colt revolvers and appurtenances. Colt somehow managed to hush it up in England and replace the order to the Russians.[32] The famous painting in Edinburgh Castle of the Argyll and Sutherland Highlanders' "Thin Red Line" at the battle of Balaklava shows a Russian cavalry officer pointing a revolver at the Highlanders (fig. 10).

By the time Samuel Colt and Elizabeth Hart Jarvis were married in Middletown, Connecticut, in June 1856, peace had prevailed for a few months in the Crimea. The happy couple partied in New York City before setting out on a transatlantic voyage, accompanied by a multilingual interpreter as well as the bride's brother and sister. They stayed almost a month in London, then toured through Belgium, the Netherlands, Bavaria, Vienna, and the Tyrol before arriving in Russia, where they spent six weeks. In Saint Petersburg they attended the coronation of Czar Alexander II, whose father, Nicholas I, had died since entertaining Colt in 1854.[33]

Many British troops had returned home to rest. The next year they would be called upon again. Some went directly to India, taking firearms, including revolvers, with them.

Sepoy Mutiny or Indian Rebellion, 1857–59

Even without government purchases, Colt benefited from the "peacekeeping" needs of individual Britons overseas. Officers and civilians headed for colonial outposts of the British Empire eagerly outfitted themselves with Colt Navy revolvers in the event of a dangerous incident. Those in India used the revolvers when embroiled from 1857 to 1859 in the Sepoy Mutiny. During two centuries in India, the British East India Company had evolved from a trading company into a quasi-government ruling over Indian principalities with an army of 257,000 sepoys (Indian soldiers) and 34,000 Europeans, who generally outranked the sepoys. In addition to the discontent of the general populace over British expropriation of native rulers' land and authority, resentments had grown among sepoys against their officers, who were increasingly bringing their families with them from Britain and enjoying privileged lives in segregated cantonments, and against Christian missionaries who denigrated the sepoys' religion. Tensions rose when sepoys were issued new Enfield rifles together with cartridges greased with animal fats that were abhorrent to both Moslems and Hindus.

One day in late March 1857 sepoy Mangel Pande's tension snapped while on parade at Barrackpore. He shot his sergeant major and the adjutant's horse and slashed the adjutant with his sword. He was hanged and his unit disbanded as collective punishment. A few weeks later eighty-five cavalry troopers at Meerut who refused to handle the new cartridges were court-martialed, stripped of their uniforms, sentenced to ten years of hard labor, and shackled. The next day a mob broke into the jail to free them and then rushed to the European cantonment, where they murdered entire families and their servants and set it on fire. The sepoys proceeded to Delhi, where they garnered reluctant support from the Bahadur Shah, the last of the Moghul rulers. Together with another mass uprising, they killed most of the Europeans and Christian Indians there. Retaliation by the British military was ferocious. Wild rumors flew, enflaming vengeance on both sides, as British and Indian women and children were butchered along with men. The rebellion spread and raged in northern parts of India for nearly two years, including an additional massacre at Cawnpore, as well as a siege and countersiege at Lucknow, where the British dug underground to guard against a breakthrough by Indian besiegers' tunnels (fig. 11).

When the British recaptured Delhi in September 1857, they spared the life of the Bahadur Shah, but not of his three sons, who were "implicated in the worst of the atrocities against the British." When they surrendered, the officer in charge, "seizing a Colt revolver . . . shot them dead one by one [and] left them where they fell."[34]

By the spring of 1858, 377 listed rebel leaders were still at large and able to raise forces among disaffected troops and local princes.[35] Loyalties and alliances among Indian factions were fluid; the rebels diminished in number as British and loyal Indian troops captured and killed them. After the rebellion was largely quelled, on 1 November 1858 the British Crown assumed direct governance of India, ending rule by the East India Company and decreeing religious toleration. The Indian Army was prudently reorganized, with a larger proportion of British to native troops, and artillery service restricted to the British. In April 1859, Tantia Topi, "the one man who might have continued to raise a rebel force," was captured and hanged.[36] On 8 July 1859, "Peace was proclaimed throughout India."[37] All told, the mutiny cost "40 million pounds and the lives of 2,034 [British] soldiers in action and another 8,987 from disease or heatstroke" plus untold numbers of murdered civilians and "native casualties."[38]

Colt's Commission to Catlin

When in England in the mid-1850s, Samuel Colt commissioned the famous but down-on-his-luck American artist George Catlin (1796–1872) to make paintings showing Catlin using various models of Colt revolving firearms

Carolyn C. Cooper

Figure 12

Augustus Hoppin, delineator

American, 1828–1896

*Apache Indians Attacking the Train
and Party*

Woodcut

John Russell Bartlett, *Personal Narrative
of Explorations and Incidents in Texas, New Mexico,
California, Sonora, and Chihuahua,*
vol. 2 (New York: D. Appleton & Co., 1854)

in hunting. Colt subsequently used these pictures in testimonial advertisements for his revolvers. Along with his fame as a painter of Native Americans, Catlin is credited in the history of environmental conservation with being a "sportsman" hunter who was "the first American—so far as we know—to suggest the national park idea."[39]

Although the formation of American rod-and-gun clubs for gentlemanly fishing and hunting became vigorous only after the Civil War, precedents had appeared decades earlier, as did books advocating the proper behavior for sportsmanlike hunting. Such sportsmen were not "commercial" or "market" hunters who slaughtered whole flocks of birds together for money, nor were they uncouth "pot" hunters who hunted for food and were glad to shoot birds on the ground rather than in the air, which required skill. Instead, good sportsmen were enjoined to be discriminating about the game they hunted and to seek quality instead of quantity. They were to make sure to kill every animal they shot rather than leave it wounded to suffer. They should eschew such tricks as shooting while lying in a floating "battery" surrounded by duck decoys or "fire hunting" with a light at night, which stunned and confused deer into standing still for easy targets.[40]

If followed, these gentlemanly hunting rules would tend to conserve wildlife and ensure that the sport could continue. They reflected old-world elitist values rather than Jacksonian common-man democracy. The port of entry for most Europeans, New York City and environs, was the habitat of sport hunters who played by these rules, and where laws were passed

early on to protect game birds.[41] Colt and Catlin were familiar with this milieu, yet both of these artistic self-inventors also were in part rebels against it. It is not obvious to which kind of hunter Colt thought Catlin's pictures would sell guns. In any case, they would appeal to the adventurous spirit of anyone interested in the wildlife of exotic places in North and South America. One such place was the Wild West that Catlin already knew and in which Colt now also took a personal interest.

Arizona and the Apaches

Well before the end of the Sepoy Mutiny, Samuel Colt had attained ample capacity at his Coltsville factory and acquired agents overseas to handle foreign sales and collect royalties from licensed foreign factories, and he had closed his London factory. For the United States market, the opening up of large formerly Mexican territories a decade earlier was drawing more Americans westward and into potential conflict with hostile Indians, creating a need for firearms for self-defense. As if to increase this demand, Colt helped form companies for land development and mining in the southernmost part of New Mexico that the United States had bought for $10 million, called the Gadsden Purchase.[42] This was within a large area on both sides of the border where marauding Apache Indians made life constantly risky for everyone—Americans, Mexicans, and other Indians.

A surveying party of the Mexican-United States Boundary Commission was among the many "trains" of horse-drawn wagons that Apaches attacked (fig. 12). The American commissioner, John Russell Bartlett, rode

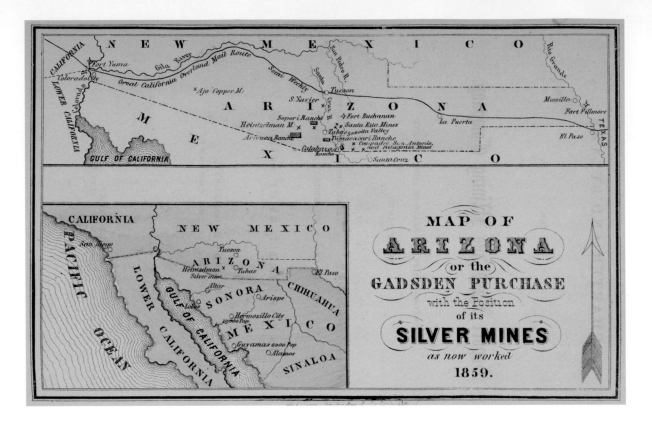

Figure 13

"Map of Arizona or the Gadsden Purchase
with the Position of its Silver Mines as now worked"
Frontispiece, John Russell Bartlett, *Charter and By-Laws of the Sopori Land
and Mining Company* (Providence, R.I.: Knowles, Anthony & Co., 1859)
Western Americana Collection, Beinecke Rare Book and Manuscript Library,
Yale University

Civil War or War Between the States

How did the American Union, cemented among former British colonies in 1787–90, come unglued by 1861? Historians differ in how they weigh economic, cultural, social, and demographic ingredients in the dissolution, but one important contributing factor was surely the speed with which Americans had spread "from sea to shining sea" without pausing for breath and circumspection. Long before this Manifest Destiny had become so manifest, the Founding Fathers established orderly procedures in the 1787 Northwest Ordinance for how and when settlers beyond the boundaries of the original states would be allowed to enjoy the stipulated governmental privileges of Territory status and eventually apply for those of statehood, which constitutionally included voting for two senators per state regardless of population. The ordinance also stipulated that slavery, which was not forbidden in the first thirteen states, would not be allowed in the states to be formed in the Northwest between the Ohio and Mississippi Rivers.[46] Beyond that, it did not look.

By 1820, when people in Maine and Missouri petitioned for statehood, states north of the Mason-Dixon Line had individually abolished slavery; the tally of states allowing or forbidding slavery was equal at eleven to eleven. A proposal in Congress to initiate gradual emancipation of slaves in Missouri upon its becoming a state was defeated in the Senate following a heated debate on the intertwined economic, cultural, and moral issues. Despite the Missouri Compromise that year in Congress, which balanced a "free" Maine against a "slave" Missouri, sectional disputes continued to rise. The rapid pace of settlement in new parts of the continent allowed little rest from the increasingly acrimonious quarrel over whether the "peculiar institution" of the South should spread, or the South should be outvoted in the Senate.

Compromises were repeatedly unmade and reshaped but never solved the problem before violence in Kansas in 1855 and John Brown's insurrection-cum-martyrdom at the Harpers Ferry Armory in 1859 spurred rearrangement of political affiliations, resulting in the emergence of a new party—the Republican—based only in the North. Republican Abraham Lincoln won the presidency, and the Union broke apart. South Carolina led the way by seceding in December 1860; on 7 February 1861 the seven southernmost states formed the Confederate States of America.

with his driver and a passenger in a carriage equipped with ten firearms, including six Colt revolvers, enabling them "in case of necessity, to discharge a round of thirty-seven shots without reloading."[43] Bartlett's years on boundary expeditions from 1850 to 1853 did not dampen his enthusiasm for the potentially prosperous farming and lucrative mining in the "Territory of Arizona or the Gadsden Purchase," even apart from its advantage for the route of a future transcontinental railroad (fig. 13).

Samuel Colt became a charter member of the Sopori Land and Mining Company and the Arizona Land and Mining Company, both incorporated by the state of Rhode Island in June 1859 with identical charters and by-laws and overlapping boards of directors who were mostly important men in Providence.[44] The secretary of both companies was John Russell Bartlett, now secretary of state of Rhode Island. Colt was a director of the Sopori Land and Mining Company. That these companies meant more to Colt than mere stock-market investments is indicated by his donation of funds and books for a library at Tubac, a settlement that was long in Spanish colonial history but at that time short of civic amenities. However, the Gadsden Purchase soon afterward became the Confederate Territory of Arizona, in large part because of Sylvester Mowry, one of Samuel Colt's colleagues in both companies, and the Civil War intervened between prospects and reality.[45]

Figure 14
Unknown artist
Trooper from Company K,
2nd Regiment U.S. Cavalry, ca. 1858–60
Ambrotype photograph
Private collection

April 15, 1861," only a few days after the war began. Colt's Army and Navy revolvers shipped to eleven Confederate destinations in those three and a half months, presumably to fill orders placed earlier, totaled 2,722.[48]

The war lasted far longer than expected, considering how much advantage the Union had over the Confederacy, both in numbers of young men (a ratio of 4.2 to 1) and of firearms (a ratio of 31 to 1).[49] The war was a voracious consumer of both. Major battles involved more than 100,000 troops at a time, leaving the dead and wounded in heaps and the countryside wasted. Colt's Patent Fire Arms Manufacturing Company joined the ranks of contractors producing Special Model 1861 single-shot muzzle-loader rifle-muskets for the U.S. Army until the armory was devastated by fire in February 1864.[50] The war ended in 1865, and the reckoning was made: 620,000 men on both sides had lost their lives—far more than in any other American war—and an estimated $20 billion had been spent killing them.[51]

Samuel Colt did not live to see peacetime. He died in 1862, leaving his wife, Elizabeth Hart Jarvis Colt, with immense wealth. She used it in rebuilding the factory, in constructing memorials to Sam and their son Caldwell, who also died young, and in charitable civic enterprises. Among her many gifts for the benefit of Hartford, she gave the Wadsworth Atheneum a new wing in which to house the firearms, artwork, and souvenirs that she and Samuel had gathered in world travels. From these, the present exhibition retells the story of arms, art, and invention.

Four more joined them after war broke out on 12 April, when Confederate cannons began shelling the federal troops in Fort Sumter at Charleston. "Peacemaking" now depended on firearms and bloodshed between West Point alumni leading blue- and gray-clad soldiers against each other in battle (fig. 14).

How did Sam Colt, a northern Democrat upholding the Union but hating "Black Republicans," disdainful of southern slavery but unwilling to risk the life of any young mechanic in fighting against it, respond to the events of early 1861? From Cuba, where he was on vacation, he wrote to Elisha Root, instructing him to "run the Armory night & day with a double set of hands. . . . Make hay while the sun shines." By 1860 Colt had produced more than 300,000 revolvers, and he certainly was game to produce more.[47] But for whom? One side or the other? Or, as he had done in Europe, for both?

The suspicion that "the Colonel was not averse to doing business with both sides" in the Civil War can be at least partly allayed by a study of shipments from the Colt factory between 25 December 1860 and 2 March 1863. The records show that "the amount of factory shipments south of the Mason-Dixon line was relatively small and they ceased altogether on

Notes

In preparing this essay, Carolyn Cooper gratefully acknowledges help from the suggestions made by Ann Brandwein, the expertise of Robert B. Gordon, and the advice of Howard R. Lamar. They are, of course, blameless for any remaining defects in the essay.

1. The Ordnance Department, established by Congress in 1812 for inspection and distribution of military supplies, took on the additional responsibility in 1815 of overseeing arms production. See Merritt Roe Smith, *Harpers Ferry Armory and the New Technology* (Ithaca, N.Y.: Cornell University Press, 1977), 105–6.
2. The other national armory was at Harpers Ferry, Virginia (now West Virginia). Interarmory coordination was also necessary; Springfield Armory took the lead in this effort. Ibid., 107.

3. Charles H. Fitch, "The Rise of a Mechanical Ideal," *Magazine of American History* 11 (1884): 517.

4. Osceola sickened and died in 1838 in prison at Fort Moultrie in Charleston, South Carolina. George Catlin painted Osceola's portrait during his imprisonment.

5. According to Ellsworth S. Grant, *The Colt Armory: A History of Colt's Manufacturing Company, Inc.* (Lincoln, R.I.: Mowbray Publishing, 1995), 19, the one hundred carbines ordered for the Army cost forty dollars apiece. This is significantly less than the $125 rifles that Jesup bought four years earlier, but still much more expensive than the single-shot muskets that the Springfield Armory and contract makers were producing.

6. The U.S. decennial census showed population increasing by a third every ten years: 7,239,881 in 1810; 9,638,453 in 1820; 12,866,020 in 1830; 17,069,453 in 1840; 23,191,876 in 1850; and 31,443,321 in 1860.

7. Samuel H. Walker to Samuel Colt, 30 November 1846, reprinted in John E. Parsons, ed., *Sam'l Colt's Own Record* (Hartford: Connecticut Historical Society, 1949), 10.

8. The Bear Flag Republic was short-lived; California was admitted to statehood in 1850.

9. Thomas Warner "improved the machinery and introduced the interchange at Whitneyville." Fitch, "Rise of a Mechanical Ideal," 525.

10. Eli Whitney, Jr., to Samuel Colt, 25 December 1846, Eli Whitney Collection, Yale University Manuscripts and Archives.

11. A draft contract with Warner in Colt's handwriting indicates a production schedule of "not less than 120 Pistols" per week. Parsons, ed., *Sam'l Colt's Own Record,* 34.

12. For an account of the battle in which Walker was killed and of the later arrival of the rest of the revolvers for Walker's company, see Waldo E. Rosebush, *Frontier Steel: The Men and Their Weapons* (Appleton, Wis.: C. C. Nelson Publishing Company, 1958), 114–24.

13. James West Davidson, William E. Gienapp, Christine Leigh Heyrman, Mark H. Lytle, and Michael B. Stoff, *Nation of Nations: A Narrative History of the American Republic,* vol. 1 (New York: McGraw-Hill, 1994), 507.

14. Donald R. Hoke, *Ingenious Yankees: The Rise of the American System of Manufactures in the Private Sector* (New York: Columbia University Press, 1990), chap. 3, 102–30.

15. The word "manufacture" derives from the Latin for "hand-making" and changed its meaning when machines were increasingly used.

16. Nathan Rosenberg, *The American System of Manufactures* (Edinburgh: Edinburgh University Press, 1969), 15.

17. Samuel Colt, "On the application of Machinery to the manufacture of Rotating Chambered-Breech Fire-Arms, and the peculiarities of those Arms," *Minutes of Proceedings of the Institution of Civil Engineers,* vol. XI, session 1851–52 (London: Institution of Civil Engineers, 1852), 44–45, quoted in Rosenberg, *American System,* 16. In fact, perfect interchangeability was an elusive goal, but together with other arms makers of his generation who adopted the American system, Colt came closer to it than the first Eli Whitney had done.

18. David A. Hounshell, *From the American System to Mass Production, 1800–1932* (Baltimore: Johns Hopkins University Press, 1984).

19. Howard L. Blackmore, "Colt's London Armoury," in S. B. Saul, ed., *Technological Change: The United States and Britain in the Nineteenth Century* (London: Methuen, 1970), 179.

20. *Household Words* 9, no. 218 (27 May 1854): 354, 356.

21. At the South Meadows factory, "The motive power is supplied by five different engines, having an aggregate of nine hundred horse power." J. Leander Bishop, *A History of American manufactures from 1608 to 1860,* vol. 2 (Philadelphia: Edward Young & Co., 1864), 739. Colt's London factory ran on one 30-horsepower engine. *Household Words,* 356; Joseph G. Rosa, *Colonel Colt, London: The History of Colt's London Firearms, 1851–1857* (London: Arms & Armour Press, 1976), 55, citing *The Expositor,* 29 October 1853.

22. Mark Twain, *A Connecticut Yankee in King Arthur's Court* (1889; reprint, New York: Harper & Row, 1963), 5.

23. Pratt and Whitney became a major producer of the so-called Lincoln milling machine, which, fitted out with different jigs and fixtures, became the workhorse of American-system industries, including the small arms industry.

24. William Hosley, *Colt: The Making of an American Legend* (Amherst: University of Massachusetts Press, 1996), 107, 115–16.

25. Ibid., 109–13, 121.

26. Rosenberg, *American System,* 199–325, 327–89, and 98–197, respectively, reprints three parliamentary commissioners' reports: "New York Industrial Exhibition. Special Report of Mr. George Wallis. Presented to the House of Commons by Command of Her Majesty, in Pursuance of their Address of February 6, 1854" (London: Harrison and Son, 1854), "New York Industrial Exhibition. Special Report of Mr. Joseph Whitworth. Presented to the House of Commons by Command of Her Majesty, in Pursuance of Their Address of February 6, 1854" (London: Harrison and Son, 1854), and the "Report of the Committee on the Machinery of the United States of America.

Carolyn C. Cooper

Presented to the House of Commons, in Pursuance of their Address of the 10th July, 1855" (London: Harrison and Sons, 1855). New York's 1853 Crystal Palace exhibition was inspired by the 1851 example in London. Whitworth and Wallis had broader terms of reference than did the Committee on Machinery, but they all reported on technology that they observed in several places on the northeast seaboard of America and considered worth emulating in Great Britain.

27. Robbins and Lawrence in Windsor, Vermont, supplied metalworking machines, and the Ames Company in Chicopee, Massachusetts, supplied gauges and machines for shaping and inletting the wooden stocks for longarms.

28. Now part of Romania.

29. The Allies also included some Sardinians.

30. These figures were for all theaters of the war. Losses in battle in the Crimea alone were: Allies, 70,000 men, Russians, 128,500. *Encyclopedia Britannica*, 11th ed. (1911), vol. 7 sv. "Crimean War," 453.

31. Rosa, *Colonel Colt, London*, 100.

32. Ibid., 96.

33. Hosley, *Colt*, 30–31.

34. John Harris, *The Indian Mutiny* (London: Hart-Davis MacGibbon, 1973), 143.

35. Richard Collier, *The Great Indian Mutiny* (New York: E. P. Dutton & Co., Inc., 1964), 340.

36. Harris, *Indian Mutiny*, 201.

37. *Encyclopedia Britannica*, 11th ed. (1911), vol. 14 sv. "India," 415.

38. Harris, *Indian Mutiny*, 202.

39. John F. Reiger, *American Sportsmen and the Origins of Conservation*, 3rd ed. (Corvallis: Oregon State University Press, 2001), 198–99.

40. Ibid., 9, 15–16, 30.

41. Ibid., 15.

42. By the treaty of Guadalupe Hidalgo in 1848 at the end of the Mexican War, Mexico, in return for $13 million, ceded its claim to Upper California and New Mexico (extending from California to Texas) and recognized the Rio Grande as the southern border of Texas. By mistake the southern border of New Mexico agreed upon was the Gila River. The Gadsden Purchase corrected the mistake.

43. John Russell Bartlett, *Personal Narrative of Explorations and Incidents in Texas, New Mexico, California, Sonora, and Chihuahua*, vol. 1 (New York: D. Appleton & Co., 1854), 48–49.

44. See "Hartford and Success" for an account of other Arizona mining companies Colt was involved in. The inclusion of "Land and" in the names of these somewhat later 1859 companies suggests a wish to encourage farming, as is explicit in their prospectuses.

45. See Sylvester Mowry, *Memoir of the Proposed Territory of Arizona* (Washington: Henry Polkinhorn, Printer, 1857) and *Arizona and Sonora*, 3rd ed. (New York: Harper and Bros, 1864; reprint, New York: Mowry Mines Company, 1904), 55–72. Mowry represented Arizona in Washington in the effort to obtain status as a U.S. Territory and military protection from Apache depredations. Frustrated, he turned to the Confederacy for these goals but suffered for the choice. In 1862 his mine was confiscated by the federal government and he was jailed for several months under suspicion of treason. The Arizona Organic Act of February 1863 redrew the boundary between New Mexico and Arizona while giving Arizona Territory status within the Union. See Howard R. Lamar, *The Far Southwest 1846–1912: A Territorial History* (New York: W. W. Norton & Co., 1970), 432–34. Separated from New Mexico and expanded northward geographically, Arizona finally became a state in 1912.

46. Davidson et al., *Nation of Nations*, 236–38.

47. Grant, *The Colt Armory*, 26, 34.

48. John E. Parsons, "New Light on Old Colts," reprinted from *The Texas Gun Collector*, 1955. Of the revolvers, 2,120 were Army pistols, 602 Navy. The number per shipment ranged from 50 to 1,110; the median was 100. For comparison, remember that the seized shipment of cotton-baled revolvers to Russia in 1855 had totaled 3,480.

49. 1860 U.S. census data: the white male population 18 to 45 years old was 4.6 million in the Union, 1.1 million in the Confederacy; the value of firearms produced was $2.29 million in the Union, $73,000 in the Confederacy. See table "Resources of the Union and the Confederacy, 1861," in Davidson et al., *Nation of Nations*, 566.

50. Colt's company produced 75,000 of these rifle-muskets. Their design, attributed to Colt's company, was based on a pattern British Enfield military musket. Norm Flayderman, *Flayderman's Guide to Antique American Firearms and Their Values* (Northfield, Ill.: DBI Books, Inc., 1977), 102, 426.

51. Davidson et al., *Nation of Nations*, 601.

Note for the Reader

Throughout this catalogue extensive use has been made of primary documents. For the most part, these documents are preserved among the Samuel Colt Papers of the Connecticut Historical Society, which are arranged in chronological order from 1801 to 1904, and here are referenced by their box numbers from 1 to 11. To a lesser degree, letters from the Records of the Colt's Patent Fire Arms Manufacturing Company, now in the Connecticut State Library and the Christopher Colt Papers in the University of Rhode Island Libraries' Special Collections, have also been cited or reproduced.

While some fair copies exist, the vast majority of Samuel Colt's outgoing correspondence and extemporaneous notes are drafts intended for transcription either by himself or a secretary. As a result, they reflect the haste with which they were written. Misspellings abound (in some instances three or more phonetic variations of a given word may appear in one letter), and grammatical niceties (such as commas, periods, and capital letters) are often lacking. Some historians have taken these errors as evidence that Colt was poorly educated. That conclusion is false, in that other letters written entirely in Colt's hand contain no errors in grammar, spelling, or syntax.

Even during his lifetime, Colt was aware that some people considered him an untutored bumpkin, and on occasion he had fun at his own expense. An excellent example of this humor is to be found scrawled across the secretarial copy of an order he sent to Milton Joslin, requesting that a presentation revolver be sent to Richard W. H. Jarvis (Colt's brother-in-law) in Middletown, Connecticut. Instead of merely initialing the order, as was his normal practice, Colt boldly signed the note vertically: "Sam Kolt / His X Mark" (fig. 1).

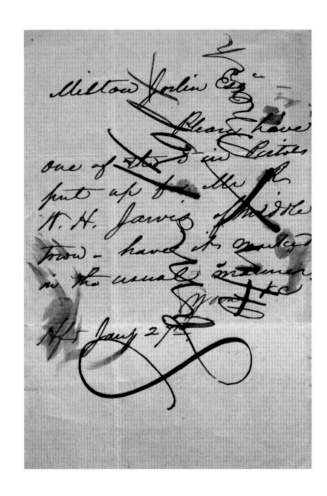

Figure 1

Letter from Samuel Colt to Milton Joslin, 27 January [1854], endorsed vertically in two lines "Sam Kolt / His X Mark." Samuel Colt Papers, Connecticut Historical Society.

Samuel Colt
Arms, Art, and Invention

In many respects Samuel Colt was more a man of the twentieth century than of the nineteenth. He championed the concept of modernism long before the word was coined. He pioneered the use of celebrity endorsements to promote his products, introduced the adjectives "New and Improved" to advertising, and demonstrated the commercial value of brand-name recognition.

Although it is often overlooked, Colt redefined the architecture of handguns. Recognizing that form plays a significant role in consumer acceptance, he designed his revolvers so that they were immediately identifiable as his product. Moreover, he adopted finishes that played upon the viewer's eye. The juxtaposition of highly polished blued steel surfaces with those emblazoned with color casehardening, as well as the pure whiteness of silver-plating, was not accidental. The play of light reflecting off the surfaces of one of his revolvers was calculated to attract customers. Colt also knew that clean symmetrical lines heightened these visual effects. As a result, he produced arms in the late 1850s and early 1860s that would not have been out of place had they been made during the Art Deco period. Indeed, his streamlined New Model series of pistols can be favorably compared to some of the best custom automobile coachwork produced in the 1930s.

Samuel Colt was also the archetype for the twentieth-century advertising executive. To demonstrate the value of his arms, he solicited and then published letters of endorsement from the celebrities of his day. The names of these individuals, primarily military officers, were known throughout the United States, and their comments were seen by the general public as an imprimatur of quality. Colt was quite possibly the first American manufacturer to use art as a marketing tool. In the mid-1850s he commissioned George Catlin to paint a series of scenes illustrating revolving pistols and rifles in use. Six of these paintings were then reproduced as lithographs for distribution to arms dealers selling Colt's products.

Above all else, Colt constantly promoted brand recognition. He traveled endlessly to establish his name as a synonym for the revolvers he made. He courted publicity of all types, whether positive or negative, to keep his name in the newspapers. On other occasions, such as his 1851 lecture to the Institution of Civil Engineers in London, he shamelessly touted the virtues of his revolvers over those designs that had preceded them.

Samuel Colt was also an innovator. In less than two decades he took an idea and transformed it into an everyday reality. While his contributions to the development of the first practical revolver are universally recognized, the process is less understood. To achieve his goal, Colt examined and refined every facet of his revolver's construction. In doing so, he secured dozens of patents, many of them for a variety of features that were never produced. Yet all of these designs reveal the workings of Colt's inventive genius.

Despite Colt's brilliance and drive, he would not have been able to realize his visions without the assistance of others. He was fortunate in being able to work with two extremely capable men who translated his ideas into reality. Between 1836 and 1841, Pliny Lawton helped Colt perfect the design of his revolver. Then from 1848 through 1862, Elisha King Root developed the means to achieve its mass production. In doing so, Colt's company introduced dedicated production lines six decades before Henry Ford. Colt also insisted that a rigid system of quality-control inspections be set in place so that purchasers of his arms could be assured of their excellence.

Colt's intellectual interests focused on more than firearms. In 1840 he invented a waterproof electric cable that could be used to detonate submerged explosives designed to protect American harbors from hostile warships. On more peaceful fronts, he actively promoted educational and social programs for his employees and their families. While some of his civic projects may have been self-serving, such as the construction of a flood-control dike along the Connecticut River by his factory, others were purely altruistic. Among these was the construction, in 1859, of a library for the residents of Tubac, Arizona, where he owned a mine. Colt also actively supported the visual arts and played a pivotal role in bringing back to Hartford the sculptures of Edward Sheffield Bartholomew after the artist died in Rome in 1858.

Often portrayed as a Horatio Alger-like character, Colt was actually a child of privilege. Yet when it suited him, he frequently professed humble origins. This ability to adapt to various surroundings made him equally at ease with workers on the factory floor and nobility in the imperial courts of Europe.

Perhaps because of his multifaceted character, Colt has been frequently dismissed as a social-climbing country bumpkin. Even in his own day, Colt's detractors branded him as a drunkard, corrupt libertine, thief, and, at the beginning of the American Civil War, a traitor. Colt relished such accusations, as they kept his name and that of his revolvers in the public eye. Indeed, on more than one occasion he circulated copies of particularly vitriolic attacks to his friends.

Samuel Colt's single-mindedness in promoting himself and his revolvers shaped his life from 1830 until his death in 1862. It also shapes this exhibition.

The exhibition is also defined by the collections from which the objects have been drawn. The majority of the pieces illustrating the evolution of revolving arms and Samuel Colt's own designs originally formed part of the inventor's personal collection. Though now divided between the Wadsworth Atheneum Museum of Art and the Museum of Connecticut History, these arms were in Colt's office when he died in 1862. They are therefore a tangible link to the man himself. In addition, this collection documents Colt's constant battles to protect his patents from both copyists and counterfeiters. Other pieces, such as the Catlin paintings and gifts Colt received from abroad, offer a glimpse into his other interests. As a counterpoint, the collection of Colt firearms assembled by his wife, Elizabeth Hart Jarvis Colt, in 1863 demonstrates Samuel Colt's posthumous contributions to the preservation of the Union during the Civil War. Thanks to their near pristine condition, these arms afford viewers an opportunity to see how Colt used color and simplicity of form to their full advantage.

Samuel Colt: Arms, Art, and Invention presents rarely viewed material while also providing visitors with a more balanced appreciation of the man who was one of the most influential Americans of the mid-nineteenth century.

The Development of Firearms up to Samuel Colt's Time

It is not known who first discovered that a mixture of four parts saltpeter, one part sulfur, and one part charcoal burns explosively when ignited by a match or spark. Credit, however, has been given at various times to the thirteenth-century English alchemist Roger Bacon, a fourteenth-century German monk named Bertholdus Niger or Berthold Schwartz, and the Chinese.

The Bacon attribution is based upon an anagram that appears in chapter eleven of his treatise "De mirabili potestate artis et naturae," written in 1242.[1] It supposedly reveals a gunpowder formula having essentially the same proportions as those described above.[2] Whether Bacon was the author of the anagram remains open to question, however, as the surviving manuscript postdates his death.

The identification of the Franciscan monk Bertholdus Niger as the inventor of gunpowder has a far longer and colorful tradition that was embroidered over centuries of retelling. As the legend goes, while living in the city of Freiburg, he attempted to transmute base elements into gold paint and accidentally stumbled upon the formula for gunpowder.[3] This event was depicted in two sixteenth-century illustrations. In the one from 1584 Bertholdus is shown testing a compound on a touchstone, whereupon his mortar unexpectedly explodes next to him.[4] The other illustration, from 1598, is far more provocative, as it shows the monk being guided in his discovery by the Devil (fig. 1).[5] In 1614 William Camden described Berthold's involvement in the discovery of gunpowder:

> If ever the witte of man went beyond belief itselfe it was in the invention of militairie or Engines of warre. Some have sayled a long course as farre as China, the farthest part of the world to fetch the invention of guns from hence, but we know the Spanish proverb "long waies, long lies...." The best approved authors agree that guns were invented in Germanie by Berthold Swarte.[6]

Several problems, however, call into question the Bertholdus Niger attribution. First, the date generally assigned to his discovery is 1354,[7] well after cannons had become known in Europe, and, secondly, there is no contemporary evidence that the monk ever existed.

Recent research has demonstrated that gunpowder was most likely invented by an unknown alchemist in China sometime during the ninth or tenth century.[8] By the eleventh century it was being used to propel arrows, and a primitive cannon made from bamboo is described in a Chinese text dated to 1132.[9]

Interestingly, metal cannons made their appearance on the battlefield in both China and Europe at about the same time. Vase-shaped cannons loaded with ballista arrows are illustrated in two manuscripts written by Walter de Milemete ("De Nobilitatibus, Sapientiis, et Prudentiis Regum" and "De Secretis Secretorum"[10]) that can be dated to 1326 or 1327, and a cannon inscribed with the date 1332 was found near Beijing in 1935.[11] Although this simultaneous appearance would appear to suggest that the construction of cannons occurred independently in both regions, the survival of a Chinese manuscript dated to 1259 that describes a rudimentary bronze cannon supports the contention that the Chinese were the first to come up with the idea.[12] The technology then traveled westward along the Silk Road to Europe.

By the early fourteenth century small cannons designed to be mounted on poles for hand use were being made in considerable quantities in China. Shortly thereafter they made their appearance in the West. These arms consisted of a simple metal tube with a socketed rear end to receive a wooden pole. They were loaded from the muzzle end with gunpowder and a projectile usually consisting of lead pellets or spherical balls. Then the piece was aimed, and the soldier holding it inserted a heated metal rod or smoldering stick into a hole drilled through the barrel's wall corresponding to where the powder charge was located.

Apart from being somewhat cumbersome, hand cannons were not particularly safe. If the bronze used in their construction was not properly cast, flaws or air bubbles could cause the piece to rupture during firing. Likewise, the varying strength of the gunpowder then being made also caused hand cannons to fail disastrously. As a result, improved methods of firing handheld firearms were quickly developed. The earliest involved fitting the barrel with a shallow pan next to the vent leading into the powder chamber. By placing some powder in this pan, the gun could be touched off by a heated rod or firebrand without placing the user's hand directly next to the barrel's breech end.

This system was quickly replaced by a lever mechanism shaped like an angular "S" that moved on a pivot at its center point. By attaching a smol-

Figure 2

Interior view of a detached wheel lock
illustrating placement of the revolving
wheel having a serrated edge,
mainspring, and pan. H. G. Houze
Collection, Cody, Wyo.

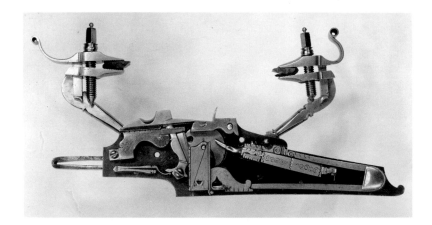

dering match cord to its forward end, the gun could be fired simply by pulling the lower arm of the lever up toward the wooden support pole, thus lowering the forward arm into the priming pan.[13] Due to their use of a smoldering cord, arms of this type were identified in contemporary references as "fire-locks."[14] Today they are referred to as matchlocks.

Improvements in bronze casting and the adoption of gunstocks that allowed firearms to be more accurately aimed from the shoulder revolutionized warfare throughout the world. Armored knights who had dominated the battlefield for centuries could be killed as easily as foot soldiers by the new weapons.

Relatively inexpensive to make and requiring little training for use, matchlock firearms became the weapon of choice for countries seeking to dominate others. They suffered one distinct disadvantage: the smoldering match cord and the exposed priming powder rendered them useless in inclement weather. Nonetheless, they remained in widespread use from the late fifteenth through the eighteenth centuries. Some measure of their popularity can be gained from the fact that due to their simplicity and ease of manufacture matchlock arms were still extensively used in some parts of the Indian subcontinent and the Far East well into the twentieth century.

For sporting purposes, however, the smoldering match warned prey of a hunter's presence. Consequently gunmakers quickly attempted to design a less visible way of firing handheld arms. This led to the development of the mechanical gunlock. The first reliable one is believed to have been invented in Italy sometime around 1500.[15] Its key component was a

spring-loaded wheel that had a serrated edge. The wheel could be wound up and then held in place by a stop-catch or sear that could be released only by the trigger. When the priming pan was filled with powder, the cock holding a piece of iron pyrite was lowered into position against the exposed surface of the wheel. When the trigger was pulled, the wheel spun against the pyrite, producing sparks that ignited the priming powder, which in turn ignited the main powder charge in the barrel. The same principle is used today in cigarette lighters. Because of their complexity, wheel locks (fig. 2) were expensive to manufacture and as a result did not see military use for most of the sixteenth century. The development of improved manufacturing processes during the first quarter of the seventeenth century did bring about more widespread use, but by that time far less costly gunlocks were available.

The first of these, known as the snaphaunce, made its appearance around 1550.[16] Like its predecessor, it used iron pyrites to produce sparks. However, in place of the serrated wheel, a pivoted arm with a concave-shaped steel was employed. When the cock was pulled back against the pressure of the internal mainspring, it was locked in position by a sear. The priming powder was then placed in the pan and the steel moved into position, where it would be hit by the iron pyrites as the cock fell forward. To keep the priming powder dry, many of these locks were fitted with pan covers that automatically opened as the cock fell. Though an improvement over the wheel lock, the snaphaunce could be put out of commission rather quickly if the steel arm was bent or otherwise knocked out of alignment.

This problem was overcome ca. 1610, when the French gunmaker Marin le Bourgeoys designed a steel arm that actually served as the priming pan cover.[17] That is, its lower end fit over the pan so that the enclosed powder was protected from moisture or wind. He also substituted a piece of flint for the iron pyrites to reduce the amount of wear on the steel that occurred from repeated use. In the flintlock system the flint scraped down the steel's face at the same time that the steel was pivoted forward exposing the priming powder. This increased the speed with which an arm could be fired and greatly improved the likelihood that it would go off.

Its relative simplicity and ease of use quickly established the flintlock ignition system as the sine qua non for all handheld firearms in Europe. Unfortunately they never achieved the level of waterproofing that sportsmen

Figure 4

Percussion caps cased with the
New Model Belt Pistol, serial no. 5726
(cat. 56). Wadsworth Atheneum
Museum of Art.

Figure 3

Exterior view of a detached flintlock
by Thomas Manton of London, ca.
1820. Stuart Mowbray Collection,
Lincoln, R.I.

required, but as the detached lock illustrated in figure 3 demonstrates, gunmakers made numerous attempts to secure that result.[18] In addition, the puff of smoke generated by the ignition priming powder often enabled game to escape.

These problems proved especially irksome to Alexander John Forsyth. A Presbyterian minister by calling and an amateur chemist by inclination, Forsyth began experimenting with various compounds that exploded by percussion. By 1798 he developed a compound using fulminate of mercury.[19] By placing a granule of this mixture on the recess of a hollow plug that went into the barrel, a loaded charge could be fired by the action of a hammer falling forward against the fulminate.

Described by some as the greatest invention since the development of gunpowder,[20] Forsyth's detonator locks rendered the flintlock obsolete. More importantly, Forsyth's invention led the way to the development of the percussion cap and later the modern self-contained metallic cartridge.

The percussion cap utilized Forsyth's fulminate granules in a different way. Invented by Joseph Egg of London in 1817, it consisted of a small copper cup that had a granule of fulminate cemented with varnish onto its interior base (fig. 4).[21] The copper cup could then be placed on a hollow nipple that was screwed into the barrel's vent plug. Impervious to water

and cheaply produced, the copper percussion cap was quickly adopted by gunmakers throughout Europe and the Americas immediately following its first appearance.[22]

In no small measure it was the development of the percussion cap that allowed Samuel Colt to design his first revolver. Had it not existed, his design would have been as unusable as those revolving arms that preceded it during the matchlock through flintlock eras.

The recognition of his indebtedness to Forsyth is plainly evidenced by Colt's purchase of examples of the inventor's earliest locks for preservation in the museum he planned. In addition to acquiring sectionalized demonstration locks designed to illustrate how the various types of Forsyth locks functioned, in 1851 Colt bought a considerable number of detached priming magazines, experimental pieces, and other detonator locks made by Forsyth's competitors. At the same time Colt also purchased, or was given, documents relating to Forsyth's work. The breadth of these acquisitions indicates an interest that extended far beyond idle curiosity.

Notes

1. British Museum, Sloane MS 2156.

2. Oscar Guttmann, *Monumenta Pulveris Pyrii* (London: Artists Press, 1906), 2–3.

3. Ibid., fig. 10.

4. J. Gole, *Des Ehrwurdigen und Sinnreiche Vatters Bertold Schwartz genandt, franciscaner Ordens, Doctor, Alchimist, und Ersinder der sreisen funst des Buchsenschieszens im Jar 1380*, etching ([Amsterdam]: n.p., 1643).

5. Joseph Boillot, *Modelles, artifices de feu et divers instrumens de guerre avec les moyens de s'en prévaloir pour assiéger, battre, surprendre et défendre toutes places ...* (Chaumont-en-Bassigny: Quentin Marechal, 1598), n.p.

6. William Camden, *Remains concerning Britaine, reviewed, corrected and encreased* (London: 1614), 238–39.

7. The date is variously recorded as 1354 and 1380.

8. Yang Hong, ed., *Weapons in Ancient China* (New York and Beijing: Science Press, 1992), 283–84.

9. Ibid., 287.

10. Library of Christ Church, Oxford, MS 92, and British Museum, Add. MS 47680.

11. Hong, *Weapons in Ancient China,* 288–89, and Howard L. Blackmore, "The Oldest Dated Gun," *Arms Collecting* 34, no. 2 (May 1996): 39–47.

12. Hong, *Weapons in Ancient China,* 287–88.

13. A marginal illustration of a soldier armed with a matchlock gun of this construction appears in the 1411 Codex MS 3069 (National Library, Vienna, reproduced in Howard L. Blackmore, *Guns and Rifles of the World* [New York: Viking Press, 1965], 9).

14. This term remained in use well into the nineteenth century and was used to describe the Japanese matchlock guns presented to Samuel Colt by the shogun Tokugawa Yoshinobu in 1854 (John S. Cunningham to Samuel Colt, 7 March 1855. Samuel Colt Correspondence, Wadsworth Atheneum Museum of Art, Bequest of Elizabeth Hart Jarvis Colt).

15. The most frequently reproduced illustration of a wheel lock dating from the early sixteenth century is that found in Leonardo da Vinci's *Codex Atlanticus* (Blackmore, *Guns and Rifles of the World,* 20).

16. An example believed to have been made in Arboga, Sweden, in 1556 is preserved in the Livrustkammaren, Stockholm (LRK 16317, old number 1341). Nils Drejholt, *Firearms of the Royal Armouries I from Gustav II Adolph to Charles XIII* (Stockholm: Livrustkammaren, 1996), 18, 20–21.

17. Torsten Lenk, *The Flintlock: Its Origin and Development,* trans. G. A. Urquhart (New York: Bramhall House, 1965), 29–31.

18. Perhaps the best and certainly the most widely copied of these attempts was the "rainproof" lock that had a priming pan with sharply cutaway sides to prevent the accumulation of moisture adjacent to the pan and the priming powder held there. The earliest patent protecting this design was issued to the London gunmaker John Prosser on 9 December 1800 (H. M. Patent Office, *Abridgements of the Patent Specifications Relating to Firearms & Other Weapons, Ammunition & Accoutrements from 1588–1858* [London: George E. Eyre and William Spottiswoode, 1859], 37, no. 2,654).

19. For a detailed account of Forsyth's experiments and preliminary lock designs, see W. Keith Neal and D. H. L. Back, *Forsyth & Co.: Patent Gunmakers* (London: G. Bell & Sons, 1969), 82–127.

20. Ibid., xiii.

21. S. James Gooding, "Joseph Egg Inventor of the Copper Cap ... ," *Arms Collecting* 36, no. 3 (August 1998): 75–79.

22. By the early 1820s this ignition system had found widespread acceptance in both England and Europe (ibid., 75–76, 78–79).

1

Hand Cannon
China
Caliber .56 in., bore length 9¾ in., overall length 13¼ in.
Date of Manufacture: mid-15th century
Private collection

The simplest and earliest form of firearms was the hand cannon. As its name implies, the arm consisted solely of a barrel that was pierced with a circular vent near its rear end, so that the powder charge loaded from the muzzle could be ignited by inserting a match cord or heated metal rod.

The first recorded hand cannons appeared in China during the twelfth century. Originally made of bamboo strengthened with lashings, they were of only limited use and were quickly replaced by others made of cast bronze. To facilitate their use, the barrels were cast with hollow sockets at the rear of the chamber wall, so they could be attached to a wooden pole by either a transverse pin or knotted cord.

As the construction of Chinese hand cannons essentially continued from the thirteenth through the late fifteenth centuries, it is impossible to accurately date examples that have been removed from their archaeological context.[1]

Note

1. The mid-fifteenth-century date assigned to this cannon is based upon the similarity of its construction to examples that can be accurately assigned to that era. Yang Hong, ed., *Weapons in Ancient China* (New York and Beijing: Science Press, 1992), 290–92. Cf. Cheng Dong and Zhong Shai-yi, *Ancient Chinese Weapons—A Collection of Pictures* (Beijing: Chinese People's Liberation Army Publishing House, 1990), 224, 230–31.

2

Matchlock Revolver

India

Caliber approximately .60 in., barrel length 27¾ in., overall length 49⅝ in.

Date of Manufacture: 18th century

Wadsworth Atheneum Museum of Art

Bequest of Elizabeth Hart Jarvis Colt, 1905.1024

1861 Inventory of Colonel Colt's Large Office

Page VI, line 23

1 Ancient Matchlock Musket with revolving Cyl (Iron) from India, fig. 2

Matchlock firearms were first made in Europe in the late fifteenth century and were so named because they used a slow-burning match cord to ignite the priming powder located in a pan next to the barrel vent. Due to their simplicity and low cost of manufacture they remained popular in Europe until the late seventeenth century, and elsewhere for a considerably longer period.

Detail of cylinder

Based upon its construction and decoration, this matchlock musket was made in India during the mid-eighteenth century. As it demonstrated one of the earliest attempts to produce a revolving cylinder arm, Samuel Colt acquired the piece for his own collection in 1851. He described the gun in his lecture of 25 November 1851 to the Institution of Civil Engineers:

Herbert G. Houze

The next match-lock arm was found, by the Author, in the possession of Messrs. Forsyth & Co., who obtained it, about twenty-four years ago, from the late Lord William Bentinck, the Governor-General of India, whence it was brought, with other curious weapons. The construction of this arm closely resembles that just described; but the workmanship is superior, and it is more elaborately ornamented. The breech, which requires to be moved by hand, has five chambers, each having a priming pan with a swing cover. The arbor is attached to the barrel which, at the end adjoining the breech, is enlarged to correspond with the diameter of the revolving chamber, to which it forms a kind of shield.

But in order to mitigate the danger, which was, no doubt, apprehended, from the simultaneous discharge of all the chambers, by the spreading of the fire, from the exploding chamber, which would be the inevitable effect of this shield, the maker has provided vents for the charges, by boring holes through the enlargement of the barrel, corresponding to the charge chambers in the revolving breech. In one respect this gun gives evidence of progress, inasmuch as the breech-arbor is more firmly secured to the stock by two square pins, thus ensuring a firmer connexion [sic] between the parts. The method of locking the breech is similar to that of the first arm described, except, that the spring for securing is fastened to the barrel instead of the stock.[1]

Note

1. Col. Samuel Colt, "On the application of Machinery to the manufacture of Rotating Chambered-Breech Fire-Arms, and the peculiarities of those Arms," *Minutes of Proceedings of the Institution of Civil Engineers, with Abstracts of the Discussions*, vol. XI, session 1851–52 (London: Institution of Civil Engineers, 1852), 32–33.

3
Snaphaunce Revolving Carbine
John Dafte
London
Caliber .46 in., barrel length 14⅜ in., overall length 33⅛ in.
Date of Manufacture: 1680–90
Wadsworth Atheneum Museum of Art
Bequest of Elizabeth Hart Jarvis Colt, 1905.1022

Although made between 1680 and 1690, this carbine uses an ignition system that was popular during the first half of the seventeenth century. The

Detail of cylinder

snaphaunce represented an intermediate step between the wheel lock and flintlock. Its name is derived from the Dutch word *snaphaan,* meaning "pecking hen." This word describes the action of the cock as it falls forward to strike the pivoted steel, or frizzen.

As the steel did not fit over the priming pan, snaphaunces were fitted with sliding pan covers that were opened either manually or by the action of the cock moving forward. In this piece the cock is fitted with an arm that automatically opens the pan cover. The hand-rotated cylinder is locked in position by a spring pin attached to the breech end of the barrel.

In Samuel Colt's 1851 lecture to the Institution of Civil Engineers he described this carbine:

> The specimen, which appears from its construction, to come next in order, was obtained by the Author from Messrs. Forsyth and Co.; it bears the evidence of English construction, as on the lock is inscribed "John Dafte, London," in characters which indicate that it is scarcely more than a century old; it may, however, be a copy of an older arm. There is evidently an attempt, in this arm, to produce a more compact weapon, for instead of having a projecting pan and steel for each chamber, recesses are made in the periphery of the breech, to form pans, and one steel was probably provided to stand over the breech, attached to the barrel. The breech, containing six chambers, is rotated by hand, and is locked when in position for firing, in the same manner as in figure 3; priming powder is also placed in a pan for each chamber, whilst the weapon is being loaded; these priming pans are each covered by a sliding plate working in parallel guides affixed to the periphery of the breech, with the intention of protecting, in a more perfect manner, the priming of the adjoining chambers, and thus preventing premature explosion. Connected with the hammer, is a small bar which projects forward, so that when the trigger is pulled, the hammer, in its descent against the steel, brings the small bar into contact with a projection on the cover of the upper priming pan, pushing it forward, and exposing the powder in the pan to the action of the sparks struck from the flint of the hammer. This arrangement has the advantage of compactness, and in this particular it may be considered a mechanical improvement on its predecessors; the stock does reach beyond the base of the breech, and the barrel is cut out

in front of the chambers to allow the balls to escape, in case of premature explosion. This arm bears evidence of being radically defective; for in consequence of the holder of the steel being fastened over one of the chambers, into which the fire would be deflected, premature explosion necessarily followed, the steel was broken off and the arm was probably rendered useless by the first discharge.[1]

After serving an apprenticeship to the London gunmakers Henry Phipps and Henry Pickfatt, John Dafte was awarded the freedom to pursue his trade by both the Worshipful Company of Blacksmiths and the Company of Gunmakers in 1668.[2] For the next nineteen years he produced work of solid but not exceptional quality.[3]

The date assigned to this carbine's manufacture is based upon the construction of the lockplate and the cock. The elongated lockplate with its well-defined terminal point, the full-bellied form of the cock, and the forward curl to its upper spur are all typical of the patterns followed by London makers between 1680 and 1690.[4]

Notes

1. Col. Samuel Colt, "On the application of Machinery to the manufacture of Rotating Chambered-Breech Fire-Arms, and the peculiarities of those Arms," *Minutes of Proceedings of the Institution of Civil Engineers, with Abstracts of the Discussions,* vol. XI, session 1851–52 (London: Institution of Civil Engineers, 1852), 35–36.

2. Howard L. Blackmore, *Gunmakers of London 1350–1850* (York, Pa.: George Shumway, 1986), 78, and H. L. Blackmore, *Gunmakers of London Supplement* (Bloomfield, Ont.: Museum Restoration Service, 1999), 60.

3. W. Keith Neal and D. H. L. Back, *Great British Gunmakers* (London: Historical Firearms, 1984), 213–17. A snaphaunce carbine with a lock signed by William Turvey (active ca. 1745), formerly in the W. Keith Neal Collection (ibid., 185–86), appears to have been built using the cylinder and barrel from a revolver identical to the example described here.

4. Neal and Back, *Great British Gunmakers,* 168–69, 173, 194.

Herbert G. Houze

Detail of cylinder

4

Collier's Patent Flintlock Revolver

Serial number 71

Caliber .46 in., barrel length 6⁷⁄₁₆ in., overall length 13⁷⁄₈ in.

Date of Manufacture: 1820–21

Wadsworth Atheneum Museum of Art

Bequest of Elizabeth Hart Jarvis Colt, 1905.995

Markings

Barrel: E. H. Collier 71 LONDON

Lockplate: E. H. Collier / 71 PATENT

Primer Magazine: E. H. COLLIER / 71 PATENT

Though not specifically listed in either of the 1861 inventories of Samuel Colt's personal offices at the Hartford factory, this revolver's case and accessories were recorded on page 7, line 9 of the Small Office inventory as follows: *1 Case & appendages for a Collier pistol.*[1]

Curiously, the pistol cylinder described and illustrated in Elisha Hayden Collier's English patent of 24 November 1818 (Number 4,315) closely resembled that of the Dafte revolver discussed on pages 27–28. That is to say, it was fitted with sliding pan covers opened by a bar connected to a rocker assembly attached to the cock.[2] Production versions of the pistol, however, were equipped with a steel having a priming powder magazine that automatically deposited a fixed amount of powder into each pan when it was brought rearward into battery (firing position).

Between 1820 and 1823, Collier maintained premises in the Strand, London. In 1824 he adopted the business name Collier & Company and moved from the Strand to the Royal Exchange.[3]

Notes

1. The 1861 inventories of Colt's large and small offices were used during the preparation of the 1887 museum inventory. They were subsequently attached to that document as pages 15 to 32 ([Anon.], "Original Draft of Inventory, of arms etc. in Museum . . . of Colt's P. F. A. Mfg. Co., Compiled Oct. 1887. . . ." Records of the Colt's Patent Fire Arms Manufacturing Company, RG 103, Administrative File, Box 61, Connecticut State Library). Properly sequenced reconstructions of both the large and

small office inventories were published with annotations in 1987 (Herbert G. Houze, "The 1861 Inventory of the Arms and Miscellaneous Material in the Office of Colonel Samuel Colt," *Armax* 1, no. 1 [Spring/Summer 1987]: 17–57, and "The 1861 Inventory of the Arms and Miscellaneous Material in the Museum Room of the Colt Factory," *Armax* 1, no. 1 [Fall/Winter 1987], 15–89). To differentiate the two documents, page numbers for the large office inventory are noted in Roman numerals. Hereafter, references and entries from both documents will be cited without source notes.

2. Elisha Hayden Collier, "Fire-arm combining Single Barrel with several Chambers, to obtain Succession of Discharges from One Loading," Letters Patent 24 November 1818, Number 4,315, enrolled 24 May 1819.

3. Howard L. Blackmore, *Gunmakers of London 1350–1850* (York, Pa.: George Shumway, 1986), 73.

5

Collier's Patent Flintlock Revolving Rifle
Serial number 125
Caliber .60 in., barrel length 27 7/8 in., overall length 47 3/4 in.
Date of Manufacture: 1821–22
Museum of Connecticut History, Hartford
Gift of the Pratt & Whitney Company Foundation, Inc., 67

Markings
Barrel: E. H. COLLIERS 125 LONDON
Lockplate: E. H. COLLIERS / 125 PATENT
Primer Magazine: 125 PATENT

1861 Inventory of Colonel Colt's Large Office
Page VI, line 25
1 Collier Rifle Revolver Flintlock –

1887 Museum Inventory Draft
67. 56 Cal Collier Revolver Flintlock 5 shot.

In his 1851 lecture to the Institution of Civil Engineers, Samuel Colt went to considerable lengths to point out the defects of revolver designs that had preceded his own. With respect to those made by Elisha Collier, however, Colt's comments were more pointed. His dismissive treatment of Collier in the preamble to the following description, while factually true, was colored by the fact that this maker had testified in support of the Massachusetts Arms Company when Colt sued the firm for patent infringement.[1]

It is not a little surprising, that the next example of a rotating chambered-breech gun, with a flint lock, patented by Elisha H. Collier (U. S. America), in 1818, should exhibit nearly all the serious defects which had doubtless been discovered, and had been, to some extent, remedied by earlier makers. The objectionable parts of this arm are the priming magazine, the flue which would conduct the fire round to different touch-holes, and the cap in front, which would direct the lateral fire into adjoining chambers. The breech is made to bear against the barrel, by means of a coiled spring, which would probably be efficient while the gun was clean, and each chamber is recessed to receive the abutting end of the barrel, with the intention of effecting a closer junction. This bearing up of the chambered-breech against the barrel is maintained, during the firing, by a bolt which is thrust forward by a cam on the spindle of the hammer, when the trigger is pulled, and would be effective for a few discharges, until the junction between the cylinder and the barrel, or the arbor on which the cylinder is turned, became foul. The valve, which forms the bottom of the priming magazine, is self-acting and supplies a certain quantity of powder to the pan, when the magazine (which forms

Herbert G. Houze

at the same time the cover of the pan, and the steel for the hammer to strike upon), is brought into its elevated position. In order to rotate the breech, the hammer is thrown back to half-cock, the breech is then drawn out of contact with the barrel, and another chamber may be turned up by hand into a line with it.[2]

Two advertising broadsides that originally accompanied this rifle or the previously described pistol later formed part of the James L. Mitchell Collection of Colt-related documents.[3]

Notes

1. Robert M. Patterson, *In the Circuit Court of the United States, District of Massachusetts. Samuel Colt vs. The Mass. Arms Company. Report on the Trial of the Above-Entitled Cause, at Boston, on the Thirtieth Day of June, A.D. 1851, Before His Honor, Levi Woodbury, Associate Justice of the Supreme Court of the United States* (Boston: White & Potter, 1851), 121–25.
2. Col. Samuel Colt, "On the application of Machinery to the manufacture of Rotating Chambered-Breech Fire-Arms, and the peculiarities of those Arms," *Minutes of Proceedings of the Institution of Civil Engineers, with Abstracts of the Discussions,* vol. XI, session 1851–52 (London: Institution of Civil Engineers, 1852), 36–37.
3. Richard A. Bourne Co., Inc., *Antique Firearms and Related Items,* 17–18 March 1982, Lot 584.

6

Forsyth's Patent Exhibition Roller Primer Gunlock
Serial number R 102
Overall length 4^{25}/$_{32}$ in.
Date of Manufacture: October 1809
Cody Firearms Museum, Buffalo Bill Historical Center, Cody, Wyo., 1983.6.1

Markings
Lockplate: -FORSYTH & CO. / -PATENT-

1861 Inventory of Colonel Colt's Large Office
Page II, lines 10–11
3 Steel models of early percussion locks by Forsyth –

1887 Museum Inventory Draft
197. Lock for Pistol showing Alex Jm Forsyth's (Pat.) variation with revolving mag primer, not autom.

As stated in the introduction to this section of the catalogue, Samuel Colt's perfection of revolving-cylinder firearms would not have been possible without the work of the Reverend Alexander James Forsyth.

Forsyth's experiments with the explosive compound fulminate of mercury eventually led him to design a gunlock using this priming mixture. In its earliest manufactured form, Forsyth's lock was fitted with a "roller primer magazine."[1] The magazine was constructed so that its body had a cavity for the priming powder, and its head contained a spring-loaded striker. When the magazine was rotated so that the body was uppermost, a small quantity of priming powder fell into a recess on the vent tube (a hollow tube entering the base of the barrel). Once the lock had been primed, the magazine was rotated so that its head was uppermost. When the hammer fell, it hit the spring-loaded striker located in the priming magazine's head. The striker then crushed the priming pellet, causing it to explode. To hold the magazine in the firing position, a spring-loaded bar catch projects through the lock plate proper just forward of the magazine.

To demonstrate the function of the priming magazine and the construction of the barrel breech, Forsyth & Company sectionalized these components so that their operation was readily evident. To facilitate the lock's use as a demonstration piece, it was originally mounted on a stand, portions of which still remain.[2] It is believed that this detached lock and the one that follows formed part of Forsyth & Company's display at the Exhibition of the Works of Art & Industry of all Nations, held in London in 1851.[3]

Although it is not known precisely when Samuel Colt purchased this lock or the other patent percussion ignition material originally in his collection, the date had to have been prior to 29 September 1852, when Forsyth & Company was dissolved.[4]

Notes

1. Alexander John Forsyth, "Apparatus for Discharging Artillery, &c. by Means of Detonating Compounds," Letters Patent 11 April 1807, Number 3,032, enrolled 3 September 1807.

2. Herbert G. Houze, "Further Notes on the Forsyth Material in the Arms Collection of Colonel Colt," *Armax* 1, no. 1 (Spring/Summer 1987): 65–66.

3. *Official descriptive and illustrated Catalogue of the great exhibition 1851* (London: William Clowes & Sons, 1851), I, 357.

4. W. Keith Neal and D. H. L. Back, *Forsyth & Co.: Patent Gunmakers* (London: G. Bell & Sons, 1969), 272.

7

Forsyth's Patent Exhibition Sliding Primer Gunlock

No serial number

Overall length $4^{25}/_{32}$ in.

Date of Manufacture: 1811

Cody Firearms Museum, Buffalo Bill Historical Center, Cody, Wyo., 1983.6.2

Markings

Lockplate: -FORSYTH- / -PATENT-

Primer: F PATENT R

1861 Inventory of Colonel Colt's Large Office

Page II, lines 10–11

3 Steel models of early percussion locks by Forsyth –

1887 Museum Inventory Draft

195. Lock for Pistol showing Alex Jm Forsyth's (Pat.) mounted on plate with handle mag primer aut. sliding

To distance the priming magazine from the point of detonation, Alexander Forsyth developed a sliding primer that moved along the same axis as the barrel. To prime the lock, the magazine was moved rearward until it was over the vent tube. This allowed a globule of fulminate of mercury to be deposited in the vent's pan. The priming magazine was then returned to its forward position. Forsyth hoped that this arrangement would prevent the accidental detonation of the priming mixture in the magazine by distancing it from the actual point of ignition. However, as the following pistol demonstrates, that was not always the case.

As with the previous detached lock, this example has a sectionalized priming magazine and barrel breech. In addition, it was also originally mounted on a stand for display purposes.[1]

Note

1. Herbert G. Houze, "Further Notes on the Forsyth Material in the Arms Collection of Colonel Colt," *Armax* 1, no. 1 (Spring/Summer 1987): 66.

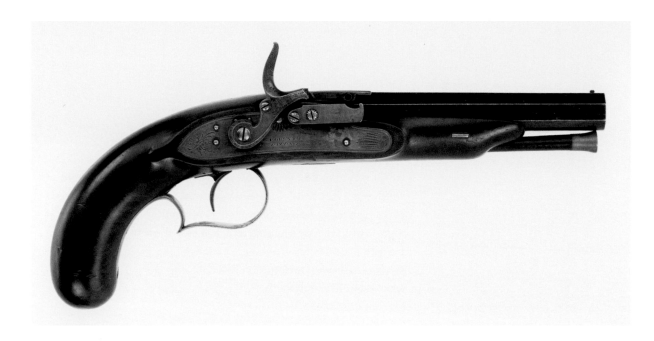

8

Forsyth Patent Sliding Primer Pistol
No serial number
Caliber .56 in., barrel length 6⅝ in., overall length 11⅝ in.
Date of Manufacture: ca. 1812
Museum of Connecticut History, Hartford
Gift of the Pratt & Whitney Company Foundation, Inc., 194

Markings
Lockplate: -FORSYTH- / -PATENT-

1861 Inventory of Colonel Colt's Large Office
Page II, line 21
1 Percussion single Barrel by Forsyth

1887 Museum Inventory Draft
194 56 Cal M L. Pistol with Alex. Jm Forsyth's Pat. Perc. Winch attachment 11/4.
1807. Mag. Primer aut. sliding

Although made as a fully functional pistol, this firearm was evidently intended solely for testing or demonstration purposes. This contention is based on the fact that the pistol's barrel was never submitted to the Worshipful Company of London Gunmakers for proof, which would have been necessary to enable it to be sold.[1]

The damage to the primer's operating rod and the absence of the sliding priming magazine suggest that the latter may have exploded during use.

Note

1. For a discussion of the Worshipful Company of Gunmakers in London and its regulations regarding the proof of firearms, see Howard L. Blackmore, *Gunmakers of London 1350–1850* (York, Pa.: George Shumway, 1986), 12–14, 18–27. Cf. Herbert G. Houze, "Further Notes on the Forsyth Material in the Arms Collection of Colonel Colt," *Armax* 1, no. 1 (Spring/Summer 1987): 66–67.

9

Porter Percussion Cap Revolving Rifle
Caliber .42 in., barrel length 33 in., overall length 51½ in.
Date of Manufacture: 1826
Wadsworth Atheneum Museum of Art
Bequest of Elizabeth Hart Jarvis Colt, 1905.1027

Unlike the preceding firearms, the cylinder of this rifle was rotated by the action of cocking the hammer. Designed by Rufus Porter of Billerica, Massachusetts, the rifle was made by Joseph H. Center in Boston in September and October 1826. In a letter to Samuel Colt dated 26 September 1836, Center described the cylinder turning mechanism:

> This gun had a revolving cylinder containing nine chambers or receivers; and the cylinder was put in motion by means of a horizontal triangle

which was mounted on a small vertical arbor, and on each point of which was a ball, which occasionally occupied a small cavity in the end of the cylinder, – two balls fitting two cavities at the same time when at rest; – and a latch which being attached by a screw to the right side of the cock projected forward over the triangle, and having a hook at the forward end which took hold of the right arm of the triangle; so that when the cock was drawn back, the triangle, and by it the cylinder was brought into another position for discharge.[1]

Although Porter never patented this design, Colt evidently became aware of its existence in 1835. Realizing that Porter could challenge the validity of his 25 February 1836 patent, Colt purchased this rifle and all production rights to the design from Porter in October 1836 for $100.[2]

The construction of the rifle's hammer is of interest, as it represents a style used only during the transition period between the flintlock and the percussion cap ignition systems. While the hammer resembles a flintlock cock whose jaws would hold a piece of flint, the present example is fitted with a cupped extension to hit the percussion cap nipples.

Notes

1. Joseph H. Center to Samuel Colt, 26 September 1836. Records of the Colt's Patent Fire Arms Manufacturing Company, RG103, Series IV, Patents 1,836–1,920, Box 45 Correspondence, File 1, Connecticut State Library.
2. Design assignments, Rufus Porter to Samuel Colt, 31 May 1836 and 1 October 1836. Records of the Colt's Patent Fire Arms Manufacturing Company, RG103, Series IV, Patents 1,836–1,920, Box 45 Correspondence, File 1, Connecticut State Library.

Detail of cylinder

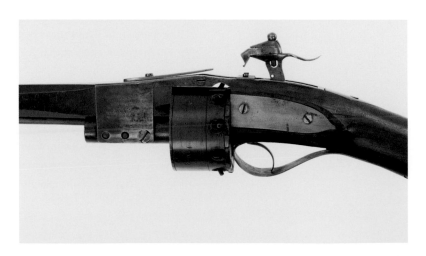

Herbert G. Houze

10

Miller Patent Percussion Ignition Revolving Rifle

No serial number

Caliber .42 in., barrel length 31¾ in., overall length 50¾ in.

Date of Manufacture: ca. 1830

Wadsworth Atheneum Museum of Art

Bequest of Elizabeth Hart Jarvis Colt, 1905.982

Markings

Barrel: J. & J. MILLER / ROCHESTER

Frame: PATENT [upper tang]

Detail of cylinder

On 11 June 1829 James and John Miller of Rochester, New York, were awarded the first United States patent for a revolver using the percussion system of ignition.[1] Unlike the preceding Porter rifle, the cylinder of this piece was revolved by hand and locked in the firing position by a spring-loaded catch located at the bottom of the shield plate in front of the cylinder.

Though made well after the introduction of metal percussion caps, the Miller rifle was designed for use with pellet primers (small globules of priming mixture) that were hand-inserted into hollow recesses cut into the cylinder at the rear of each chamber. When these primers were crushed by the action of the hammer falling, they exploded, sending a jet of flame into the chamber beneath them.

It is likely that this rifle is the same as the one presented in evidence by Samuel Colt's attorney during the infringement action brought against the Massachusetts Arms Company in 1851 (see "Counterfeits, Infringements, and Competitors," pp. 124–25).[2]

Notes

1. Prior to late 1836, United States patents were not assigned registry numbers and consequently are identified only by date.

2. Robert M. Patterson, *In the Circuit Court of the United States, District of Massachusetts. Samuel Colt vs. The Mass. Arms Company. Report on the Trial of the Above-Entitled Cause, at Boston, on the Thirtieth Day of June, A.D. 1851, Before His Honor, Levi Woodbury, Associate Justice of the Supreme Court of the United States* (Boston: White & Potter, 1851), 56.

11

Richardson Four-Barrel Percussion Cap Pistol
No serial number
Caliber .45 in., barrel length 2⁷/₈ in., overall length 9 in.
Date of Manufacture: 1825–30
Museum of Connecticut History, Hartford
Gift of the Pratt & Whitney Company Foundation, Inc., 209

Markings
Frame: RICHARDSON / MANCHESTER

1861 Inventory of Colonel Colt's Small Office
Page 9, line 6
1 4 barreled pistol radial barrels -

1887 Museum Inventory Draft
209. .43 Cal. Percussion cap multibarrel pistol, rifled, shoots from four barrels diverging simultaneously. Made by Richardson, Manchester

Without question the most rudimentary of all multishot weapons are those constructed with more than one barrel. While most firearms of this type are fitted with separate locks for each barrel, one type was designed specifically to fire all its barrels in unison. Known during the flintlock and percussion periods as "volley guns," these multibarreled weapons were particularly suited for several purposes. Those made with a cluster of somewhere between eight and fourteen small-caliber barrels were used by sportsmen to hunt game birds.[1]

Larger-caliber versions were designed for an entirely different purpose. Issued to marines and sailors aboard warships, these eight- or ten-shot volley guns were used to sweep the decks of other ships during close engagements.[2] In effect they increased the firepower of a vessel by the number of barrels each gun incorporated.

One of the more unusual applications of the "volley gun" principle was what is now known as the "duck's foot pistol." This name derives from the splayed-out barrels that from above resemble the webbed foot of a duck. Made and carried in pairs, these weapons were particularly favored by ship's officers because they offered an effective means to discourage or quell mutinies.

Although most "duck's foot pistols" date from the flintlock era, this pistol was originally made for use with percussion caps. Unfortunately little is known about its maker, James Richardson, other than the fact that he worked as a cutler, gunsmith, and surgical instrument maker in Manchester, England, from 1793 to 1830.[3]

Notes

1. Col. Thomas Thornton, *A Sporting Tour through France &c.* (London: Longman, Hearst, Rees and Orme, 1806), I, 9, and the plate following 71.
2. Howard L. Blackmore, *British Military Firearms 1650–1850* (London: Herbert Jenkins, 1961), 91–93.
3. De Witt Bailey and Douglas A. Nie, *English Gunmakers: The Birmingham and Provincial Gun Trade in the 18th and 19th Century* (London: Arms and Armour Press, 1978), 102.

Herbert G. Houze

From Navigator to Arms Designer, 1814–1836

Samuel Colt was born on 14 July 1814, the third son and fourth child of Hartford silk manufacturer Christopher Colt and his first wife, Sarah Caldwell.[1] Apart from some posthumous and probably apocryphal stories, little is known about Samuel's childhood.[2] However, given his father's position, he most likely lived quite comfortably until his mother died on 16 June 1821. Following her death, Samuel, along with his three brothers and three sisters, was apparently cared for by one of his father's relatives until Christopher Colt's marriage to Olivia Sargeant in late 1823 or early 1824.[3]

Samuel Colt was evidently educated at home until he enrolled at the Amherst Academy in Amherst, Massachusetts, in early June of 1830 to study navigation, and it is from this period that the earliest documentary evidence concerning Colt's life has survived. His departure for Amherst was a source of concern for his stepmother, as she sent him a letter containing her advice not only about his planned vocation but also how he should behave.

Ware Cottage 15th June 1830

Dear Samuel,
We received your letter today and we all feel gratified that you have located your self where you can acquire a suitable knowledge of Navigation, I hope you will—improve all your time, save what is necessary for exercise & relaxation, that you may prosecute your Studies with renewed energy & vigour.

Your Father informed me this noon that Mr. Lawrence was in the village, that he had invited him to here this after noon. he wished me to write you that, Mr. Lawrence, had no doubt but you could have the Situation desired aboard that Ship—he has seen the Captain & had conversation with him favourable to you obtaining your wishes, provided you qualify your self—You see then Samuel, that self-application is necessary to the gratification of your inclination in your favourite pursuit and a thorough knowledge of Navigation will be a great advantage to you in a voyage upon the Seas. . . .

Now when making choice of your occupation it is time to pause and reflect, you stand as it where upon an eminence, a given point of time, for you to take your stand. . . . Give up the low frivolous pursuits of a boy—and determine at once you will pursue the steps of Manhood. Cultivate the Virtues that adorn & dignify the Man, have a strict regard to honesty & integrity of Character. . . .

I feel it a duty encumbent on me to admonish you before you go out into the World exposed to many hurtful temptations . . . your extreme youth will expose you to much that is eval—but I pray & hope you may be preserved blameless.[4]

Aside from demonstrating a truly affectionate relationship between Samuel Colt and his stepmother, this letter reveals that the future inventor had a long-standing interest in going to sea. On a personal note, Olivia Colt's comment regarding the necessity for self-application suggests that the young man did not always faithfully attend to his studies.

On 23 June Olivia Colt wrote to her stepson again. On this occasion she told him that a family friend, Samuel Lawrence, had "applied to Capt Jones owner of the ship Corvo Capt Spalding for Calcutta to sail in about a month & Capt Jones will take you. he speaks highly of the situation, to be absent about ten months."[5]

Samuel Colt's residence at Amherst Academy was to end shortly thereafter. In a letter dated 22 July 1864 written by Edward Dickinson, a professor at the academy, to Colt's first biographer, Henry Barnard, the young lad's departure is described as follows:

My Dear Sir,
Your letter of yesterday, is just rec'd. I well recollect the main incidents of the celebration enquired about; tho' I never before knew that the celebrated Hartford Sam. Colt was the hero of that occasion.

A young wild fellow of the name of Colt, of Ware, was a member of our Academy & joined with other boys of Academy Lodge, on College Hill, in firing cannon, early in morning of 4th July. (the day of the week, I can't tell.)

Some of the officers of College interfered & tried to stop the noise. Colt, as Prof. Fisk ordered him not to fire again, and placing himself, as the story was told, the next day near the mouth of the gun, swung his match, & cried out "a gun for Prof. Fiske." & touched it off—The Prof. Enquired his name—& he replied, "his name was Colt, & he could Kick like Hell"—He soon left town, for good. This was the account given at the time—& has after been repeated here.[6]

The image of an impetuous and willful youngster revealed traits that were to characterize Samuel Colt's life ever afterward.

Shortly after Samuel Colt returned from Amherst, arrangements were finalized for his going to sea as a member of the crew aboard the brig *Corvo.* This was not without some expense on Christopher Colt's part, as his son had to be totally equipped at a cost of $91.24.[7] Although this may seem a very small amount today, in 1830 dollars it was more than twice the mean monthly wage paid to skilled armorers at the Springfield Armory.[8] In current funds it would equal approximately $1,900.[9] This level of financial commitment indicates that Christopher and Olivia Colt were quite willing to further their son's advancement.

When the *Corvo* sailed from Boston on 2 August 1830, Samuel Lawrence wrote Christopher Colt that "the last time I saw Sam he was in a tarpaulin checkd . shirt & duck trousers on the fore topsail yard loosing the topsail, this was famous at first gain off. The Capt & Super cargo will give him good advice if required & instruction in seamanship, he is a manly fellow & I have no doubt will do credit to all concerned, he was in goods spirits on departure."[10]

Although it is not known when Samuel Colt returned to the United States, it most likely occurred in either May or June of 1831. This date is based upon Olivia Colt's remark in her letter of 23 June 1830 telling Samuel that the *Corvo* would be at sea for "about ten months."

It was during this voyage that Samuel Colt had the epiphany that J. Massey Rhind later romantically re-created for a monument commissioned by Elizabeth Hart Jarvis Colt. While watching the action of the *Corvo*'s wheel, Colt realized that the same method of locking the wheel in a fixed position could be applied to a revolving multiple-barrel firearm. To demonstrate this concept, Colt carved models of the primary parts out of scrap wood to physically illustrate their form and function (fig. 1). Although it has always been assumed that these wood models represented those of a revolving cylinder arm, such was not the case. The original model components and the first pistol constructed after their design by Anson Chase of Hartford were both based upon a multiple-barrel design now known as a pepperbox. This is confirmed not only by the dimensional ratios of the surviving wood models of the arbor pin and supposed "cylinder" (3 in. to 1¹⁵/₁₆ in.) but also by Samuel Colt's own words. In 1842 he stated

Figure 1

Models of an arbor pin, barrel group, and hammer carved out of wood by Samuel Colt while he was aboard the brig *Corvo* in 1831. Long believed to represent parts of a revolving cylinder pistol, the length of the arbor pin (3 in.) in relation to the supposed cylinder pistol (1¹⁵/₁₆ in.) indicates they are models for a pepperbox that had a revolving group of barrels. These pieces were given by Colt to the Hartford gunmaker Anson Chase in late 1831 to serve as guides in the construction of a prototype pepperbox (see figs. 2 and 3). Following Colt's suit against the Massachusetts Arms Company in 1851, they were apparently returned to him by Chase. Wadsworth Atheneum Museum of Art (1905.1072.1-3).

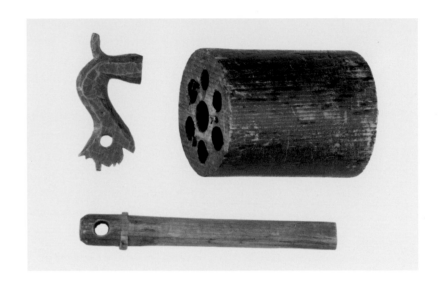

that he had "never made pistols with more than one barrel except at first, about ten years ago, and then only kept them as models."[11] Nine years later, in 1851, Colt described his first revolver in far greater detail when he appeared before the Institution of Civil Engineers in London.

> The first arrangement, contrived by the Author, was the combination of a number of barrels, to rotate upon a spindle, by the act of cocking the lock, and similar in construction to those now generally made; but from the weight and bulk of the arm, it soon appeared better to have only a rotating cylinder containing several chambers, and to discharge through one barrel.[12]

Despite the loss of this pistol during test firing,[13] details of its construction are depicted in three elevational drawings (figs. 2 and 3).[14] Prepared for use as evidence in Samuel Colt's patent infringement case against the Massachusetts Arms Company,[15] the primary view clearly illustrates Colt's separate ratchet collar mounted around the arbor pin connecting the barrel group to the pistol's frame assembly. Based upon the design schematics, the mechanism's operation can be described as follows: when the hammer

Herbert G. Houze

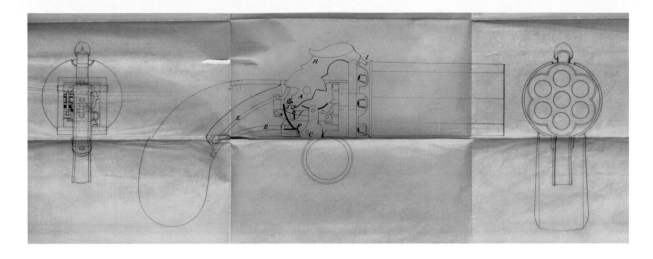

Figure 2

Pen and ink drawing of the pepperbox revolver invented by Samuel Colt in 1830. Samuel Colt Papers, Connecticut Historical Society.

was pulled back or cocked, a link on the mainspring pushed a lever connected to the turning pawl or hand downward; the movement of this link pushed the pawl upward so that it engaged one of the turning collar's ratchets; to ensure this engagement, the pawl moved against a curved flat spring; when the ring trigger was pulled rearward, its upper arm below the pivot point forced the pawl downward, thereby turning the barrel group one-sixth of a full rotation; further rearward movement of the trigger disengaged the sear holding the hammer at full cock, allowing it to fall forward to hit the percussion cap on the nipple of the uppermost barrel.

Figure 3

Detail of the drawing illustrated in fig. 2.

Despite its complicated lockwork, Colt's pepperbox design was revolutionary. For the first time in the development of cylinder breech firearms, a multishot weapon had been designed that allowed its user to automatically rotate the cylinder by the simple action of the hammer. In addition, by employing the percussion ignition system, the barrels coming into firing position were ready for immediate use rather than having to be separately primed. The design did, however, have one drawback: it lacked a mechanism to lock the barrel group in alignment with the barrel at the moment of discharge.

By December 1831 Colt had decided to abandon the multiple-barrel concept in favor of one having a revolving cylinder attached by an arbor pin between a firearm's frame and barrel. In contrast to the pepperbox, Colt's first revolving rifle, made by Anson Chase in December 1831, incorporated a number of improvements. The ratchet collar attached to the cylinder arbor pin was turned by a pawl connected to an operating lever that

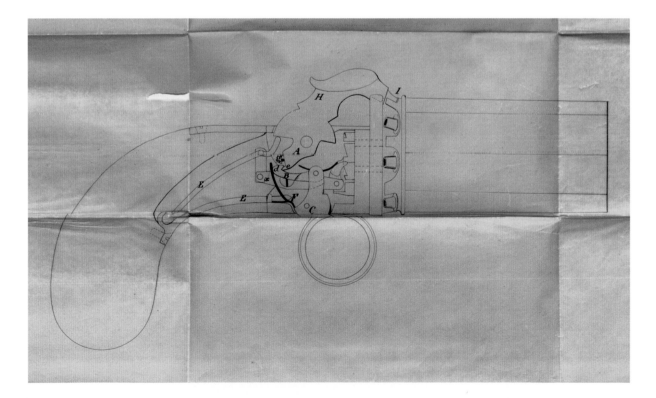

also cocked the hammer. To ensure the proper alignment of the cylinder during firing, it was held in place by a longitudinally acting pin that engaged round recess stops cut into the rear face of the cylinder. When the rifle was cocked, the hammer could be released by a conventional trigger.

Having finally made a workable revolving cylinder arm, Colt began laying plans for development of the design. To finance the work necessary to perfect the initial design, Colt left home again to seek his fortune. It is evident that he did not reveal the nature of his future plans to his father, since on 30 March 1832 Christopher Colt wished him well, whether he chose to go "into a store, or go to Sea, or join in any kind of manuf-ing."[16]

It is unknown whether Samuel Colt had already decided to give demonstrations of nitrous oxide, or laughing gas, as a means of making a living. Similarly, the reasons for his choosing this occupation are also unknown. He adopted the stage name of "Dr. Coult" and by late 1832 was presenting lectures on this subject. For the next three years "Dr. Coult" traveled the eastern seaboard from the Carolinas to the British colony of Nova Scotia, entertaining audiences with his demonstrations of "Exhilarating Gas."

Given the repetitious nature of these lectures, Colt quickly established a set introduction, which he put in writing sometime in 1832 or 1833.

Ladies & Gentlemen

If you wil give me your attention for a few minuits, I wil commence the evenings entertainment with a few intraductary remarks.

Nitrous Oxide, or the Prot Oxide of Azot. which is more genarally known by the name Exhilarating Gas, was discoverd by Dr. Priestly in 1772, but it was first acurateley investigated by Sir Humphrey Davy in 1799. . . .

Sir Humphrey Davy. first shode that by breathing a few quarts of it contand in a Silk bag for too or three minuits effects analagus to those occasioned by drinking formented liquors were produced. Individuals who differ in temperament, are however, as one might expect differantly effected.

It effects uppon some people are truly ludricus, producing involuntary muscular motion, & a propensity for leaping & Running. In others involuntary fits of laughter & in all high spirrits & the most exquisately pleashourable sensations. without any subsequent feelings of debillity. . . .

Agreable to my usual custum, I wil enhale the first dose of Gas myself, in order to show you that it is purfectly pure, & that there need be no fear of inhaling it—I would observe to all pursons who inten taking the Gas, this evening, to dispose of their nives, or other weppins, preaveous to there taking it, in order to gard against an accident, altho I do not apprehend any danger for I have never had an accident hapin.[17]

Despite his disclaimer, Colt's exhibitions were not always without incident. In a letter written to Colt on 10 September 1851 by his old friend the sculptor Hiram Powers, one such incident was described:

I shall never forget the *gas,* at the old museum, nor your sly glances at the ropes stretched around the columns, when about to snatch the gas bag from the huge blacksmith, who glowered so threatenly at you, while his steam was getting up—nor his grab at your coat tail as, frog like, you leaped between the ropes—[18]

The rest of Powers's letter is also of interest, as it raises the tantalizing possibility that the sculptor may have been involved in the construction of some of Colt's earliest prototypes.

I remember your telling me in Washington that at that very time you were elaborating in your mind—the great invention you have since given the world. . . . I have not forgotten my old mechanical pursuits, and I have a shop near here—Turning-lathe, forge &c—& I spend much of my leisure time in this way—I have invented several improvements in working marble and plaster of Paris one of them you shall one of these days—for it embraces much of your own art—it could not fail to be very useful to you—

While Colt's income from this enterprise was somewhat erratic (he apparently charged fifty cents admission per person and had to meet rental fees of about five dollars per night plus the cost of lighting),[19] he spent every spare penny on having models of his firearms made. For the first two years, 1832 and 1833, he commissioned work from a number of different gunmakers. Though Anson Chase of Hartford was still favored, in those towns where Colt had extended runs, he hired local smiths. As this arrangement was less than perfect, in 1834 he entered into a relationship with A. T. Baxter of Baltimore to do most of the work.

In all, thirteen gunmakers or smiths, as well as one engraver and one draftsman, were to be involved, between 1831 and 1835, in the preparation of Colt's first models. What is remarkable about this work is the amount of money Colt spent in developing his idea. From December 1831 through mid-August 1835 he invested a total of $1,362.73½ in the production of ten pistols, seven rifles, and one shotgun. Although this may not appear to be a substantial amount, in today's funds it would be equivalent to approximately $28,500, and even greater expenses were yet to come.

To ensure that his revolver designs were properly protected, on 24 July 1835 Henry L. Ellsworth, commissioner of the U.S. Patent Office, advised Colt to secure an English patent before filing elsewhere.[20] The reason for doing so pertained to a peculiarity of British law that precluded the awarding of a patent to any invention that had been previously protected in another country. Acting on this advice, Colt booked passage on a ship bound for Liverpool on 24 August 1835.[21] On 22 October, just over three months after his twenty-first birthday, Colt was granted patent number 6,909 for his improvements in the construction of revolving firearms.[22] He then went to France, where he filed an identical patent application on 16 November 1835.[23]

Colt spent $676.50 to secure his English patent and $341 to obtain the French one. Factoring in the other expenses involved (passage to Europe, lodgings, and so forth), the total cost for his trip and the patents was $1,912 (equivalent to nearly $40,000 today).[24] In addition, Colt paid William Parker of London twelve shillings (three dollars) on 29 October 1835 for "Polishing Blueing & Hardening Work of a Gun," as well as "To Engraving Scroll work on Do."[25]

Quite apart from the financial investment Colt had made (totaling approximately $68,000 in 2004 funds), the development process was remarkable for a number of other reasons. Traveling in America between 1831 and 1835, he faced dangers that do not exist today. He stayed in boardinghouses of varying quality and gave public lectures, where he was exposed on more than one occasion to cholera.[26] Although Colt does not mention it in any of his surviving letters, he probably also visited towns and cities that were experiencing outbreaks of smallpox and yellow fever. Nonetheless, he persevered, single-mindedly pursuing his dream.

This determination, though admirable in some ways, had its darker side. No matter what the reasons, Colt would not be deterred from seeing his wishes translated into steel and wood. This trait was demonstrated in his dealings with numerous gunsmiths, most notably John Pearson. In a letter dated 26 January 1836, Colt directed Pearson to purchase a number of items to be used in constructing a new pocket pistol.[27] Although he enclosed a draft for fifty dollars, the remainder of the letter was not well received by Pearson. On 1 February Pearson severely rebuked the young inventor for offering him ten dollars in wages for a twelve-hour day, an amount Pearson viewed as an insult.[28] Pearson also cautioned Colt that he was "neither willing to Hazard my Time or money on your work any more."[29] The draft of Colt's response, dated 5 February 1836, reiterated his previous orders and addressed Pearson's concerns only in the next to last paragraph. The actual letter, however, did contain additional money for the distraught gunsmith.

> Sir
> I have only five minutes to devote to you as the male is about to be closing.
> Refer to my letter to you containing the draft for fifty Dollars & I you wil see what are my wishes. Doo as I requested there. Occupy Mr Evit's shop insted of O'Brian's it being probable I shal put one or more hands at work [with y]ou soon.
> Send me the Shot gun by the [first S]team Boate. after having had the Colt heds engraved & purchased what articles nessessary in its use.
> Give me credite for the inclosed draft of Seventy Five Dollars, a part of which appropriate to the purch of Tools & other necessaries for the commencement of your work & the [rest—deleted] ballance to purchase wat articles you should chance need while at work & in the payment of your wages as they come due make your expenses as late as possible.

Tel Brown I shal probably want want him to go to work with you about the first of March. Dont be alarmd about your wages nothing shal be rong on my part. But doo well for me & you shal fare wel—[30]

Samuel Colt's financial condition following his trip to Europe was even worse than it had been before he left. He had used up every cent he had to his name and exhausted those who previously had been disposed to lend him money. Yet his long-term prospects were improving. During his absence, his cousin Dudley Selden, an attorney, had apparently agreed to help finance the construction of a factory in his hometown of Paterson, New Jersey, to manufacture Colt patent revolvers. In addition, Selden took care of the legal niceties involved in formally organizing a company to oversee its operation. This, however, did not answer Colt's immediate needs. Three days after returning from Europe, on 10 January 1836, he drafted the following letter to his father:

The state of my affairs are such that I cant go to Paterson or stay here a weeke Longer without I rais $1000. which is intially out of my power to doo by any proppersitions or—& can offer to Mr Selden He says however that he will try to negotiate at Bank two of your notes of $500. each drawn at Three & Four months & requests them made payable as per indosed scrip.

There is no doubt but that before they fall due I will be able to meete them I hope therefore that you will forward them to me at the Aster House by the next mail as they are my only relyance[31]

Although in the letter Colt actually sent he substantially lowered the amount he wanted to borrow, his request was not well received by his father. Indeed, Christopher Colt's response of 11 February was somewhat terse.

Your favour of the 10th Jny. is recd and contents noted, with all the aid you have thru the introduction of your Cosin Selden and such friendly advice as you will receive of Mr. Ellsworth I have no doubt you will be able realise all the funds you will require from Government or from the Army & Navy departments—After you have obtained a favorable report from the Military or Navy department I hope you will get the News papers in Washington to press the inventor a little & send me a paper—

I think it will be well for you to take orders from Gen. Of the South and West for Rifles & Pistols to be manufd. in New jersey (as soon as you can get underway) and forward to them in the way they shall order let each subscriber pay on submitting enaugh to pay expense of Manufg. & leave something for the inventor—

In the mean time I hope I hope a charter will be granted you in New jersey that will enable [you—deleted] us to git up a Compy. In New York—

I annex my Draft on Mr. Selden for 300$ as requested bu trust you will not dispose of it if you can get along with out it—

I think you had best remain in Washington untill you get something appropriated that you can depend upon unless it important for you to return to New jersey and N York immediately—

. . . you will be likely to meet Mr. Whiting in Washington for Texas If he has Cash he may wish to hand some to you for Rifles & Pistols to be forward to him in Texas—[32]

Christopher Colt's remarks concerning Samuel Whiting were prophetic, as Samuel had already received an order from that gentleman. Sent on 1 January 1836, Whiting's letter had been held during the inventor's absence by John Mason, Samuel Colt's closest friend in Washington. It is interesting to note that Whiting did not seem concerned about the cost of a Colt revolving shotgun, as that subject was not mentioned. It is apparent, however, that he was in a hurry.

Will you please finish as convenient one Repeating Gun of Extra Large Bore to carry from 30 to 35 largest size Buck Shot 3 or 4½ in chamber to be made of the best materials in a plain neat manner & to be put up in a neat plain case with all apparatus &c marking—please have the name of Major S. Whiting engraved on the Gun—when completed write Wm. H. Whiting New Orleans & he will inform you where to send it—[33]

Through the efforts of John Mason, Colt was also able to secure a trial of his revolving arms from the U.S. Navy Commissioners' office. In their letter of notification dated 24 February 1836, the commissioners requested that Colt supply a Trial Board "with one Musket, one Rifle and two pistols, fitted in a plain but substantial manner without ornament; one of the pistols to be of the size of our common ship pistols, and the other that of a pocket pistol."[34]

Unfortunately the orders placed by Major Whiting and the Navy Commissioners were to result in renewed tensions between Samuel Colt and John Pearson, who was to construct the arms requested. Although Colt had access to the money his father had sent him on 11 February, he continued to treat Pearson cavalierly. On 27 March Pearson wrote Colt that he "was greatly disapointed after waiting 3 weeks for a letter and money you make nothing at disapointing me but you do not like I should disapoint you."[35] The payment situation did not improve in the following month, as Pearson sent Colt another scathing letter on 23 April.

> Mr S. Colt
>
> Sir I am sorry I am under nessesity of writing to you for I have waited untill my Patience and money is all gone, For money I have Borrowed untill I am ashamed to ask again for I do not know when I can Pay again. I can Place no confidence in what you write me, as you said you was to receive $1000 on the 18th inst—after which you should come on imediately but here is satirday and you are not come yet nor very likely not one foot nearer than you was when you last wrote, You Pretended to be in a Devil of a hurry when you wrote but not to send any money, I do not know what you think, but know what I think, I did not serve you so when you sent for the rifles to be finished but I worked night and day almost so I would not disapoint you, and what have I got for it—why vexation and trouble, if I had not sent you the 2 rifles you could but serve me so, If you was disapointed in getting the money, you might have Borrowed as much as would satisfy me as you say you have got through all the difficulty.[36]

Pearson closed his letter with the statement that he was "in a Devil of a ill humor and not without cause."

Unbeknown to Pearson, Colt was in no position to advance the funds requested. Since May 1835, when he left the lecture circuit to concentrate on promoting and patenting his revolvers, Colt had been borrowing money to finance those efforts. Indeed, prior to his departure for England, he had given promissory notes to his second cousin, Roswell Lyman Colt of Pater-

son, and pawned the cased shotgun made in January 1835 and one pistol.[37] Between 10 January and 9 June 1836, he borrowed an additional $2,064.50 (approximately $40,000 in today's funds) from his father and Dudley Selden.[38] Some of this money was evidently used to pay Pearson, as Colt's accounts indicate that the gunsmith received $240 between 23 January and 2 March 1836. Pearson's assistant, F. H. Brask, was paid a total of $133.25 over the same period.[39] The outstanding amounts due Pearson that occasioned his letter of 23 April, however, were not paid until after 14 June, when Colt received a $2,000 advance against the production royalties he was to receive from the newly formed Patent Arms Manufacturing Company.[40] To say the least, it was not an auspicious beginning for that company.

If there was one bright spot for Colt in early 1836, it was the issuance on 25 February of his first United States patent for an "Improvement in Fire-Arms."[41]

Notes

1. For Samuel Colt's genealogy, see Appendix One.

2. Numerous accounts of Colt's early interest in firearms have been published (e.g., Henry Barnard, *Armsmear: The Home, the Arm, and the Armory of Samuel Colt* [New York: Privately published, 1866]); however, none of these appeared during the inventor's lifetime, nor did Colt ever write about his early interests.

3. While the date of Christopher Colt's marriage to Olivia Sargeant is unknown, it predated the birth of their first child, William Upson Colt, on 25 October 1824.

4. Olivia Colt to Samuel Colt, 15 June 1830. Samuel Colt Papers, Box 1, Connecticut Historical Society.

5. Olivia Colt to Samuel Colt, 23 June 1830. Samuel Colt Papers, Box 1, Connecticut Historical Society.

6. Edward Dickinson to Henry Barnard, 22 July 1864. Samuel Colt Correspondence, Wadsworth Atheneum Museum of Art, Bequest of Elizabeth Hart Jarvis Colt.

7. Among the items purchased for the voyage were an almanac, compass, jackknife, and mattress, as well as bedding, a quadrant, and a seaman's chest (Samuel Lawrence to Christopher Colt, 2 August 1830. Samuel Colt Correspondence, Wadsworth Atheneum Museum of Art, Bequest of Elizabeth Hart Jarvis Colt).

8. Felicia Johnson Deyrup, *Arms Makers of the Connecticut Valley: A Regional Study of the Economic Development of the Small Arms Industry, 1798–1870*, Smith College Studies in History 33 (Northampton, Mass.: Smith College, 1948), 242.

9. This amount is based upon the conversion factors provided by the Consumer Price Index.

10. Samuel Lawrence to Christopher Colt, 2 August 1830. Samuel Colt Correspondence, Wadsworth Atheneum Museum of Art, Bequest of Elizabeth Hart Jarvis Colt.

11. This statement was made by Samuel Colt in testimony he gave during the murder trial of his brother John. Thomas Dunphy and Thomas J. Cummins, *Remarkable Trials of all Countries: Particularly of the United States, Great Britain, Ireland and France; with Notes and Speeches of Counsel* (New York: Diossy & Co., 1867), 256.

12. Samuel Colt, "On the application of Machinery to the manufacture of Rotating Chambered-Breech Fire-Arms, and the peculiarities of those Arms," *Minutes of Proceedings of the Institution of Civil Engineers, with Abstracts of the Discussions*, vol. XI, session 1851–52 (London: Institution of Civil Engineers, 1852), 38.

13. Robert M. Patterson, *In the Circuit Court of the United States, District of Massachusetts. Samuel Colt vs. The Mass. Arms Company. Report of the Trial of the Above-Entitled Cause, at Boston, on the Thirtieth Day of June, A.D. 1851, Before His Honor, Levi Woodbury, Associate Justice, of the Supreme Court of the United States* (Boston: White & Potter, 1851), 229.

14. Pen and ink drawing on tissue paper, n.d. [1851]. Samuel Colt Papers, Box 11, Folder 9 (Drawings), Connecticut Historical Society.

15. The draftsmanship and type of paper are more consistent with a production date of 1851 than with the 1830s.

16. Christopher Colt to Samuel Colt, 30 March 1832. Samuel Colt Correspondence, Wadsworth Atheneum Museum of Art, Bequest of Elizabeth Hart Jarvis Colt.

17. Samuel Colt, "Ladies & Gentlemen," n.d. [1832–33]. Samuel Colt Papers, Box 9, File 4, Connecticut Historical Society.

18. Hiram Powers to Samuel Colt, 10 September 1851. Samuel Colt Correspondence, Wadsworth Atheneum Museum of Art, Bequest of Elizabeth Hart Jarvis Colt.

19. Colt was quoted an evening's rental fee of five dollars for the "Franklin Hall" in Portsmouth, New Hampshire, or Rhode Island in 1834 (Locke & Robinson to Samuel Colt, 26 September 1834. Samuel Colt Correspondence, Wadsworth Atheneum Museum of Art, Bequest of Elizabeth Hart Jarvis Colt). This fee did not include lighting, for which sperm whale candles were available at a cost of thirty-three cents per pound of oil or one dollar per gallon.

20. Henry L. Ellsworth to Christopher Colt, 24 July 1835. Samuel Colt Papers, Box 1, Connecticut Historical Society.

21. Samuel Colt "Expendatures . . . ," 6 March 1835. Samuel Colt Papers, Box 1, Connecticut Historical Society.

22. Samuel Colt, Letters Patent for "Revolving Fire-arms," 22 October 1835, enrolled 30 October 1835, Number 6,909.

23. Préfecture du Département de la Seine, No. 6024 du Registre des Brevets: Proces-Verbal de depot de Pièces pour un Brevet issued to Samuel Colt, 16 November 1835. Samuel Colt Papers, Box 1, Connecticut Historical Society.

24. Samuel Colt, "Expendatures . . . ," 6 March 1835, 5–6.

25. Receipt of William Parker to Samuel Colt, 29 October 1835. Samuel Colt Papers, Box 1, Connecticut Historical Society.

26. Samuel Colt to Christopher Colt, 30 November 1834. Samuel Colt Papers, Box 1, Connecticut Historical Society.

27. Samuel Colt to John Pearson, 26 January 1836. Samuel Colt Papers, Box 1, Connecticut Historical Society.

28. John Pearson to Samuel Colt, 1 February 1836. Samuel Colt Papers, Box 1, Connecticut Historical Society.

29. Ibid.

30. Samuel Colt to John Pearson, 5 February 1836. Samuel Colt Papers, Box 1, Connecticut Historical Society.

31. Samuel Colt to Christopher Colt, 10 January 1836. Samuel Colt Papers, Box 1, Connecticut Historical Society.

32. Christopher Colt to Samuel Colt, 11 February 1836. Samuel Colt Papers, Box 1, Connecticut Historical Society.

33. S. Whiting to Samuel Colt, 1 January 1836. Samuel Colt Papers, Box 1, Connecticut Historical Society.

34. Jn. Honyer (?), Navy Commissioners' Office to Samuel Colt, 24 February 1836. Samuel Colt Papers, Box 1, Connecticut Historical Society.

35. John Pearson to Samuel Colt, 27 March 1836. Samuel Colt Papers, Box 1, Connecticut Historical Society.

36. John Pearson to Samuel Colt, 23 April 1836. Samuel Colt Papers, Box 1, Connecticut Historical Society.

37. Samuel Colt, "Expendatures . . . ," 6 March 1835, 7.

38. Ibid.

39. Ibid., 6.

40. Ibid., 7.

41. U.S. Patent Office. Samuel Colt, "Improvement in Fire-Arms," Number 138, issued 25 February 1836.

Herbert G. Houze

12

Prototype Revolving Rifle

No serial number

Caliber .36 in., barrel length 35½ in., overall length 54¼ in.

Date of Manufacture: 1831–32

Wadsworth Atheneum Museum of Art

Bequest of Elizabeth Hart Jarvis Colt, 1905.1032

Detail of right frame with
smoke door open

Although this rifle was reworked after its manufacture, the major components (the frame, internal lockwork, cylinder, and barrel) are likely those made for Samuel Colt by Anson Chase of Hartford in December 1831 and January 1832.[1] This assertion is based on the somewhat unsophisticated construction of the lock and the mechanism used to rotate the cylinder. For example, the spring bearing against the trigger sear is awkwardly mounted in a sideways position within the frame, and the ratchet collar that revolves the cylinder is of cogwheel rather than toothed construction.

The rifle is cocked and its cylinder rotated by means of the lever mounted to the rear of the trigger. During the lever's final movement it causes a locking bolt to move forward so that it engages a recess cut in the rear face of the cylinder.

The rifle can then be fired by pressing the trigger. While the internal hammer is of conventional construction, its head or tip does not strike the cylinder's nipples. Instead it hits a spring-loaded striker or firing pin located within the forward wall of the frame. This striker then transmits the pressure of the hammer's momentum against the nipples.

This rifle has several other features that are unique to its construction. The right side of the nipple shield is fitted with a hinged and pierced trapdoor that allows access to the nipples for capping, as well as the ventilation of combustion gases. The left side of the shield is likewise perforated with vents. The cover plate in front of the cylinder has a loading aperture with a sliding brass access panel.

Based upon wood inserts set into the bottom of the stock to the rear of the existing trigger guard tang, it is apparent that the guard was replaced on at least two occasions. It is also possible that the butt stock was replaced after the rifle's original manufacture.

Note

1. Anson Chase to Samuel Colt, Receipts for "work on Rifle," 12 December 1831 and 7 January 1832. Samuel Colt Papers, Box 1, Connecticut State Library.

13

Prototype Revolving Rifle

No serial number

Caliber .30 in., barrel length 34½ in., overall length 52⅛ in.

Date of Manufacture: 1832

Wadsworth Atheneum Museum of Art

Bequest of Elizabeth Hart Jarvis Colt, 1905.1028

Overall left

The conventionally positioned internal lockwork of this rifle identifies it as being the second one made by Anson Chase for Samuel Colt. Completed sometime in December 1832,[1] it incorporates a cylinder locking mechanism entirely different from the previously described prototype. In place of the horizontally acting bolt that engaged cutout recesses in the rear of the cylinder, this rifle has a locking bolt set within the frame's body directly below the cylinder. Actuated by a levered arm, the upper surface of this bolt rises to enter round stops cut into the cylinder's circumference when the hammer is cocked. It is not known whether this cylinder lock was originally installed by Chase or is a later modification. The latter is entirely possible, as it is evident that John Pearson restocked the piece.[2] Moreover, when that work took place (July 1835), all of Colt's prototypes were being fitted with vertically acting cylinder bolts.

The engraved foliate scrollwork found on the nipple shield is believed to have been executed by Richard B. Henshaw of New York City.[3]

While the barrel of this rifle was previously attributed to Pearson,[4] it was in fact salvaged from another gun, made by J. Pan of Aachen, Sweden.

Notes

1. Anson Chase to Samuel Colt, Invoice, 30 December 1832. Samuel Colt Papers, Box 1, Connecticut Historical Society.

2. The scrolled finger spur to the rear of the trigger guard is a hallmark of Pearson's work. Although it frequently serves merely as the terminal of the guard, in this instance it is the head of a threaded bolt that secures the upper tang of the frame, as well as the mainspring. The presence of the silver patchbox indicates that the stock work was done after 8 July 1835, when Colt purchased two patchboxes of this type from Edward Tryon of Philadelphia (Edward Tryon to Samuel Colt, Receipt for "2 Electrum heal plates &c," 8 July 1835. Samuel Colt Papers, Box 1, Connecticut Historical Society).

3. Robert M. Patterson, *In the Circuit Court of the United States, District of Massachusetts. Samuel Colt vs. The Mass. Arms Company. Report of the Trial of the Above-Entitled Cause, At Boston, on the Thirtieth Day of June, A.D. 1851, Before His Honor, Levi Woodbury, Associate Justice of the Supreme Court of the United States* (Boston: White & Potter, 1851), 255.

4. R. L. Wilson, *The Paterson Colt Book: The Early Evolution of Samuel Colt's Repeating Arms* (Palo Alto, Calif.: Strutz-LeVett Publishing Co., n.d. [2002]), 25.

Herbert G. Houze

14

Prototype Revolving Rifle

No serial number

Caliber .52 in., barrel length 34 in., overall length 53 in.

Date of Manufacture: 1834

Wadsworth Atheneum Museum of Art

Bequest of Elizabeth Hart Jarvis Colt, 1905.1030

Overall left

In early 1834 Samuel Colt engaged the services of A. T. Baxter in Baltimore to construct his sample pistols and rifles.[1] As Baxter apparently maintained a relatively large shop, he assigned the work to one of his employees, John Pearson.

This rifle was one of the first arms produced by Baxter and Pearson. It represents a major improvement over the preceding prototypes due to its use of a cocking and rotation lever located in front of the trigger. The repositioning of the lever allowed use of a simpler hammer, which improved the transmission of the lever's momentum to the internal lockwork. Another design change involved the use of a rectangular-headed locking bolt in place of the round one previously used. To accommodate this change, the locking recesses cut in the cylinder's circumference were altered to the same form.

As with the previous Chase-made rifle, this piece is believed to have been engraved by Richard B. Henshaw of New York,[2] and it is fitted with a salvaged barrel.[3]

Notes

1. A. T. Baxter to Samuel Colt, Receipt for work on rifles and pistols, 24 May 1834. Samuel Colt Papers, Box 1, Connecticut Historical Society.

2. Robert M. Patterson, *In the Circuit Court of the United States, District of Massachusetts. Samuel Colt vs. The Mass. Arms Company. Report of the Trial of the Above-Entitled Cause, At Boston, on the Thirtieth Day of June, A.D. 1851, Before His Honor, Levi Wood-*

bury, Associate Justice of the Supreme Court of the United States (Boston: White & Potter, 1851), 255.

3. In this instance the barrel was made by an individual named Worley and is so marked on the right side immediately forward of the breech. Given the absence of a given name or initial, it is impossible to positively identify Worley as either an American or English barrel smith.

15

Prototype Revolving Shotgun

Serial number 5

Caliber .66 in., barrel length 30⅜ in., overall length 49⅝ in.

Date of Manufacture: 1834–35

Wadsworth Atheneum Museum of Art

Bequest of Elizabeth Hart Jarvis Colt, 1905.1025

Markings

Cheek piece escutcheon: S. Colt P. T.

Overall left

Detail of engraved inscription

Detail of cylinder

Of all the early Colt prototypes, this shotgun is the best documented. Its construction was begun in late 1834 and completed in the third or fourth week of January 1835.[1] The work was primarily carried out by John Pearson under the direction of Charles C. C. O'Brian.[2] In a letter to Pearson dated 23 January 1835 Colt requested that the shotgun be put up in a suitable wooden case with all the accessories necessary for its use (cap primer, shot bag, cleaning rods, etc.). In addition, Colt noted:

> I forgot to mention I wished you to have the ornament on the stock ingraved. Take it to the ingraver underneath the museum or some other good ingraver & have him ingrave the Colts heads in the center of which I want my name (S Colts P.T.) Engraved.[3]

On 10 February 1835 Pearson informed Colt that he had taken the gunstock to be engraved.[4] The work was carried out by an artist surnamed Medeitry, who charged Pearson $1.50.[5] The finished shotgun, case, and accessories were subsequently shipped to Colt in Richmond, Virginia, on 26 February 1835.[6] In the autumn of 1835 Colt took this shotgun with him to England, where he had it refinished and the frame engraved by the London gunmaker William Parker.[7]

Herbert G. Houze

Due to its rather substantial caliber, the barrel of the gun was secured to the frame not only by a transverse pin passing through the forward end of the cylinder arbor and a set screw in the front cylinder plate but also by two longitudinal bolts located on either side of the cylinder. These reinforcing bolts are attached at the rear by screws entering the frame, and their tips are threaded to receive capstan nuts. To facilitate capping, the right side of the nipple shield is provided with a sliding access aperture.

Notes

1. Samuel Colt to John Pearson, 23 January 1835, and Charles C. C. O'Brian to Samuel Colt, Invoice for work done on shotgun, 26 January 1835. Samuel Colt Papers, Box 1, Connecticut Historical Society.

2. Samuel Colt to John Pearson, 23 January 1835. Samuel Colt Papers, Box 1, Connecticut Historical Society.

3. Ibid.

4. John Pearson to Samuel Colt, 10 February 1835. Samuel Colt Papers, Box 1, Connecticut Historical Society.

5. Medeitry to John Pearson, Bill "for Engraving Gun with Colt Heads & name," 14 February 1835. Samuel Colt Papers, Box 1, Connecticut Historical Society.

6. Maryland & Virginia Steam Boat Company to John Pearson, Bill of Lading, 26 February 1835. Samuel Colt Papers, Box 1, Connecticut Historical Society.

7. William Parker to Samuel Colt, Invoice, 29 October 1835. Samuel Colt Papers, Box 1, Connecticut Historical Society.

16

Prototype Revolving Rifle

No serial number

Caliber .36 in., barrel length 32¾ in., overall length 49¼ in.

Date of Manufacture: 1835

Wadsworth Atheneum Museum of Art

Bequest of Elizabeth Hart Jarvis Colt, 1905.968

Markings

Barrel: S. Colt P. T.

See catalogue 17 for a discussion of this rifle.

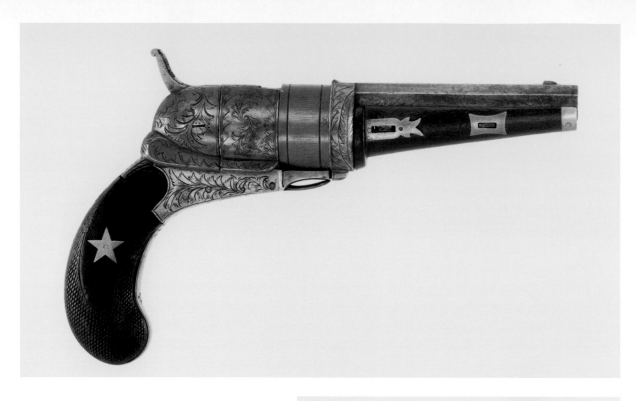

Overall disassembled

17

Prototype Revolving Pocket Pistol

No serial number

Baltimore, Md.

Caliber .33 in., barrel length 3¹¹/₁₆ in., overall length 7¾ in.

Date of Manufacture: 1835

Wadsworth Atheneum Museum of Art

Bequest of Elizabeth Hart Jarvis Colt, 1905.1014

The construction of this rifle (cat. 16) and pistol (cat. 17) indicates that they were made at the same time. Both have the same stepped contours along the lower frame beneath the cylinder and identically formed cylinder front plates. In addition, the exterior dimensions of the pistol's barrel at the breech correspond to those of the rifle's muzzle. This detail allows the two pieces to be identified with instructions Colt sent to John Pearson on 16 January 1835.

> Purchase of Mr O'Brian the small rifled barrel that I spoke of when in Baltimore price Five Dollars. From the small end of it cut a barrel of a [small—deleted] pocket pistol of the sise of the first pare you made for me.[1]

While the engraving found on the rifle parallels that attributed to Richard B. Henshaw of New York, the decoration on the pistol is from an entirely different hand. It might have been decorated by the unknown Baltimore engraver who did some work charged to Colt's account by A. T. Baxter in July 1835.[2]

The pistol's cylinder is of note, as the chambers are counterbored, so that the diameter of the lower section where the powder would be placed is smaller than the mouth where the bullet would be set. The advantage of this design is that it automatically prevented the accidental overcharging of the chambers with gunpowder. If too much powder was introduced into a chamber, the bullet would not seat on the concave step where the interior diameters changed. This would cause it to protrude from the chamber's mouth, thereby preventing the reassembly of the pistol. By ensuring that a proper powder charge was used at all times, Colt was attempting to make certain that the cylinders of his samples never failed during use.

Notes

1. Samuel Colt to John Pearson, 16 January 1835. Samuel Colt Papers, Box 1, Connecticut Historical Society.
2. A. T. Baxter to Samuel Colt, Invoice for "Engraving Pistol," 18 July 1835. Samuel Colt Papers, Box 1, Connecticut Historical Society.

18

Prototype Revolving Holster Pistol

No serial number

Caliber .53 in., barrel length 8 3/16 in., overall length 13 5/16 in.

Date of Manufacture: 1835–36

Wadsworth Atheneum Museum of Art

Bequest of Elizabeth Hart Jarvis Colt, 1905.989

Overall left

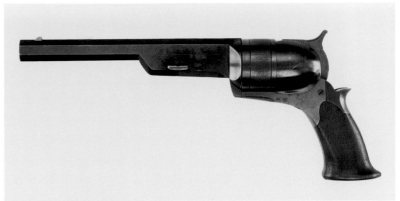

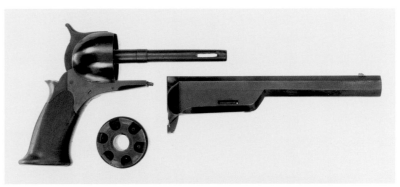

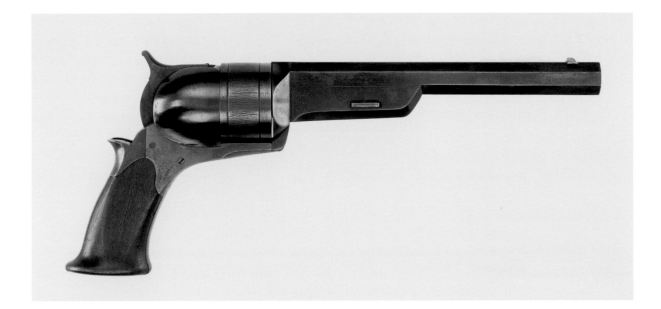

Overall disassembled

Without question the most aesthetically pleasing of all the Colt prototypes is the Holster Pistol made by John Pearson. In many respects the lines of this revolver would not have been out of place had it been made in the 1930s, a century after its actual manufacture. Its curved lines and angular surfaces interact against each other in a manner that is reminiscent of Art Deco automobile coachwork.[1]

As the accompanying drawing demonstrates, the Pearson Holster Pistol did not always possess the aesthetic balance it now has. When first made in 1835, it was fitted with a shorter barrel having an angled and truncated bolster below its breech. A filled keyhole slot in the back strap indicates that the pistol was originally fitted with a detachable shoulder stock.

At Colt's request, in March 1836, Pearson modified the pistol's grip and fitted it with a new longer barrel. These alterations were necessitated by a letter Colt had received from the U.S. Navy Board of Commissioners. In agreeing to test his revolvers, the board specified that Colt furnish them with "one Musket, one Rifle and two pistols, fitted in a plain but substantial manner without ornament; one of the pistols to be of the size of our common Ship pistols, and the other that of a pocket pistol."[2] That Pearson carried out this work is confirmed in a letter to Colt dated 27 March 1836. In response to Colt's complaint that

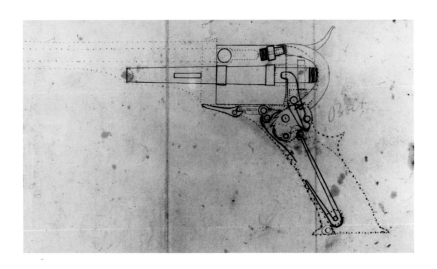

Cat. 18a. Pen and ink drawing, ca. 1835, of the Pearson prototype Holster Pistol illustrating the original form of its barrel and grip. Records of the Colt's Patent Fire Arms Manufacturing Company, Connecticut State Library.

Pearson had not followed his instructions, Pearson replied, "I have not Done any but that Large one I have alter'd the Handle and finished it"[3] (cat. 18a).

Apart from filling the keyhole slot, Pearson fitted fuller grips with flared lower edges to counterbalance the increased weight from the barrel. He also installed a cap box on the bottom of the grip. While the dimensions of this Holster Pistol approximated those of the U.S. Navy Pistol adopted in 1826 (an overall length of 13¼ in. and barrel length of 8⅝ in.), its caliber was slightly smaller (.52 vs. .54 in.).[4] That one point notwithstanding, in comparison with the single-shot flintlock pistol and the percussion version that followed in 1842, Colt's revolver was light-years ahead.

Notes

1. For example, the lines of this pistol can be favorably compared to the coachwork carried out by the Italian firm of Figoni & Falaschi for Delahaye.

2. Jn. Honyers (?), Navy Commissioners' Office to Samuel Colt, 24 February 1836. Samuel Colt Papers, Box 1, Connecticut Historical Society.

3. John Pearson to Samuel Colt, 27 March 1836. Samuel Colt Papers, Box 1, Connecticut Historical Society.

4. Robert M. Reilly, *United States Military Small Arms 1816–1865* (Baton Rouge, La.: Eagle Press, 1970), 176–77.

19

Prototype Revolving Rifle

No serial number

Caliber .53 in., barrel length 32 in., overall length 49¼ in.

Date of Manufacture: 1836 (?)

Wadsworth Atheneum Museum of Art

Bequest of Elizabeth Hart Jarvis Colt, 1905.1026

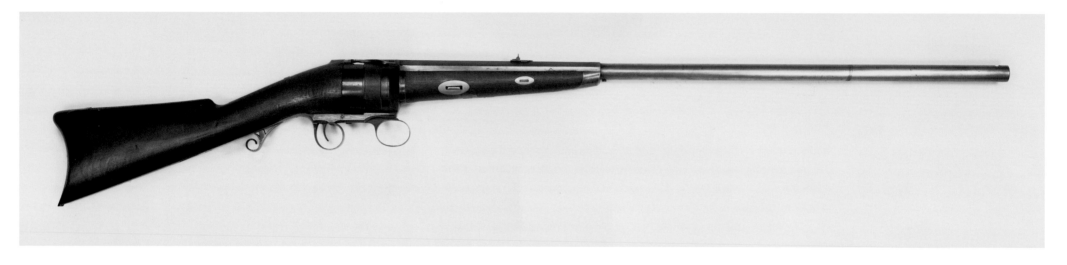

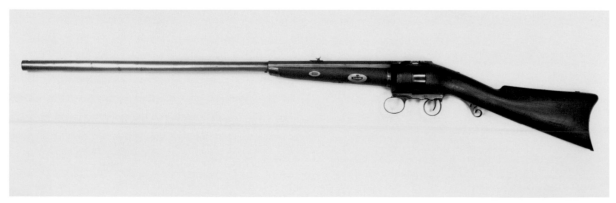

Given the caliber and absence of any ornamentation, this rifle may have been made in response to the U.S. Navy Board of Commissioners' request for a plain revolving rifle in February 1836.[1] However, the lack of any records describing the arms submitted by Colt for testing prevents a positive identification.

Note

1. Jn. Honyer (?), Navy Commissioners' Office to Samuel Colt, 24 February 1836. Samuel Colt Papers, Box 1, Connecticut Historical Society.

Overall left

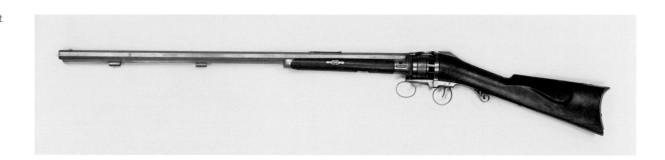

20

Prototype Revolving Rifle

No serial number

Caliber .35 in., barrel length 30⅝ in., overall length 47⅞ in.

Date of Manufacture: 1836

Wadsworth Atheneum Museum of Art

Bequest of Elizabeth Hart Jarvis Colt, 1905.1021

In preparation for the tooling up of the Patent Arms Manufacturing Company's factory in Paterson, New Jersey, John Pearson built several arms that were to serve as model pieces.

This rifle essentially established the pattern for what was to become known as the Number 1 Rifle. Having had some of his prototypes chain-fire (that is, multiple chambers going off in succession) due to the construction of the nipple shield and the plate in front of the cylinder, Colt dispensed with these two components. He also abandoned the vertically operating cylinder bolt in favor of the earlier design locking the cylinder from the rear. Given these refinements, it is likely that this rifle was made toward the very end of Pearson's employment by Colt, in June 1836.

The Paterson Era, 1836–1841

Samuel Colt's dream of quantity production moved closer to reality on 5 March 1836, when the State of New Jersey issued a charter to the Patent Arms Manufacturing Company.[1] Actual production, however, did not begin until December 1836. This delay was caused by the need to build a factory, install its machinery, and refine Colt's revolver designs for manufacture.

Located in Paterson, the Patent Arms Manufacturing Company was in many respects a family affair, as its capitalization had been drawn from relatives of the extended Colt family or their immediate friends.[2] As a result, there was a vested interest in seeing the concern become a successful business. A key element in ensuring its success was the hiring of a competent manager or superintendent to oversee the factory's operation. Fortunately the person chosen was an extremely gifted mechanic named Pliny Lawton.[3] Originally from Massachusetts, Lawton was the ideal choice for the position, as he had extensive experience in the manufacturing field. Moreover, he was a man of considerable abilities, who over the next six years was to prove indispensable to Colt in translating the inventor's design concepts into hard steel.

Under the terms proposed by Colt on 9 March 1836 and approved by the company on 30 May, Colt was to receive a royalty advance of $6,000 against his fifty percent share of the firm's net annual profits.[4] Once manufacture had actually begun, it was also stipulated that Colt was to receive a yearly stipend of $1,000 to promote his revolvers.[5]

The first model to enter production was the Number 1 Revolving Rifle in late 1836.[6] Shortly thereafter, in January 1837, manufacture of the Number 1 Pocket Pistol commenced.[7] By the end of that year four models were in production, and a balance sheet prepared by Colt to calculate his potential royalties indicated that nearly one thousand arms had already been made.[8] Of that number, two hundred were Number 1 Rifles, five hundred were Number 1 Pistols, approximately two hundred were Number 2 Pistols, and the remainder were Number 2 Rifles. The balance sheet drawn up by Colt indicated that five hundred Number 2 Rifles were to be made; however, that quantity was never realized. This shortfall in production was most likely caused by undercapitalization, as Colt noted that an additional $12,000 needed to be spent to complete the arms then called for.[9] One other entry in Colt's account is of interest, as it documents Dudley Selden's financial involvement with the company. Aside from owning stock, he apparently had advanced the concern an additional $16,000 to enable it to commence operations.[10]

Throughout the first year of operation, the company was plagued by stagnant sales. Hoping to improve the situation, Samuel Colt used letters of introduction from Henry L. Ellsworth, commissioner of the U.S. Patent Office, as well as other Washington contacts, to secure a trial of his revolving rifles by the U. S. Army.[11] Conducted at the U.S. Military Academy, West Point, New York, in June 1837, the trial produced results that were, to say the least, disastrous. The review officers reported that Colt's arms were "entirely unsuited to the general purposes of the service."[12]

Colt did achieve a minor success in May 1838, when Maj. Gen. Thomas Jesup authorized the purchase of fifty Number 1 Rifles for use by troops under his command in Florida.[13] Although payment for this unorthodox order was delayed,[14] its receipt enabled the Patent Arms Manufacturing Company to survive at a time when it was hard-pressed for operating capital. From Samuel Colt's perspective, the most important aspect of this sale involved the field reports submitted by troops armed with his rifles. In contrast to the findings of the West Point trial board, Jesup's men indicated that the rifles were completely suitable for service use and not susceptible to failure.[15] Buoyed by this success, Colt began lobbying government officials for more purchases.

Despite his best efforts, no new contracts were forthcoming. This had a profound effect on Colt's income, which was based in part on royalties. But to increase those royalties, he had to spend money beyond his stipend courting potential buyers. The direct consequence of this situation was spiraling debt. To support himself and more importantly his efforts to secure sales, in 1837 Colt began borrowing money against future royalties from the Patent Arms Manufacturing Company.[16] These advances were not freely dispensed. On 1 March 1837 Dudley Selden cautioned Colt that he was far too liberal in his spending: "It seems to me that you use money as if it were drawn from an inexhaustible mine."[17] Such admonishments had little effect on Colt's behavior, as these funds made it possible for him to continue his sales efforts.

As the following production and sales summary demonstrates, 890 arms had been sold out of a total production of 1,992 by 1 July 1839.[18]

	No 1 Rifle	No 2 Rif	No 1 P	No 2 &3	No 5	Carbine	Shot Gun
[Sold]	158-	40-	128-	433-	118	8-	5
Made	201-	200	490-	700-	201-	100-	100-
[Net]	43	160	262 [*sic*] 267		83	92	95

While these sales figures were not outstanding, they did indicate that Colt was producing more and more income for the company.

In his zeal to secure sales, Colt sometimes engaged in somewhat problematic activities. Although it is not known what sort of inducement Colt offered to the U.S. Army's chief of ordnance, Col. George Bomford, in late 1838 to approve a proposed purchase contract, its disclosure to the company management in Paterson brought an immediate response. In a letter dated 6 January 1839, Dudley Selden, one of the firm's principal shareholders and its treasurer, expressed his displeasure to Colt in no uncertain terms:

> I will not become a party to a negotiations with a public officer to allow him compensation for aid in securing a contract with the government The suggestion with respect to Col Bumford is dishonorable in every way. and if you write me I trust it will relate to other topics.[19]

Chastised but not cowed, Colt continued to promote his revolvers in Washington. In these efforts he drew upon one character trait that was to serve him well throughout his life: persistence. To secure letters of endorsement, he evidently had to badger some officers. For example, he had to press Lt. Col. William S. Harney of the 2nd Regiment of U.S. Dragoons for an assessment of the Number 1 Ring Lever Rifles that his command had used during the Seminole War. On 6 February 1839 Colt finally received the report he had so dearly wanted.

> In answer to the many inquiries which you make of me respecting the Rifles of your Invention that I have had in my possession some Twelve or Fifteen months I have the pleasure to state that they have surpassed my expectations, (which were great) in every particular. They have had much hard service in Florida, & with the exception of two of the fifty, they are all in good order. Those two are by no-means irreparable.

It is my honest opinion that no other Guns than those of your invention will be used in a few years.[20]

In the years to come, letters such as that written by Harney would be used by Colt in advertising brochures, newspaper submissions, and supporting documents sent to government agencies. Indeed, it could be said that Colt perfected the use of endorsements as a promotional tool.

In 1839 Colt had to confine his sales efforts to demonstrations. These were not always easily arranged, and as his report of 12 March 1839 to the president and directors of the Patent Arms Manufacturing Company indicates, various methods were used to secure participation.

> devoted my whole time to establish the merits of our Carbine with the Officers of the Army and Navy to effect which my first move was to send every Officer then at Washington a printed Note of invitation to attend the Shooting and other experiments to be tried with our Carbine appointing a time and place for that purpose—those that attended were highly delighted many of whom shot the Arm themselves and the next day I met some of the Officers by appointment who were present at the exhibition and we drafted a recommendation and petition of which the enclosed is a Copy and obtained the signatures of most of the Officers present at the Shooting Match which being only a portion of the Officers then in the City rendered it necessary to adopt further means of getting the signatures of others before we could expect to carry our point with the Secretary and as it was impossible to get their names to the paper by simply showing them the Carbine and equally impossible to induce most of them to attend a Public Shooting Match and I being determined at any expence and the hazard of the pecuniary inconvenience to which I am now consequently subjected—to effect the object I danced constant attempting on them until with the aid of a few friends I had already made I got them one by one to ride with me a few Miles in the Country to the Race Course where after sundry trials and invitations to dinner I succeeded in convincing most of them of the superiority of my arms and added their signature to the paper.[21]

Figure 1

Line engraving illustrating the operational relationship of the hammer, hand, pawl, and cylinder of a standard-production Colt revolver. Wadsworth Atheneum Museum of Art.

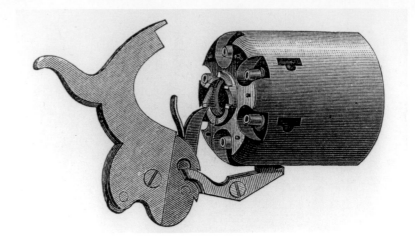

In addition to providing invitations to dinner, Colt freely used alcoholic beverages to influence his guests. For example, during the January to February promotional campaign he purchased forty-six bottles of beer, brandy, sherry, and Madeira from the liquor dealer Edward Simms of Washington.[22]

Colt's methods did produce results, and on 6 March 1839 he submitted a "Recommendation for a trial of Repeating Arms" signed by thirty-two serving officers to Secretary of War Joel R. Poinsett.[23] Attesting to the breadth of Colt's contacts is the inclusion among the petition's signatories of five major generals, four colonels, and one former state governor. Although not immediately acted upon, this March recommendation eventually led to the purchase of two hundred carbines in 1841.[24]

Despite Colt's success in securing these sales, his reliance upon distilled spirits as a marketing tool displeased Dudley Selden. Indeed, two years earlier, Selden had written Colt that he had "no belief in undertaking to raise the character of your gun by old Madeira."[25]

Aside from freely spending money to promote his arms, Colt lived beyond his means in other ways. To present an image of prosperity in Washington, he not only dined fashionably but also dressed the part. As a result, between 2 July 1838 and 18 May 1839 he ran up a bill of $290.75 at his tailor, George Andrews.[26]

Colt's freewheeling methods and his largesse in using company funds eventually soured his relationship with many of his earlier supporters. This was particularly true of Dudley Selden, who had attempted on many occasions to rein Colt in.[27] Realizing that his entreaties were falling on deaf ears, in 1838 Selden secured approval from the company's stockholders to arrange a new contractual relationship with Colt. After an exchange of numerous offers and counterproposals, Colt relinquished his position as an employee of the company and instead became its agent.[28] Moreover, four-fifths of the royalties due Colt were to be retained by the company to repay his outstanding debts.[29] This had the immediate effect of reducing the negative cash flow previously generated by Colt, while at the same time putting the inventor in an even more precarious financial position. Aside from being cut off from a ready income, he was responsible not only for his own expenses but also for those relating to the firm's New York City store at 155 Broadway.

Although his correspondence with the officers of the company remained cordial after this date, circumstantial evidence suggests that Colt had already realized that it was not in his best interests to share all his thoughts with the firm. This is particularly true of improvements he had developed in 1838. In preparing a caveat, or a request for design protection, filed with the U.S. Patent Office in October of that year, Colt described an entirely new method of effecting the rotation of a revolver's cylinder (fig. 1), which differed from that protected by his 25 February 1836 patent.

> Improvements in the lock.—The pin (a) is substituted for fig. 3 in the old patent. The pin b, is to hold the cylinder in place, and it is withdrawn in the act of half cocking. The body of it is split so as to connect it into a spring c, in a hand, or pall, which falls into the ratchet d, this projection d; on this ratchet passes into a accompanying opening in the the [sic] bore of the cylinder. The hand c, rises in the act of cocking the gun and pushes the cylinder round. In the old patent the ratchet teeth were on the side of the ratchet, and to obtain the requisite motion the parts had to be complicated, three pins having been used where one now serves the purpose; this arrangement will make the foundation for claim, which is constituted essentially of the change in the ratchet; the change in the arm which pushes the cylinder round, and the change in the bolt b, that holds the cylinder.[30]

Yet when he filed his application in early 1839 to secure patent protection for the other improvements described in the October 1838 caveat, he intentionally omitted any mention of the pawl and hand design.[31] Although Colt's reasons for doing this are unknown, they may represent an attempt on his part to retain control over a design that he knew would eventually be of considerable value. This motive probably prompted Colt to conceal another refinement he had developed for his revolvers in 1837.

Herbert G. Houze

Figure 2

Line engraving accompanying the published version of Samuel Colt's lecture to the Institution of Civil Engineers in 1851 illustrating the angles of gas deflection provided by chamfering the mouths of a cylinder's chambers. Wadsworth Atheneum Museum of Art.

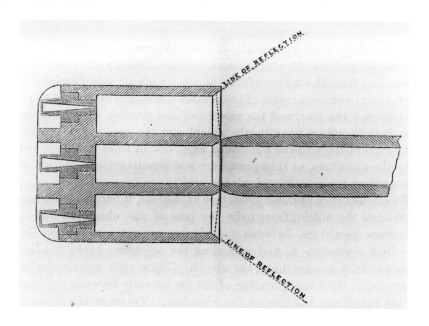

This invention involved the chamfering of the cylinder chamber mouths to reduce the possibility of combustion gases igniting adjacent chambers when a revolver was fired (fig. 2).[32] Though seemingly of little importance, this design feature was to prove critical in the later success of Colt's pistols.[33]

With the resignation of Dudley Selden as the company's treasurer in 1839, Colt's position became even more precarious. Selden's replacement was a New York hardware dealer and importer named John Ehlers.[34] Although Ehlers initially supported Colt, they quickly came to a parting of the ways. To a large extent, Ehlers's antipathy was caused by a series of gifts Colt made in late May 1840 to various officers and public officials who had arranged the carbine trials of the previous year. In all, a total of eleven pistols and three longarms were distributed as gifts.[35]

An additional five pistols were to be presented, but their intended recipients refused to accept them. Among the latter was Capt. David E. Twiggs, who thanked Colt for his kind offer but declined, stating that he had been "actuated by no other motive than strict justice to an invention which I think reflect great credit on the inventor, and will prove a valuable acquisition to the Service."[36]

After June 1840, Colt's relationship with Ehlers deteriorated steadily, and by the end of the year his continued association with the Patent Arms Manufacturing Company was in serious jeopardy.

Notes

1. Organization of what was to become the Patent Arms Manufacturing Company began in late 1836 while Samuel Colt was abroad. During that period his father, Christopher, contacted a number of potential investors, including Dudley Selden.

2. Among the initial stockholders was Christopher Colt, as well as his cousins Elisha Colt, Roswell Colt, and Dudley Selden (Samuel Colt, "List of Stock Holders in Patent Arms Mg. Co. Augt. 1837." Samuel Colt Papers, Box 1, Connecticut Historical Society).

3. Pliny Lawton was hired in late March 1836 at the suggestion of Christopher Colt. Samuel Colt evidently met Lawton in his official capacity as factory superintendent in April (Samuel Colt to Christopher Colt, 6 April 1836. Colt Family Papers, MSG no. 78, Series II, Christopher Colt, Sr., Business Correspondence, Box 11, Folder 3, University of Rhode Island Libraries Special Collections).

4. Samuel Colt to Dudley Selden, 9 March 1836, and Dudley Selden to Samuel Colt, 31 May 1836. Samuel Colt Papers, Box 1, Connecticut Historical Society.

5. Ibid.

6. Pliny Lawton to Samuel Colt, 21 or 27 December 1836. Samuel Colt Papers, Box 9, File 3, Connecticut Historical Society.

7. Pliny Lawton to Samuel Colt, 8 February 1837. Samuel Colt Papers, Box 1, Connecticut Historical Society. Difficulties were evidently experienced in bringing this model into production, as Lawton asked Colt in August 1837 to return the sample he had borrowed because it was needed to commence manufacture (Pliny Lawton to Samuel Colt, 3 August 1837. Samuel Colt Papers, Box 1, Connecticut Historical Society).

8. Samuel Colt, [Production and Expenditure Summary], n.d. [December 1837]. Samuel Colt Papers, Box 9, "Notes & Figures" Folder, Connecticut Historical Society.

9. Ibid.

10. Ibid.

11. Christopher Colt to Samuel Colt, 28 January and 15 February 1837; Henry L. Ellsworth to Samuel Colt, 15 and 23 March 1837. Samuel Colt Papers, Box 1, Connecticut Historical Society.

12. Samuel Colt to Jesse Hoyt, 2 October 1837. Samuel Colt Papers, Box 1, Connecticut Historical Society.

13. This purchase was in large part due to the lobbying of Col. William S. Harney (Col. William S. Harney to Samuel Colt, 22 December 1837. Samuel Colt Papers, Box 2, Connecticut Historical Society).

14. Samuel Colt to Christopher Colt, 22 May 1838. Colt Family Papers, MSG no. 78, Series II, Box 11, File 5, University of Rhode Island Libraries Special Collections.

15. Col. William S. Harney to Samuel Colt, 6 February 1839. Samuel Colt Papers, Box 2, Connecticut Historical Society.

16. Dudley Selden to Samuel Colt, 1 March 1837. Samuel Colt Papers, Box 1, Connecticut Historical Society.

17. Ibid.

18. Samuel Colt, "Sales up to 1 July 1839." Samuel Colt Papers, Box 2, Connecticut Historical Society.

19. Dudley Selden to Samuel Colt, 6 January 1839. Samuel Colt Papers, Box 2, Connecticut Historical Society.

20. Lt. Col. William S. Harney to Samuel Colt, 6 February 1839. Samuel Colt Papers, Box 2, Connecticut Historical Society.

21. Samuel Colt to Daniel Holsman, 12 March 1839. Samuel Colt Papers, Box 2, Connecticut Historical Society.

22. Edward Simms to Samuel Colt, Account Statement, 8 March 1839. Samuel Colt Papers, Box 2, Connecticut Historical Society.

23. Samuel Colt to the Hon. Joel R. Poinsett, 6 March 1839, and "Recommendation for a trial of repeating arms," 6 March 1839. Samuel Colt Papers, Box 2, Connecticut Historical Society.

24. Lt. John McLaughlin to Samuel Colt, 21 January 1841, and Col. George Bomford to Samuel Colt, 26 February 1841. Samuel Colt Papers, Box 3, Connecticut Historical Society.

25. Dudley Selden to Samuel Colt, 1 March 1837. Samuel Colt Papers, Box 1, Connecticut Historical Society.

26. George Andrews to Samuel Colt, Account Statement, 21 May 1839. Samuel Colt Papers, Box 2, Connecticut Historical Society.

27. Dudley Selden to Samuel Colt, 1 March 1837. Samuel Colt Papers, Box 1, Connecticut Historical Society.

28. The specific details of the 24 August 1838 agreement are listed in Samuel Colt's deposition taken 20 September 1841 in support of his "Bill of Complaint" filed in the Chancery Court of New Jersey (Samuel Colt Papers, Box 3, Connecticut Historical Society). Copies of Colt's proposals are to be found in Folder 4, Box 9 of the Samuel Colt Papers in the Connecticut Historical Society.

29. Ibid.

30. Samuel Colt to the commissioner of U.S. Patents, n.d. [October 1838]. Samuel Colt Papers, Box 9, Folder 1, Connecticut Historical Society.

31. Although Colt later allowed the Paterson company to manufacture revolvers utilizing the improved design, its ownership never passed to the firm. It remained Colt's property under the terms of the 1838 caveat until he included a description of the improved pawl and hand's operation in the claims for his patent Reissue Number 124 of 24 October 1848.

32. Samuel Colt to H. L. Ellsworth, 28 March 1837. Samuel Colt Papers, Box 1, Connecticut Historical Society.

33. Chamfered cylinder chamber mouths were first used by Colt on production arms in 1847, and he described the improvement in detail in his 1851 lecture to the Institution of Civil Engineers in London.

34. The first mention of Ehlers as company treasurer appears in a letter dated 11 October 1839 (John Ehlers to Christopher Colt, 11 October 1839. Colt Family Papers, MSG no. 78, Series II, Box 12, Folder 11, University of Rhode Island Libraries Special Collections). By March 1841 Ehlers owned 325 shares, or over ten percent of the Patent Arms Manufacturing Company's stock (Samuel Colt, "List of Stockholders in Pt Arms Mang Company March 17.1841." Samuel Colt Papers, Box 3, Connecticut Historical Society).

35. Samuel Colt, List of Presentation Arms, May 1840. Samuel Colt Papers, Box 9, File 1, Connecticut Historical Society.

36. Capt. David E. Twiggs to Samuel Colt, 28 May 1840. Samuel Colt Papers, Box 2, Connecticut Historical Society.

Herbert G. Houze

21

Prototype Belt Pistol

No serial number

Caliber .29 in., barrel length 4⅛ in., overall length 7¹⁵⁄₁₆ in.

Date of Manufacture: 1836

Wadsworth Atheneum Museum of Art

Bequest of Elizabeth Hart Jarvis Colt, 1905.1013

Overall left with knife open

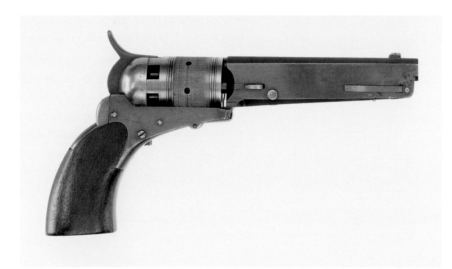

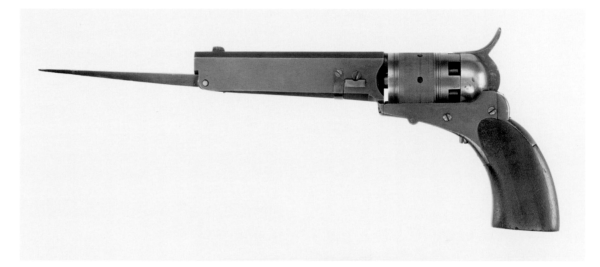

During the summer and early autumn of 1836 Samuel Colt reworked his original pistol design to improve both its function and ease of actual manufacture. One of the arms made at this time is this Belt Pistol. Based upon its overall configuration and similarity to later Patent Arms Manufacturing Company products, it was probably constructed by the firm's superintendent, Pliny Lawton. Drawings made before the pistol's completion indicate that it was to be fitted with

a forward cylinder plate; however, that feature was omitted when the prototype was made.[1] Colt explained the reason for this design change when he presented his 25 November 1851 lecture on revolving firearms to the Institution of Civil Engineers in London.

> but when he enclosed the rear, and the mouths of the rotating chambers, the fire, being confined beneath the shield and the cap, was communicated successively to the percussion caps, and in front was conveyed into the chambers, so that premature and simultaneous explosion of the charges necessarily took place.[2]

In common with several of the prototype pistols made by John Pearson of Baltimore, this pistol is fitted with a folding knife or dirk blade beneath the barrel.

The most distinctive and technically interesting feature of this piece involves the design of the cylinder locking mechanism. It consists of a pivoted bolt that rises and falls through the action of a stud mounted on the right side of the hammer's base. When the hammer is cocked, the stud lowers the bolt's head, allowing the cylinder to rotate. After the rotation has begun, the bolt is released by the hammer and under spring pressure again comes into contact with the cylinder circumference, so that it engages a locking recess upon full cock. Although this design was not used in any of the Patent Arms Manufacturing Company's products, Colt later employed the system when he received the

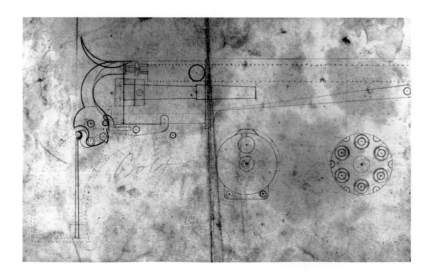

Cat. 21a. Pen and ink drawing, ca. 1836, of the prototype Belt Pistol. Records of the Colt's Patent Fire Arms Manufacturing Company, Connecticut State Library, Hartford.

contract to produce Holster Pistols in 1847 and included it in his patent extension application of 1848 (cat. 21a).[3]

Notes

1. Drawings for this pistol are preserved in the Records of the Colt's Patent Fire Arms Manufacturing Company, RG 103, Administrative File, Design Drawings, Box 62 (No. 12). The reverse of this drawing is inscribed in Colt's hand, "Mr Lawton." The drawing for a similar revolver without a folding bayonet is in the Samuel Colt Papers of the Connecticut Historical Society (Box 9, Drawings Folder).

2. Samuel Colt, "On the application of Machinery to the manufacture of Rotating Chambered-Breech Fire-Arms, and the peculiarities of those Arms," *Minutes of Proceedings of the Institution of Civil Engineers, with Abstracts of the Discussions*, vol. XI, session 1851–52 (London: Institution of Civil Engineers, 1852), 40.

3. U.S. Patent Office. Samuel Colt, "Improvement in Revolving Fire-Arms," Reissue No. 124, 24 October 1848.

Shortly after construction began on the Patent Arms Manufacturing Company's factory in Paterson, New Jersey, Samuel Colt went to Baltimore in June 1836 to collect the machinery and tooling that had been used there to make the final series of prototypes.[1]

Despite an unfavorable test report issued by the U.S. Army Ordnance Department in 1837[2] and the fact that the Number 1 Rifle's bore diameter was less than half the size of the muskets then in service, Colt was able to sell the government a small lot of these rifles. At the urging of Lt. Col. William S. Harney, Maj. Gen. Thomas Jesup purchased fifty revolving rifles for use by troops under his command in Florida in May 1838.[3] These rifles performed admirably, and Colt received numerous letters extolling their military value.[4] Their performance in Florida, however, did not prompt the federal government to place any additional orders for rifles of this design.

The Number 1 Rifle did see service with the Republic of Texas Army. In late 1839 the fledgling republic purchased 120 rifles.[5] It is believed that this order, as

22

Number 1 Rifle

Serial number 189

Caliber .34 in., barrel length 31⅞ in., overall length 44⅛ in.

Date of Manufacture: 1838

Wadsworth Atheneum Museum of Art

Bequest of Elizabeth Hart Jarvis Colt, 1905.969

well as others placed by the republic that year for Number 5 Holster Pistols and Carbines, resulted from lobbying efforts on Colt's behalf by Samuel Whiting, who had purchased a prototype rifle in January 1836.[6] Whiting, a Hartford native, had moved to Texas in 1825, and after the establishment of the republic, he served as a purchasing agent for its military forces and briefly as an envoy to Washington.[7]

The Number 1 Rifle did find a following among sportsmen, and by 1 July 1839 the company had sold 158 of the 201 that had been made.[8]

It is likely that this rifle was one of the "10 old rifles Patterson make" listed in the 1861 inventory of Colonel Colt's Large Office (page VI, line 32).

Notes

1. Samuel Colt to Christopher Colt, 17 June 1836. Samuel Colt Papers, Box 1, Connecticut Historical Society.

2. Samuel Colt to Jesse Hoyt, 2 October 1837. Samuel Colt Papers, Box 1, Connecticut Historical Society.

3. William S. Harney to Samuel Colt, 22 December 1837. Samuel Colt Papers, Box 1, Connecticut Historical Society.

4. William S. Harney to Samuel Colt, 6 February 1839. Samuel Colt Papers, Box 2, Connecticut Historical Society.

5. Samuel Colt to Edward Custice, 16 December 1839. Samuel Colt Papers, Box 2, Connecticut Historical Society.

6. Samuel Whiting to Samuel Colt, 1 January 1836. Samuel Colt Papers, Box 1, Connecticut Historical Society.

7. *Handbook of Texas Online,* s.v. "Whiting, Samuel," http://www.tsha.itexas.edu/handbook/online/articles/WW/fwh40.html (accessed 2 June 2005).

8. Samuel Colt, "Sales up to 1 July 1839." Samuel Colt Papers, Box 2, Connecticut Historical Society.

23

Number 1 Pocket Pistol
Serial number 7
Caliber .28 in., barrel length 2½ in., overall length 5½ in.
Date of Manufacture: 1840
Wadsworth Atheneum Museum of Art
Bequest of Elizabeth Hart Jarvis Colt, 1905.1059

Markings
Barrel: Patent Arms M'g. Co. Paterson N.J.-Colt's Pt.
Turn-screw: Patent Arms M'g. Co. Paterson N.J.-Co
Flask: Patent Arms M'g Co Paterson N-J Colt's Pt.
Capper: Colt's Patent. Patent Arms M'g. Co. Paterson. N.J.

The first revolving pistol to be produced by the Patent Arms Manufacturing Company of Paterson, New Jersey, was appropriately named the Number 1. Introduced in 1837, this tiny five-shot pistol was designed purely for self-defense.

Perhaps because of its small size and caliber, sales were abysmal. A production and sales summary prepared on 1 July 1839 indicated that of the 490 pistols made to that date, only 128 had been sold.[1] Consequently, a significant number of these pistols were still in stock when Pliny Lawton redesigned the cylinders for all the company's revolvers. To improve their looks and prevent fragments of exploded percussion caps from jamming the cylinder in place, Lawton rounded "the cone ends of all our cylinders."[2] As a result, almost three-quarters of the production run were fitted with cylinders having rounded rear shoulders rather than the straight- or square-angled style originally used.

Three of the accessories accompanying this pistol are of note, as their construction and method of use were protected by Samuel Colt's U.S. Patent Number 1,304, issued on 29 August 1839.[3] The specific items are the combination powder flask and bullet dispenser located below the pistol's butt, the circular percussion cap dispenser with the embossed lid, and the combination loading tool-turn screw-nipple cleaner located below the bullet mold. The design of the combination powder flask allowed all five chambers of the cylinder to be charged with powder simultaneously and then likewise loaded with balls by turning the flask over. The cap dispenser was driven by an internal spiral spring that fed one percussion cap at a time from its reservoir to an aperture at its lower end. The combination tool's purpose was to properly seat the bullets into each chamber after the cylinder had been positioned on its arbor. The turn screw tip fit into a slot cut in the arbor, and the swiveled plunger could then be levered into each chamber's mouth. The ring-tipped projection at the tool's other end is a needle for cleaning the nipples of powder or combustion residue. Interestingly, the design of the bullet mold with a handle for the sprue cutter (the top plate that cuts off excess lead) was described in Colt's 29 August 1839 patent specifications but not claimed.

This cased revolver is probably the one recorded on page 11, line 21 of the 1861 inventory of Colonel Colt's Small Office: "1 case contg. Small Patterson pistol & appendages."

Pliny Lawton was a fervent believer in the potential of the Number 1 Pistol[4] and began making cases for them that were "bound so much like a book as to

deceive the most observing—with titles varyous (say Common Law of Texas, the Tourists Companion, Elmers digest being A law book &c &c)."[5]

Notes

1. Samuel Colt, "Sales up to 1 July 1839." Samuel Colt Papers, Box 2, Connecticut Historical Society.
2. Pliny Lawton to Samuel Colt, 28 April 1840. Samuel Colt Papers, Box 2, Connecticut Historical Society.
3. U.S. Patent Office. Samuel Colt, "Improvements in Fire-Arms and in the Apparatus Used Therewith," Number 1,304, issued 29 August 1839.
4. Pliny Lawton to Samuel Colt, 3 April 1840. Samuel Colt Papers, Box 2, Connecticut Historical Society.
5. Pliny Lawton to Samuel Colt, 28 April 1840. Samuel Colt Papers, Box 2, Connecticut Historical Society.

24

Number 3 Belt Pistol
Serial number 186
Caliber .34 in., barrel length 5½ in., overall length 9¹³/₃₂ in.
Date of Manufacture: 1838
Wadsworth Atheneum Museum of Art
Bequest of Elizabeth Hart Jarvis Colt, 1905.1005

Markings
Barrel: Patent Arms M'g Co Paterson N-J. Colt's Pt.

The Number 3 Belt Pistol was made from 1837 to 1840. Early examples, such as the one illustrated here, were fitted with cylinders having a squared or flat rear shoulder, while those produced toward the end of manufacture had cylinders with rounded rear shoulders like the preceding Number 1 Pocket Pistol. Based upon a production and sales summary prepared on 25 March 1839, five hundred revolvers of this pattern were made.[1]

Sales of the Number 3 Belt Pistol were much better than for its smaller counterpart, and the summary noted above records that 317 had been sold as of that date.[2] This pistol was totally refinished at some later time. As a result, the cylinder scene and markings were partially erased.

Notes

1. Samuel Colt, "Sales up to 1 July 1839." Samuel Colt Papers, Box 2, Connecticut Historical Society.
2. Ibid.

25

Number 5 Holster Pistol
Serial number 984
Caliber .36 in., barrel length 9 in., overall length 13 in.
Date of Manufacture: 1840
Wadsworth Atheneum Museum of Art
Bequest of Elizabeth Hart Jarvis Colt, 1905.1009

Markings
Barrel: Patent Arms M'g. Co.Paterson, N.J.-Colt's Pt.

The most popular of all the Patent Arms Manufacturing Company revolvers was the Number 5 Holster Pistol, produced from 1838 to mid-1840. It also has the distinction of being the first revolving pistol ever purchased by a govern-

ment for military service. In April 1839, 180 Number 5 Holster Pistols were purchased by the Republic of Texas for use by its navy.[1] In December 1841 the U.S. Navy purchased one hundred revolvers for issuance to its Pacific Squadron.[2] In August 1845, some three years after the collapse of the Patent Arms Manufacturing Company, the U.S. government bought fifty additional Number 5 pistols from the New York dealer John Ehlers.[3]

As a result of its use by the navy of the Republic of Texas, this model was popularly called the "Texas Holster Pistol," and revolvers with .36 in. bores were known thereafter as being of "Navy caliber."

Given the splendid decoration of this revolver, it was probably used by Samuel Colt as an exhibition or promotional piece. Although it is not specifically mentioned in the 1861 inventories of either Colonel Colt's Large or Small Offices, circumstantial evidence suggests that it may be the pistol listed in the 1861 inventory of Colt's Small Office on page 6, line 11: "Patterson Navy Pistol concealed trigger Colt's."

The basis for this assertion lies in the twelve-dollar valuation assigned to the pistol when it was inventoried. The same valuation was given to the "Case with Patterson 6 in with extra long barrel" recorded on line 16. As the valuation of the cased revolver with an extra barrel and presumably all accessories was equal to that of the previously listed "Patterson Navy Pistol," the latter must have had some special features, such as engraving.

Notes

1. John Fuller to C. B. Zabriskie and I. Dean to Samuel Colt, 1 April 1839. Samuel Colt Papers, Box 2, Connecticut Historical Society. This purchase was probably made at the suggestion of Samuel Whiting (see notes for the Number 1 Rifle [cat. 22]).
2. Samuel Colt, Sales Summary, "about the middle of Decr 1841." Samuel Colt Papers, Box 3, Connecticut Historical Society.
3. Philip R. Phillips and R. L. Wilson, *Paterson Colt Pistol Variations* (Dallas: Jackson Arms, 1979), 93.

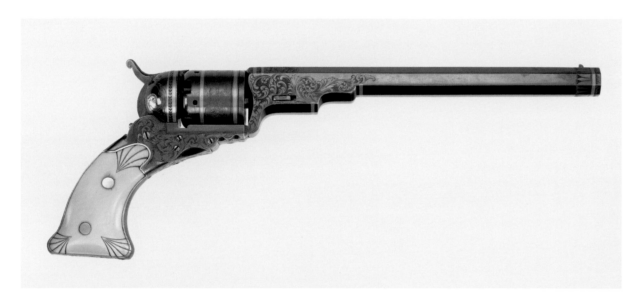

Overall top

Overall left

26

Patent Arms Manufacturing Company Carbine

Serial number 118

Caliber .525 in., barrel length 24 3/8 in., overall length 42 in.

Date of Manufacture: 1839

Wadsworth Atheneum Museum of Art

Bequest of Elizabeth Hart Jarvis Colt, 1905.970

Markings

Barrel: Patent Arms M'g Co. Pa[terson], N.J.-Colt's Pt. [right side]

In response to the poor sales for the Number 1 and 2 Rifles, Samuel Colt developed a conventionally constructed longarm with an exposed hammer in 1838. Although scheduled to enter production that year, problems encountered in its manufacture delayed the new model's introduction until 1839.[1]

Next to the Number 5 Holster Pistol, the Carbine was the most popular of all Paterson-made Colt revolvers. The first major sale was to the Republic of Texas, which purchased 180 Carbines for its navy in April 1839 and at the same time ordered an equal number of Number 5 Holster Pistols.[2] The U.S. Army Ordnance Department ordered one hundred Carbines in March 1841.[3] The U.S. Navy followed suit in December 1841, purchasing one hundred Carbines.[4] The final government purchase occurred in August 1845, when the Navy Department purchased an additional one hundred Carbines from John Ehlers of New York City.[5]

Patent Arms Manufacturing Company carbines were to play a role in one of New England's lesser-known crises. Facing open rebellion from supporters of Thomas W. Dorr, who advocated broader state suffrage, Rhode Island Governor Samuel Ward King agreed to arm a company of carabineers being raised in New York City by a former Rhode Island resident, James N. Olney. Olney purchased fifty carbines from John Ehlers and then proceeded to Rhode Island. After the Dorrites were defeated at the so-called battles of Chepatchet on 28 June 1842 and Pawtucket the following day, the carabineers then went to Prov-

idence, where they were formally disbanded on 4 July 1842. Their carbines were turned over to the state's quartermaster general, and though some were presented to officers and men of the company, the majority remained in storage until 1848. In mid- or late 1848 Samuel Colt purchased these carbines with the intention of selling them overseas. To make them more marketable, the original cylinder turning mechanisms were removed and the cylinders fitted with ratchets.[6]

Although most of the carbines Colt acquired in 1848 were modified, a small number were left untouched. It is not known whether this carbine was originally part of the Rhode Island group. It is likely, however, that it was one of the Patent Arms Manufacturing Company carbines listed on page I, line 22, of the 1861 Inventory of Colonel Colt's Large Office: "23 Colt's Rifles Old pattern with & without lever ramrods."

Notes

1. The problems associated with bringing this model into production are detailed in letters written to Colt by Pliny Lawton on 3 January 1839 and to Dudley Selden on 5 January 1839 (Samuel Colt Papers, Box 2, Connecticut Historical Society). Production output was so low that in February 1839 the company's New York City agent, C. B. Zabriskie, had to ask Colt to send him one of the sample carbines as soon as he was finished with it because no others were available (C. B. Zabriskie to Samuel Colt, 22 February 1839. Samuel Colt Papers, Box 2, Connecticut Historical Society).

2. John Fuller to C. B. Zabriskie and I. Dean to Samuel Colt, 1 April 1839. Samuel Colt Papers, Box 2, Connecticut Historical Society.

3. Col. George Bomford to Samuel Colt, 26 February 1841. Samuel Colt Papers, Box 3, Connecticut Historical Society.

4. Samuel Colt, Sales Summary, "about the middle of Decr 1841." Samuel Colt Papers, Box 3, Connecticut Historical Society.

5. Philip R. Phillips and R. L. Wilson, *Paterson Colt Pistol Variations* (Dallas: Jackson Arms, 1979), 93.

6. Herbert G. Houze, *Colt Rifles & Muskets from 1847 to 1870* (Iola, Wis.: Krause Publications, 1996), 26–43.

Samuel Colt in New York, 1841–1846

The collapse of the Patent Arms Manufacturing Company has traditionally been blamed on Samuel Colt's extravagance and the actions of the firm's treasurer, John Ehlers, who owned ten percent of its stock. While it is true that both men played pivotal roles in the firm's demise, other factors were also at play.

In many respects it is a wonder that the company survived as long as it did, given the economic climate of the United States in those years. Chartered on 5 March 1836, the company weathered the Panic of 1837, when banks throughout the country failed due to a lack of gold reserves to cover their deposits. Two years later the firm emerged unscathed from the Panic of 1839, when bills of exchange, or unsecured letters of payment similar to today's checks, were discounted as much as forty percent because of the collapse of cotton prices. It also endured the deep economic depression that gripped the United States from 1837 onward.

The company's success was primarily based upon sales to one geographic region: the Republic of Texas.[1] When that market became satiated in 1840, sales declined precipitously. Faced with mounting financial obligations exacerbated by dwindling sales, it was inevitable that the Patent Arms Company would fail. Its end, however, was hastened by the actions of John Ehlers.

Fed up with Samuel Colt, Ehlers decided to rid the company of his presence. On 20 August 1841 he met with two other stockholders, J. D. Miller and Edward A. Nicoll, to seize Colt's patent rights. Acting as a pro tem board of directors, they passed a resolution authorizing the sale of Colt's patents to satisfy certain debts he owed to the company.[2] Beginning on 23 August, notices were published in various New York City newspapers advising the public that a three-fourths interest in Colt's patent rights would be sold on 15 September.[3]

Upon learning of the pending public auction, Colt hired the law firm of McCown & Clark to determine not only the legality of Ehlers's actions[4] but also whether any indebtedness existed.[5] Colt had long suspected that Ehlers was concealing sales in order to reduce the royalties due, but he had no proof. Now on the advice and with the participation of counsel, he could demand to see the firm's books. It proved to be a difficult task, as Ehlers gave one excuse after another as to why he could not turn them over to Colt or his representatives.[6] Perhaps sensing that Colt's actions might prove successful, Ehlers set about removing all the company's finished arms from its office at 155 Broadway in New York. Some were transferred to Herman LeRoy Newbold in satisfaction of a supposed debt, and the remainder, amounting to 260 carbines, 340 pistols, and 210 rifles, were moved to Ehlers's own store.[7] Outraged by this act of theft, Colt considered placing the following advertisement in the New York newspapers.

> Absconded
> A Jerman calling himself John Ehlers, about fifty years of age, five feet eight inches high, the upper part of his head balled short locks of yellow curly hair on the back & sides of his head, faice round, figure stout & vulgar looking
>
> The person above described has been imployed as the chief clerk & Treasurer of the Patent Arms Manufacturing Co & has of a suden absented him self without the knowledge of the President or stockholders of said Company after taking from there armoury at Paterson New Jersey & there Store 155 Broadway New York from fifty to Seventy five thousand dollars worth of Colts Repeating Fire Arms & other property
>
> Any information that can be furnished of the mustirous movements of said individual or the disposition he may have made of said property will be very thankfully received by the undersigned & measures shall be taken at the earliest meeting of the stockholders of said Company to sutably reward the person who shall [. . .][8]

Dissuaded by cooler heads from further inflaming matters, Colt instead sought legal relief and requested from the Chancery Court of New Jersey an injunction forbidding the sale.[9] This was granted in early September 1841, and for the next few months the affairs of the Patent Arms Manufacturing Company remained in a state of suspended animation.

Samuel Colt, however, was busy with a new project. In 1840, or perhaps a little earlier, he had conceived an idea for protecting American ports from enemy warships by means of submerged mines that could be electrically detonated from shore. Realizing that his future prospects with the Patent Arms Manufacturing Company were dim at best, he set about promoting his system for harbor defense. Drawing upon the contacts he had made in Washington in the late 1830s, Colt was able to secure support for

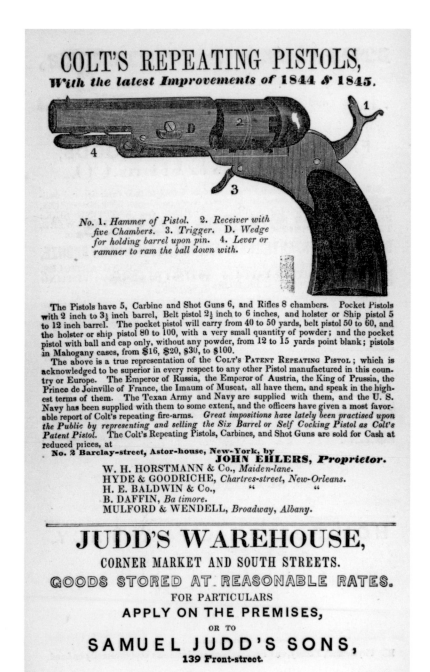

the development of the "Submarine Battery" from Secretary of the Navy Abel P. Upshur.[10] With this in hand he formed the Sub-Marine Battery Company and began securing subscriptions for its stock.[11] Resembling nothing more closely than a crayon, Colt's mine consisted of a tin tube containing anywhere from one hundred to two hundred pounds of black powder that was anchored to the sea floor at a predetermined depth.[12] To detonate the mine, Colt proposed using a spark created by an electromagnetic telegraph wire. While in theory the plan appeared relatively simple, the development of suitable waterproofing for the telegraph wires took some time. In perfecting its design, Colt achieved the distinction of having invented the first underwater electrical cable.[13]

During the same period that witnessed the founding of the Sub-Marine Battery Company and Colt's attempts to develop new sources of income, he had to cope with a major distraction. In New York City on 17 September 1841 his older brother, John Colt, had murdered Samuel Adams, the printer of an accounting textbook he was writing. What made the crime even more heinous was the fact that John Colt had used an axe and then attempted to cover up the deed by shipping the body in a trunk to New Orleans. The trial was originally scheduled to begin in November 1841, but was delayed until the end of January of the following year. Given the lurid details of the murder, which included John Colt's involvement with an attractive and very pregnant woman,[14] the press coverage was immense. Daily accounts of the proceedings were published not only in local New York newspapers but also reprinted in countless other states. Numerous witnesses, including his brother Samuel, were called before the bench. Based upon the evidence and John Colt's own confession, he was found guilty and sentenced to death. His attorneys, one of whom was his cousin Dudley Selden, pursued every avenue of appeal, but none were successful, and an order was issued that John Colt be hung on 18 November 1842. After marrying his mistress and bidding adieu to Samuel and others, John Colt cheated the hangman's rope by committing suicide.[15]

Capitalizing on Samuel Colt's preoccupation with his brother's trial and his growing involvement with the Sub-Marine Battery Company, John Ehlers decided to play his final card concerning the Patent Arms Manufacturing Company's future. To prevent any examination of the company's books and to rid himself permanently of Colt, he decided to close the Pater-

Herbert G. Houze

son firm. Because of the general financial climate of the time, Ehlers encountered little to no opposition. At a special meeting of the firm's directors on 4 January 1842, he convinced those present "to liquidate & wind up the Concern,"[16] and two weeks later, on 18 January, the measure was approved by a majority of the stockholders.[17]

Despite its dissolution, the Paterson factory continued for a brief period of time to assemble and finish arms that were in the final stages of production. As the company no longer existed, the marking dies were altered to delete the phrase "Mfg Co" after the words "Patent Arms." By mid-April 1842 this work had been completed and the Paterson factory ceased all production.[18] It was not until some eight months later, however, that the final act of the firm's closure was played out.[19] On 9 December a public auction was held in New York City to sell the company's most liquid assets, which consisted primarily of unassembled pistol, rifle, shotgun, and carbine parts. Not surprisingly, John Ehlers bought the lion's share. In doing so, he secured parts for 536 pistols, as well as 150 to 160 carbines, rifles, and shotguns. More importantly, under the terms of the sale, the purchaser also received full rights to assemble and finish those arms (fig. 1).[20]

Although Colt had briefly considered having his revolvers made under license by the N. P. Ames Company of Cabottsville, Massachusetts,[21] he abandoned that idea in favor of further development of his underwater mine and the construction of tinfoil cartridges that he had first developed in late 1838.[22]

By the late spring of 1842 Colt had perfected the design of the mine and began making preparations for an exhibition of its effectiveness.[23] Originally scheduled for late May off Castle Garden (Ellis Island) in New York Harbor, the test of the underwater mine was delayed until 4 July because of a lack of explosives.[24] Immediately following the annual Independence Day fireworks display, Colt set off his mine by remote control. To the astonished delight of the assembled crowd, the hulk of a sailing ship that was either anchored or towed into position above the mine was lifted out of the water by the explosion and sank.[25] A month and a half later, on 20 August, Colt repeated the experiment in the Potomac River. Due to its location and the number of luminaries present, this demonstration received far greater press coverage. One of the more widely reproduced accounts was written by the correspondent for the *New York Journal of Commerce*.

Colt was stationed, with his apparatus, at a point on the shore near Alexandria, five miles from the vessel to be operated on.

The signal for firing the battery was to be given from the Arsenal, and was to be two Paixhan guns, fired in quick succession.

At the flash of the second gun, Colt pulled the trigger, and simultaneously with the report of the gun, a magnificent and astonishing spectacle was presented to us.

The water around the vessel was upheaved, and rose in a vast and majestic column, to an astonishing height—a gigantic jet d'core—a marine volcano. No comparison can give an adequate idea of its grandeur.

As to the vessel, she was not visible in the mass of foam and water; but the thousands of small, dark splinters into which she was shredded, were seen raising with the upper mass of the column, into the air.[26]

Additional demonstrations in September and October 1842 further proved his weapon's effectiveness.[27] However, contracts from the U.S. government did not materialize, and Colt soon lost interest in the entire project.

Colt turned his attention to perfecting the tinfoil cartridges he had originally designed for use in his revolvers.[28] Realizing that they could be adopted for naval use, he began making larger-caliber samples for government testing. Aside from being waterproof, these cartridges possessed another virtue. Their tinfoil wrapping made them resistant to premature explosion when they were exposed to embers remaining in a cannon barrel that had not been properly swabbed after firing.[29] Following an extensive series of trials in 1843, Colt received contracts for his tinfoil cartridges from the U.S. Navy and Revenue Service.[30] The purchase of tinfoil cartridges by the U.S. Revenue Service was to be expected, given its operations. In contrast to the Navy, revenue cutters during the 1840s were far more likely to engage in actual combat. This was due to their assigned task of preventing contraband cargo from being smuggled into the United States by sea.

Using the income derived from the tinfoil cartridges, Colt decided to explore other uses of Samuel F. B. Morse's telegraph cable—this time for more peaceful pursuits than setting off underwater mines. A year after

Morse had completed the first successful long-distance telegraph line, in 1844, from Baltimore to Washington, D.C., Colt proposed building a similar line from Sandy Hook, New Jersey, to New York in order to transmit shipping news to the city. In many respects Colt's concept was prescient, as he realized that local merchants would pay for information about the arrival time and cargo of vessels due to enter New York Harbor. After securing the rights to build such a line from the Morse Telegraph Company on 8 May 1845,[31] Colt undertook obtaining the necessary financing to bring about its completion. He was successful in convincing the New York merchant industrialist William Robinson of the idea's merit, and the two formed a partnership on 28 September 1845.[32] The Colt & Robinson New York and Offing Electro-Magnetic Telegraph Company initially installed wires from its office in Dorr's (later Post's) Granite Building at the rear of the Merchants' Exchange in lower Manhattan to the westernmost point of Coney Island.[33] The firm later extended the line to the Fire Island Light, but its goal to connect the New Jersey coast with New York City was never realized.

Despite the partial success of this venture, Colt never abandoned his hope of reentering the arms field. In this regard the election of President James K. Polk in 1844 proved to be a godsend. His policies sought to transform the United States from an inward-looking country to one that would exercise its "Manifest Destiny." As a result, wars with Great Britain over the Oregon Territory boundaries and with Mexico as a result of the annexation of Texas were very real possibilities. The likelihood of these conflicts meant that the nation would need new firearms for all branches of the armed services, which would offer Colt the perfect opportunity to press for the adoption of his patented revolvers.

At first Colt planned to resurrect the Patent Arms Manufacturing Company, but these hopes were firmly laid to rest in January 1846, when his father refused to back the project.[34] In a sense Christopher Colt's decision was a blessing in disguise, as it allowed Samuel time to design an improved revolving pistol. In contrast to the revolvers made previously, the revised design was of a substantially larger caliber and was fitted with a conventional rather than a folding trigger set within a protective guard. Lacking the necessary tools to produce an actual sample, Colt took his drawings to the New York gunmakers Blunt & Syms for translation into steel and wood.[35] Completed during the autumn of 1846, the sample Holster

Pistol was immediately sent to Washington for review by the War Department. Though favorably received, it was not until Capt. Samuel H. Walker of the U.S. Mounted Riflemen viewed the piece on 2 December that government adoption became a possibility.[36]

Recognizing its military value, Walker suggested changes in the revolver's design and then pressed for its acceptance by the government. Having received approval from Secretary of War William L. Marcy to purchase one thousand of the new revolvers, Walker and Colt signed a memorandum of agreement on 4 January 1847 to manufacture that quantity.[37] Colt then approached Eli Whitney, Jr., of Whitneyville, Connecticut, to produce the revolvers incorporating Walker's improvements. Whitney accepted the proposition, and Colt duly subcontracted their manufacture.[38]

Whitney was able to tool up for the pistols in a remarkably short time and made the first delivery on 7 June.[39] A month later, on 6 July, the entire contract had been fulfilled.[40] With its completion, Colt's fortunes had at last begun to brighten.

Notes

1. It is estimated that sales to this region amounted to approximately twenty percent of the Patent Arms Manufacturing Company's total output.

2. Patent Arms Manufacturing Company, Minutes of Board of Directors' Meeting, 20 August 1841. Samuel Colt Papers, Box 3, Connecticut Historical Society. The money generated by the sale of Colt's patent rights most likely was to be used to satisfy Dudley Selden's claims against the company arising from advances he had made to the concern between 1837 and 1839 (Samuel Colt to Christopher Colt, 3 August 1841. Colt Family Papers, MSG no. 78, Series II, Box 11, Folder 6, University of Rhode Island Libraries Special Collections).

3. Samuel Colt, Deposition taken before B. W. Vandervoot, 20 September 1841, Bill of Complaint, Chancery Court of New Jersey, 14–15. Samuel Colt Papers, Box 3, Connecticut Historical Society.

4. The legality of Ehlers's actions was questionable, as he and Miller owned only 345 shares out of the three thousand then outstanding. The amount of Nicoll's interest is unknown, as his name does not appear on the 17 March 1841 list of stockholders (Samuel Colt, List of Stockholders in Pt Arms Mang Company March 17.1841. Samuel Colt Papers, Box 3, Connecticut Historical Society).

Herbert G. Houze

5. Whether Colt was indebted to the company was a moot point because debts, if they existed, could not be recovered by the sale of his patent rights. This was due to the fact that the company never filed the necessary assignments with the U.S. Patent Office (Samuel Colt to H. L. Ellsworth, 4 September 1841, and H. L. Ellsworth to Samuel Colt, 6 September 1841. Samuel Colt Papers, Box 3, Connecticut Historical Society).

6. John Ehlers to McCown & Clark, 23 August 1841. Samuel Colt Papers, Box 3, Connecticut Historical Society.

7. Samuel Colt, Deposition, Bill of Complaint, Chancery Court of New Jersey, 17. The removal of these arms was also occasioned by Dudley Selden's threat to attach them as payment for the monies owed him by the Patent Arms Manufacturing Company (Samuel Colt to Christopher Colt, 3 August 1841. Colt Family Papers, MSG no. 78, Series II, Box 11, Folder 6, University of Rhode Island Libraries Special Collections).

8. Samuel Colt, "Absconded," n.d. [August–September 1841]. Samuel Colt Papers, Box 9, File 4, Connecticut Historical Society.

9. Elias B. D. Ogden, Bill of Complaint, Chancery Court of New Jersey, 2 September 1841. Samuel Colt Papers, Box 3, Connecticut Historical Society.

10. Samuel Colt to the Hon. Abel P. Upshur, 24 November 1841. Samuel Colt Papers, Box 3, Connecticut Historical Society.

11. Among the subscribers were Samuel L. Southard (two hundred fifty shares), William Gibbs McNeill (two hundred shares), George W. Whistler (fifty shares), Roswell L. Colt (twenty shares), and John A. Morrill (ten shares). Under the terms of the subscription, Colt received twenty-five percent of the total share price of fifty dollars upon each owner's signature (Sub-Marine Battery Company Subscription Agreement, 18 December 1841. Samuel Colt Papers, Box 3, Connecticut Historical Society).

12. Samuel Colt, New London Torpedo Exn. (drawing), 1842. Samuel Colt Papers, Box 3, File 5, Connecticut Historical Society.

13. Although others were later to claim this distinction, none could prove that their designs predated 1843. Nevertheless, controversy surrounded Colt's development of a practical submarine telegraph cable until the late 1850s. In England questions lingered even longer due to the writings of the essayist T. P. Shaffner. However, he was finally convinced that Colt had indeed been first, and he abandoned further attempts to prove British origin for the invention (Charles F. Dennet to T. P. Shaffner, 7 March 1861. Samuel Colt Papers, Box 8, Connecticut Historical Society).

14. The identity and subsequent history of John Colt's wife, Caroline Henshaw, has been the subject of considerable speculation over the years. She has been described as German, even though her surname was definitely of English origin and her family was from Philadelphia, where her son, Samuel Caldwell Colt, was born in November 1841. On 3 November 1841 John Colt's trial was postponed due to "the absence of a material witness, Caroline M. Henshaw, who is at the point of confinement in Philadelphia" (*Brooklyn Eagle*, "The trial of Colt. . . ," 3 November 1841, 2). It has also been said that she later married Friedrich von Oppen under the assumed name of Julia Leicester. As von Oppen's wife, Isabella, was born in 1835, her identification with Caroline Henshaw is a statistical impossibility. For further information regarding Julia Leicester, see Appendix One.

15. For contemporary accounts of the trial, see [C. Frank Powell] *An authentic life of John C. Colt, now imprisoned for killing Samuel Adams, in New York, on the seventeenth of September, 1841* (Boston: S. N. Dickinson, 1842), and "Colt's Trial," *Brooklyn Eagle*, 21–28 January and 19 November 1842, 2. A slightly edited version of the actual trial transcripts was published in Thomas Dunphy and Thomas J. Cummins, *Remarkable Trials of all Countries: Particularly of the United States, Great Britain, Ireland and France: with Notes and Speeches of Counsel* (New York: Diossy & Co., 1867), 226–310.

16. John Ehlers to Samuel Colt, 6 January 1842. Samuel Colt Papers, Box 3, Connecticut Historical Society.

17. Ibid., and Christopher Colt to Samuel Colt, 13 January 1842. Samuel Colt Papers, Box 3, Connecticut Historical Society.

18. Thomas A. Emmett to Samuel Colt, 21 April 1842. Samuel Colt Papers, Box 3, Connecticut Historical Society.

19. The decision to fully liquidate the Patent Arms Manufacturing Company's holdings took place at a stockholders' meeting held on 19 September 1842 (Samuel Colt to Christopher Colt, 14 September 1842. Colt Family Papers, MSG no. 78, Series II, Box 11, Folder 6, University of Rhode Island Libraries Special Collections).

20. "Public Sale," 9 December 1842. Samuel Colt Papers, Box 3, Connecticut Historical Society.

21. Samuel Colt to William Ball, 26 December 1841. Samuel Colt Papers, Box 3, Connecticut Historical Society.

22. Assigning a date of 1838 to the development of the tinfoil cartridge is based on the fact that Samuel Colt filed a caveat with the U.S. Patent Office to protect the design pending formal application for a patent on 8 March 1839. Samuel Colt to the Commissioner of Patents, 8 March 1839. Samuel Colt Papers, Box 2, Connecticut Historical Society.

23. Samuel Colt to William Gibbs McNiell, 17 May 1842. Samuel Colt Papers, Box 3, Connecticut Historical Society.

24. Samuel Colt to Colonel Bankhead and Commodore Perry, 22 May 1842, and Samuel Colt to the Editors of *The Sun, New Era*, etc., 4 June 1842. Samuel Colt Papers, Box 3, Connecticut Historical Society.

25. Samuel Colt to the Hon. A. P. Upshur, 5 July 1842. Samuel Colt Papers, Box 3, Connecticut Historical Society.

26. Among the newspapers reprinting this report was the *Brooklyn Eagle* (23 August 1842, 2). Prior to retiring on the night of 20 August, Samuel Colt wrote to his father: "This has been the most tryumfant day of my life" (Samuel Colt to Christopher Colt, 20 August 1842. Colt Family Papers, MSG no. 78, Series II, Box 11, Folder 6, University of Rhode Island Libraries Special Collections).

27. One of these exhibitions was held in association with the 15th Fair of the American Institute held in New York City. To demonstrate the submarine battery's power, on 18 October 1842 Colt destroyed a 260-ton vessel being towed across the harbor (George C. De Kay to Samuel Colt, 20 October 1842. Samuel Colt Papers, Box 3, Connecticut Historical Society). In a letter inviting Gen. William Worth to witness the event, Colt poetically described his intention to "send an old hulk of some three hundred tones on a voyage of discovery to the moon" (Samuel Colt to Gen. William Worth, 13 October 1842. Samuel Colt Papers, Box 3, Connecticut Historical Society).

28. The caveat filed by Colt on 8 March 1839 (see note 22 above) described only tinfoil cartridges suitable for small arms.

29. The danger posed by combustion remnants in cannon barrels endangered not only those loading the piece but also quite often anyone nearby. If a charge detonated before it was fully rammed home, the combustion gases would raise breech pressures to the point where a cannon's walls might rupture. It is believed that this is exactly what happened on 28 February 1844 when the gun known as "The Peacemaker" aboard the USS *Princeton* exploded. In what was definitely a cruel and tragic twist of fate, one of the bystanders killed was Secretary of State Abel P. Upshur, who had approved the purchase of Colt's tinfoil cartridges while serving as secretary of the navy.

30. A considerable amount of the correspondence between Samuel Colt and the U.S. Navy Board of Ordnance from 1842 to 1845 is preserved in the Samuel Colt Papers, Boxes 3 and 4, Connecticut Historical Society.

31. Samuel Colt and Samuel F. B. Morse, Letter of Agreement, 8 May 1845. Samuel Colt Papers, Box 5, Connecticut Historical Society.

32. Samuel Colt and William Robinson, Articles of Partnership, 28 September 1845. Samuel Colt Papers, Box 5, Connecticut Historical Society.

33. New York and Offing Electro-Magnetic Telegraph, blank transmission sheet, n.d. [1845–46]. Samuel Colt Papers, Box 5, Connecticut Historical Society.

34. Samuel Colt to Christopher Colt, 18 January 1846. Samuel Colt Papers, Box 6, Connecticut Historical Society.

35. In testimony given during Colt's action against the Massachusetts Arms Company in June 1851 Orison Blunt made the following statement regarding this revolver: "The first pistol made on this model was made in my shop for Mr. Colt to exhibit to Captain Walker, in January, A.D., 1848" (Robert M. Patterson, *In the Circuit Court of the United States. Samuel Colt vs. The Mass. Arms Company. Report of the Trial of the Above-Entitled Cause, at Boston, on the Thirtieth Day of June, A.D. 1851, Before His Honor, Levi Woodbury, Associate Justice, of the Supreme Court of the United States* [Boston: White & Potter, 1851], 105). As the model was shown to Walker on 2 December 1847, the date of "January, A.D., 1848" cited by Blunt may refer to when the pistol was fitted with a six-chambered cylinder.

36. Samuel Colt to Capt. Samuel H. Walker, 3 December 1846. Samuel Colt Papers, Box 6, Connecticut Historical Society.

37. Samuel Colt and Capt. Samuel H. Walker, Memorandum of Agreement, 4 January 1847. Samuel Colt Papers, Box 6, Connecticut Historical Society.

38. Charles T. Haven and Frank A. Belden, *A History of the Colt Revolver and the Other Arms Made by the Colt's Patent Fire Arms Manufacturing Company from 1836 to 1940* (New York: Bonanza Books, 1940), 278–79.

39. Samuel Colt to Capt. William A. Thornton, 7 June 1847. Samuel Colt Papers, Box 6, Connecticut Historical Society.

40. Samuel Colt to the Hon. William L. Marcy, 6 July 1847. Samuel Colt Papers, Box 6, Connecticut Historical Society.

Herbert G. Houze

a revolution, depending upon the number of chambers. While deceptively simple in design, the machining of the ratchet teeth and the length of the pawl's arm were critical to the revolver's proper functioning. A slight variation in their precise measurements would result in the cylinder being under or over rotated, which could cause misfires if the nipples were out of alignment with the hammer. Should the revolver happen to discharge with a cylinder chamber out of line with the barrel, the user risked injury from flying particles of soft lead shaved from the side of the ball or bullet as it forced its way into the barrel.

Although Colt first designed a cylinder with integral ratchets in 1832 or 1833,[1] problems encountered in its manufacture evidently led him to abandon the concept until 1838 or early 1839, when he filed a caveat with the U.S. Patent Office describing its operation.[2]

Aside from a sample model made after Colt's first design, the earliest firearm having a cylinder with an integral ratchet was a carbine made by Pliny Lawton during the summer of 1840. This piece is described briefly in a letter written by Lawton to Colt on 9 September 1840.

> I left in the afternoon for the State of Ohio where I am now going to *sniff* the fresh air & try my skill at shooting having A gun of my own prepared with shot barrel a cylinder ½ inch bore 6 charges & A Rifle barrel & cylinder (short) with 8 charges 87 to the lb. which will set in the same lock the ratchets being fast in the cylinders.[3]

Despite the fact that Colt had illustrated the principle in a full-scale drawing of another carbine with a hinged barrel, dated 4 December 1840,[4] it was not until 1848 that he included a description of the mechanism in a patent application. In the specifications filed to support the reissue of his 25 February 1836 patent, Colt specifically claimed that cylinder rotation could be effected by "the ratchet teeth, or the equivalent thereof, may be made directly on a projection of the breech [i.e., the cylinder], or in the end thereof, or on any part connected with the breech, as convenience may dictate."[5]

27

Improved Belt Pistol

Serial number 22

Caliber .34 in., barrel length 4½ in., overall length 7⅞ in.

Date of Manufacture: 1842

Wadsworth Atheneum Museum of Art

Bequest of Elizabeth Hart Jarvis Colt, 1905.1060

Markings

Barrel: Patent Arms Paterson N-J Colt's Pt.

In an ironic turn of events, the final product of the Paterson factory could have saved the company from failure if it had appeared earlier. This assertion is based on the fact that the Improved Belt Pistol utilized an entirely new and far superior method of turning the cylinder than had previously been used. In place of the rotating collar mounted around the base of the cylinder pin, a series of ratchet teeth were machined into the rear face of the cylinder. By mounting the pawl or hand so that it moved through a slot cut in the frame's recoil shield, it could engage the ratchet teeth directly. Thus, as the hammer was cocked, the cylinder stop was released and the pawl moved upward so that its tip engaged a ratchet, thereby rotating the cylinder one-fifth or one-sixth of

Disassembled view

As the inscription die used to mark the barrel of this revolver was reworked to delete the abbreviation "Mfg Co" after the words "Patent Arms," the date of manufacture can be fixed to the period immediately following the dissolution of the company on 11 January 1842. While it is unknown exactly how many arms were assembled during the period when the firm was winding down its business, it probably numbered less than fifty pieces.

Unfortunately for Colt, most of the Pocket and Belt Pistols made on this principle were assembled by John Ehlers from the parts he acquired at the auction of the Patent Arms Manufacturing Company's assets held on 9 December 1842, which were sold by Ehlers without any financial benefit to Colt.[6]

The accessories accompanying this revolver are of note, as variations of two were later used by Colt. A larger version of the combination nipple wrench-screwdriver was supplied with the Holster Pistols delivered to the U.S. Army under his contract of 4 January 1847, and the plunger powder flask reappeared as an accessory for the New Model series of longarms introduced in 1855.

Notes

1. An elevational drawing illustrating this pistol can be dated to 1832–33 on the basis of the revolver's profile and other details of its construction. Records of the Colt's Patent Fire Arms Manufacturing Company, RG103, Administrative File, Box 62, Connecticut State Library.
2. Samuel Colt, Caveat Application, n.d. [1838–39]. Samuel Colt Papers, Box 9, File 1, Connecticut Historical Society.

3. Pliny Lawton to Samuel Colt, 9 September 1840. Samuel Colt Papers, Box 2, Connecticut Historical Society.
4. Records of the Colt's Patent Fire Arms Manufacturing Company, RG103, Administrative File, Box 62, Connecticut State Library.
5. U.S. Patent Office, Samuel Colt, of Hartford, Connecticut, "Improvement in Revolving Fire-Arms," Reissue No. 124, 24 October 1848, p. 3.
6. John Ehlers heavily advertised these arms between 1844 and 1846. For example, see the illustrated advertisements published in *Doggett's New York Business Directories* for 1844–45 and 1845–46 (New York: J. Doggett, Jr., 1844 and 1845), 22 and n.p. respectively.

28

Prototype Holster Pistol
No serial number
Caliber .47 in., barrel length 7 in., overall length 13³/₈ in.
Date of Manufacture: 1846
Museum of Connecticut History, Hartford
Gift of the Pratt & Whitney Company Foundation, Inc., 243

1861 Inventory of Colonel Colt's Small Office
Page 6, line 10
1 old army Pistol Different pat 8 sided barrel Patterson

1887 Museum Inventory Draft

243 47 Cal Imitation O.M. Paterson Colt, 7"

Sometime during the autumn of 1846 Samuel Colt commissioned Blunt & Syms of New York to build a prototype of the improved revolver he had designed that summer.[1] Unlike the models produced during the Paterson era, this pistol was not fitted with a folding trigger but rather with a conventional one set within a protective guard. It was also of a substantially larger caliber and weight (3 pounds, 13 ounces).

Upon its completion, Colt submitted the pistol to Secretary of War William L. Marcy for consideration.[2] On 2 December 1846 Colt showed it to Capt. Samuel H. Walker of the U.S. Regiment of Mounted Riflemen.[3] Colt could not have chosen a more qualified individual to judge the merits of his improved revolver. During his service with the Texas Rangers Captain Walker had used a Patent Arms Manufacturing Company Number 5 Holster Pistol in action at Walker's Creek in 1844. It is also likely that he was familiar with the Colt carbines that had been issued to units of the Republic of Texas armed forces in 1839. Drawing upon this past experience, Walker recognized the prototype's potential value as a military sidearm and agreed to support Colt's efforts to press for its adoption by the U.S. government. At the same time he also pointed out deficiencies in the design that would need to be corrected before the pistol was suitable for use in the field. Among the alterations he subsequently suggested were a redesigned front sight, a finer rear sight, the installation of a loading

Overall left

lever, and, most important of all, a new grip configuration. Although the prototype had a grip based upon that used on the Patent Arms Manufacturing Company's Number 5 Holster Pistols, Walker stated on 17 February 1847, "The handle of pistol is rather short & not quite full enough, and must be increased a little

in length and thickness."[4] He repeated his concern about that point in a letter to Colt dated 28 April 1847: "I hope you have made the alteration in the Britch that I suggested as the handle is very imperfect being so short that a suitable grip cannot be taken to enable you to hold it steady enough to shoot with much accuracy."[5]

While the sight and grip changes were easily effected, the loading lever proved to be a greater challenge. On 18 January 1847 Colt wrote to Walker, advising him, "There are some difficultes about adapting my pistols to the elongated Ball in the operation for loding I shall have to see you on the subject as soon as I get the loading operatos made & I must have from you authorraty to make the loding operatus different from what we origeonally determined upon."[6] Colt's frustration with the loading lever is even more apparent in his letter to Walker of 23 January 1847:

> I have been bothered to deth in endevering to lode the cillinders with the conical ball by means of the old fashioned leaver and have abandoned it as a bad job. There must be a leaver attached to the barrel upon a new plan which will work purpindicular otherwise you never can get your balls strate into the cillinder. I am now getting up a moddle to work that way and I know it is the best way, and you cant but be pleased with it.[7]

Immediately following the completion of this model, Colt submitted it to Walker for his approval. Once that had been secured, Walker, acting on behalf of the U.S. government, prepared a memorandum of agreement concerning production of the new Holster Pistols. Shortly after Colt signed this document, on 4 January 1847,[8] he began making arrangements to manufacture the pistols. As the text of the contract included a statement specifying that the revolvers were to be made with an "additional sixth chamber in the cylinder," it would appear that this prototype was originally fitted with a five-chambered cylinder.

Notes

1. Robert M. Patterson, *In the Circuit Court of the United States, District of Massachusetts. Samuel Colt vs. The Mass. Arms Company. Report of the Trial of the Above-Entitled Cause, at Boston, on the Thirtieth Day of June, A.D. 1851, Before His Honor, Levi Woodbury, Associate Justice of the Supreme Court of the United States* (Boston: White & Potter, 1851), 105–6.

2. Samuel Colt to John H. Offley, 1 December 1846, and Samuel Colt to Col. John Mason, 1 December 1846. Box 1982/47, folders 36 and 10. Samuel Hamilton Walker Papers. Archives and Information Services Division, Texas State Library and Archives Commission.

3. Samuel Colt to Capt. Samuel H. Walker, 3 December 1846. Samuel Colt Papers, Box 6 Connecticut Historical Society.

4. Capt. Samuel H. Walker to Samuel Colt, 17 February 1847. Samuel Colt Papers, Box 6 Connecticut Historical Society.

5. Capt. Samuel H. Walker to Samuel Colt, 28 April 1847. Samuel Colt Papers, Box 6, Connecticut Historical Society.

6. Samuel Colt to Capt. Samuel H. Walker, 18 January 1847. Samuel Colt Papers, Box 6, Connecticut Historical Society.

7. Samuel Colt to Capt. Samuel H. Walker, 23 January 1847. Samuel Colt Papers, Box 6, Connecticut Historical Society.

8. Samuel Colt and Capt. Samuel H. Walker, Memorandum of an agreement, 7 January 1847. Samuel Colt Papers, Box 6, Connecticut Historical Society.

29

U.S. 1847 Holster Pistol
Serial number 1020 (cylinder 1019)
Caliber .44 in., barrel length 9 in., overall length 15½ in.
Date of Manufacture: 1847
Wadsworth Atheneum Museum of Art
Bequest of Elizabeth Hart Jarvis Colt, 1905.988

Markings
Barrel: ADDRESS SAML COLT NEW-YORK CITY
Barrel lug (right side): U.S. / 1847
Cylinder: COLT'S PATENT / MODEL U.S.M.R.

1861 Inventory of Colonel Colt's Small Office
Page 6, line 9
1 old army Pistol (Patterson?)

As Colt did not have a manufacturing facility of his own, he assigned the 4 January 1847 contract from the U.S. government for one thousand Holster Pistols to Eli Whitney, Jr., of Whitneyville, Connecticut, for completion.

Although mechanically the same as the preceding prototype, the revolvers made by Whitney incorporated all of the improvements suggested by Captain Walker. Measuring 15½ inches overall and weighing 4 pounds, 9 ounces unloaded, the Colt-Whitneyville Holster Pistol was a formidable as well as a massive weapon. In view of the eventual issuing of these contract revolvers to troopers of the U.S. Regiment of Mounted Riflemen, they were assigned serial numbers reflecting the regiment's composition. They were stamped with the abbreviation "Co." for company, followed by the letter designation of that unit (A, B, C, D, or E) and an issuance number (usually 1, 2, 3, etc.).

Although military arms were normally devoid of ornamentation, Colt decided that the cylinders of these revolvers should be engraved with an image illustrating a skirmish that Samuel Walker had described to him in a letter dated 30 November 1846.[1] In that action that took place in July 1844, a contingent of Texas Rangers, armed with Paterson-manufactured Holster Pistols, routed a much larger force of hostile Comanche Indians. Sometime in early March 1847 Colt commissioned Waterman L. Ormsby of New York to engrave a roll die depicting an abbreviated detail of the engagement between bracketed cartouches containing the legends COLT'S PATENT and MODEL U.S.M.R.[2] The decision to use this image was in many respects a stroke of genius on Colt's part, as two of the Rangers involved were John Coffee Hayes and Samuel Walker, both officers in the Regiment of Mounted Riflemen.

Herbert G. Houze

Detail of cylinder

Shortly after the first deliveries of the revolvers, beginning in June 1847, Colt had Whitney complete a series of pistols for private distribution.[3] To differentiate these arms from those made for the Army, they were serial numbered from 001 upward. With the exception of two that were sent to the New York firm of Moore & Baker for sale,[4] all the pistols with serial numbers between 1001 and 1020 were presented to officers of the U.S. Army and Navy. Among the recipients were Capt. Samuel H. Walker, Col. John Coffee Hayes, Col. William S. Harney, Capt. Charles G. Alvarado Hunter, U.S.N., Maj. Gen. Winfield Scott, Col. Parsifer Smith, Maj. Gen. Zachary Taylor, Col. John W. Tibbatts, Col. David E. Twiggs, and Maj. Gen. William Worth.[5] Based upon James B. Colt's correspondence with his brother Samuel, the above revolvers were shipped to Veracruz, Mexico, aboard

Overall left

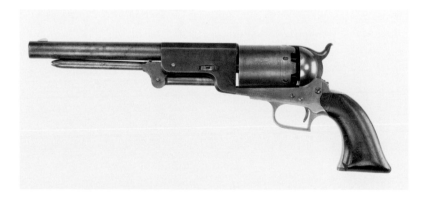

the *Martha Washington*.[6] Immediately after the ship's arrival at Veracruz on 4 August 1847, the revolvers were distributed to their respective recipients by Capt. E. G. Elliott, the port's acting quartermaster.[7]

Although this revolver (assembled from the frame, barrel, and butt of number 1020 and the cylinder from pistol number 1019) has traditionally been identified as having belonged to Capt. Samuel H. Walker, this attribution was recently questioned. In 1998 Philip Schreier of the National Firearms Museum presented a persuasive argument that the pistols received by Walker in 1847

were those with serial numbers of 1009 and 1010.[8] In support of this identification, Schreier used documents written immediately following Walker's death in October of that year and information provided by the captain's descendants. Having posited a lineage for these two revolvers, Schreier then turned his attention to number 1019/1020. The primary thrust of his assertion that this revolver could not have belonged to Captain Walker involved the character of Lt. Bedney F. McDonald, the officer who gave it to Colt in 1848 or 1852.[9] According to Schreier, McDonald was a charlatan who had abandoned his military duties in Mexico in 1848 to "chase his fortunes" in the California gold fields.[10] In 1860 he wrote a fawning letter to Colt concerning the establishment of an arms factory in his native state of Georgia, also mentioning the pistol he had given to the inventor. Moreover, for reasons Schreier does not make clear, he intimates that McDonald acquired number 1019/1020 after it had become obsolete in the early 1850s.[11]

Contemporary evidence does not support the first allegation. McDonald did not go to California from Mexico; instead he went to Washington, D.C. This is confirmed by a newspaper report published in the *Georgia Telegraph* on 1 February 1848, noting that the "gallant young officer arrived here [Macon] on Thursday last, from Vera Cruz," and that "after spending two days with his relatives in this city, left for Washington."[12] Given McDonald's meritorious service in Mexico, it must be assumed that he was traveling under orders and not absent without leave.[13]

The second point raised by Schreier concerns McDonald's letter to Colt dated 4 January 1860. In this letter, as cited by Schreier, McDonald stated: "I regret to have to say to you that the pistols you were kind enough to present to me during the War with Mexico were burnt in California—I hope you have the pistol I let you have that Capt Walker left me when he was killed in a good

Cat. 29a. Concluding paragraph of Bedney McDonald's letter of 4 January 1860 to Samuel Colt containing the interlinear insertion of the word "killed." Samuel Colt Papers, Connecticut Historical Society.

Cat. 29b. English-manufactured "Escopeta" presented by Bedney F. McDonald to Samuel Colt, ca. 1848. Museum of Connecticut History.

state of preservation."[14] However, there is a problem with this transcription. The word "killed" was an interlinear addition written in a hand quite distinct from that of McDonald; witness the construction of the letter "k" and the dot over the "i" in the accompanying photograph (cat. 29a).[15] Consequently the closing sentence should read: "I hope you have the pistol I let you have that Capt Walker left me when he was in a good state of preservation." The phrase "a good state of preservation" therefore refers to Walker, not the pistol. While not common, the expression was used during the first half of nineteenth century to indicate a state of good health.[16] It is entirely possible that this meaning was unknown to whoever annotated McDonald's letter and therefore interpreted as a reference to the pistol.

While unmentioned in Schreier's article, Samuel Colt's response of 12 January 1860 to McDonald's letter written eight days earlier is of some interest.[17] Its contents and wording indicate a level of familiarity between the two men. Moreover, Colt refers to McDonald's having lost his presentation pistols "by fire in San Francisco," a point not mentioned in the letter of 4 January. Colt also injected humor into the letter, referring to his home, Armsmear, as "my 'shanty' here in Hartford."[18] Comments of this nature appear only in letters that Colt wrote to friends, not business or casual acquaintances.

Returning to the revolvers presented by Samuel Colt to Captain Walker, Schreier states that they were received on 5 October 1847, when Samuel Walker wrote to his brother, Jonathon Thomas Walker: "I have just received a pair of Colt's pistols which he sent to me as a present."[19] In fact, this letter cannot be used to prove the date when the pistols came into Walker's possession, but rather only the date when he informed his brother of the gift. It is known that the pistols arrived in Veracruz on 4 August and were distributed immediately by Capt. E. G. Elliott, as confirmed in a letter of thanks sent to Colt by Maj. Gen. Zachary Taylor on 17 August.[20] Further evidence of this fact is provided by a letter dated 12 August 1847, sent to Colt by Capt. Floyd Waggaman stating that he

had seen the pair of revolvers sent to Captain Hayes.[21] As Walker was in camp relatively near Veracruz, it is extremely unlikely that he did not receive his pistols until some two months later. Furthermore, given the special relationship that existed between Walker and Colt, it is inconceivable that the latter would have slighted his friend by presenting examples of the new revolver to other senior officers but not to him.

With respect to McDonald's claim that Walker had given him the pistol numbered 1019/1020, there is no doubt that the two officers knew each other. McDonald was awarded a brevet commission for his conduct during the Battle of Huamantla, where Walker was killed (cat. 29b).[22]

Two pieces of circumstantial evidence tend to support McDonald's claim. First, serial number 1019/1020 exhibits no evidence of having been used. It not only retains a significant amount of its original blued and case-hardened finish, but the barrel's interior is mirror bright, indicating it was fired rarely or not at all. Likewise, the cylinder chambers and nipple recesses exhibit no evidence of combustion corrosion. It is in almost the same condition as it was when it left Eli Whitney's factory. This absence of any sign of use tends to indicate that the weapon was put aside for some reason shortly after it was made. Second, contrary to Schreier's statement that Colt would not have known whether number 1019/1020 had gone to Walker because he did not keep track of serial numbers,[23] docketed annotations listing numbers on some of his correspondence prove otherwise.[24] Consequently, a ruse would have been quickly unmasked.

Given all of this, what is to be made of the Walker identification? Walker was instrumental in perfecting the Whitney-manufactured Holster Pistol's design, so it is highly probable that Colt sent his friend additional revolvers and Walker, in turn, gave one of them to McDonald. If this were the case, Captain Walker may have had several pairs of Holster Pistols in his possession other than those returned to his family after his death.

Herbert G. Houze

Notes

1. Capt. Samuel H. Walker to Samuel Colt, 30 November 1846. Samuel Colt Papers, Box 6, Connecticut Historical Society.

2. Eli Whitney, Jr., Revolving Pistol of Saml Colt [account summary prepared on or immediately after 19 May 1847]. Samuel Colt Papers, Box 6, Connecticut Historical Society.

3. The revolvers called for in the government's contract were evidently completed by the third week of May 1847, when Eli Whitney, Jr., prepared the account cited immediately above. Actual deliveries began on 7 June 1847 (Samuel Colt to Capt. William A. Thornton, 7 June 1847. Samuel Colt Papers, Box 6, Connecticut Historical Society).

4. Moore & Baker to Samuel Colt, 31 July 1847. Records of the Colt's Patent Fire Arms Manufacturing Company, RG103, Business File, Series III, Incoming Correspondence, Box 8, Connecticut State Library. This letter requests additional revolvers from Colt because the firm had sold the two previously sent.

5. This list is based on the following correspondence: Samuel Colt to Col. William S. Harney, n.d. [7 June 1847]; Samuel Colt to Maj. Gen. Winfield Scott, n.d. [7 June 1847]; Samuel Colt to Maj. Gen. Zachary Taylor, n.d. [7 June 1847]; Samuel Colt to Col. Jack Hayes, 3 June 1847; Samuel Colt to Col. David E. Twiggs, 10 June 1847; James B. Colt to Capt. Samuel H. Walker, 28 July 1847; Samuel Colt to Capt. Charles G. A. Hunter, 23 August 1847; Samuel Colt to Col. John W. Tibbatts, n.d. [September–October 1847]. Samuel Colt Papers, Boxes 6 and 9, File 3 (undated letters), Connecticut Historical Society.

6. James B. Colt to Samuel Colt, 9 July 1847. Records of the Colt's Patent Fire Arms Manufacturing Company, RG103, Business File, Series III, Incoming Correspondence, Box 8, Connecticut State Library.

7. Capt. G. A. Elliott to Samuel Colt, 2 August 1847. Records of the Colt's Patent Fire Arms Manufacturing Company, RG103, Business File, Series III, Incoming Correspondence, Box 8, Connecticut State Library.

8. Philip Schreier, "Walker's Walkers—The Colt Walker Revolvers of Captain Samuel H. Walker, Texas Ranger," *Man at Arms* 20, no. 3 (May/June 1998): 30–39.

9. McDonald could have given this revolver to Colt in February or March 1848 when both were in Washington or alternatively in 1852 when Colt visited San Francisco.

10. Ibid., 39.

11. Ibid.

12. *Georgia Telegraph,* "Lieut. Bedney F. McDonald," 1 February 1848, 1. This article also notes that McDonald was the son of Charles J. McDonald, governor of Georgia from 1839 to 1843, and that he had studied law at Oglethorpe University.

13. McDonald initially served as a sergeant in the Georgia Regiment of Volunteers. He subsequently was appointed 2nd lieutenant in the U.S. Third Regiment in May 1847 and was brevetted (awarded a 1st lieutenant's commission) "for gallant and meritorious service" during the occupation of Huamantla on 9 October 1847, where Captain Walker met his death (Francis B. Heitman, *Historical Register and Dictionary of the United States Army* [Washington, D.C.: U.S. Government Printing Office, 1903], I, 662).

14. The transcription used by Schreier was first published in James L. Mitchell, *Colt: A Collection of Letters and Photographs about the Man—the Arms—the Company* (Harrisburg, Pa.: Stackpole Company, 1959), 99, and later in R. L. Wilson, *The Arms Collection of Colonel Colt* (Bullville, N.Y.: Herb Glass, 1964), 16. Authorship of the interlinear addition can be attributed on the basis of the handwriting to Colt's personal secretary, L. H. Goodman. Why it was done, however, remains a matter of speculation.

15. Bedney F. McDonald to Samuel Colt, 4 January 1860. Samuel Colt Papers, Box 8, File 1, Connecticut Historical Society.

16. For example, "Sally [a horse] has recover'd and is now in a fine state of preservation" (Thomas N. Radenhurst, *Letters* [Montreal: n.p., 1850], 81 [letter dated 4 April 1844]).

17. Samuel Colt to Bedney F. McDonald, 12 January 1860. Samuel Colt Papers, Box 8, File 2, Connecticut Historical Society.

18. Ibid.

19. Schreier, "Walker's Walkers," 33.

20. Maj. Gen. Zachary Taylor to Samuel Colt, 17 August 1847. Wadsworth Atheneum Museum of Art, Bequest of Elizabeth Hart Jarvis Colt.

21. Capt. Floyd Waggaman to Samuel Colt, 12 August 1847. Records of the Colt's Patent Fire Arms Manufacturing Company, RG103, Business File, Series III, Incoming Correspondence, Box 8, Connecticut State Library.

22. McDonald later gave Colt a souvenir of that action, which was noted in the 1861 Inventory of Colonel Colt's Small Office as "An 'Escopeta' [a short carbine] taken from Mexican lancer Flint lock 76 Cal" (page 4, line 15). When this weapon, now in the Colt Collection of the Museum of Connecticut History, was cleaned some years ago, in its barrel was found a piece of Colt company stationery having the following notation: "Escopeta from Huamantla give Col C by Lt. McDonald" (cat. 29b). That a relationship existed between the two men is also demonstrated by the fact that McDonald sent Colt a testimonial letter praising the U.S. Model 1847 Holster Pistol sometime in 1848. An extract from the letter was published as Abstract II in *Senate Committee on Military Affairs, Memorial of Samuel Colt, on the subject of his repeating fire-arms.* 30th Cong., 2nd sess., 1849, S. Rep. 296, 4.

23. Schreier, "Walker's Walkers," 35.

24. Horstmann, Sons & Drucker to Samuel Colt, 1 November 1847 (annotation dated 2 November 1847). Records of the Colt's Patent Fire Arms Manufacturing Company, RG103, Business File, Series III, Incoming Correspondence, Box 8, Connecticut State Library.

Hartford and Success

As the Whitneyville-made Holster Pistols began to reach the final stages of manufacture in April 1847, Samuel Colt's confidence increased almost exponentially. Although his optimism had yet to be substantiated by the use of his revolvers in action, he began to contemplate their production in greater quantities.

Others also evidently believed that the new pistol would be a commercial success. In response to a now lost letter of inquiry, E. E. Marcy of Hartford informed Colt that a Mr. Brimley of that city would rent Colt a building suitable for manufacturing arms at an annual rent of $250.[1] More importantly, Marcy conveyed that Brimley was anxious to see Colt set up business in Hartford.

> He is desirous that you should come here & take it and will expend any amount of money in enlarging the building &c &c—He wished me to say to you that he would do *every thing*, but furnish an engine to induce you to come & set up here—[2]

The inducement to locate his factory in Hartford was strengthened on 12 May 1847, when Marcy informed Colt that the rental property would be only temporary, as he was willing to provide land to Solomon Porter for the construction of a much larger facility.[3] Although Marcy stated that the funding for this project had yet to be raised, he made it clear that the citizens of Hartford were "all anxious to establish manufactories in our midst and when we get the grand Canal done here, we shall become a little the 'Smartest city' this side of Birmingham."[4]

Despite these offers, Colt remained somewhat cautious about his future plans. Indeed, he explored the possibility of having his arms made either at his own factory or by an independent maker in New York City. To those ends he contacted his cousin Dudley Selden and the firm of Blunt & Syms.[5] Whether these overtures were genuine or merely a ruse to disguise his true intentions is not known. However, the dates of the Blunt & Syms correspondence suggest the latter.[6]

Whatever the case, the production and royalty agreement offered to Colt by Blunt & Syms on 4 September 1847 must have reassured the inventor that he had reached the right decision on manufacturing his pistols at his own factory.[7] Certainly he knew that the profits from such a venture would exceed the amounts offered by Blunt & Syms.[8]

Colt probably decided to set up business in Hartford in August 1847, when the postmaster in New Haven, Connecticut, began forwarding all of his correspondence to Hartford.[9] By 23 September he had evidently already entered into an agreement to rent Brimley's building at 33 Pearl Street, as he wrote Capt. Charles Hunter: "I am off this morning for Hartford Connecticut where I have an establishment for making my Arms."[10]

Although the first Holster Pistols to be assembled in Hartford were made using surplus parts from the Whitneyville venture, by October 1847 Colt began shipping revolvers that combined both old and newly manufactured components.[11] Shorter in length and incorporating a greatly improved loading lever latch, these pistols won an immediate following. While the initial orders were normally for one or two, as word of the availability of these new revolvers spread, bulk orders began to be received. Interestingly, the first of these was not from New York City, where several dealers were actively promoting Colt's revolvers, but from Philadelphia. On 30 September 1847 the firm of Magee Faber & Company sent Colt a letter requesting twelve pistols at twenty-five dollars each plus six sets of accessories (bullet molds, powder flasks, and nipple wrenches).[12] Colt's net profit on this order, after allowing a discount for cash, was $314.28.[13]

The margin for profit on smaller orders was substantially more, as the price charged for single pistols with plain brass mounts (that is, back straps and trigger guards) was thirty dollars, and those with silver-plated mounts cost thirty-five dollars, minus a ten percent discount for cash payments.[14]

The level of production at the Pearl Street works during its first two months of operation can be gauged to a certain extent from serial numbers that Colt recorded in his correspondence file. For example, two Holster Pistols with serial numbers 1069 and 1071 were sent to Horstmann, Sons & Drucker on 2 November 1847,[15] and number 1104 was delivered to John Mason, Jr., on 4 October.[16] The disparity between the numbers and their nonsequential order was due to the fact that the revolvers sold to Horstmann were from stock, whereas the one delivered to Mason was a special order made specifically at the request of the secretary of the navy. Their sequencing aside, the numbers indicate that the Pearl Street factory was turning out approximately one hundred revolvers a month during the autumn of 1847.

It is worth noting that Samuel Colt did not forget the contributions made by Capt. Samuel Walker to the success of his revolvers. In response to an order received from W. Huntington of Cincinnati, Ohio, dated 11 November 1847, Colt wrote: "I can furnish a few of the 6 chambered Holster pistols of my construction at this time cal'd the Walker modle."[17]

That Colt had begun contemplating the manufacture of smaller-caliber revolvers in 1847 is demonstrated by the following comments he made in letters to J. Leigh, Horstmann, and W. Huntington:

In about one month I can send you a pare of Belt pistols weighing about 3¾ lbs. each. . . .

. . . I shall have an other size receptiv for the belt rady for market in a short time, & also a pocket sise in cource of a few months— . . . .

. . . will be able to furnish a small supply of the sise adapted to the belt in a month or six weeks time can also supply a sise reseptiv to the pocket in about three or four months.[18]

Despite these hopes, subsequent events would delay introduction of the Pocket Pistol until mid-1848 and the Belt Pistol until 1851.

Although Colt had first approached Secretary of War William L. Marcy about a second contract for one thousand Holster Pistols in July 1847, it was not until 2 November that the contract was issued.[19] The receipt of this contract had the immediate effect of shelving any plans Colt had for the production of civilian models. However, the purchase price of twenty-five dollars per pistol to be paid by the government more than made up for any delays the order caused. By reinvesting the profits, Colt was able to retool his Pearl Street factory for the production of Pocket Pistols almost immediately after the government contract was fulfilled in the late summer of 1848.

The immense and widespread popularity of Colt's revolvers led to an ever-increasing number of orders that the Pearl Street armory was hard-pressed to fill.[20] Fortunately at approximately the same time Solomon Porter completed the building on Grove Lane that E. E. Marcy had first mentioned to Colt on 12 May 1847.[21] By maintaining his lease on the Pearl Street property on a monthly basis after it expired in September 1848, Colt gradually moved his operations to the Porter building without disrupting production. As the Grove Street facility had substantially more floor space, Colt was able to expand his manufacturing capabilities to meet the back orders that had arisen from the increased demand for his revolvers. He also began work on improving their design.

He had hired Elisha K. Root in 1848 to oversee the armory's operations and to serve as its chief mechanic.[22] The choice of Root was propitious, as he became an invaluable asset to Colt over the next fourteen years. Root's involvement with the fledgling concern also demonstrated Colt's intention to involve only relatives in its administration; Root's wife, Matilda, was Colt's cousin.[23]

As sales grew, so did Colt's disposable income. In contrast to his free-spending ways of the Paterson era, he reinvested this income in his factory. New tools were purchased and patents secured. The excess was invested in promoting his revolvers both at home and, more importantly, abroad.

Colt's first efforts to secure foreign sales for his revolvers were made in the autumn of 1849, when he visited Europe and Constantinople, the capital of the Ottoman Empire.[24] Although Colt had some success in Europe, notably an agreement with the Austro-Hungarian government that would allow it to manufacture copies of his revolvers on a royalty basis for five years,[25] his trip to Constantinople produced no results. Colt did, however, have an audience with the Turkish sultan, at which he and his traveling partner, Samuel F. B. Morse, were presented with gifts.[26] This European trip marked Colt's entrance onto the world stage.

The tour had one lasting consequence. Colt's ability to secure audiences with important government officials was apparently hampered by his status as a private citizen. As a result, on his return to Connecticut, he sought a militia commission from Governor Thomas H. Seymour. On 2 May 1850 Seymour appointed Colt a lieutenant colonel and aide-de-camp to the captain general of the State of Connecticut.[27] Shortly thereafter, the inventor had new barrel inscription dies cut that read: ADDRESS COL. SAML COLT NEW-YORK U.S. AMERICA (fig. 1).

A year later Colt firmly established his presence abroad when he displayed an array of his pistols and a few remodeled revolving carbines at the 1851 Exhibition of the Works of Art & Industry of all Nations held in London.[28] In addition to receiving considerable press coverage, the display resulted in Colt's being invited to present a lecture on revolvers to the Institution of Civil Engineers in London on 25 November, for which he was later awarded the Telford Medal and an associate membership the following year.[29]

Much to dismay of his landlord, Solomon Porter, Colt decided in late 1851 that the time had come to have his own factory. To achieve this goal, in early 1852 he began buying land south of Hartford in an area known as the South Meadows.[30] As the South Meadows lay within the Connecticut River's natural flood plain, Colt proposed building a dike along the river's edge to prevent the area from being inundated. Although this plan was greeted with some skepticism, Colt was not to be deterred. To ensure the project's success, he hired the country's best hydrologist, Capt. Alexander Hamilton Bowman, to design the dike and oversee its construction.[31] After it was completed, Colt set about building his armory. His foresight would be validated in 1854, when the Connecticut River flooded a large portion of downtown Hartford, including the Porter building housing the Colt works. In contrast, the dike shielding the South Meadows held, and the area remained dry.

In 1853 Colt became an international arms maker when he opened his Pimlico factory in London. Employing approximately three hundred workers, it was the largest private firearms manufactory in England. The venture attracted considerable press coverage.

COLT'S PISTOL MANUFACTORY IN LONDON.—
Col. Colt is astonishing the English at his new pistol manufactory in London. Twelve months since he had possession of one of the buildings fitted up for the accommodation of the contractors for the new houses of Parliament, at the northern end of Vauxhall Bridge. The building is 258 feet long, of three floors, well constructed, and is now called "a smart machine shop." The numerous machines employed are almost exclusively of American manufacture; and the leading operations are conducted by American mechanics from the pistol manufactory at Hartford, Conn. Out of the three hundred employed, fifty are Yankees, to "show the British how." A few days since, MR. BUCHANAN, the American Minister, visited the establishment and addressed and complimented the operatives. He expressed great satisfaction and pleasure, and said the institution was an honor to the United States as well as to Great Britain.[32]

Colt's rising fortunes were to suffer a setback in 1854, when he tried to solidify his position in the United States by seeking an extension of his reissued patent of 1848. His detractors mounted a well-orchestrated campaign implying that Colt had sought to bribe members of Congress with monetary gifts from a secret $15,000 fund maintained by the industrialist's attorney, Edward N. Dickerson.[33] Prodded by press attacks, Congress ultimately began a formal inquiry into the charges.[34] Although Colt was exonerated, the patent extension failed because of adverse publicity. Even though Colt was unsuccessful, he relished every minute of the controversy and sent to his friends for light reading copies of the more vicious attacks penned by the "hounds who are howling at us."[35] He had learned that anything that kept his name or his revolvers in the public eye was good publicity no matter how negative.

The opening of the new armory on Vandyke Avenue in 1855 demonstrated Colt's emergence as one of the country's great industrialists. Physically dominating the southern skyline of Hartford, the building also served as a constant reminder that the city was changing. The change was to have a far more profound effect upon its owner. In order to recoup his sizable investment in the facility, estimated by some as in excess of $400,000, Colt spent ever-increasing amounts of time promoting his products.

From 1855 onward, Colt traveled incessantly, but he did take a break from work in June 1856, when he married Elizabeth Hart Jarvis, the daughter of a prominent Hartford minister.[36] Yet even their honeymoon trip to Europe involved business. Invited to attend the coronation of Russia's Czar Alexander II, the couple journeyed to Saint Petersburg, where Colt met with members of the czar's government in the hope of securing an arms contract.[37] His efforts were successful, leading to a very lucrative contract to supply all the tools and fixtures needed to manufacture a copy of his Belt Pistol at the Tula Arsenal southeast of Moscow.[38]

While Colt was abroad, plans that he had set in motion before his departure to seek a charter for a public company, to be known as the Colt's Patent Fire Arms Manufacturing Company, were finalized. To ensure that he maintained complete control of this new entity, Colt instructed the treasurer and bookkeeper, Milton Joslin, to divide one hundred of the three hundred authorized shares among various company officials and to hold the remainder in Colt's name.[39]

After returning home, Colt embarked on a new venture that was to further increase his fortunes. At the suggestion of two acquaintances who were mining engineers, S. H. Lathrop and Herman Ehrenberg, Colt purchased a controlling interest in the Sonora Exploration & Mining Company and the Santa Rita Mining Company in Tubac, Arizona. Although Charles D. Poston, an Arizona politician, and Ehrenberg, the concern's putative owners, may have viewed Colt as a passive partner, in June 1858 he dispatched his brother-in-law, Richard Jarvis, to Arizona to protect his interests.[40] In April 1859 Colt took control of both mines and formed the Arizona Mining Company.[41] Aside from supplying a large quantity of arms for the defense of these holdings, Colt was interested in improving the cultural atmosphere of Tubac. To achieve this, he provided funds to build a library and then arranged for a wide selection of books to be sent to the mining town.[42]

It was also in 1859 that Colt erected a factory on the South Meadows property to process willow branches, obtained from trees planted on the dike, to make articles of furniture and household goods.[43] To ensure that his employees there were properly housed, he built homes in the immediate vicinity, as well as a community center and library.[44] Colt's interest in the welfare and continuing education of his workers was most likely the result of his having seen the positive effects of "Worker Societies" in England, as well as in the German states.

The same year witnessed another patent-reissue petition that Colt expected to be contentious. The patent involved in this instance, however, was not one that had been awarded to Colt. Rather, it involved E. K. Root's Patent Number 13,999 of 25 December 1855. While the major claim of that patent, involving a method for turning the cylinder by means of an operating rod, was of little consequence to Colt, he had considerable interest in the added claim for a rack and gear loading lever, as he planned to incorporate the design in all the new models then under development.[45] To ensure that the reissue was granted, Colt was willing to spend far more to "grease the rails" than he had done in 1854 when his patent extension was denied. On 12 December 1859 he wrote to his agent, Maj. William H. B. Hartley:

> I have a note to day from Captain Joe Comstock of which I enclose a copy the party refered to is a distinguished leder in the republican party & has pledged his support to our patent extensions, which if he actes in good faith united with the influence Mr Corwin may be able to bring to bear upon the Congress we may be successful & for which I am willing to pay handsome contingent fees. I have once said that I would concent to bend myself to pay in all $50,000 to General Kerryman when the patent extension has become a law & this sum should be eaqually divided between the Republicans & Democrats.[46]

Although Colt had been actively involved in local politics since purchasing the South Meadows, in 1860 he publicly supported the Democratic candidate for president, Stephen A. Douglas. Much has been written in the past of this support and Colt's supposed "Southern leanings."[47] That Colt had countless friends in the southern states cannot be denied, for many of the officers who first supported the adoption of his revolvers in the 1830s and 1840s were from the region. However, Colt's feelings about slavery were at odds with the views of most of those gentlemen. As early as 1849 he had publicly voiced his repugnance for the practice. Describing some of what he had seen in Constantinople, Colt wrote that "the condition of slavry ther I find particuly abhorent."[48] In 1860 he made those sentiments a matter of public record, when he had one thousand copies of an abolitionist sermon printed for distribution to his employees and their families.[49]

The question then arises as to why he continued to sell arms to the southern states after it became evident they were likely to secede. The simple answer is that he was obliged to by federal law. Both southern and northern states placed orders under the provisions of what is known as the Militia Act, approved by the U.S. Congress on 25 April 1808.[50] This act allowed individual states to order arms for their militias subject to the approval of the U.S. Army's Ordnance Department. As a result, all the orders Colt fulfilled had the official sanction of the government in Washington and in many cases were forwarded from the Ordnance Department. More-over, had Colt not complied with the requests, he would have been subject to government penalties. Until the federal government announced that a state of war existed between the United States and the Confederate States of America, Colt continued to process southern orders placed under the auspices of the Militia Act. He did, however, begin to delay such shipments in 1861, much to the consternation of some of his oldest friends.[51]

Despite attacks in the press and anonymous letters exposing his sup-posed southern sympathies,[52] Colt's loyalty to the Union was beyond ques-tion. In April 1861 he organized and equipped a volunteer unit that was subsequently officially recognized as the 1st Regiment Connecticut Rifles.[53]

The outbreak of war was to have a profound effect upon Samuel Colt and his factory. He directed all his attention to securing contracts from the federal government, as well as from individual northern states. At the same time, Elisha K. Root brought the armory up to full production. The strain on both men eventually led to their deaths. Colt's passing, however, took place much earlier than Root's.[54]

Public concern about Colt's health first arose in late November 1858, when a rumor was circulated announcing his death.[55] Although the announcement was somewhat premature, by late 1860 close attention was being paid to the inventor's health not only by his family but also by the residents of Hartford.[56] Suffering from what was variously described as gout or rheumatism, Colt had spells of good health broken by relapses throughout 1861.[57] By the end of the year he was worn out, and shortly after Christmas he caught a cold that led to his final illness on 9 January 1862. Three days later Colt died at his home, Armsmear.[58]

Notes

1. E. E. Marcy to Samuel Colt, 2 May 1847. Records of the Colt's Patent Fire Arms Manu-facturing Company, RG103, Business File, Series III, Incoming Correspondence, Box 8, Connecticut State Library.

2. Ibid.

3. E. E. Marcy to Samuel Colt, 12 May 1847. Records of the Colt's Patent Fire Arms Manufacturing Company, RG103, Business File, Series III, Incoming Correspondence, Box 8, Connecticut State Library.

4. Ibid.

5. Samuel Colt to Dudley Selden, 15 July 1847. Samuel Colt Papers, Box 6, Connecticut Historical Society.

6. Both of the Blunt & Syms letters postdate Colt's decision to begin manufactur-ing arms in Hartford. Blunt & Syms to Samuel Colt, 4 September and 29 Septem-ber 1847. Records of the Colt's Patent Fire Arms Manufacturing Company, RG103, Business File, Series III, Incoming Correspondence, Box 8, Connecticut State Library.

7. Ibid., 4 September 1847.

8. The royalties quoted by Blunt & Syms amounted to ten dollars per Holster Pistol (less the cost of accessories) and fifty cents per other size pistol (ibid.).

9. Letters addressed to Colt in New Haven by Captain Waggaman were forwarded to Hartford (Capt. Floyd Waggaman to Samuel Colt, 12 and 24 August 1847. Records of the Colt's Patent Fire Arms Manufacturing Company, RG103, Business File, Series III, Incoming Correspondence, Box 8, Connecticut State Library). Colt's change of address may have occurred as early as the first week of August 1847 in that a letter sent to him by the firm of Canfield & Robbins on 9 August was sent directly to Hart-ford (Canfield & Robbins to Samuel Colt, 9 August 1847). Records of the Colt's Patent Fire Arms Manufacturing Company, RG103, Business File, Series III, Incoming Corre-spondence, Box 8, Connecticut State Library.

10. Samuel Colt to Capt. Charles G. A. Hunter, 23 August 1847. Samuel Colt Papers, Box 6, Connecticut Historical Society.

11. For example, the revolver serial number 1104, submitted for testing by the U.S. Navy on 4 October 1847, was built using a combination of new parts and compo-nents made at Whitneyville. John Mason, Jr., to Samuel Colt, 21 September 1847 (docketed annotation in Colt's hand dated 4 October 1847). Records of the Colt's Patent Fire Arms Manufacturing Company, RG103, Business File, Series III, Incoming Correspondence, Box 8, Connecticut State Library.

12. Magee Faber & Company to Samuel Colt, 30 September 1847. Records of the Colt's Patent Fire Arms Manufacturing Company, RG103, Business File, Series III, Incoming Correspondence, Box 8, Connecticut State Library.

13. Ibid. (docketed note dated 24 October 1847).

14. Samuel Colt to Horstmann, Sons & Drucker, 23 October 1847. Records of the Colt's Patent Fire Arms Manufacturing Company, RG103, Business File, Series II, Outgoing Correspondence, Box 6, Connecticut State Library.

15. Horstmann, Sons & Drucker to Samuel Colt, 1 November 1847 (docketed annota-tion in Colt's hand dated 2 November 1847). Records of the Colt's Patent Fire Arms

Herbert G. Houze

Manufacturing Company, RG103, Business File, Series III, Incoming Correspondence, Box 8, Connecticut State Library.

16. John Mason, Jr., to Samuel Colt, 21 September 1847 (docketed annotation in Colt's hand dated 4 October 1847). Records of the Colt's Patent Fire Arms Manufacturing Company, RG103, Business File, Series III, Incoming Correspondence, Box 8, Connecticut State Library.

17. W. Huntington to Samuel Colt, 11 November 1847 (undated docketed annotation in Colt's hand). Records of the Colt's Patent Fire Arms Manufacturing Company, RG103, Business File, Series III, Incoming Correspondence, Box 8, Connecticut State Library.

18. Samuel Colt to J. Leigh, 23 October 1847, and Samuel Colt to Horstmann, Sons & Drucker, 23 October 1847. Records of the Colt's Patent Fire Arms Manufacturing Company, RG103, Business File, Series II, Outgoing Correspondence, Box 6, Connecticut State Library. W. Huntington to Samuel Colt, 11 November 1847 (undated docketed annotation).

19. Samuel Colt to the Hon. William L. Marcy, 16 July 1847. Records of the Colt's Patent Fire Arms Manufacturing Company, RG103, Business File, Series II, Outgoing Correspondence, Box 6, Connecticut State Library; Charles T. Haven and Frank A. Belden, *A History of the Colt Revolver and the Other Arms Made by Colt's Patent Fire Arms Manufacturing Company from 1836 to 1940* (New York: Bonanza Books, 1940), 290–91.

20. Beginning in 1848 and continuing through the early 1850s, Colt received a tremendous number of orders from California. Demand for his revolvers in the gold fields was so great that they often changed hands for amounts ranging from $250 to $500 (The Hon. T. Butler King to the Hon. James Wilson, 26 February 1850. Wadsworth Atheneum Museum of Art, Bequest of Elizabeth Hart Jarvis Colt).

21. E. E. Marcy to Samuel Colt, 12 May 1847. Records of the Colt's Patent Fire Arms Manufacturing Company, Connecticut State Library.

22. Elisha K. Root was hired by Samuel Colt in November 1848.

23. Matilda Colt was the fourth child of Elisha Colt (1778–1827) and Lucretia Ann Davis (ca. 1780–1820). Elisha and Samuel Colt shared the same grandfather, Benjamin Colt (1738–1781).

24. The *firmin*, or transit permit issued to Colt by the sultan of Turkey in 1849 is preserved in the collections of the Wadsworth Atheneum Museum of Art, Bequest of Elizabeth Hart Jarvis Colt.

25. The majority of the revolvers made under license at Innsbruck were issued to officers of the Austrian Navy and were finished in a manner identical to that of cat.

86. Cased and more highly polished examples were available for private purchase to those who secured government warrants.

26. Samuel Colt and Samuel F. B. Morse, [Private Claim] Reimbursement on duties paid on presents from the Sultan of Turkey, 31st Congress, Bill No. R.19 (*Digested Summary and Alphabetical List of Private Claims which have been Presented to the House of Representatives from the First to Thirty-First Congress* [Washington, D.C.: U.S. Government Printing Office, 1853], 371).

27. Governor Thomas H. Seymour, Commission of Appointment to Samuel Colt, 2 May 1850. Wadsworth Atheneum Museum of Art, Gift of Mrs. E. Sanderson Cushman, 1964.455.

28. *Official descriptive and illustrated Catalogue of the great Exhibition* (London: William Clowes & Sons, 1851), III, 1454.

29. Samuel Colt, "On the application of Machinery to the manufacture of Rotating Chambered-Breech Fire-Arms, and the peculiarities of those Arms," *Minutes of Proceedings of the Institution of Civil Engineers; with Abstracts of the Discussions*, vol. XI, session 1851–52 (London: Institution of Civil Engineers, 1852), 30–50. The Telford Premium Medal is illustrated and described in cat. 127.

30. Quitclaim deeds for the property purchased at this time are preserved in the Samuel Colt Papers, Boxes 6 and 11, Connecticut Historical Society.

31. Alexander Hamilton Bowman (1803–1865) graduated from the U.S. Military Academy, West Point, in 1825 and had a distinguished military career as an engineer. Among the many projects he was responsible for were Fort Sumter in Charleston Harbor, South Carolina, and the U.S. Assay Office in New York City.

32. *New York Daily Times*, "Colt's Pistol Manufactory in London," 2 December 1853, 8.

33. The instigator of this campaign was Horace H. Day, who under a variety of names submitted letters for publication in the *New York Herald* during the first two weeks of January 1854. As a lobbyist for opposing interests, Day's motives were rather transparent, a fact that Edward N. Dickerson, Colt's attorney, took full advantage of when he sent a detailed exposé to the editor of the *Herald* on 19 January 1854 (reproduced in U.S. House of Representatives, *Report No. 353 Colt Patent, &c., &c., 33d Congress, 1st Session* [Washington, D.C.: U.S. Government Printing Office, 3 August 1854], 37–42).

34. The findings of the select committee investigating the charges were noncommittal on the question of whether Colt had actually attempted to bribe members of Congress.

35. Edward N. Dickerson to Samuel Colt, 15 January 1854. Samuel Colt Papers, Box 7, Connecticut Historical Society.

36. Elizabeth Hart Jarvis (1826–1905) was the daughter of the Reverend William Jarvis and Elizabeth Miller Hart.

37. Samuel Colt to Milton Joslin, 2 September 1856. Records of the Colt's Patent Fire Arms Manufacturing Company, RG103, Business File, Series III, Incoming Correspondence, Box 10, Connecticut State Library, and Samuel Colt to Milton Joslin, 30 September 1856. Samuel Colt Papers, Box 7, Connecticut Historical Society.

38. William Jarvis to William Jarvis, Jr., 5, 12, and 26 April 1858. William Jarvis Letters, MSS Coll. 70425, Connecticut Historical Society.

39. Samuel Colt to Milton Joslin, 30 September 1856. Samuel Colt Papers, Box 7, Connecticut Historical Society.

40. William Jarvis to William Jarvis, Jr., 7 June 1858. William Jarvis Letters, MSS Coll. 70425, Connecticut Historical Society.

41. William Jarvis to William Jarvis, Jr., 4 April 1859. William Jarvis Letters, MSS Coll. 70425, Connecticut Historical Society.

42. For a complete account of the arms sent and other details concerning Samuel Colt's involvement with Tubac, Arizona, see Herbert G. Houze, *Colt Presentations from the Factory Ledgers 1856–1869* (Lincoln, R.I.: Andrew Mowbray Inc., 2003), 47–56.

43. William Jarvis to William Jarvis, Jr., 14 November 1859 and 7 January 1860. William Jarvis Letters, MSS Coll. 70425, Connecticut Historical Society.

44. These facilities were located in an area that was known as the German Village or Coltsville.

45. U.S. Patent Office, E. K. Root, of Hartford, Connecticut, "Improvements in Revolving Fire-Arms," Reissue no. 846, 1 November 1859, 2.

46. Samuel Colt to Maj. William H. B. Hartley, 12 December 1859. Samuel Colt Papers, Box 7, Connecticut Historical Society.

47. In particular, it has repeatedly been suggested that Colt harbored southern sympathies and actively acted on behalf of the secessionist states. William Hosley, *Colt: The Making of an American Legend* (Amherst: University of Massachusetts Press, 1996), 95–97. Cf. James L. Mitchell, *Colt: A Collection of Letters and Photographs about the Man—the Arms—the Company* (Harrisburg, Pa.: Stackpole Company, 1959), 31–84.

48. Samuel Colt to Andrew T. Allen, 6 December 1849. Allen Family Papers, Private collection.

49. William Jarvis to William Jarvis, Jr., 30 December 1860. William Jarvis Letters, MSS Coll. 70425, Connecticut Historical Society.

50. Summary accounts of the arms ordered by individual states between 1856 and 1861 under the 1808 Militia Act are to be found in the National Archives, Records of the Office of the Chief of Ordnance, Entry 118—Distribution of Arms Under Militia Act, RG-156, vol. 5, 53–103.

51. For example, an order for five hundred Belt Pistols placed on behalf of Maj. Benjamin McCulloch on 25 March 1861 was declined by Colt's Patent Fire Arms Manufacturing Company. Maj. William H. B. Hartley to Lewis Wigfall, 26 March 1861. Private collection.

52. *New York Times*, "A Revolving Patriot," 26 April 1861, 4, and "A Member of V. C. [Vigilant Committee]" to Samuel Colt, 15 April 1861. Formerly James L. Mitchell Collection (Richard A. Bourne Co., Inc., *Antique Firearms and Related Items* [17–18 March 1982], Lot 621).

53. The costs of raising this unit were partially underwritten by the Colt company (Colt's Patent Fire Arms Manufacturing Company, Journal A, 493, Doug Donnelly Collection). On 16 May 1861 Samuel Colt was appointed colonel of the regiment by Governor William W. Buckingham (Governor William W. Buckingham, Commission of Appointment to Samuel Colt, 16 May 1861. Wadsworth Atheneum Museum of Art, Gift of Mrs. E. Sanderson Cushman, 1964.455).

54. Elisha K. Root died on 1 September 1865.

55. William Jarvis to William Jarvis, Jr., 22 November 1858. William Jarvis Letters, MSS Coll. 70425, Connecticut Historical Society.

56. William Jarvis to William Jarvis, Jr., 30 October, 26 November, and 17 December 1860. Ibid. On page 4 of the 17 December letter mention is made of the rumors concerning Colt's health that were then circulating in Hartford.

57. William Jarvis to William Jarvis, Jr., 3 January, 13 January, 27 March, 6 August 1861; 9 January 1862. Ibid. The recurrent nature of his illness suggests that Colt may have suffered from malaria contracted during one of his many trips to Cuba.

58. William Jarvis to William Jarvis, Jr., 12 January 1862. Ibid.

both surplus parts from Whitneyville and newly made components. The Hartford Holster Pistol was a marked improvement over its predecessor. As shown in the accompanying drawing prepared for his first advertising broadside and a later caveat filed with the U.S. Patent Office (cat. 30a), the revolver was not only shorter in length but also had a more secure loading lever catch. With the awarding of a second contract for one thousand Holster Pistols from the U.S. Army on 2 November 1847, production at the fledgling Hartford factory was focused solely on their production.

Once revenues began to be received after delivery of these Holster Pistols to the government in June 1848, Colt turned his attention to the production of a revolver more suited for civilian use. Brought to market in either September or early October 1848, the five-shot .31 caliber Pocket Pistol was greeted with considerable enthusiasm despite the fact that it was not fitted with an attached loading lever.[1] This omission was quickly corrected, and a revised version was placed in production in 1849.

Offered in a variety of barrel lengths, between 3 and 6 inches, slightly more than 15,500 were made before the model was replaced by a redesigned variation in 1850. To emphasize the Pocket Pistol's potential value as a self-defense sidearm, Colt had Waterman L. Ormsby engrave a cylinder roll die with a fanciful scene of a stagecoach passenger warding off would-be robbers.

Note

1. The exact date of this model's introduction is unknown. Initial demand was evidently rather strong, as none could be sent to Colt while he was in Washington, D.C., in December 1848 (Samuel Colt to Maj. Gen. W. J. Worth, 2 December 1848. Samuel Colt Papers, Box 6, Connecticut Historical Society).

Cat. 30a. Record copy of the pen and ink drawing submitted to the U.S. Patent Office by Samuel Colt with his caveat request of 16 September 1848. Private collection.

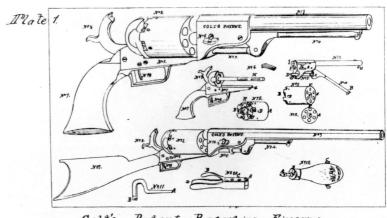

30

Pocket Pistol

Serial number 4786

Caliber .31 in., barrel length 3 in., overall length 7⅞ in.

Date of manufacture: 1848

Museum of Connecticut History, Hartford

Gift of the Pratt & Whitney Company Foundation, Inc., 280

Markings

Barrel: ADDRESS SAML COLT NEW YORK CITY

Cylinder: COLTS PATENT

1861 Inventory of Colonel Colt's Small Office

Page 1, line 6

Pocket Pistol 2½ in. [altered to *3 in.*]

1887 Museum Inventory Draft

280 .31 caliber 5 shot 3 inch barrel Colt Police [sic] *Has seen service 4786*

When Samuel Colt began production at the 33 Pearl Street factory in mid-October 1847, his attention was focused on the finishing and assembly of existing Holster Pistol components that had been shipped to Hartford from the works of Eli Whitney, Jr., in Whitneyville, Connecticut. By the beginning of October, however, he had begun to manufacture a hybrid pistol that incorporated

31
Bullet Mold
No serial number
Overall length 4 in.
Date of Manufacture: 1848–50
Museum of Connecticut History, Hartford
Gift of the Pratt & Whitney Company Foundation, Inc., 1152

Markings
Sprue cutter: COLT'S / PATENT

Before the introduction of fixed ammunition (that is, cartridges that combined the primer or ignition agent, powder charge, and bullet in one unit), firearm owners had to use loose powder and ball to load their pistols or rifles. Consequently, arms makers provided purchasers with the accessories they needed to use, whatever firearm they bought. In the percussion period these tools consisted of a combination screwdriver/nipple wrench, a powder flask, and a bullet mold. Of these, the most important was the mold, as it was made to cast either round balls or conical bullets of the precise size matching the caliber of the arm it accompanied.

Later examples of the bullet molds made by the Colt company for its .31 caliber Pocket Pistol were fitted with a movable steel plate covering the mold chambers, called the sprue cutter. By pushing it to the side after lead had been poured into the mold, the excess lead was automatically cut off from the bases of the ball and bullet that had just been made.

32
Experimental Holster Pistol
No serial number
Caliber .44 in., barrel length 7½ in., overall length 13⅞ in.
Date of Manufacture: 1849
Museum of Connecticut History, Hartford
Gift of the Pratt & Whitney Company Foundation, Inc., 285

Markings
Barrel: COLT'S PATENT

1861 Inventory of Colonel Colt's Small Office
Page 5, line 28
1 Army Pistol Barrel jointed to frame

1887 Museum Inventory Draft
285 .44 Cal. 6 shot 7½ barrel Colt Holster Pistol. Experiml. Frame with hinge below & in front of cyl. marked & engraved Colt's Patent.

Shortly after Colt's Pearl Street factory began full-scale production, the inventor turned his attention to the development of potential improvements. The first of these involved a design that he had first worked on some eight years earlier. In an effort to reduce the fouling of the cylinder pin arbor by the residue resulting from the combustion of black powder during firing, he proposed using a fully enclosed arbor. This design also allowed him the opportunity to hinge the barrel

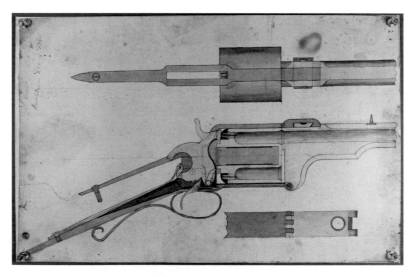

Cat. 32a. Pen, ink, and watercolor drawing of a hinged-barrel revolving carbine, 4 December 1840. Records of the Colt's Patent Fire Arms Manufacturing Company, Connecticut State Library.

Herbert G. Houze

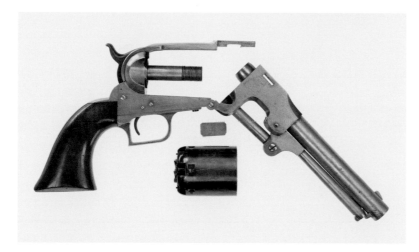

Overall right with barrel lowered

ment provided a more stable connection between the barrel and the frame, Colt's concept of a hinged-barrel revolver never advanced beyond the experimental stage. Other inventors, however, were to follow his lead, and by the mid-1870s hinged-barrel revolvers were being mass-produced in the United States as well as abroad.

This revolver would be little more than a passing curiosity if it were not for its cylinder. In contrast to its companion pieces illustrated in the patent specifications, as well as all the production revolvers that preceded it, the cylinder stop recesses are not of round or oval form. Instead they are rectangular, with the leading or left side having a well-defined straight bearing wall. The other wall is cut away so that the spring-loaded cylinder stop automatically engaged the recessed catch, a feature described by Colt in his 1 September addendum to a caveat he filed with the U.S. Patent Office on 28 August 1848.[2] This change was brought about by problems encountered with the earlier circular and oval stop recesses. When the stop or the edges of the recesses became worn, the cylinder would not always lock with the chambers in proper alignment with the axis of the bore. If this occurred during actual use, it could result in either a misfire caused by the hammer not hitting the percussion cap on the nipple or, if the cap was fired, the lead bullet being shaved as it forced its way into the barrel. Since neither of these results was conducive to a user's confidence in the weapon, the problem had to be quickly addressed. The use of rectangular cylinder stops was adopted for production in late 1849, and Colt was awarded a U.S. patent for their design on 10 September 1850 (Number 7,629). It is worth noting that this locking system is still used today by many arms manufacturers.

Notes

1. Samuel Colt, pen, ink, and watercolor drawing, 4 December 1840. Records of the Colt's Patent Fire Arms Manufacturing Company, RG 103, Administrative File, Design Drawings, Box 62, Connecticut State Library. While the form of these cylinder stops resembled those used on the later pre-Paterson prototypes, their depth and area were increased. In addition, the stop bolt acted through an aperture cut in the frame that prevented any lateral movement.

2. Samuel Colt to the Commissioner of Patents, 1 September 1848. Records of the Colt's Patent Fire Arms Manufacturing Company, RG 103, Legal File, Series IV, Patents, Box 45, Connecticut State Library.

assembly directly to the frame instead of using a horizontal key that passed through the barrel lug and forward end of the cylinder arbor. While this method of construction would allow the cylinder to be easily removed for reloading or cleaning, it had one major disadvantage. As the barrel was not supported by the arbor at its rear end, it could easily be knocked out of alignment if the pistol was dropped or the muzzle struck against a hard object.

Despite this, several different models were made to test hinge attachment systems. The earliest and most complicated of these are illustrated in the specifications drawings enrolled with Samuel Colt's U.S. Patent Number 7,613, issued 20 September 1850. The system employed in this revolver closely parallels that first designed by Colt in 1840, in that the barrel is secured to the frame's top strap by a simple dovetail key (cat. 32a).[1] Although this arrange-

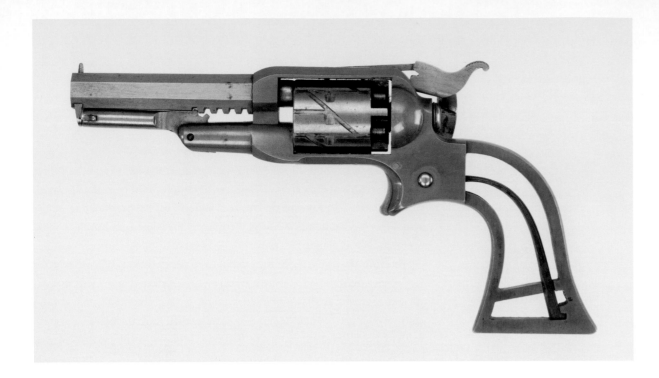

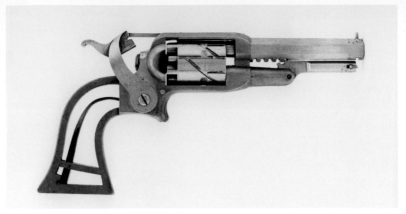

Cat. 33a. Experimental Pocket Pistol, identical in design, with the hammer in the cocked position. Museum of Connecticut History.

33

Experimental Pocket Pistol
Serial number 5
Caliber .265 in., barrel length 3 in., overall length 7 in.
Date of Manufacture: 1849–50
Wadsworth Atheneum Museum of Art
Bequest of Elizabeth Hart Jarvis Colt, 1905.1001

Markings
None except serial number

1861 Inventory of Colonel Colt's Small Office
Page 4, line 26
Small NM Pistol with slide and Grooves
or
Page 5, line 27
5 Models (Iron & brass) illustrating slides & grooves marked 97 98 92

Perhaps one of the most novel approaches to ensuring the proper alignment of the cylinder's chambers to the barrel's bore was that developed by Elisha K. Root during the autumn of 1849. Based in part on designs first patented by Otis Whittier in 1837 and Elijah Jaquith in 1838 (both of which were later purchased by Root),[1] his solution utilized a sliding pin mounted in a slot cut in the frame's top strap to engage grooves cut into the cylinder's surface.

Attached to the nose of the hammer by a linked operating rod, the pin moved back and forth as the hammer was drawn rearward or when it fell forward. This movement in turn was transmitted to the cylinder by the angled lower point of the pin riding within the exterior grooves. When the hammer was cocked, the pin's tip automatically moved into the oblique grooves causing the cylinder to rotate. Then, as the pistol was fired, the pin's tip slid forward along the perpendicular groove parallel to the center line of the chamber. This arrangement ensured that the cylinder and barrel were perfectly aligned (cat. 33a).

The revolver illustrated here incorporates an improvement of Root's basic design developed by Colt. To allow the pistol to be safely carried while loaded, intermediate perpendicular grooves join the oblique channels so that the hammer could be moved forward from the half cock position to rest on the shoulders of the cylinder between the nipple recesses.

Although Root did not patent the pin and groove design until 1855, he filed a caveat describing its construction with the U.S. Patent Office on 9 December 1849.[2] Similarly, Colt did not seek official protection for his contributions until 1856, even though he had filed a caveat on 21 January 1851.[3]

The design was actually impractical, as any dirt or fouling in the grooves would have rendered the revolver inoperable. Nonetheless, a considerable number of sample prototypes were made in 1849 and 1850. Superficially similar, they all differ in the construction of their cylinder pins, the location of the hammer, and, more importantly, Colt's rack-and-pinion loading lever.

While the hinged loading lever then being used in production arms was serviceable, it did have one weakness. As the movement of the plunger (the rod entering the cylinder chambers) was controlled by a lever, the pressure it exerted against bullets being loaded could vary with the strength of the user. As a result, the soft lead conical bullets or round balls being chambered were often accidentally deformed. This drastically affected a revolver's accuracy and was a problem that needed to be addressed. The physics of the rack-and-pinion or creeping lever system allowed bullets to be seated in the cylinder's chambers with only a moderate amount of pressure on the forward lever arm. In addition, the spacing of the rack cuts allowed the rearward movement of the plunger to be controlled in such a way that a constant level of pressure was applied to each bullet. To ensure the rack-and-pinion lever's proper operation, a number of factors had to be examined. Consequently, sample revolvers were made up with rack grooves cut into the lower surface of the barrel or drilled with holes to receive the pinions, while others had the rack cut into the plunger rod.

The four most promising designs, including one that consisted of a threaded plunger moved by a fixed nut, were described and illustrated in the caveat filed by Colt on 21 January 1851.[4]

Notes

1. Eli Miller and Thadeus Miller to E. K. Root, Assignments of Patent Interests, 22 October 1850. Records of the Colt's Patent Fire Arms Manufacturing Company, RG 103, Legal File, Series III, Patent Assignments, Box 45, Connecticut State Library.

2. E. K. Root to the Commissioner of Patents, 9 December 1849. Records of the Colt's Patent Fire Arms Manufacturing Company, RG 103, Legal File, Series IV, Patents, Box 45, Connecticut State Library.

3. Samuel Colt to the Commissioner of Patents, 21 January 1851. Records of the Colt's Patent Fire Arms Manufacturing Company, RG 103, Legal File, Series IV, Patents, Box 45, Connecticut State Library.

4. Ibid.

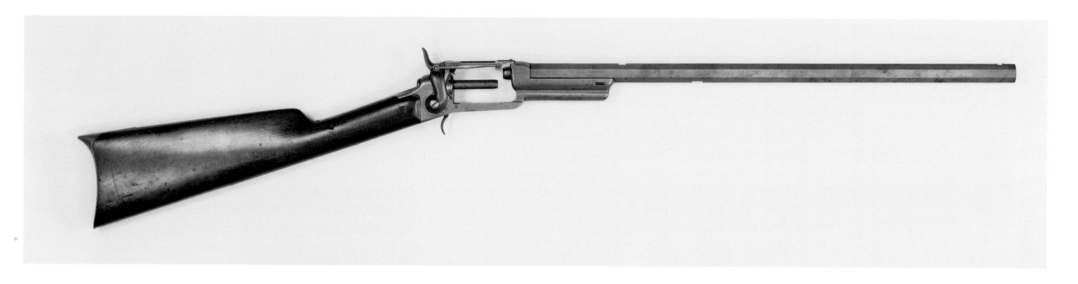

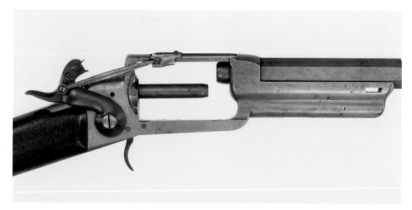

Detail of receiver

34

Experimental Rifle

No serial number

Caliber .38 in., barrel length 32¼ in., overall length 43 in.

Date of Manufacture: 1849/1850

Museum of Connecticut History, Hartford

Gift of the Pratt & Whitney Company Foundation, Inc., 65

This fragmentary rifle demonstrates a slightly different method of revolving the cylinder. Instead of having an operating rod set into the top strap of the frame over the cylinder, it is mounted along the strap's right side. This arrangement would have been less susceptible to fouling but would have been difficult to keep clean during field use.

The design of the cylinder pin corresponds to those illustrated in Samuel Colt's U.S. Patent Number 7,613, issued 3 September 1850.

35

Experimental Pocket Pistol

No serial number

Caliber .28 in., barrel length 5 in., overall length 10⅛ in.

Date of Manufacture: 1850

Museum of Connecticut History, Hartford

Gift of the Pratt & Whitney Company Foundation, Inc., 266

Markings

Barrel: -ADDRESS SAML COLT- / NEW YORK CITY

Cylinder: Col. Colt 1850

1887 Museum Inventory Draft

266 31 Cal, 6 shot, Colt, 5" b. oct., rack & pin ram., highly engraved and blued

cylin moves to left

cones on top

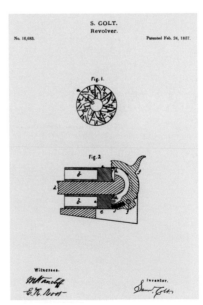

Cat. 35a. Drawing enrolled with Samuel Colt's U.S. Patent No. 16,683, issued 24 February 1857, illustrating the turning grooves machined into the rear face of a revolver cylinder. U.S. Patent and Trademark Office, Washington, D.C.

Of all the experimental designs developed during the first years of the Hartford factory's operation, this example is perhaps the most interesting, as it embodies a number of novel features. Aside from being of solid frame construction, the cylinder is unlike those used in any other Colt revolver. Instead of the percussion cap nipples being placed in line with the chambers, they are set at angles along the exterior rear circumference. Their location in this position was dictated by the fact that the entire rear face of the cylinder is cut with radiating channels or grooves to allow its rotation by a pivoted driving pin attached to the base of the

Herbert G. Houze

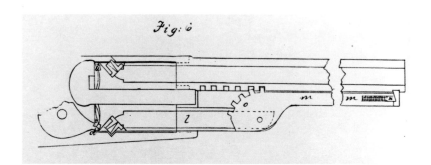

Cat. 35b. Record copy of a pen and ink caveat drawing submitted to the U.S. Patent Office on 21 January 1851 by Samuel Colt. Records of the Colt's Patent Fire Arms Manufacturing Company, Connecticut State Library.

hammer. When the pistol is cocked, the driving pin moves upward within prescribed channels, causing the cylinder to rotate. As it falls forward, the pin automatically is repositioned into a different channel (cats. 35a–c).

The method of securing the cylinder is also noteworthy. Instead of a fixed or removable cylinder pin, it is fitted with a spring-loaded captive pin having a concave forward end and a domed rear. When the cylinder is inserted into position, it is held in place by a separate locking pin mounted in the forward vertical wall of the frame beneath the barrel. When the locking pin is moved rearward, it engages the cylinder pin, causing it in turn to move rearward. This action allows the domed end of the cylinder pin to engage a recess cut in the face of the recoil shield. To prevent the cylinder pin from becoming disengaged, the locking pin is held in place by a setscrew mounted in the left side of the frame's forward vertical wall. As the pistol was intended to be used as a patent model, it was constructed so that the operation of the rack-and-pinion loading lever was fully exposed.

While the cylinder turning mechanism was described and illustrated in a caveat filed by Samuel Colt with the U.S. Patent Office on 21 January 1851,[1] formal protection was not sought until 1857.[2] Colt never filed a caveat or patent application for his novel captive cylinder pin design.

Notes

1. Samuel Colt to the Commissioner of Patents, 21 January 1851. Records of the Colt's Patent Fire Arms Manufacturing Company, RG 103, Legal File, Series IV, Patents, Box 45, Connecticut State Library.

2. U.S. Patent Office. Samuel Colt, "Improvement in Many-Chambered Rotating-Breech Fire-Arms," Number 16,683, issued 24 February 1857.

Cat. 35c. Colt advertising broadside, ca. 1853, illustrating the cylinder scenes roll-engraved on Pocket, Belt, and Holster Pistols. Connecticut Historical Society.

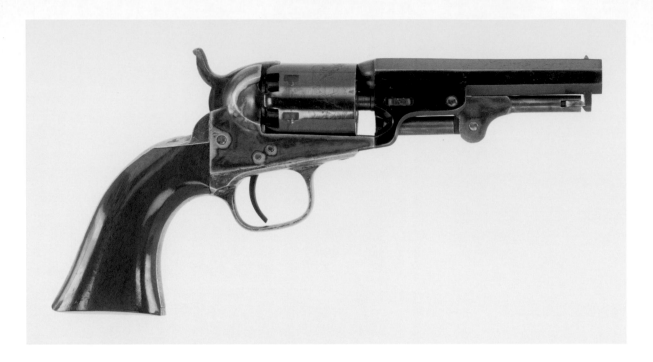

36

Pocket Pistol

Serial number 233154

Caliber .31 in., barrel length 4 in., overall length 9 in.

Date of Manufacture: 1863

Wadsworth Atheneum Museum of Art

Bequest of Elizabeth Hart Jarvis Colt, 1905.994

Markings

Barrel: ADDRESS COL. SAML COLT NEW-YORK U.S.AMERICA

Cylinder: COLT'S PAT.

Frame: COLTS / PATENT

This revolver, though of later date, is a typical example of the improved pistols manufactured at the Colt armory on Grove Lane after it entered full production in 1851. The small size of the Pocket Pistol and its availability with a 4-, 5-, or 6-inch barrel made it an immensely popular sidearm. As a result, by the time production ceased in 1872, more than 300,000 had been made.

This revolver originally formed part of the memorial collection assembled by Elizabeth Hart Jarvis Colt and is listed on page 213 of the Colt's Patent Fire Arms Manufacturing Company's Serial Number Ledger 4 under the date 30 May 1863.

37

Sample Patent Verification Belt Pistol

No serial number

Caliber .36 in., barrel length 7 7/16 in., overall length 13 1/16 in.

Date of Manufacture: November 1851

Derek Povah Collection

Markings

Barrel: SAMUEL COLT BREVETE A PARIS

1861 Inventory of Colonel Colt's Small Office

Page 1, line 5

1 Navy Pistol marked in French

Despite Colt's hope that production of a Belt Pistol would begin in late 1847,[1] the model was not introduced until 1851. The cylinders of this model were roll-engraved with a scene depicting action between warships of the Republic of Texas and Mexico that occurred on 16 May 1843. This, combined with their caliber, prompted the model to also be given the name "Navy Pistol."

Although the revolver illustrated here has long been regarded as a French copy or counterfeit of a Colt Belt Pistol, it is actually something entirely different.

Detail of barrel inscription

Herbert G. Houze

In order to satisfy French patent laws, verification samples of patented designs had to be submitted to government officials within six months of a patent's issuance. To satisfy these requirements, William E. Newton, Colt's European patent attorney, initially hired a Parisian gunmaker to build a sample in September 1851, based upon the enrolled patent drawings.[2] However, the arrangements came to naught when this maker, whose name is not known, became "terribly frightened at the amount of work in it" and withdrew from the project.[3] As a result, Newton decided to have the verification sample made from "the pieces of the one you let me have."[4]

Problems were evidently encountered in carrying out this plan, as Newton informed Colt in November 1851 that the maker he had engaged to do the work, Louis-François Devisme, had to make "a barrel following your plan" before the pistol could be finished.[5]

Interestingly, the cylinder of this revolver was roll-engraved with an unfinished die that did not include the standard COLT'S PATENT / No. panel.

Notes

1. Samuel Colt to J. Leigh, 23 October 1847. Records of the Colt's Patent Fire Arms Manufacturing Company, RG 103, Business File, Series III, Incoming Correspondence, Box 8, Connecticut State Library.
2. William E. Newton to Samuel Colt, 20 September 1851. Records of the Colt's Patent Fire Arms Manufacturing Company, RG 103, Business File, Series III, Incoming Correspondence, Box 8, Connecticut State Library.
3. William E. Newton to Samuel Colt, 24 September 1851. Records of the Colt's Patent Fire Arms Manufacturing Company, RG 103, Business File, Series III, Incoming Correspondence, Box 8, Connecticut State Library.
4. Ibid.
5. William E. Newton to Samuel Colt, November 1851. Records of the Colt's Patent Fire Arms Manufacturing Company, RG 103, Business File, Series III, Incoming Correspondence, Box 8, Connecticut State Library.

38

Belt Pistol with "Attachable Breech"
Serial number 128519/S
Caliber .36 in., barrel length 7½ in., overall length 13 in., overall length with stock 25½ in.
Date of Manufacture: 1862
Wadsworth Atheneum Museum of Art
Bequest of Elizabeth Hart Jarvis Colt, 1905.984A,B

Markings
Barrel: ADDRESS SAML COLT NEW.YORK CITY
Cylinder: COLT'S PATENT
Frame: COLTS / PATENT

When the .36 caliber Belt Pistol was introduced in 1851, it proved to be an immediate success. As its relatively light weight (2 pounds, 10 ounces) made it an ideal personal sidearm, the model saw service throughout the world.

This example is fitted with a detachable shoulder stock, or "Attachable Breech" of the type covered by Samuel Colt's U.S. Patent Number 22,696, issued on 18 January 1859. Attachable stocks enabled revolvers to be used as shoulder arms. This not only improved accuracy but also allowed their more efficient use by mounted horsemen.

This pistol-carbine originally formed part of the memorial collection assembled by Elizabeth Hart Jarvis Colt and is listed on page 156 of the Colt's Patent Fire Arms Manufacturing Company's Serial Number Ledger 4, under the date 31 December 1862.

39

Holster Pistol

Serial number 15016

Caliber .44 in., barrel length 7½ in., overall length 14 in.

Date of Manufacture: 1856

Wadsworth Atheneum Museum of Art

Bequest of Elizabeth Hart Jarvis Colt, 1905.992

Markings

Barrel: ADDRESS SAML COLT NEW.YORK CITY-

Cylinder: MODEL U.S.M.R. / COLT'S PATENT

Frame: COLTS / PATENT

Dating from 1856, this Holster Pistol resembles those first made by Colt at his Hartford factory in 1848. The model initially produced had a square-back trigger guard and oval cylinder stops. In 1850 the latter were replaced with rectangular stops, and in 1851 the rear bow of the trigger guard was given a rounded profile. In comparison with the Holster Pistol made in Whitneyville, this example weighs 4 pounds, 2½ ounces instead of 4 pounds, 9 ounces. It is also approximately 1¼ inches shorter in length.

Manufacture of this model was discontinued on 18 September 1861, when Colt issued an order stating, "I want no more of these Arms for the present."[1]

Note

1. [Samuel Colt] "Orders &c. Col. Colt," 2. Records of the Colt's Patent Fire Arms Manufacturing Company, RG 103, Business File, Series VI, Production Records 1856–1928, Box 24A, Connecticut State Library.

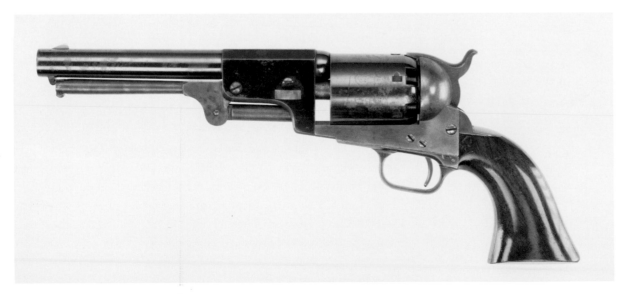

Overall left

Herbert G. Houze

40

Experimental Belt Pistol

No serial number

Caliber .36 in., barrel length 7½ in., overall length 13¾ in.

Date of Manufacture: ca. 1852–53

Museum of Connecticut History, Hartford

Gift of the Pratt & Whitney Company Foundation, Inc., 286

Markings

None

1861 Inventory of Colonel Colt's Small Office

Page 6, line 13

1 of first models for large New Model Pistol

1887 Museum Inventory Draft

286 36 Cal 6 shot 7½ oct Rifle frame pistol experiment. unfin.

Approximately a year after manufacture of the .36 caliber Belt Pistol had begun, Samuel Colt commenced work on a new series of experimental revolvers. Realizing that solid frame design was structurally superior to those then in production, Colt used this type of frame in his revised design. The prototype's lockwork with an exposed side hammer was derived from E. K. Root's experimental pocket pistols of 1849 and 1850. The enclosed cylinder pin first seen in Colt's hinged barrel and 1850 Pocket Pistol was also used. The pistol was fitted with a rack-and-pinion loading lever, now missing, of the type used in the earlier series of experimental pistols.

While the design was an improvement over those currently offered by Colt, its development was not pursued beyond the experimental stage. The reasons for this may have involved either the extensive retooling costs its manufacture would have entailed or the weight of a Holster Pistol made in the same pattern. This prototype did, however, demonstrate the practicality of the enclosed cylinder pin design. As a result, this feature was patented by Colt in 1857.[1]

Note

1. U.S. Patent Office. Samuel Colt, "Improvement in Many-Chambered Rotating-Breech Fire-Arms," Number 18,678, issued 24 November 1857.

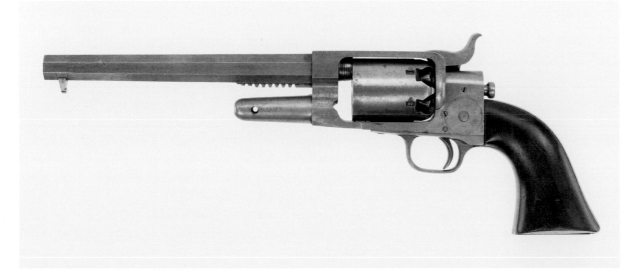

Overall left

41

New Model Pocket Pistol

Serial number 17170

Caliber .265 in., barrel length 3½ in., overall length 7⅞ in.

Date of Manufacture: 1857–58

Museum of Connecticut History, Hartford

Gift of the Pratt & Whitney Company Foundation, Inc., 295

Markings

Barrel: COLT'S / PATENT; ADDRESS COL. COLT / HARTFORD CT. U.S.A.

Cylinder: COLT'S PATENT / No. 17170

1887 Museum Inventory Draft

295 27 Cal. 5 shot Colt New Model Pocket oct 3½, marked 17170 sceleton [sic]

By 1854 Colt and E. K. Root had finally developed a solid frame side-hammer revolver design that was suitable for production. Introduced the following year, arms of this type were made in two forms: a diminutive Pocket Pistol and a Rifle.

Weighing slightly more than one pound, the Pocket Pistol immediately attracted considerable attention. It was not a long-term success because of its relatively small caliber, and users often found the cylinder pin difficult to remove. The resulting complaints caused Colt to revisit its design on more than one occasion. The .265 caliber New Model Pocket Pistol remained in production until 1861, when it was replaced by a revised .31 caliber version. During the seven years this model was manufactured, a total of approximately 28,000 were made.

Serial number 17170 is of particular note, as it has been "skeletonized" to reveal the internal construction and operation of the pistol's lockwork. "Skeletonized" revolvers were first made by Colt following his visit to the Exhibition of the Works of Art & Industry of all Nations, held in London in 1851. Aside from seeing sectionalized Forsyth gunlocks, Colt encountered a number of other exhibitors who displayed arms in various stages of manufacture or cut open to reveal their construction.[1] Impressed by the fascinated reaction of visitors, Colt realized that "skeletonized" arms would be ideal promotional tools. Upon his return to the United States, he had examples of his existing product line made up in this form. Thereafter, "skeletonized" pistols and rifles always formed part of the displays he mounted at both local and international trade exhibitions.[2]

Based upon the serial number of this revolver, it was probably made for display at the American Institute of New York's 1858 exhibition.

Notes

1. In addition to Forsyth & Company, the Birmingham maker J. R. Cooper & Co. exhibited a twelve-barrel revolving pepperbox that had one side of the stock "removed to show the working parts of the lock" (*Official descriptive and illustrated Catalogue of the great Exhibition* [London: William Clowes & Sons, 1851], I, 355). Among the makers displaying arms in their various states of manufacture were Bertonnet, Boss, and George and John Deane (ibid., III, 1174; I, 353).

2. Two other New Model Pocket Pistols, serial numbers 17117 and 17236, were also "skeletonized" by the Colt company for exhibition purposes (Robert Q. Sutherland and R. L. Wilson, *The Book of Colt Firearms* [Kansas City, Mo.: R. Q. Sutherland, 1971], 151).

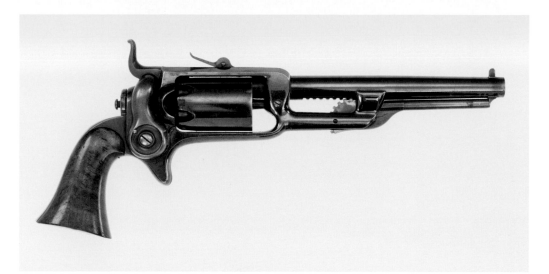

42

Sample Patent Verification Pistol

No serial number

Caliber .36 in., barrel length 7½ in., overall length 13¾ in.

Date of Manufacture: 1855

Museum of Connecticut History, Hartford

Gift of the Pratt & Whitney Company Foundation, Inc., 282

Markings

None

1861 Museum Inventory

Page 8, line 2

1 Berlin imitation of N. M. pocket p (larger)

1887 Museum Inventory

282 .36 Cal. 6 shot 7½ Colt Revolver Exp. Model R & p. r. with frame like Colt Revolv. Rifle

Long identified as an experimental prototype for a side-hammer Belt Pistol, this revolver is in fact a patent verification sample made by the Berlin gun-maker Theodor Gehrmann to substantiate the claims contained in Samuel Colt's Prussian patent application of 1855.

Details concerning the sample's manufacture and cost are contained in a series of letters written to Colt's London office by his Berlin agent, C. F. Wappen-hans. On 7 March 1855 Wappenhans notified Colt that "Mr. Gehrmann who is making the said pistol promised yesterday to have finished it in 14 days sure, so that I have already informed the Ministry in order to get the necessary cer-tificate that the patent is really executed in Prussia."[1] The pistol was completed

prior to June 1, when Wappenhans informed Luther P. Sargeant in London that "the patent commissioners have examined the pistol, and found it correspond-ing with the patent granted thereon, so that now every thing is right and the patent law completely satisfied."[2] Theodor Gehrmann charged Wappenhans 70.25 Prussian thalers for his work.[3] As the rate of exchange for Reich thalers to pounds sterling quoted by Wappenhans in his letter of 10 July was 6.17.4, the patent verification sample cost approximately 12 pounds, or sixty dollars. While this may seem a trifling amount, it would be equivalent to more than $6,000 in today's currency.

A full description of Colt's Prussian patent was published under the title "Die Fabrik Kleiner Feuerwaffen des Obristen Colt" in *Polytechnisches Journal* 140 (Stuttgart, 1856): 81–92, 161–69, pl. 2, figs. 1–11, and pl. 3, figs. 1–11.

Notes

1. C. F. Wappenhans to Col. Luther P. Sargeant, 7 March 1855. Records of the Colt's Patent Fire Arms Manufacturing Company, RG 103, Business File, Series III, Incoming Correspondence, Box 10, Connecticut State Library.

2. C. F. Wappenhans to Col. Luther P. Sargeant, 1 June 1855. Records of the Colt's Patent Fire Arms Manufacturing Company, RG 103, Business File, Series III, Incoming Corre-spondence, Box 10, Connecticut State Library.

3. C. F. Wappenhans to Col. Luther P. Sargeant, 10 July 1855. Records of the Colt's Patent Fire Arms Manufacturing Company, RG 103, Business File, Series III, Incoming Corre-spondence, Box 10, Connecticut State Library.

43

New Model Rifle

Serial number 804

Caliber .36 in., barrel length 27 in., overall length 46¼ in.

Date of Manufacture: 1857

Wadsworth Atheneum Museum of Art

Bequest of Elizabeth Hart Jarvis Colt, 1905.977

Markings

Barrel: COLT'S PT. / 1856 / ADDRESS COL. COLT / HARTFORD CT. U.S.A.

1861 Inventory of Colonel Colt's Small Office

Page 11, line 6

1 Rifle revolving with lubricator on side

During the same period when Colt and Root were experimenting with solid frame side-hammer pistols, several prototype rifles were also made using the design. The construction proved to be ideal, and in 1856 the New Model Rifle was placed in production. Intended solely for hunting and, therefore, of relatively small caliber, the new rifle met with a mixed reaction. Some sportsmen praised its accuracy and versatility, while others claimed it was of little practical value. Approximately one thousand were made.

The earliest New Model Rifles were fitted with trigger guards having finger spurs forward and rearward of their bows. These spurs were intended to indicate the proper position where the rifle was to be held by the user's supporting hand (that is, beneath the cylinder, not in front of it). The rifles were also equipped with a spring-loaded lubricating syringe on the side of the barrel lug. The purpose of this device was to allow a small amount of oil or other lubricant to be deposited on bullets chambered in the cylinder. Apart from reducing friction during firing, this film at the mouths of the chambers prevented ignition flashover where adjacent chambers were set off by the combustion gases escaping around the breech of the barrel. The lubricator design was subsequently patented by Colt (U.S. Patent Number 16,716, issued 3 March 1857).

Detail of left side, from lubricator to behind cylinder

Herbert G. Houze

44

New Model Rifle

Serial number 582

Caliber .44 in., barrel length 31⁵/₁₆ in., overall length 49⁷/₈ in.

Date of Manufacture: 1858

Wadsworth Atheneum Museum of Art

Bequest of Elizabeth Hart Jarvis Colt

Accession number 1905.976

Markings

Frame: COLT'S PT. / 1856 / ADDRESS COL. COLT / HARTFORD CT. U.S.A.

Cylinder: PATENTED SEPT. 10th 1850

Cylinder pin: PATENTED MAY 4th 1858

Frame: PATD NOV. 24 1857

In response to requests for a larger-caliber revolving rifle, Colt introduced a reworked model in 1858. In contrast to the earlier version, the new rifle had a wood forearm and a fluted cylinder. It also was fitted with an improved cylinder pin patented by Colt (U.S. Patent Number 20,144, issued 4 May 1858).

45

Plunger Powder Flask

No serial number

Overall length 7½ in.

Date of Manufacture: 1857–58

Museum of Connecticut History, Hartford

Gift of the Pratt & Whitney Company Foundation, Inc.

No accession number

Markings

None

1861 Inventory of Colonel Colt's Small Office

Page 5, line 13

1 spring Powder flask EKR's Patern

One of the rarest accessories made by the Colt's Patent Fire Arms Manufacturing Company prior to the American Civil War is the plunger powder flask. Designed by Elisha K. Root for use with New Model Rifles, it had a nozzle that fitted into the mouth of the cylinder's chambers.[1] By pushing the plunger located on the bottom plate of the flask downward, a set amount of gunpowder was released into the bulbous neck of the flask's spout. This powder in turn was deposited into the cylinder chamber.

As the amount of powder delivered into the cylinder chambers was fixed by the flask's construction, it offered a distinct advantage over common flasks that provided variable amounts. Because flasks of this type were expensive to manufacture, they normally were used only with presentation arms.

Note

1. E. K. Root did not seek patent protection for this style of plunger flask because it was merely an improved version of a flask designed by Samuel Colt. Colt's flask had a body of globular form and was fitted with a similar spout. He described and illustrated the design in a caveat filed with the U.S. Patent Office on 29 March 1850 (Records of the Colt's Patent Fire Arms Manufacturing Company, RG 103, Legal File, Series IV, Patents, Box 45, Connecticut State Library). Colt filed applications with the U.S. Patent Office on 29 March and 17 April 1856 (ibid.) to protect a slightly different plunger flask, but these were evidently denied, as no patent was issued. Colt was successful, however, in obtaining a British patent for the design (Patent Number 908, issued 16 April 1856).

46

New Model Carbine

Serial number 7

Caliber .56 in., barrel length 18 in., overall length 36½ in.

Date of Manufacture: 1857

Wadsworth Atheneum Museum of Art

Bequest of Elizabeth Hart Jarvis Colt, 1905.972

Markings

Frame: COL.COLT HARTFORD CT. U.S.A.

Upper tang of frame: COLTS / PATENT Nov. 24 1857

Work on the .56 caliber version of the New Model Rifle began in early 1856, but it did not enter full-scale production until 1858. Exasperated by the delay, Colt in June 1856 began to think about manufacturing the model at his factory in London in the belief that "I will be suner able to get them in market from here sooner that I can elsewhere."[1] Nonetheless, he continued to press E. K. Root to begin production in Hartford:

Mr. Root must put all his forces upon the New Moddle Rifle & smalest pistol that can possible be employed & let the wirk accumulate at the jigging machines if it must & put into the mashine Department a lot of jigging machines at once to meet the emergency I direct his whole forces upon there early completion.[2]

Colt's concerns about the delay in manufacturing the .56 caliber version were well founded, as the model proved to be quite popular.[3]

Notes

1. Samuel Colt to Milton Joslin, 20 June 1856. Samuel Colt Papers, Box 7, Connecticut Historical Society.

2. Ibid.

3. Approximately 8,950 New Model .56 caliber carbines, muskets, and rifles were manufactured during the variation's term of production (Herbert G. Houze, *Colt Rifles & Muskets from 1847 to 1870* [Iola, Wis.: Krause Publications, 1996], 167).

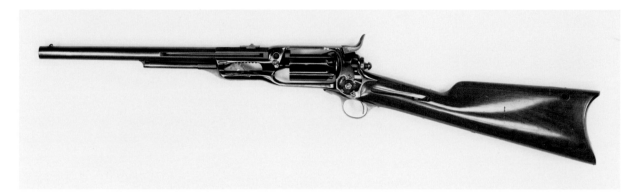

Overall left

47
New Model Carbine
Serial number 326
Caliber .56 in., barrel length 15 in., overall length 33¾ in.
Date of Manufacture: 1858
Wadsworth Atheneum Museum of Art
Bequest of Elizabeth Hart Jarvis Colt, 1905.983

Markings
Frame: COL.COLT HARTFORD CT. U.S.A.
Upper tang of frame: COLTS / PATENT Nov. 24 1857

1861 Inventory of Colonel Colt's Large Office
Page IV, line 29, addendum B
1 Skeleton Rifle

To demonstrate the internal construction and the mechanics of their operation, several New Model Carbines were extensively skeletonized.[1] Though effective educational tools, skeletonized arms were and remain prohibitively expensive to make. The precision machining required to maintain the structural integrity of the finished arms raises the cost of manufacture by a factor of at least ten above complete examples.[2]

Based upon this carbine's serial number, it was probably made in 1858 for exhibition at the New York American Institute.

Notes
1. A skeletonized .44 caliber New Model Carbine, serial number 687, is preserved in the Colt Collection of the Museum of Connecticut History (accession number 64).
2. In 1981 William Talley of the Winchester Repeating Arms Company calculated the cost of skeletonizing a Model 70 Sporting Rifle at a multiple of twelve above normal cost (Winchester Repeating Arms Company, "Cost Analysis" memorandum, January 1981. Author's collection).

Details of skeletonized areas,
right and left sides

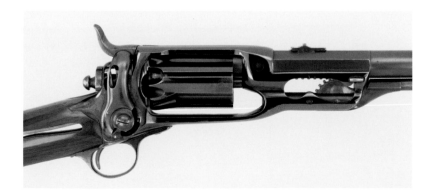

In contrast to the highly polished surfaces of civilian arms, those destined for military service had a less reflective finish similar to that found on this carbine.

48

New Model Carbine

Serial number 852

Caliber .56 in., barrel length 15 in., overall length 33¼ in.

Date of Manufacture: 1858–59

Wadsworth Atheneum Museum of Art

Bequest of Elizabeth Hart Jarvis Colt, 1905.978

Markings

Frame: COL. COLT HARTFORD CT. U.S.A. [top strap]

COLT'S PATENT / Nov. 24th 1857 [upper tang]

PATD. NOV. 24, 1857 [by cylinder pin aperture]

Cylinder: PATENTED SEPT. 10th 1850

Cylinder Pin: PATENTED MAY 4th 1858

Trigger Guard: 56 CAL.

1861 Inventory of Colonel Colt's Small Office

Page 4, line 13

Colt's rifle blue finish 56 Cal complete

49

New Model Shotgun

Serial number 261

Caliber .60 in., barrel length 27 in., overall length 45½ in.

Date of Manufacture: 1860

Wadsworth Atheneum Museum of Art

Bequest of Elizabeth Hart Jarvis Colt, 1905.979

Markings

Frame: COL. COLT HARTFORD CT. U.S.A. [top strap]

COLT'S PATENT / Nov. 24th 1857 [left side]

PATD. NOV. 24, 1857 [by cylinder pin aperture]

Cylinder: PATENTED SEPT. 10th 1850

Cylinder Pin: PATENTED MAY 4th 1858

Trigger Guard: - CAL.

The New Model Shotgun entered production in October 1859. Not surprisingly, it was given a lukewarm reception by sportsmen more accustomed to single- and double-barrel shotguns. Due to this lack of interest, production was discontinued in late 1860 or early 1861 after about three hundred had been made.

Herbert G. Houze

50

Experimental "Reduced Weight" Holster Pistol

Serial number 2

Caliber .44 in., barrel length 8 in., overall length 14 in.

Date of Manufacture: ca. 1857–58

Museum of Connecticut History, Hartford

Gift of the Pratt & Whitney Company Foundation, Inc., 247

Markings

None except serial number

1861 Inventory of Colonel Colt's Small Office

Page 10, line 11

1 Experimental Holster pistol for reducing weight

1887 Museum Inventory Draft

247 44 Cal. Colt 7½ Old m. holster P. Experim to reduce weight

Samuel Colt's first approach to making his revolvers more attractive to potential customers involved reducing their weight. This was a particularly critical factor with respect to the Holster Pistol, which weighed four pounds, two ounces. By recontouring the barrel, cylinder, and frame he was able to substantially lessen the pistol's net weight. The alteration of the barrel involved rounding the breech and reducing the width of the lower lug. In addition, the loading groove was deepened and extended to include the left side of the lug. These changes allowed the forward section of the frame beneath the cylinder to be similarly thinned. The pistol's weight was further reduced by cutting the rear shoulders of the recoil shield forward and longitudinally fluting the cylinder between the chamber walls. As a result of these changes, the revolver illustrated here weighs three pounds, eleven ounces, some seven and a half ounces less than the version then in production.

A second series of "Reduced Weight" Holster Pistols was made up in mid-1858 having rack-and-pinion loading levers instead of the hinged type found on this example.[1]

Note

1. Serial number 1 from the second series of "Reduced Weight" Holster Pistols with rack-and-pinion-style loading levers is illustrated and described in *Illustrated Catalogue: A. E. Brooks Collection of Antique Guns, Pistols, Etc.* (Hartford: Case, Lockwood and Brainard, 1899), no. 139, 28, and Frank M. Sellers, *The William M. Locke Collection* (East Point, Ga.: Antique Armory, 1973), 56. Serial number 2 was later owned by Colt's son Caldwell and is described and illustrated in Robert Q. Sutherland and R. L. Wilson, *The Book of Colt Firearms* (Kansas City, Mo.: R. Q. Sutherland, 1971), 158.

Overall left

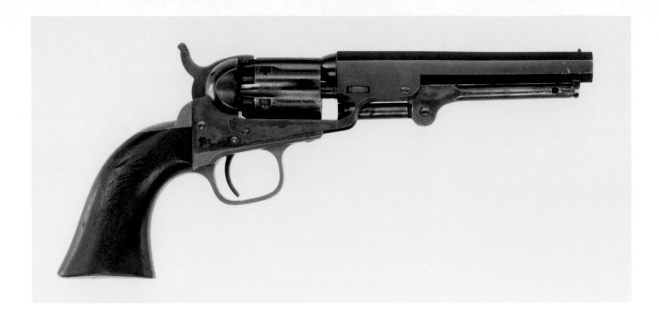

51

Experimental "Reduced Weight" Pocket Pistol
Serial number 1
Caliber .31 in., barrel length 5 in., overall length 10⅞ in.
Date of Manufacture: 1857–58
Museum of Connecticut History, Hartford
Gift of the Pratt & Whitney Company Foundation, Inc., 273

Markings
Barrel: ADDRESS SAML COLT / HARTFORD.C.T.
Cylinder: None
Frame: COLT'S / PATENT

1861 Inventory of Colonel Colt's Small Office
Page 10, line 18
1 old model pocket small bore corrugated Cyl.

1887 Museum Inventory Draft
273 31 Cal, 5 shot, Colt Pocket, 5 oct., No 1, first one with corrugated cyl.

Despite the fact that savings in weight would have been marginal at best, test samples of both "Reduced Weight" Pocket and Belt Pistols were also made at this time. In contrast to the Holster Pistol, the modification of these revolvers involved only the fluting of their cylinders.

52

Experimental "Enlarged Caliber" Belt Pistol
Serial number 3
Caliber .40 in., barrel length 5½ in., overall length 11 in.
Date of Manufacture: 1858
Wadsworth Atheneum Museum of Art
Bequest of Elizabeth Hart Jarvis Colt, 1905.1008

Markings
Barrel: -ADDRESS SAML COLT NEW-YORK CITY-
Cylinder: COLT'S / PATENT NO. 3
Frame: COLT'S PATENT

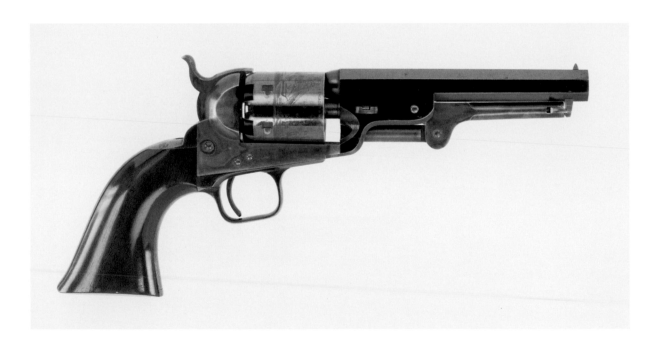

A second approach explored by Colt in making his pistols more marketable involved rechambering the Belt model from .36 to .40 caliber. The incentive for this line of experimentation lay in its minimal retooling costs. However, as a .40 caliber pistol would have directly competed with both the existing Belt and Holster Pistol models, the design was not developed in this form beyond the experimental stage.

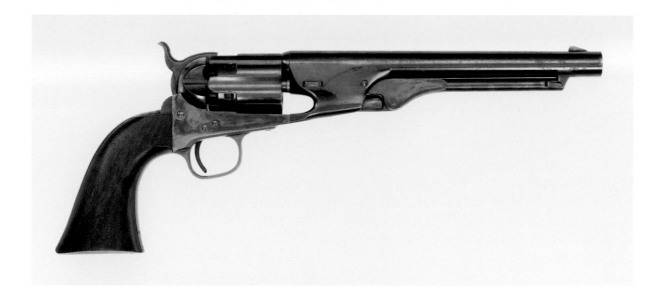

Overall left

53

Experimental "Enlarged Caliber" Belt Pistol

Serial number 5

Caliber .44 in., barrel length 7½ in., overall length 13 in.

Date of Manufacture: 1858

Museum of Connecticut History, Hartford

Gift of the Pratt & Whitney Company Foundation, Inc., 254

1861 Inventory of Colonel Colt's Small Office

Page 10, line 13

1 old model Navy with fluted Cyl Round barrel Enlarged bore

1887 Museum Inventory Draft

254 44C., 6 sh., Colt Army, 7½ marked 5

The first "Enlarged Caliber" program was not an entirely fruitless endeavor, for Colt realized that the Belt Pistol's frame could be modified to accept a rebated .44 caliber cylinder.

The process of rebating, or constructing a cylinder with front and rear diameters of different sizes appears to have been developed during the summer of 1858. The reduction of the cylinder's rear was possible due to its relative thickness around the nipple recesses and base of the chambers. In addition, this section of the cylinder was not subject to excessive pressure during firing. Consequently, Colt redesigned the .44 caliber cylinder so that it would fit in a Belt Pistol with a lower frame that was cut away to accept the slightly larger forward end of the rebated cylinder. To further reduce the weight of the revolver, the cylinder was milled with longitudinal flutes in the same manner as the "Reduced Weight" series of prototypes.

Although the original samples were fitted with hinged loading levers, at least two later examples were fitted with rack-and-pinion levers. The latter pistols established the design patterns for the New Model Holster Pistol, introduced in 1860.

54

Prototype New Model Holster Pistol

Serial number 6

Caliber .44 in., barrel length 8 in., overall length 14 in.

Date of Manufacture: 1859

Wadsworth Atheneum Museum of Art

Bequest of Elizabeth Hart Jarvis Colt, 1905.1000 (current location unknown)

Markings

None except serial number

Drawing upon the information gained during the "Enlarged Caliber" program, Colt designed two completely remodeled Holster Pistols in 1859. The first of these, as illustrated here, incorporated a streamlined barrel, hinged loading lever, and a rebated and fluted cylinder. In addition, the pistol's frame was shortened slightly and cut to accept the new cylinder. To improve handling, the sample revolvers were fitted with a slightly longer grip. The second design differed only in having the samples equipped with rack-and-pinion loading levers and Belt Pistol-size grips.

Based upon the serial numbers found on surviving examples, it would appear that fewer than ten revolvers of both patterns were made.[1]

Note

1. Serial number 3 from this series of prototypes was formerly in the collection of William M. Locke (Frank M. Sellers, *The William M. Locke Collection* [East Point, Ga.: Antique Armory, 1973], 129). Serial number 5 is preserved in the Colt Collection of the Museum of Connecticut History (accession number 254).

55

New Model Holster Pistol with "Attachable Breech"
Serial number 1617
Caliber .44 in., barrel length 8 in., overall length 14 in., overall length with stock 26½ in.
Date of Manufacture: 1860
Wadsworth Atheneum Museum of Art
Bequest of Elizabeth Hart Jarvis Colt, 1905.986

Markings
Barrel: -ADDRESS SAML COLT HARTFORD CT.-
Cylinder: PAT.SEPT 10th 1850 / 1617
Frame: COLTS / PATENT

1861 Inventory of the Colonel Colt's Large Office
Page X, line 9
1 New Model Army pistol with breech attachment

Manufacture of the New Model Holster Pistol with a rack-and-pinion loading lever began in late February 1860. Originally produced with fluted and rebated cylinders similar to those on the original prototypes, fluting was discontinued in 1861, when it was discovered that the process structurally weakened the cylinders to the point that if the chambers were overcharged, their walls would crack when the pistol was fired. The circular profile of the forward section allowed the cylinders to be roll-engraved with Ormsby's scene depicting a naval engagement, previously used on the Belt model.

By the time the New Model Holster Pistol was discontinued in 1873, well over 200,000 had been made. Of that number, almost 130,000 were purchased by the U.S. government for use during the Civil War.

To allow the pistol to be used as a shoulder-held arm, it is fitted with an "Attachable Breech" or stock of the type patented by Colt (U.S. Patent Number 22,626, issued 18 January 1859).

56
New Model Belt Pistol
Serial number 5726
Caliber .36 in., barrel length 7½ in., overall length 13 in.
Date of Manufacture: 1861
Wadsworth Atheneum Museum of Art
Gift of Mrs. Charles W. Butler, 1932.5

Markings
Barrel: ADDRESS COL. SAML COLT NEW-YORK U.S. AMERICA
Cylinder: COLT'S PATENT NO 5726
Frame: colt's / patent
Back Strap: Wm. Faxon / with Compliments of Col. Colt

In the autumn of 1861 Samuel Colt began distributing specimens of his arms to various military and naval officers who might be in the position to support the purchase of his revolvers by the U.S. government. Based upon surviving examples, it appears that approximately one hundred Pocket, Belt, and Holster Pistols were specially made and encased for distribution. While many of these were given a highly polished finish, others were engraved with foliate scrollwork.

This example was prepared for William Faxon, a Hartford native who was chief clerk of the U.S. Navy Department. Unfortunately Faxon did not receive the revolver until after Colt's death on 9 January 1862. For this reason, his letter of thanks, dated 5 February 1862, to Hugh Harbison, secretary of the Colt company, is quite poignant.

> I acknowledge the receipt this morning, per Adams' Express, in accordance with previous advices, of a Navy pistol, and all accompaniaments. It is indeed a splendid present and I accept it with great pleasure, and with many thanks, in the spirit in which it is tendered. Sincerely lamenting the death of him whose name is inscribed upon it, and with very kind regards to yourself and other officers of the company.[1]

Included among the accessories accompanying the pistol was a linen cleaning cloth printed on both sides with detailed instructions describing the proper use and maintenance of Colt revolving pistols and rifles. Few of these printed cleaning cloths have survived, and it is not known whether they were distributed with standard production Colt revolvers or just with presentation pieces.

The New Model Belt Pistol was designed in early 1860 and entered full-scale production in November of the same year.[2]

Notes

1. Richard A. Bourne Co., Inc. Public Auction Antique Firearms and Related Items (17 and 18 March 1982), Lot 693 (illustrated with the incorrect lot identification 690).
2. Samuel Colt to the Hon. J. B. Floyd, 10 May 1860. Records of the Colt's Patent Fire Arms Manufacturing Company, Business File, Series II, Outgoing Correspondence, Box 6, Connecticut State Library.

Overall right, out of case

57

Prototype New Model Police Pistol

Serial number 1

Caliber .36 in., barrel length 5½ in., overall length 10½ in.

Museum of Connecticut History, Hartford

Gift of the Pratt & Whitney Company Foundation, Inc., 275

Markings

Barrel: ADDRESS COL. SAML COLT NEW-YORK U.S. AMERICA

Cylinder: COLT'S PATENT NO 1

Frame: COLT'S / PATENT

1861 Inventory of Colonel Colt's Small Office

Page 10, line 14

2 Experimental Pistols First made of the enlarged caliber Pocket

1887 Museum Inventory Draft

275 36 Cal, 5 shot, Colt Pocket 4⁹/₁₆" r.b., No 1, first O.M.P. enlarged calibre

The last revolver to be designed by Samuel Colt before his death was the .36 caliber Pocket Pistol having the same lines as the New Model Belt and Holster Pistols.

The production version, first manufactured in December 1860, had a semi-fluted cylinder. While fluting had been abandoned on the cylinders of six-shot New Model Holster Pistols due to the structural weakness it could cause, that problem did not exist in the New Model Police Pistols. Their cylinders had only five chambers; hence, the amount of metal between each was substantially thicker than that found on the Holster Pistols. This allowed Colt to improve the cylinder's profile by scalloping the forward portion of the cylinder between the chambers. Since this had little effect on the revolver's weight, its purpose was wholly aesthetic.

Herbert G. Houze

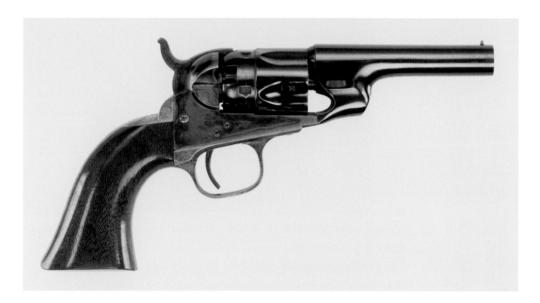

58
New Model Police Pistol
Serial number 4160
Caliber .36 in., barrel length 3½ in., overall length 8½ in.
Date of Manufacture: 1861
Wadsworth Atheneum Museum of Art
Bequest of Elizabeth Hart Jarvis Colt, 1905.993

Markings
Barrel: ADDRESS COL SAML COLT NEW-YORK U.S.AMERICA
Frame: COLTS / PATENT
Cylinder: PAT.SEPT.10th 1850
Trigger Guard: 36 CAL

1861 Inventory of Colonel Colt's Small Office
Page 8, line 26
1 Model pistol without ramrod

In 1861 the Colt company manufactured an extremely limited number of Police Pistols designed to be carried in the owner's pocket.[1] Weighing twenty-three and a half ounces unloaded, the model is readily distinguished not only by its short barrel but also by the absence of an attached loading lever. This omission prevented the pistol from becoming snagged in a pocket lining when being drawn.

In the "LIST OF PRICES FOR COLT'S NEW ARMS on and after January 1st, 1861" this model was priced at fourteen dollars, complete with a separate "Plain Ramrod."[2]

It is entirely possible that examples of the New Model Belt and Holster Pistol may also have been made in this configuration, as loading ramrods suitable for their use are found in the fused masses of revolver parts recovered after the 1864 Colt armory fire (see "Samuel Colt's South Meadows Armory," fig. 19).

Notes
1. It has been estimated that fewer than fifty 3½ in.-barrel New Model Police Pistols were made in 1861 (R. L. Wilson, *The Arms Collection of Colonel Colt* [Bullville, N.Y.: Herb Glass, 1964], 39).
2. Ibid., xxii.

Figure 1

Illustration of Samuel Colt's display at the Exhibition of the Industry of all Nations at the Crystal Palace, New York City, published in *Gleason's Pictorial Drawing-Room Companion,* November 1853. Wadsworth Atheneum Museum of Art.

Samuel Colt's Prize and Presentation Medals

When silver and gold medals are mentioned today, we almost immediately associate them with success at the Olympic Games. In the nineteenth century they indicated success of a different kind, recognizing an invention or product deemed worthy of merit.

The awarding of medals struck in precious metals first occurred in France during the Consulate period following the Revolution of 1789. At the government-sponsored industrial exposition held in Paris in 1801 a jury awarded certificates of merit and bronze, silver, or gold medals to those exhibitors whose products exemplified French industry.[1] This practice continued at subsequent French industrial expositions, as well as at those organized elsewhere in Europe.[2]

In the United States industrial exhibitions were first sponsored by trade associations or learned societies, such as the Massachusetts Charitable Mechanics Institute, the Franklin Society of Philadelphia, and the American Institute in New York City. Samuel Colt was keenly aware of the importance of prize medals to the public because they represented

endorsement of a product. Consequently, he regularly exhibited his revolvers, cartridges, and other designs at the expositions held in Boston and New York City (fig. 1).[3]

Colt also recognized that prize medals were especially useful in marketing his arms in Europe. He wrote to his cousin Elisha Colt in July 1849:

> Thees medles we must get & I must have them with me in Europe to help make up the reputation of my arms as soon as I begin to make a noyes about them & I must get duplicates of the old ones that have been lost all these things go a grate ways in Europe & it would pay for a special trip to America to secure them if they cannot be got without my presence there.[4]

To display and easily transport the medals he had won, Colt had one of the Buehl pistol cases made in 1849 fitted with trays.[5] Lined in plush velvet, the bottom of the box was fitted with recesses to hold medals, and the interior edges had a step so that an upper tray could be installed. Rather than being of solid construction, the latter was pierced to allow thirteen medals to be viewed from both sides. Although the majority of the medals housed in this box were prize awards, three were not. One was Colt's most prized possession, the Telford Premium Medal, awarded to him in 1852 by the Institution of Civil Engineers in London; the second was a portrait medal given to him by Czar Alexander II; and the third was a portrait medal presented by King Victor Emmanuel II of Italy, all of which are discussed in "Samuel Colt and the World" (pp. 183–99).

At the time of Samuel Colt's death, this box and the medals it contained were in the Cabinet of Presents located in the Music Room at Armsmear.

Herbert G. Houze

Notes

1. For a complete listing of artisans who were awarded medals or certificates of merit at the 1801 exposition, see *Seconde Exposition Publique des Produits de l'Industrie Française. Proces-Verbal des opérations du Jury nommé par le Ministre de l'interieur pour examiner les Produits de l'Industrie française mis à l'Exposition des jours complementaires de la neuvième année de la République* (Paris: L'Imprimerie de la République, an 10 [1802]), 7–32.

2. The proliferation of medal awards at the European industrial expositions between 1819 and 1849 prompted organizers of the 1851 Exhibition of the Works of Art & Industry of all Nations to be held in London to limit awards to three categories: an Honourable Mention certificate, a bronze Prize Medal, and a bronze Council Medal (*Exhibition of the Works of Art & Industry of all Nations, 1851. Reports of the Juries. . .* [London: William Clowes & Sons, 1851], i–ii).

3. In a letter to his cousin Elisha Colt concerning the Buehl boxes, Colt specifically states that he wishes "to have specimens of our arms prepared as above & exibated in these boxes boxes [*sic*] at the anual fairs of the American Institute [N.York—deleted] & the Mecanicks institutes of N. Yor, also the fares to be held this fall in Boston & Philadelphia & any other places where they award gold medals in premium for the best inventions" (Samuel Colt to Elisha Colt, 18 July 1849. Records of the Colt's Patent Fire Arms Manufacturing Company, RG 103, Business File, Series III, Incoming Correspondence, Box 8, Connecticut State Library).

4. Ibid.

5. The date when these boxes were manufactured can be fixed from the following account contained in Colt's letter of 18 July 1849 cited above:

> Since here I have engaged with an artist making designs for Pistol cases of a peculiar description of inlade wood called by the Austrans "Buhl" & have left orders & money for making & paying for the following number & sises vis
>
> 5 Boxes for Large sise pistols in Pares

5	"	"	"	"	single
10	"	"	"	"	in Pares assorted
5	"	"	"	"	3in single
5	"	"	"	"	4in "
5	"	"	"	"	5in "

> 35" in all & for which I want you to have made show Pistols, put up in the most elegant stile possible. The cases or boxes will be most beutaful specemens of inlade work ever seen in America. I want the pistols intend for these to be as good as can be made. Some of the boxes will be finished & rady for shipment in about six weeks.

Interior

59

Buehl Box

Vienna, Austria

Rosewood, ivory, mother-of-pearl, brass, and silver

13³/₈ x 6³/₄ x 2³/₄ in.

Date of Manufacture: 1849

Wadsworth Atheneum Museum of Art

Bequest of Elizabeth Hart Jarvis Colt, 1905.1255

Reverse

60

American Institute of New York Gold Medal, 1837

"AWARDED TO Samuel Colt For the best many chambered cylinder Rifle"

George Hampden Lovett

Diameter 1⅛ in.

Wadsworth Atheneum Museum of Art

Bequest of Elizabeth Hart Jarvis Colt, 1905.1514

61

American Institute of New York Gold Medal, 1841

"AWARDED TO Samuel Colt For a REPEATING CARBINE"

George Hampden Lovett

Diameter 1⅛ in.

Wadsworth Atheneum Museum of Art

Bequest of Elizabeth Hart Jarvis Colt, 1905.1511

62

American Institute of New York Gold Medal, 1844

"AWARDED TO Samuel Colt For his invention in rendering Cartridges safe and waterproof"

George Hampden Lovett

Diameter 1⅛ in.

Wadsworth Atheneum Museum of Art

Bequest of Elizabeth Hart Jarvis Colt, 1905.1510

63

American Institute of New York Silver Medal, 1845

"AWARDED TO Samuel Colt For the best GUNS, RIFLES, PISTOLS AND POWDER FLASKS"

George Hampden Lovett

Diameter 2 in.

Wadsworth Atheneum Museum of Art

Bequest of Elizabeth Hart Jarvis Colt, 1905.1509

This medal was one of the replacement pieces Samuel Colt asked his cousin Elisha Colt to secure in July 1849.[1] Its identification as such is based on the fact that the medal was struck in silver rather than gold and Colt was not awarded a prize at the American Institute exhibition of 1845. The award for best firearms and accessories was given to John Ehlers for his display of Colt patent revolvers.

Note

1. Samuel Colt to Elisha Colt, 18 July 1849. Records of the Colt's Patent Firearms Manufacturing Company, RG 103, Business File, Series III, Incoming Correspondence, Connecticut State Library

64

American Institute of New York Gold Medal, 1850

"AWARDED TO SAMUEL COLT FOR THE BEST REVOLVING PISTOLS"

George Hampden Lovett

Diameter 1⅛ in.

Wadsworth Atheneum Museum of Art

Bequest of Elizabeth Hart Jarvis Colt, 1905.1512

Herbert G. Houze

65

American Institute of New York Gold Medal, 1855

"AWARDED TO Samuel Colt For the best Revolving Rifles & Pistols"

George Hampden Lovett

Diameter 1⅛ in.

Wadsworth Atheneum Museum of Art

Bequest of Elizabeth Hart Jarvis Colt, 1905.1513

Reverse

66

Exhibition of the Works of Art & Industry of all Nations, Bronze Exhibitor's Medal, 1851

London

William Wyon

Diameter 1¾ in.

Wadsworth Atheneum Museum of Art

Bequest of Elizabeth Hart Jarvis Colt, 1905.1098

Reverse

67

New York Crystal Palace International Exhibition Medal, 1853

Silver

George Hampden Lovett

Diameter 2³⁄₁₆ in.

Wadsworth Atheneum Museum of Art

Bequest of Elizabeth Hart Jarvis Colt, 1905.1097

68

Connecticut State Agricultural Society Gold Medal, 1855

"Samuel Colt for Pistols"

George Hampden Lovett

Diameter 1¹⁄₁₆ in.

Wadsworth Atheneum Museum of Art

Bequest of Elizabeth Hart Jarvis Colt, 1905.1516

Reverse

69
Exposition Universelle Silver Medal, 1855
Paris
Albert Barre
Diameter 2⁵⁄₁₆ in.
Wadsworth Atheneum Museum of Art
Bequest of Elizabeth Hart Jarvis Colt, 1905.1092

70
Hartford County Agricultural Society Gold Medal, 1856
"Awarded to Col Samuel Colt for Pistols 1856"
Diameter 1³⁄₁₆ in.
Wadsworth Atheneum Museum of Art
Bequest of Elizabeth Hart Jarvis Colt, 1905.1517

71
Universal Society for the Encouragement of Arts & Industry Bronze Medal, 1856
London
"Awarded to Col. S. Colt of Hartford Conn. London 30th June 1856"
Desaide Roquelay
Diameter 2⁷⁄₁₆ in.
Wadsworth Atheneum Museum of Art
Bequest of Elizabeth Hart Jarvis Colt, 1905.1091

Reverse

72
Exhibition of the Works of Art & Industry of all Nations, Honourable Mention Bronze Medal, 1862
London
Leonard Charles Wyon
Diameter 2¹⁵⁄₁₆ in.
Wadsworth Atheneum Museum of Art
Bequest of Elizabeth Hart Jarvis Colt, 1905.1090

Reverse

Reverse

The Emergence of the Metallic Cartridge Era

One of the major criticisms leveled at Samuel Colt by contemporary historians is that he did not appreciate or understand the dramatic change that self-contained metallic cartridges would bring about in firearms construction.[1] This assertion is baseless. Colt's correspondence and directives demonstrate that the opposite is true.

The development of self-contained metallic cartridges, wherein the projectile, propellant, and priming agent are contained in a copper casing instead of being loaded separately, began shortly after the Reverend Alexander James Forsyth invented his percussion gunlock.[2] Cartridges were not a new phenomenon, as various firearms makers since the sixteenth century had made pieces that could be loaded at the breech with separate chambers (metal tubes having their own priming pan and steel or percussion nipple) that could be inserted into the barrel.[3] A sportsman equipped with a pistol, shotgun, or rifle using this system could carry any number of these chambers, each loaded with powder and ball or shot, so that when the weapon was fired, it could be readied for reuse simply by withdrawing the used chamber and inserting a new one. Owing to the cost of making supplemental chambers with identical dimensions, the number of arms made for their use was limited. In 1809 the Swiss balloonist Samuel Johannes Pauley designed a breech-loading gun that used a self-obturating cartridge (one that sealed the barrel breech).[4] Constructed with a soft metal base and paper walls, the cartridge was fired by a separate firing pin striking the primer set into the cartridge's base.[5]

Improvements on Pauley's basic concept followed two different paths. In Germany Johann Nikolaus von Dreyse, who had worked for Pauley in Paris, developed a cartridge with the primer located at the base of the projectile. It was fired by a needle-like firing pin passing through the cartridge's powder charge until it hit the primer. Patented in England on 15 December 1831,[6] the needle-fire cartridge was adopted for military use by the Prussian Army in 1840.[7]

In Paris Casimir Lefaucheux developed an entirely different type of cartridge, which did not rely upon a long-stroke firing pin for ignition. Instead, he proposed using a copper cartridge that had a pin set into the casing's side at right angles immediately above the base. When inserted into a gun barrel, the pin extended above the barrel's surface and could be hit by the hammer when it fell. This caused the pin to strike either a percussion cap or pellet glued inside the cartridge. Patented in France on 31 March 1835,[8] the cartridge was subsequently known in Europe by its inventor's name and in the English-speaking world by the descriptive term pin-fire.

In their original forms neither cartridge was readily practical, and the needle-fire cartridge was particularly ill suited for revolvers due to its firing pin. Nevertheless, both Dreyse and Lefaucheux designed pistols using cartridges of both types.

Although the exact date when Samuel Colt became aware of these cartridges is unknown, it is certain that he saw examples of both systems when he visited the 1851 Exhibition of the Works of Art and Industry of all Nations in London. Needle-fire arms were exhibited by Falisse & Trapmann of Liège, Theodore Gehrmann of Berlin, J. B. Gleichauf of Hanau, the Royal Gun Manufactory Oberndorf, and M. W. Sears of London.[9] In addition, the partnership of Dreyse & Collembusch, which had been formed to manufacture these cartridges, also was an exhibitor.[10] Casimir Lefaucheux displayed examples of his pin-fire arms in the French court at the exhibition and was awarded a Prize Medal for Works in Precious Metals.[11] It should be noted that the Parisian gunmaker Louis Mathieu exhibited a double-barrel shotgun that used the more recently developed center-fire cartridge.[12]

Presentists would no doubt argue that Colt should have immediately seized upon this new technology and retooled his factory for the production of cartridge arms. However, this argument assumes that the level of cartridge reliability approached that of the percussion cap system. In fact, it did not, and would not do so for some years to come.

Despite the technical limitations of metallic cartridges, one maker, Casimir Lefaucheux' son Eugene, pressed forward with the design. On 27 April 1854 he was granted a patent in England for a revolver using pin-fire cartridges. The text of the patent extract is of interest, as it describes a cylinder having chambers bored completely through so that cartridges could be loaded from the rear without having to disassemble the revolver.[13]

When Eugene Lefaucheux submitted his patent application for this design to the French government on 15 April 1854, the enrolled drawing illustrated a Colt Belt Pistol altered for use with pin-fire cartridges.[14] Interestingly, arms historians have taken little notice of this drawing, and none have pursued the question of why Lefaucheux selected a Colt revolver as his model.

The contents of two letters written to Samuel Colt by Eugene Lefaucheux in late 1854, combined with correspondence from Colt's patent attorneys, J. N. McIntire and Charles M. Keller, in which they discuss an American patent issued in 1855 to Rollin White covering a similar cylinder design, suggest that there is more to the matter than first meets the eye. Lefaucheux's correspondence of 6 November and 18 December clearly indicates that the machinery installed in his Paris factory was purchased from Colt.[15] That Lefaucheux was the first French arms maker to use the "American System of Manufacturing" has been recognized for some time. That he used Colt machinery has not. Moreover, the letter of 18 December implies that the machinery to be used at the Tula works in Russia to manufacture Lefaucheux patent revolvers also was to be supplied by Colt.[16] These letters prove that Colt was not only aware of the self-contained metallic cartridge revolvers but also profiting from their manufacture, albeit in a somewhat removed fashion.

The McIntire and Keller letters to Colt indicate that the inventor was at least entertaining the idea of challenging Rollin White's bored-through cylinder patent. Although undated, internal evidence suggests that McIntire's note was written in late 1855.

> White has 5 patents and many claims, but the only claim covering any *broad* feature is *1st claim* of pat. No. 12.648. dated apl. 3rd. 1855.— This claim covers the construction of a rotating cylinder with chambers extending "right through."

> It strikes me the French had used and published something of this sort *before* 1855—I'll look at the *French* Publications and other Books in Washington—and inform you on this subject.[17]

Charles M. Keller's letter succinctly summarized the tack Colt planned to take.

> New York, Sept. 8. 1859.
> Col. Saml. Colt
> Hartford—Conn.
>
> Dear Sir
> I have carefully examined the rotating cylinder of Mr. White's patent bearing the date the 3rd day of Apr. 1855 and find it is a direct infringement on the patent of Mr. Johnson [Lefaucheux's London patent agent] granted in England the 27th day of Apr. 1854 and the Brevet d'invention awarded Mr. Lefaucheux in France the 10th day of June 1854. I am of the considered opinion that Mr. White's claims can be set aside if suit is brought.
>
> Respectfully yrs.
> Charles M. Keller
> Counsellor at Law[18]

It is therefore apparent that a challenge to White's claims would be based on the fact that his design for a bored-through cylinder was neither novel nor new—two essential points in securing a U.S. patent. As Colt's interest was more than academic, he authorized the manufacture of two sample metallic cartridge revolvers in 1855. The first was a Holster Pistol altered for use with pin-fire cartridges (cat. 76) and the second a Belt Pistol designed to fire Dreyse-pattern cartridges (cat. 78).[19]

The existence of these two revolvers, together with the McIntire and Keller letters, inevitably leads one to ask why Colt did not pursue the patent challenge and produce cartridge revolvers. Simply put, it was not in his best interests at that time. By late 1859 the political climate in the United States was unsettled, and Colt had more than enough orders for percussion cap weapons to keep his armory running at full capacity. Consequently, it would have been folly to close and retool his factory for an as yet unproven new cartridge revolver. Furthermore, in contrast to the readily available powder, ball, and percussion caps used in the arms he then made, metallic cartridges were still a novelty sold only in the largest cities. Whatever the true influence of these factors, the manufacturing of metallic cartridge revolvers became a moot point when the Civil War began in April 1861.

Notes

1. "The greatest blunder of Sam Colt's career was his failure to recognize the significance of the metallic cartridge" (William Hosley, *Colt: The Making of an American Legend* [Amherst: University of Massachusetts Press, 1996], 45).
2. The development of self-contained cartridges having either copper or paper cases was entirely made possible by Forsyth's work with fulminate of mercury. This

Herbert G. Houze

compound could be used in globular form as a primer pellet or infused into a paper wafer that could be pasted into a vent in a cartridge's base. In either case, ignition was caused by the fulminate being struck by a firing pin mounted within an arm's lock work.

3. Given the care with which auxiliary chamber inserts had to be made and their attendant cost, it is not surprising that the first firearms using them were made for ruling monarchs. The earliest examples date from approximately 1535 and were made for Henry VIII of England. In the inventory of Henry's property they were noted as being in the possession of the royal armorer, Erasmus Kirkener, at Greenwich (Society of Antiquaries, MS 129, fol. 435v, transcribed in David Starkey, ed., *The Inventory of King Henry VIII, Society of Antiquaries, MS 129, and British Library, MS Harley 1419, The Transcript* [London: Society of Antiquaries, 1998], 160).

> 8313 Item A Chamber pece blacke vernysshed with A fier locke and A blacke stocke A purse of blacke lether with flaske and Touche boxe of blacke vellet.
>
> 8314 Item one Chamber grauen and guilte with A fier Locke and A blacke stocke coured with blacke Lether A purse of blacke vellet A white horne garnisshed with Copper and guilte and A Touche boxe of copper and guilte. . . .
>
> 8318 Item A white Tacke with A fier locke and A guilte flower with A Chamber A blacke purse of vellet and blacke horne Iron and guilte.

In contrast to the above, which were wheel locks (i.e., having a "fier locke"), the 1553-dated breech-loader owned by Ferdinand II of Austria was a matchlock (Erwin Schalkhausser, *Handfeuerwaffen Jagdewehre Schreibenbuchsen Pistolen. Kataloge des Bayerischen Nationalmuseums*, XIX [Munich: Deutscher Kunstverlag, 1988], 14–16, pl. 1).

4. Pierre Jarlier, *Répertoire d'arquebusiers et de fourbissurs français* (St.-Julien-du-Sault: François-Pierre Lobies, 1976), 212–13. Obturation, or the sealing of the barrel's breech end to prevent the rearward venting of the propellant's combustion gases, was achieved by using soft copper for cartridge cases. When exposed to heat and pressure, the copper expanded within the barrel, thereby sealing it. Copper was used in both the Pauley system and in a slightly later breech-loader designed by Pottet-Delcusse (Antoine-Marie Heron de Villefosse, *Des métaux en France. Rapport fait au jury central de l'exposition des produits de l'industrie française de l'année 1827 sur les objets relatifs à la metallurgie* [Paris: Huzard, 1827], 182–83).

5. This design was patented in France on 29 September 1812. In Pauley's English patent of 1816 the cartridge is described as a "culot" (Jean Samuel Pauley, "Apparatus and Arrangements for Discharging Fire-arms by means of Condensed Air; also Cartridges applicable thereto," 4 August 1814, Number 4,026, enrolled 12 November 1814).

6. Abraham Adolphe Moser (a communication), "Improvements in Certain Descriptions of Fire-Arms," Letters Patent Number 6,196, enrolled 15 December 1831 (H. M. Patent Office, *Abridgements of the Patent Specifications relating to Firearms & Other Weapons, Ammunition & Accoutrements from 1588–1858* [London: George Eyre and William Spottiswoode, 1859], 78–79).

7. Hans-Dieter Gotz, *Militargewehre und Pistolen der deutschen Staaten 1800–1870* (Stuttgart: Motorbuch Verlag, 1978), 290–95.

8. Ministre du Commerce et du Travaux publics. Brevet de Perfectionnement et d'Addition, No. 6348 du 7 Janvier 1835, 4ème Brevets d'Invention, de perfectionnement et d'importation, au brevet du 28 janvier 1833.

9. *Official descriptive and illustrated Catalogue of the great Exhibition* (London: William Clowes & Sons, 1851), III, 1156 (Falisse & Trapmann); III, 1052 (Gehrmann); III, 1097 (Gleichauf); III, 1115 (Oberndorf); and, I, 363 (Sears).

10. Ibid., III, 1085.

11. Ibid., III, 1239, and *Exhibition of the Works of Art & Industry of all Nations, 1851. Reports of the Juries. . .* (London: William Clowes & Sons, 1852), 519.

12. *Official descriptive and illustrated Catalogue of the great Exhibition*, III, 1207.

13. John Henry Johnson (a communication), "Improvements in Revolving Fire-arms," Letters Patent Number 955, enrolled 27 April 1854 (H. M. Patent Office, *Abridgements of the Patent Specifications*, 162–63).

14. Ministre du Commerce et du Travaux publics. Brevet d'Invention No. 19380 du 10 juin 1854.

15. Eugene Lefaucheux to Samuel Colt, 6 November and 18 December 1854. Formerly John H. Hintlian Collection (present whereabouts unknown). The letter of 6 November acknowledges receipt of "pistol machinery from Brussels" and the payment of 3,280 pounds sterling to Colt's account at Baring Brothers in London. The second is a brief letter of thanks for Colt's gift of a translated copy of the lecture he gave in 1851 to the Institution of Civil Engineers in London (Samuel Colt [trans. O. Squarr], *De l'application des Machines à la fabrication des Armes à Feu à Culasse Tournantes et à leurs Systèmes Particuliers* [Brussels: Imprimerie et Lithographie des Beaux-Arts for Charles Manby, F.R.S., 1854]).

16. Lefaucheux to Colt, 18 December 1854. The passage in question reads: "M. Jean of your acquaintance departs tomorrow for Tula. He knows your machinery well and will supervise the workers."

17. J. N. McI[ntire]. to [Samuel Colt], n.d. [1855]. Samuel Colt Papers, Box 7, Connecticut Historical Society.

18. Charles M. Keller to Samuel Colt, 8 September 1859. Connecticut State Library.

19. Interestingly, the Philadelphia arms dealer Joseph C. Grubb was to make the following suggestion in 1860 describing a similar method for altering percussion cap revolvers for use with metallic cartridges, which Colt employed in making the pinfire prototype: "I ommitted to suggest whether your N. Model could not by cutting off say ½ an inch of the forward end of the Cylinder (nipples included) be without much trouble turned into a cap and ball arm. This style of arm should certainly in your improvements secure your attention. It must become a very favorite thing" (Joseph C. Grubb to Maj. William B. Hartley, 1 May 1860. Samuel Colt Papers, Box 8, Connecticut Historical Society). It should be noted that the phrase "cap and ball," now used to describe percussion cap firearms, was originally employed to identify arms chambered for metallic cartridges.

jecting from the base. The internal end of the striker rested against either a percussion cap or a globule of fulminate of mercury, so that the propellant charge could be ignited by the action of the hammer hitting the pin.[2] Despite their obvious advantages over the percussion cap system with its loose powder and ball, pin-fire cartridges did have some drawbacks. They had to be carefully loaded, so that the exposed portion of the pin sat within notches cut in the rear face of the cylinder, and they had to be stored in such a way that the pins did not become dislodged from the cartridge casings.

In 1855 Eugene Lefaucheux exhibited a selection of his cartridge revolvers at the Exposition Universelle in Paris. In recognition of their merits and his contribution to the French arms industry, Lefaucheux was awarded a *médaille d'honneur* by the exhibition's judges.[3]

Given the low serial number of this revolver, it is quite possible that it was purchased by Samuel Colt when he visited the exhibition in October 1855.[4]

Notes

1. John Henry Johnson (a communication), "Improvements in Revolving Fire-Arms," Letters Patent Number 955, enrolled 27 April 1854 (H. M. Patent Office, *Abridgements of the Patent Specifications relating to Firearms and Other Weapons, Ammunition & Accoutrements from 1588–1858* [London: George Eyre and William Spottiswoode, 1859], 162–63), and Ministre du Commerce et du Travaux publics, Brevet d'Invention No. 19380 du 10 juin 1854.

2. Abraham Adolphe Moser (a communication), "Improvements in Certain Descriptions of Fire-Arms," Letters Patent Number 6,196, enrolled 15 December 1831 (H. M. Patent Office, *Abridgements of the Patent Specifications*, 78–79).

3. *Exposition Universelle de 1855. Rapports du Jury Mixte Internationale* (Paris: Imprimerie Imperiale, 1856), I, 45.

4. C. F. Wappenhans to Col. L. P. Sargeant, 1 June 1855. Records of the Colt's Patent Fire Arms Manufacturing Company, RG 103, Business File, Series III, Incoming Correspondence, Box 10, Connecticut State Library.

73

Lefaucheux Cartridge Revolver
Serial number 25
Caliber .35 in., barrel length 7⁹/₁₆ in., overall length 12¾ in.
Date of Manufacture: 1854–55
Museum of Connecticut History, Hartford
Gift of the Pratt & Whitney Company Foundation, Inc., 388

Markings
Barrel: INV LEFAUCHEUX BRVETE 25

1861 Inventory of Colonel Colt's Small Office
Page 4, line 7
Small Lefaucheux Pistol Revolver

1887 Museum Inventory Draft
388 35 Cal, 6 sh, 7.6 oct Lefaucheux Brev Paris.25

The first revolver chambered for self-contained metallic cartridges was patented in England on 27 April 1854 and in France on 10 June 1854 by Eugene Lefaucheux.[1] In contrast to percussion cap revolvers having cylinders with chambers closed at the rear to enable them to be charged from the front, Lefaucheux's design utilized a cylinder that had chambers open from front to rear. This allowed copper-cased "cartouches à broche," or pin-fire cartridges to be inserted or removed from the rear. Designed by Casimir Lefaucheux, Eugene's father, pin-fire cartridges were so named because of the striker pro-

Herbert G. Houze

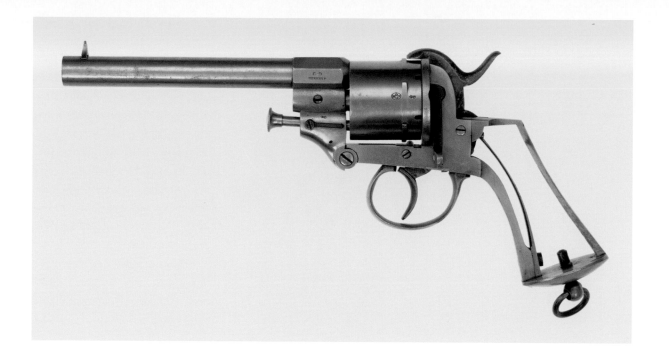

74

Delvigne Cartridge Revolver

Serial number 253

Caliber .45 in., barrel length 5¾ in., overall length 10⅞ in.

Date of Manufacture: 1861

Museum of Connecticut History, Hartford

Gift of the Pratt & Whitney Company Foundation, Inc., 379

1861 Inventory of Colonel Colt's Small Office

Page 4, line 8

Large Lefaucheux Pistol Revolver

1887 Museum Inventory Draft

379 43 Cal, 6 sh, 5¾" b. DA, for Lefaucheux Cartrs, marked 253, G.D.Liege. unf.

Although this hinged barrel revolver was made by Gustave Delvigne in Liège,[1] its design was patented on 6 April 1861 by the Parisian gunmaker Nicolas Vivario Plomdeur.[2] Aside from being of a fairly substantial caliber, this pistol would have been of interest to Samuel Colt because of the locking mechanism used to secure the barrel in place. The rearmost portion of the cylinder arbor extends into a slot cut in the forward wall of the frame. To unlock the arbor from the closed position, a transverse bar with an operating lever mounted on the left side of the frame is rotated rearward. This moves the bar into a position where a cutout section on its internal arm no longer bears against the cylinder arbor, thereby allowing the cylinder and barrel to pivot forward. When the

action is open, cartridges can be removed from the cylinder chambers by the ejector rod, which is normally threaded into the barrel bolster immediately above the hinge point.

Notes

1. Gustave Delvigne (1799–1876) was a renowned engineer and gunmaker who maintained premises in both Liège and Paris (Pierre Jarlier, *Répertoire d'arquebusiers et de fourbisseurs français* [St.-Julien-du-Sault: François-Pierre Lobies, 1976], 81).

2. One of the schematic drawings enrolled with Vivario's Patent Number 49,166 is reproduced by Chris C. Curtis in *Système Lefaucheux* (Santa Ana, Calif.: Armslore Press, 2002), 233.

hollow rim of its cartridge's base.[2] Despite their advantages, rim-fire cartridges initially met with considerable skepticism. Objections were raised about the number of misfires encountered due to uneven deposits of priming in cartridge rims and their small caliber, which made arms chambered for such cartridges unsuitable for hunting or military use.

Despite the development of improved manufacturing methods that spun the priming mixture into cartridge rims by centrifugal force, problems associated with metallurgy delayed the production of more reliable large-caliber rim-fire cartridges until approximately 1862.[3] Even then, some makers of rim-fire weapons, such as the New Haven Arms Company, which manufactured the famous sixteen-shot Henry Rifle, were so discouraged by the lack of conformity in cartridges produced by different firms that they established their own production lines.[4]

The pistol illustrated here is of significance, as it dates from either 1858 or 1859, shortly after medium-caliber rim-fire cartridges began being made. Its maker, D. Renotte,[5] patented the hammer safety that allows the hammer's tip to be locked against the frame when the pistol is loaded.

75

Renotte Cartridge Revolver

No serial number

.35 caliber, barrel length 7⅜ in., overall length 12 in.

Date of Manufacture: 1858–59

Museum of Connecticut History, Hartford

Gift of the Pratt & Whitney Company Foundation, Inc., 380

Markings

Barrel: D RENOTTE / BREVETE

1861 Inventory of Colonel Colt's Small Office

Page 4, line 10

Renatte French pistol like Lefaucheux

1887 Museum Inventory Draft

380 35 Cal, 6 sh., 7⅜" oct-, r.f., with safety hammer, D Renotte.B.unf.

While the design of the bored-through cylinder needed for rear-loading cartridges was rigidly held in the United States by Springfield, Massachusetts, arms makers Smith & Wesson,[1] no such controls existed in England or Europe because Eugene Lefaucheux allowed his patent to be freely used. Consequently, European and British arms designers were able to exercise their inventive talents on a scale not found in the United States.

Among the first cartridges to be developed after the introduction of the pin-fire system was one that had the priming compound located within the

Notes

1. Roy G. Jinks, *History of Smith & Wesson* (North Hollywood, Calif.: Beinfeld Publishing, Inc., 1977), 34–37.

2. In the United States Smith & Wesson attempted to control the manufacture of rim-fire cartridges through the following patents: Horace Smith and Daniel B. Wesson, "Improvement in Cartridges," Number 11,496, issued 8 August 1854, and "Improvements in Priming Metallic Cartridges," Number 27,933, issued 17 April 1860. These efforts were hampered by the fact that the Springfield concern did not own the rights to its 1854 patent, which belonged to Oliver F. Winchester, who had their unrestricted assignment as part of the assets of the Volcanic Repeating Arms Company after its failure. When Smith & Wesson tried to reassert their rights in 1863, Winchester pointedly reminded them that the rights had been forfeited in 1856 (Oliver F. Winchester to Smith & Wesson, 20 April 1863. *New Haven Arms Company Letter Press Book*, 237. Winchester Arms Collection Archives, Buffalo Bill Historical Center).

3. The improvements in the manufacture of rim-fire cartridges were brought about in large part by the necessities of the Civil War. To ensure the proper functioning of the rifles they were manufacturing, individuals such as Christopher Spencer of Boston and Oliver F. Winchester of New Haven began to manufacture ammunition that could withstand the rigors of field service. More reliable priming mixtures were introduced, and heavier- gauge copper was used to construct the cartridge casings.

4. Oliver F. Winchester to Crittenden & Tibballs, 15 April 1863. *New Haven Arms Company Letter Press Book*, 233 and 237.

5. It does not appear that Renotte fully prosecuted this patent as no comments regarding its issuance have been found in any of the contemporary English, French, or German patent sources. Moreover, the design was subsequently used by other markets (for example, Eugene Lefaucheux) without any reference to Renotte.

Herbert G. Houze

change would have involved the form of the hammer's nose. Indeed, when the Colt's Patent Fire Arms Manufacturing Company began production of rim-fire revolvers in 1871, large numbers of percussion cap pistols were altered in much the same manner as this pistol.

76

Colt-Lefaucheux Holster Pistol
No serial number
Caliber .44 in., barrel length 7½ in., overall length 14 in.
Date of Manufacture: 1854–55
Museum of Connecticut History, Hartford
Gift of the Pratt & Whitney Company Foundation, Inc., 351

Markings
Barrel: ADDRESS SAML COLT NEW YORK CITY

1861 Inventory of Colonel Colt's Small Office
Page 4, line 9
Colt's pistol Cylinder bored through

1887 Museum Inventory Draft
351. 44 Cal, 6 shot, 7½ semi oct. Colt's old Holster Pistol Altered for Lefaucheux pin cartr. rear load.

The earliest-known Colt metallic cartridge revolver is a Holster Pistol modified for use with pin-fire cartridges. The ease with which this could be accomplished is demonstrated by the fact that the only changes made to this revolver involved the installation of a new cylinder, hammer, and space plate to the face of the frame's recoil shield. As a loading lever was no longer needed, it was removed from this test sample.

Although made for pin-fire cartridges, the alterations seen in this pistol could have been applied to an arm chambered for rim-fire rounds, as the only

77

Comblain Pepperbox
Serial number 18
Caliber .28 in., barrel length 2⁹/₁₆ in., overall length 7³/₈ in.
Date of Manufacture: ca. 1855
Wadsworth Atheneum Museum of Art
Bequest of Elizabeth Hart Jarvis Colt, 1905.1003

Markings
Frame: D J COMBLAIN / BREVETE

1861 Inventory of Colonel Colt's Small Office
Page 8, line 23
1 revolving barrel pistol French

In form this pistol resembles a typical percussion cap pepperbox of the early 1850s. However, it was not designed for use with loose powder and ball. Rather, it is chambered for combustible Dreyse-pattern cartridges that were loaded from each barrel's muzzle. Combustible cartridges were made with paper cases that had been treated with a burning agent so that they were entirely consumed upon firing.

It is likely that Colt purchased this pistol to study its internal action during one of his visits to Europe. Its maker, Hubert-Joseph Comblain, later achieved fame as a designer of breech-loading rifles.[1]

Note

1. Pierre Jarlier, *Répertoire d'arquebusiers et de fourbisseurs français* (St.-Julien-du-Sault: François-Pierre Lobies, 1976), 65, and Claude Gaier, *Four Centuries of Liège Gunmaking* (London: Sotheby, Parke Bernet Publications, 1976), fig. 175.

78

Colt-Dreyse Belt Pistol
Serial number 55366
Caliber .36 in., barrel length 7½ in., overall length 13 in.
Date of Manufacture: 1855
Museum of Connecticut History, Hartford
Gift of the Pratt & Whitney Company Foundation, Inc., 352

Markings
Barrel: ADDRESS SAML.COLT NEW.YORK CITY -
Cylinder: COLTS PATENT / NO 5366
Frame: COLTS / PATENT

1887 Museum Inventory Draft
352. 36 Cal, 6 shot, 7½ oct. Colt's Navy. Altered for Needle Cartrs of Dreyse. 55366

The date and authorship of this revolver's alteration for use with Dreyse-pattern cartridges are revealed in correspondence exchanged between the Colt company's Berlin representative, C. F. Wappenhans, and Col. Luther P. Sargeant in London. In a letter dated 1 June 1855, Wappenhans informed Sargeant that

> Mr Gehrmann has not yet finished the one of the needle guns ordered by Mr. Colt; he promises to get every thing ready in a week or two. As I understand that Mr. Colt is coming to Paris to see the exhibition, it would perhaps be as well to send the said pistols & three needle guns to Cologne or some other place at the disposal of Mr Colt.[1]

Since this pistol was constructed using components made in Hartford, it appears that Theodore Gehrmann's work entailed only the reworking of the revolver's hammer and cylinder. This involved fitting the hammer's nose with a pivoted striker that would pierce a Dreyse-pattern cartridge and hit the primer located at the base of its bullet. To allow the insertion of cartridges into the cylinder, the rear section with the nipples was cut off and replaced with a perforated disc of the same diameter as the remaining portion of the original cylinder. In addition, a loading groove was machined into the right side of the frame's recoil shield. Although the mechanics of this system were suitable for bolt-action longarms, it was impractical for pistols because of the delicate nature of the striker needle and its awkward operation.

Note

1. C. F. Wappenhans to Col. L. P. Sargeant, 1 June 1855. Records of the Colt's Patent Fire Arms Manufacturing Company, Business File, Series III, Incoming Correspondence, Box 10, Connecticut State Library.

Herbert G. Houze

Counterfeits, Infringements, and Competitors

With all due apologies to Charles Caleb Colton, imitation is not always the sincerest form of flattery. In the business world, it is often theft.

In common with countless other successful artists, authors, and inventors, once Samuel Colt's revolvers achieved a measure of popularity, he was beset by copyists. While some of his competitors demonstrated considerable ingenuity, a number of them followed the simple expedient of counterfeiting his arms. Colt may have admired the former, but he held the latter group in utter contempt.

Although few gunmakers produced copies of his earliest designs, those made at Paterson, New Jersey, because of their complexity, the simpler Hartford pistols were another matter. Within two years of their introduction, numerous Belgian makers were busy manufacturing revolvers that, for all intents and purposes, appeared to be Colt products. The most insidious of these were fraudulently marked with Colt's name.

Colt's personal feelings about these counterfeits are clearly seen in the draft of a letter sent to A. W. Spies & Company, one of his New York agents, on 1 February 1853.

> I have seen samples of arms that are infringements upon my Patents they are sed to have been made in Liege & are the most infurnal productions I ever have looked at & better calculated to kill behind [than] before. Under no circumstances shall I permit such arms to be sold where [I] to receive a premeum, or Royalty, of five times the price of one of my [own] make.[1]

Aside from notifying his own distributors, Colt also instructed his attorney to prepare a general notice for the public. The announcement published in the *New York Daily Times* was unambiguous.

> COLT'S PISTOLS—NOTICE!—Dealers in Fire Arms are hereby notified that imitations of COLT'S ARMS, manufactured in Europe, and closely resembling the genuine are now imported into the United States for sale. As the sale of any such arms would be an infringement of Col. Colt's patent, and as the spurious arms are offered for genuine Colt's pistols, this notice is given to put dealers and purchasers on their guard. Any person found importing or selling such arms, or any others, made in violation of Col. Colt's patent, will be prosecuted.

> SAMUEL COLT.
> New York, Feb. 15, 1853.[2]

In large part, Colt's problems were self-inflicted. To comply with Belgian patent law, he had authorized the manufacture in Liège of verification samples demonstrating the hinged loading lever and the cylinder locking system.[3] These samples were later used as models for the production of copies by a number of gunmakers in Liège, then Europe's largest arms-making center. By mid-1851 the production of counterfeit revolvers had reached the point that impelled Colt to dispatch his London patent attorney, William E. Newton, to Liège in order to resolve the issue. Writing to Colt on 21 September 1851, Newton reported: "I don't know whether I should say it causes me pleasure or regret to inform you that not one but several manufacturers here have made the arms for exportation."[4] After circulating a notice that Colt's designs were protected under Belgian patent law, Newton hired Monsieur Devos-Sera to act as Colt's agent in Liège.[5] Devos-Sera's primary task was to oversee the licensed manufacture of Colt Patent revolvers in Liège that were equal in quality to the Hartford product. In addition, he was to mark those revolvers made under license with a die stamp reading "Colt Brevete," provided by Newton.[6] It was also Devos-Sera's responsibility to ensure that none of the Colt-pattern pistols made in Liège were intended for export.[7] Despite Colt's assurances to Spies that "I shall never consent to have them imported into the United States; be they ever so well constructed. & shall proscut anay person who offers them for Sail to the full extent of the law,"[8] quantities of Belgian, as well as German, counterfeits began to reach the New York market in early 1853. Devos-Sera had failed in his mission on all counts.

To protect his interests, Colt instructed his attorney, Edward N. Dickerson, to issue a notice to the major arms dealers in Boston, New York, and Philadelphia.

> 57 CHAMBERS STREET.
> NEW-YORK Feb.15th, 1853.

> SIR:
> I am informed that Pistols, made in imitation of COLT'S ARMS, are now imported into this country from Germany, and, other places in

Europe, and offered for sale here. You are hereby notified that the importation or sale of any such arms is a violation of COL. COLT's patent; and that all persons found engaged in such violation, will be prosecuted at once.

EDW'D N. DICKERSON,
Of Counsel with Sam'l Colt[9]

Even as Colt threatened legal action against sellers of the counterfeit pistols, he was exploring other avenues to limit their negative economic impact. Despite having been burned by the arms makers of Liège, he decided to give them one more opportunity to cooperate with him. This uncharacteristic move involved supplying specific makers with partially finished revolver components, as well as the tooling necessary for their manufacture. To implement this arrangement, Colt instructed John Sainthill, who had replaced the luckless Devos-Sera in early 1853, to begin negotiations with various Liège makers.[10] In theory this appeared to be an ideal solution, as Colt could rid himself of obsolete tooling and components that were no longer needed, while at the same time reaping revenue from what would otherwise have been merely scrap. Furthermore, the ten-franc royalty payment instituted by Newton would remain in effect.

The arrangement initially worked rather well. On 15 September 1853 Sainthill notified Charles F. Dennett, Colt's London agent: "The workmanship of the Pistols has greatly improved and some are really very respectable and creditable to their Makers."[11] However, unauthorized copies continued to be made despite the best efforts of Colt and Sainthill.[12]

It is likely that Colt's offer to the Liège makers was based on his previous successful efforts to license the production of his pistols. In 1849 he had entered into an agreement with the Austro-Hungarian government authorizing the manufacture of revolvers based on his patents at its primary arsenal, the Kaiserliche Konigliche Privilegierten Machinen Fabrik in Innsbruck. Over the five-year period of the license, slightly more than one thousand .34 and .36 caliber revolvers were produced for private sale.[13] Colt later sold the Imperial Russian government all the machines and tooling necessary to manufacture his Belt Pistol at the Tula small arms factory southeast of Moscow.[14]

Patent Infringements

Infringements—arms incorporating design features that were protected by patents awarded to Colt—were another problem the inventor had to deal with. In 1851 rumors began to circulate that two former Colt workmen had begun to manufacture infringements in Springfield, Massachusetts. To determine the validity of these stories, Colt sent the following letter to his cousin Henry Sargeant on 5 May 1851:

> Dear Sir
> I want a good specemin of the Pistols now being made by the Mass Arms Co. at Chicopee falls, & also one of those now making in the south part of Springfield by Messrs Yong & Levet of N York & Mr Warner. Will you du me the favour to purchase a specemin pistol from each of the above named establishments & forward the same to me today or tomorrow if possible & draw upon me for there cost. I do not want them to know the arms are for me. I want them immediately & you will confer a grate favour on me by getting & forwarding them as soon as you can, & much oblige[15]

The arrival of these revolvers (cat. nos. 87 and 100) in Hartford was to set the stage for one of the greatest patent battles.

In late May 1851 Colt filed suit against the Massachusetts Arms Company, alleging that its production of revolvers based on the designs of Daniel B. Wesson and Daniel Leavitt infringed on his patents. The major points of litigation involved Wesson and Leavitt's use of a cylinder rotated by the action of cocking the pistol's hammer, a hammer-actuated cylinder locking system, and the cylinder shoulders between the nipple recesses—all features protected by Colt's 1835 patent, which had been reissued on 24 October 1848 and extended for an additional seven years on 10 March 1849.[16]

The trial in Boston was closely followed by the press, who regaled the public with sordid accounts of how evidence had been fabricated by the defendants and official documents changed in the U.S. Patent Office to bolster their claims.[17] After Colt won the case in October 1851, he took the unusual step of having the trial transcripts published in their entirety.[18] Although the jury hearing the case did not award monetary damages, Colt's attorney, Edward N. Dickerson, secured a $15,000 settlement from the Massachusetts Arms Company.[19] The firm, however, continued to manufacture revolvers that Colt considered to be infringements. As a result, while Colt was in Europe, Dickerson filed suit on his behalf in October 1852 against two of the Massachusetts Arms Company's principals, Hiram Terry and Edwin Leavitt.[20] This action was heard before the U.S. Circuit Court for the District of New York and was extensively covered by the city's major newspapers. And again evidence concerning fraudulent exhibits and tampering with Patent Office files was made public.[21] As before, the court found in Colt's favor.

Immediately following the verdict, Dickerson distributed the following notice to the trade:

NOV. 10th. 1852

SIR—

You will please to take notice to desist forthwith from the sale of any REPEATING FIRE ARMS, in which rotation, or locking and releasing, are produced by combining the breech with the lock; or in which the cones are separated by partitions, or set into recesses; except such as are made by Col. Colt, at Hartford.

All rotary arms constructed with such combinations, whether made by the Springfield Arms Co., by Young & Leavitt, by Allen & Thurber, by Blunt & Syms, by Marstin & Sprague, by Bolen, or by any other person, are a plain violation of Col. Colt's patent; and I shall proceed against you and hold you responsible for damages, if you persist in the sale of any such arms.[22]

Needless to say, this circular had a chilling effect upon the American arms industry. The Worcester, Massachusetts, company of Allen & Thurber, which produced pepperboxes, was particularly worried and approached Dickerson to secure some sort of accommodation. Realizing that a settlement with Allen & Thurber was more to Colt's advantage than a protracted lawsuit, Dickerson entered into negotiations with the company. On 29 December 1852 an agreement was reached, and a new circular was distributed, signed by Allen & Thurber and by Dickerson on behalf of Colt.[23] Although it specifically noted that Colt had not waived his rights to reinstitute a suit against Allen & Thurber, it notified the trade that they would not be subject to any sanctions should they decide to sell the latter company's arms.

Although Dickerson secured a payment of $15,000 from Allen & Thurber in return for a promise not to pursue a patent infringement case, Samuel Colt was livid when he learned of the agreement after he returned from Europe in late January 1853.[24] In response to an evidently scathing letter written by Colt on 29 March 1853, when he was once again in England,[25] Dickerson responded that the arrangements with Allen & Thurber were "a mere suspension of hostilities, until a permanent arrangement can be made, or until we desire to renew the fight."[26] After outlining various courses of action, Dickerson then gave Colt the following advice:

Nothing is easier than to get into a big law suit; but there are many easier things than to get out again successfully: Your *luck* as I suppose you will call it, has been hitherto very good—better than *any other inventor* in America by far, but it may turn, an another suit may bring out something which we know not of, and which may destroy us. . . . I advise you to let this affair of A & T stand just where it now is till you come home.[27]

Colt heeded his attorney's advice, and the Allen & Thurber settlement was formalized following Colt's return to the United States on 27 June 1853.[28]

Colt's willingness to pursue legal action against manufacturers producing infringements did have one positive effect. Their production virtually ceased, and it was not until 1859 that measures had to be taken against other makers. That litigation involved infringements of Colt's patents of 10 September 1850 and 24 November 1857.[29]

Competitors

While Colt was by far the largest manufacturer of civilian arms during the 1850s, he faced ever-increasing competition as the decade progressed. This was particularly true after his patent covering the use of a hammer-actuated pawl and cylinder stop expired on 24 October 1856. Although some of the firms producing revolvers had relatively limited outputs, others posed a serious challenge to Colt's market dominance. Chief among these were the resurgent Massachusetts Arms Company of Chicopee Falls,

Massachusetts; E. Remington of Ilion, New York; and Eli Whitney, Jr., of New Haven, Connecticut. Colt kept abreast of their activities by purchasing representative examples of their products on the open market. He also actively collected revolvers made in England and Europe. Colt's interest in acquiring copies as well as infringements was well known among those who sold his arms. For example, on 1 October 1850 the New York gun dealer, as well as manufacturer, Blunt & Syms sent Colt a letter regarding a piece they had just purchased or taken in trade.

> We have a pistol in store said to have been manufactured in Australia which is an exact copy of your Holster Pistol except the Barrel is 5½ inches long 75 bore and the stock steel mounted (a size of pistol which you ought to make) of very good workmanship and better lever rod than yours which supposing would be of more interest to you than to ourselves, we have reserved it and will give it to you in exchange for a plated Holster pistol complete. There is accompanying it a wrench, mould, cones & powder measure.[30]

By the time Colt died, in January 1862, a myriad of other makers had begun production of revolvers intended for federal forces. None of these manufacturers were to prove a lasting threat, and "Colonel Colt's Great Northern Armoury"[31] would dominate the American arms industry for decades to come.[32]

Notes

1. Samuel Colt to A. W. Spies & Co., 1 February 1853.

2. *New York Daily Times*, "Colt's Pistols—Notice!" 15 February 1853, 7.

3. William E. Newton to Samuel Colt, 20 September 1851. Records of the Colt's Patent Fire Arms Manufacturing Company, RG 103, Business File, Series III, Box 8, Connecticut State Library.

4. William E. Newton to Samuel Colt, 21 September 1851. Records of the Colt's Patent Fire Arms Manufacturing Company, RG 103, Business File, Series III, Incoming Correspondence, Box 8, Connecticut State Library.

5. William E. Newton to Samuel Colt, 24 September 1851. Records of the Colt's Patent Fire Arms Manufacturing Company, RG 103, Business File, Series III, Incoming Correspondence, Box 8, Connecticut State Library.

6. Ibid.

7. Ibid.

8. Samuel Colt to A. W. Spies & Co., 1 February 1853.

9. Edward N. Dickerson, Printed Notice to the Arms Trade, 15 February 1853. Samuel Colt Papers, Box 7, Connecticut Historical Society.

10. Samuel Colt to John Sainthill, [?] March 1853. Records of the Colt's Patent Fire Arms Manufacturing Company, RG 103, Business File, Series II, Outgoing Correspondence, Box 6, Connecticut State Library.

11. John Sainthill to Charles F. Dennett, 9 September 1853. Records of the Colt's Patent Fire Arms Manufacturing Company, RG 103, Business File, Series III, Incoming Correspondence, Box 9, Connecticut State Library.

12. The copying of Colt's designs was not confined to makers in Belgium, France, and Germany. Prior to Colt's sale of revolver machinery to the Imperial Russian government, creditable copies of his Belt and Holster Pistols were being made at Tula (Valentin Mavrodin, *Fine Arms from Tula Firearms and Edged Weapons in the Hermitage, Leningrad* [New York: Harry N. Abrams, 1977], nos. 131, 132, and 137). In Finland, M. Wetzer of Helsingfors, produced approximately one hundred Colt-pattern Belt Pistols (Butterfield & Butterfield, *Sale Number 6157A European Military Revolvers from the Estate of Rolf H. Muller* [6 December 1994], Lot 2519).

13. Samuel Colt to Elisha Colt, 12 June 1849. Records of the Colt's Patent Fire Arms Manufacturing Company, RG 103, Business File, Series III, Incoming Correspondence, Box 8, Connecticut State Library.

14. William Jarvis to William Jarvis, Jr., 5, 12, and 26 April 1858. William Jarvis Letters, MSS Coll. 70425, Connecticut Historical Society.

15. Samuel Colt to Henry Sargeant, 5 May 1851. Samuel Colt Papers, Box 6, Connecticut Historical Society.

16. Robert M. Anderson, *In the Circuit Court of the United States. Samuel Colt vs. The Mass. Arms Company. Report of the Trial of the Above-Entitled Cause, at Boston, on the Thirtieth Day of June, A.D. 1851, Before His Honor, Levi Woodbury, Associate Justice, of the Supreme Court of the United States* (Boston: White & Potter, 1851), 18, 42–43.

17. Ibid., 241.

18. It is believed that the press run did not exceed one hundred copies. A facsimile edition was published by Martin Rywell in 1953 under the title *The Trial of Samuel Colt* (Harriman, Tenn.: Pioneer Press).

19. Edward N. Dickerson to Samuel Colt, 30 April 1853. Samuel Colt Papers, Box 7, Connecticut Historical Society.

20. *New York Daily Times*, "COLT'S REVOLVERS," 13, 14, 18, and 19 October 1852.

Herbert G. Houze

21. For example, see Charles M. Keller's comments concerning the origin of the patent model of the Colborne revolver admitted in evidence by Terry and Leavitt's counsel, Mr. Staples (*New York Daily Times,* "COLT'S REVOLVERS," 13 October 1852, 6).

22. Edward N. Dickerson, Printed Notice to the Arms Trade, 10 November 1852. Samuel Colt Papers, Box 7, Connecticut Historical Society.

23. Samuel Colt, "Copy of printed Circular," 29 December 1852. Samuel Colt Papers, Box 7, Connecticut Historical Society.

24. Colt annotated a copy of the second circular Edward N. Dickerson issued, on 29 December 1852 (reproduced below): "Jany 24, inquired of Dickerson / Jany 28 inquired of Sargeant } What means this circular" (Samuel Colt Papers, Box 7, Connecticut State Library).

> Sir:
>
> Under an arrangement made between ALLEN & THURBER and MR. COLT this day, the notice heretofore given you not to sell ARMS manufactured by Allen & Thurber is hereby withdrawn. You will be required, however, to observe the requirements of the said notice in respect to all other Rotary Arms.
>
> EDW'D N. DICKERSON.

25. This letter is referred to in Dickerson's response of 27 April 1853, cited below.

26. Edward N. Dickerson to Samuel Colt, 27 April 1853. Samuel Colt Papers, Box 7, Connecticut Historical Society. It should be noted that this letter is annotated on the first page as follows: "No date. Supposed to have been written about April 30.1853 S.C." The letter's actual date follows Dickerson's signature on page 8.

27. Ibid.

28. Colt arrived in New York aboard the SS *Baltic* from Liverpool on 27 June 1853 (National Archives, *Passenger Lists of Vessels Arriving at New York, New York, 1820–1897.* Micropublication M237. Roll 128, List Number 615, Line 29).

29. The individuals and companies sued in 1859 included Allen & Wheelock, the Manhattan Fire Arms Manufacturing Company, North & Savage, A. Pliers, the Phenix Armory (William M. Marston), E. Remington, and James Warner (Samuel Colt, "CAUTION. To Manufacturers, Merchants, and Purchasers generally, of Rotatin Breech Chambered Fire Arms," 24 November 1859. Formerly in author's collection).

30. Blunt & Syms to Samuel Colt, 1 October 1850. Records of the Colt's Patent Fire Arms Manufacturing Company, RG 103, Business File, Series III, Incoming Correspondence, Box 8, Connecticut State Library.

31. John A. McLaren to Robert McLaren, 1 June 1862. Private collection.

32. Upon Colt's death in 1862, Elisha K. Root was appointed president of the Colt company. Following Root's death in 1865, Richard W. H. Jarvis (Elizabeth Colt's brother) became president and remained in that position until 1901.

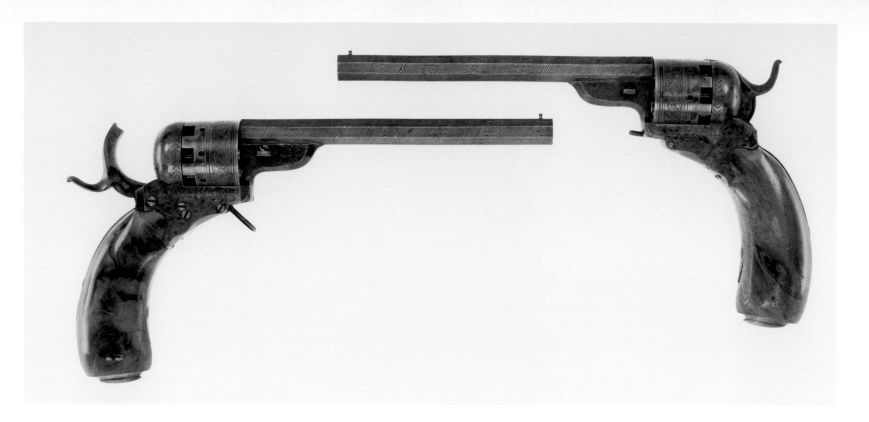

79

Counterfeit Patent Arms Number 3 Belt Pistols

No serial numbers

Caliber .36 in., barrel length 6⅞ in., overall length 10½ in.

Date of Manufacture: ca. 1845

Museum of Connecticut History, Hartford

Gift of the Pratt & Whitney Company Foundation, Inc., 227 and 228

Markings

Backstrap: JULES LEMARCHE / A LIEGE

1861 Inventory of Colonel Colt's Small Office

Page 7, line 8

1 Case 2 revolvers & appendages by Lamarche Liege

1887 Museum Inventory Draft

227. Old .32 Cal. Colt revolvers. Paterson N.J. Model 8 shot, oct: damasacus barrel

228. 6⅞" long, percussion cap One of first made in quantity

Due to their involved mechanics, counterfeits of Colt's earliest revolvers are relatively rare. This pair of pistols can more accurately be described as copies because no attempt was made to deceive a purchaser into thinking they were genuine Colt products. Apart from being signed by Lemarche, they have grips of typical European form and barrels of Damascus steel. The production of Damascus steel barrels involved the winding of multiple strips of iron around a mandrel or rod and then hammer-welding the strips together to form a solid tube. When etched with acid, as is the case with these barrels, the pattern of the forged steel is revealed. Though attractive, Damascus barrels were not as strong as those made from fluid or forged steel. Consequently they gradually lost favor as the nineteenth century progressed. While it is likely that these revolvers were made during the mid- to late 1840s, Colt purchased them in December 1860.[1]

Note

1. Colt's Patent Fire Arms Manufacturing Company. Journal A (1 January 1856–31 December 1862), 326. D. Donnelly Collection.

80

Counterfeit Colt Pocket Pistol

Serial number X-1

Caliber .32 in., barrel length 3 1/4 in., overall length 7 1/8 in.

Date of Manufacture: ca. 1853

Museum of Connecticut History, Hartford

Gift of the Pratt & Whitney Company Foundation, Inc., 343

Markings

None

1861 Inventory of Colonel Colt's Small Office

Page 10, line 26

1 Counterfiet of Colt's old model pocket (cocks with trigger)

1887 Museum Inventory Draft

343. 31 Cal. 5 shot, 3 1/4" oct. b. d.A. Maker not known. Marked XI

This revolver is not only an infringement of Colt's patents but also of the U.S. patent awarded to Robert Adams of London. The latter, Number 9,694, issued 3 May 1853, protects the double-action operation of this pistol, where the rearward movement of the trigger cocks the revolver and at the same time turns the cylinder. Typical of many counterfeits, it is unsigned by its maker. Circumstantial evidence suggests that it may have been made by Benjamin J. Hart & Brother of New York City.[1]

Note

1. Frank M. Sellers and Samuel E. Smith, *American Percussion Revolvers* (Ottawa, Ont.: Museum Restoration Service, 1971), 76–78.

81

Counterfeit Colt Belt Pistol

No serial number

Caliber .354 in., barrel length 7 7/16 in., overall length 12 7/8 in.

Date of Manufacture: 1857–58

Museum of Connecticut History, Hartford

Gift of the Pratt & Whitney Company Foundation, Inc., 333

Markings

Frame: A. PLIERS / BREVETE

1861 Inventory of Colonel Colt's Large Office

Page I, line 6

1 French Revolver (A. Pliers)

1887 Museum Inventory Draft

333. .354 Cal. 6 shot, 7.40" oct. barrel, A. Pliers' Pat. France

Incorporating details of both the Paterson and Hartford era Colt revolvers, the Pliers Belt Pistol was identified by Colt's patent attorney as a direct infringement of his client's patent of 10 September 1850 due to its use of shoulders between the cylinder's nipple recesses.[1] Pliers's Belgian patent of 17 June 1856 protected the dual use of a cleaning rod as a cylinder pin.

The fact that Colt included this infringement in his 24 November 1859 advisory notice to dealers suggests that revolvers of this type were then being offered for sale in New York City.[2]

Notes

1. Charles M. Keller to Samuel Colt, 8 September 1859. Connecticut State Library.
2. Samuel Colt, "Caution To Manufacturers, Merchants, and Purchasers of Rotating Breech Chambered Fire Arms," 24 November 1859. Connecticut State Library.

Given the close similarity between this revolver and the first Colt Belt Pistols made in Hartford, it is likely that at least in part it was made using obsolete parts sent by Colt to Liège. As the revolver is stamped with the maker's mark, N.G., on the cylinder, as well as elsewhere, it can be identified as a product of N. Gilon's shop.

The notation that this piece was a counterfeit in the 1861 inventory of Colt's office indicates that despite being marked "Colt Brevete," no royalty for its manufacture was paid to either Colt or his Liège agent. Under the licensing agreements that Colt's patent agent, William E. Newton, had negotiated with Liège makers in 1851, a fee of ten francs was to be paid to Colt for every copy they produced.[1] Some manufacturers avoided paying the royalty by fraudulently marking some of their Colt-pattern revolvers with "Colt Brevete" die stamps they made themselves.[2] N. Gilon evidently was one of these makers.

In contrast to Hartford-manufactured Colt Belt Pistols, this revolver's cylinder is roll-engraved with a maritime scene depicting fishing boats.

Notes

1. William E. Newton to Samuel Colt, 24 September 1851. Records of the Colt's Patent Fire Arms Manufacturing Company, RG 103, Business File, Series III, Incoming Correspondence, Box 8, Connecticut State Library.

2. Samuel Colt to John Sainthill, [?] March 1853. Records of the Colt's Patent Fire Arms Manufacturing Company, RG 103, Business File, Series II, Outgoing Correspondence, Box 6, Connecticut State Library.

82
Counterfeit Colt Belt Pistol
Serial number 3
Caliber .36 in., barrel length 7³/8 in., overall length 13¹/16 in.
Date of Manufacture: 1853–54
Museum of Connecticut History, Hartford
Gift of the Pratt & Whitney Company Foundation, Inc., 264

Markings
Barrel: COLT / BREVETE

1861 Inventory of Colonel Colt's Small Office
Page 8, line 20
1 Counterfiet Colt's P-

1887 Museum Inventory Draft
264. 36 Cal, 6 shot, Colt Navy 7³/8 oct., 3, brevete

83

Counterfeit Colt Belt Pistol

Serial number 5014

Caliber .36 in., barrel length 7½ in., overall length 13 in.

Date of Manufacture: ca. 1855

Museum of Connecticut History, Hartford

Gift of the Pratt & Whitney Company Foundation, Inc., 263

Markings

Barrel: COLT / BREVETE

1861 Inventory of Colonel Colt's Large Office

Page I, line 14

1 Counterfiet (French) Navy pistol No 5014

1887 Museum Inventory Draft

263. 36 Cal, 6 sh, Colt Navy, 7½ oct. marked 5014, Brevete engraved.

Liège gunmakers quickly changed the construction of their counterfeits to reflect the revised form of the Colt Belt Pistol introduced in 1853. Consequently, this revolver has a trigger guard bow with a fully rounded form rather than one having a vertical rear wall.

This example bears the maker's marks of N. Gilon, who was licensed by Colt to manufacture copies for domestic sale in Belgium. However, this pistol postdates the expiration of the agreement and therefore falls into the category of counterfeit.

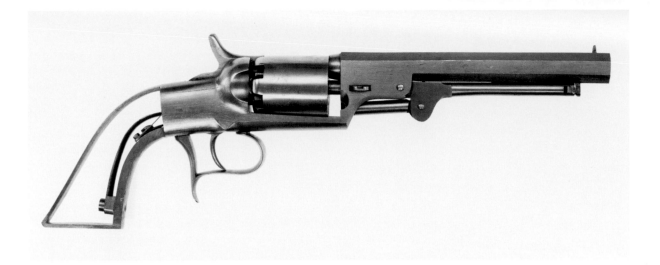

Overall left

84
Counterfeit Colt Belt Pistol
No serial number
Caliber .35 in., barrel length 7½ in., overall length 13 in.
Date of Manufacture: 1856–57
Museum of Connecticut History, Hartford
Gift of the Pratt & Whitney Company Foundation, Inc., 339

Markings
Barrel: CH CHARLIER / BREVETE

1861 Inventory of Colonel Colt's Small Office
Page 7, line 22
Revolver by Charlier

1887 Museum Inventory Draft
339. 35 Cal., 6 shot, 6½ Ch. Charlier Brevete.unf.

Perhaps no other Liège counterfeiter was more vexing to Colt than Charles Charlier. This unfinished counterfeit was secured by Colt for use as evidence in a successful attempt to prosecute the Liège maker for infringement of the inventor's Belgian patent of 1849.[1]

Aside from the construction of the revolver's frame and trigger guard, it closely resembles Colt's Hartford Belt Pistol. In addition to being an infringement, the pistol has a frame made of cast iron, which is relatively brittle and liable to crack when subjected to repeated strain, such as that generated by the recoil of firing. Colt was well aware of the dangers posed by using cast iron and described pistols made with it as being "better calculated to kill behind [than] before."[2]

Notes
1. Frederick von Oppen to Samuel Colt, 6 July 1859. Records of the Colt's Patent Fire Arms Manufacturing Company, RG 103, Business File, Series III, Incoming Correspondence, Box 10, Connecticut State Library.
2. Samuel Colt to A. W. Spies & Co., 1 February 1853. Records of the Colt's Patent Fire Arms Manufacturing Company, RG 103, Business File, Series II, Outgoing Correspondence, Box 6, Connecticut State Library.

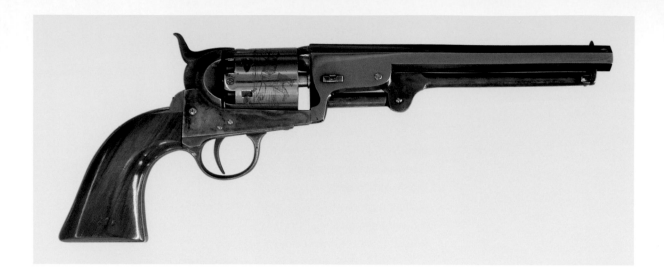

Barrel inscription

Herbert G. Houze

85

Belgian Manufactured Colt Belt Pistol
Serial number 7891
Caliber .36 in., barrel length 7½ in., overall length 13 in.
Date of Manufacture: ca. 1860
R. C. Romanella Collection

Markings
Barrel: COLT / PATENT [stamped]; Devisme arqer Bte a Paris [engraved]
Grips: 3270 [right side]

During the 1850s France was by far the largest market for Belgian-produced copies and counterfeits of Colt revolvers. While unsigned counterfeits were widely distributed there, established arms dealers avoided those arms in favor of licensed copies. This was especially true of the Parisian arms makers who fully appreciated Colt's efforts to defend his patent rights against usurpers because they faced the same problems.

This licensed copy of a Hartford Belt Pistol was retailed by the Parisian gunmaker Louis-François Devisme. The presence of a partially obliterated London Gun Makers Company view mark on the left side of the barrel lug is of note, as it may indicate that the barrel was made at Colt's Pimlico factory in London and sent in an unfinished state to Liège for assembly.

In contrast to Hartford or London Belt Pistols, those made in Liège often had their cylinders roll-engraved with vignettes of more local interest. In this case the scene depicted is a horse race.

86

Koenigliche Kaiserliche Privelegierten Machinen Fabrik Colt's Patent Belt Pistol
Serial number 143
Caliber .36 in., barrel length 5⁵⁄₁₆ in., overall length 11½ in.
Date of Manufacture: 1850
Wadsworth Atheneum Museum of Art
Bequest of Elizabeth Hart Jarvis Colt, 1905.1011

Markings
Frame: K:K:PRV:MASCH:FABR: / INNSBRUCK [right side]
PATENT 1849 [left side]

1861 Inventory of Colonel Colt's Small Office
Page 7, line 24
K. K. Prv Or Pry Insbruck Pistol

The first Colt revolvers to be manufactured under license in Europe were those made by the Imperial Austro-Hungarian arms factory in Innsbruck. Although it has been stated that the majority of the revolvers made in Innsbruck were issued to officers and men of the Imperial Navy, no substantive evidence for this has been found.[1] Based on surviving examples, the majority were apparently produced for private sale to individual officers and civilians under permission warrants granted by the government.

The Innsbruck Colt Belt Pistols have somewhat more awkward profiles than their Hartford counterparts and were available in both .36 and .34 caliber. Approximately one thousand were made before the five-year licensing agreement expired in 1855.

Note

1. Robert Q. Sutherland and R. L. Wilson, *The Book of Colt Firearms* (Kansas City, Mo.: R. Q. Sutherland, 1971), 143.

87

Wesson & Leavitt Holster Pistol
No serial number
Caliber .40 in., barrel length 6¾ in., overall length 13⅞ in.
Date of Manufacture: 1848
Museum of Connecticut History, Hartford
Gift of the Pratt & Whitney Company Foundation, Inc., 314

Markings

Barrel: LEAVITTS / PATENT and MANUFACTURED BY / WESSON, STEVENS & MILLER HARTFORD. CT. [top strap over cylinder]

1861 Inventory of Colonel Colt's Small Office
Page 7, line 23
Leavitt's patent Pistol

1887 Museum Inventory Draft
314. 36 Cal. 7 shot 6⁵⁄₁₆" Leavitt's Pat. Made by Wesson, Stevens & miller. Hartfd. Conn.

Only a very few examples of this revolver were made in Hartford by Wesson, Stevens & Miller before its manufacture was taken over by the Massachusetts Arms Company of Chicopee.[1] The revolvers produced by that firm were essentially of the same form except for an improved barrel catch designed by Edwin Wesson.[2]

It is highly probable that this pistol was one of the firearms purchased by Henry Sargeant in early May 1851 at the request of his cousin Samuel Colt.[3] Following an examination of its lockwork, Colt filed suit against the Massachusetts Arms Company for patent infringement. The case, heard in the U.S. Circuit Court for the District of Massachusetts in Boston, alleged that the revolvers then being made by the Massachusetts Arms Company incorporated three features protected by Colt's reissued U.S. patent of 24 October 1848 (Number 124). The specific points of contention involved the use of a revolver's hammer to rotate the cylinder, a cylinder lock or bolt acting in concert with the hammer, and the placement of the percussion cap nipples in recesses located at the rear of the cylinder.[4]

Although the court found in Colt's favor, the Massachusetts Arms Company continued production. This necessitated a second suit, filed in New York City against two principals of the company.[5]

Notes

1. Frank M. Sellers and Samuel E. Smith, *American Percussion Revolvers* (Ottawa, Ont.: Museum Restoration Service, 1971), 186.
2. U.S. Patent Office. Edwin Wesson (Edwin G. Ripley, Administrator), "Method of

Overall left

Connecting the Hammer with the Cylinder of a Revolving Fire-Arm," Number 6,669, issued 28 August 1849.

3. Samuel Colt to Henry Sargeant, 5 May 1851. Samuel Colt Papers, Box 6, Connecticut Historical Society.

4. *In the Circuit Court of the United States, District of Massachusetts. Samuel Colt vs. The Mass. Arms Company. Report of the Trial of the Above-Entitled Cause, at Boston, on the Thirtieth Day of June, A.D. 1851, Before His Honor, Levi Woodbury, Associate Justice of the Supreme Court of the United States* (Boston: White & Potter, 1851), 12–13.

5. *New York Daily Times,* "COLT'S REVOLVERS," 13, 14, 18, and 19 October 1852.

88

Allen & Wheelock Pocket Pistol
Serial number 12
Caliber .32 in., barrel length 4 in., overall length 9⅞ in.
Museum of Connecticut History, Hartford
Gift of the Pratt & Whitney Company Foundation, Inc., 327

Markings
Barrel: ALLEN & WHEELOCK.WORCHESTER.MASS.U.S.; ALLEN'S PT'S JAN. 13.DEC 15 1857

1861 Inventory of Colonel Colt's Large Office
Page I, line 9
1 Allen & Wheelock do [Revolver] 4" (pr $10)

1887 Museum Inventory Draft
327. .32 Cal., 5 shot, 4" oct Allen's Pat 13/1 15/12. 57. Allen & Wheelock. Worcester mass

The patent dates cited in the barrel inscription refer to Ethan Allen's U.S. Patent Numbers 16,367, issued 13 January 1857, and 18,836, issued 15 December 1857. The first covers the construction of a loading lever having a racked lower surface that is actuated by pinions machined into the forward arm of a hinged trigger guard.[1] The second patent described a mechanism for locking the cylinder in place during firing.[2]

This revolver is described as an infringement of Samuel Colt's 24 November 1857 patent in a cautionary notice dated 24 November 1859 that was distributed to manufacturers, dealers, and the general public.[3] The basis for identifying it as an infringement was its use of a rear-mounted cylinder pin.

Notes

1. U.S. Patent Office. Ethan Allen, "Improved Fire-Arm," Number 16,367, issued 13 January 1857.

2. U.S. Patent Office. Ethan Allen, "Improvement in Revolving Fire-Arms," Number 18,836, issued 15 December 1857.

3. Samuel Colt, "CAUTION To Manufacturers, Merchants, and Purchasers of Rotating Breech Chambered Fire Arms," 24 November 1859. Connecticut State Library.

89

Manhattan Fire Arms Manufacturing Company Belt Pistol
Serial number 302
Caliber .31 in., barrel length 3¹⁵/₁₆ in., overall length 5¾ in.
Date of Manufacture: 1858–59
Museum of Connecticut History, Hartford
Gift of the Pratt & Whitney Company Foundation, Inc., 324

Markings
Barrel: MANHATTAN FIRE ARMS / MANUFG.CO.NEW YORK

1861 Inventory of Colonel Colt's Large Office
Page I, line 7
1 Revolver Manhattan Fire Arms Co (4" pr 9.75)

1887 Museum Inventory Draft
324. .31 Cal., 5 shot, 4" oct. Imitation Colt's O. M. Pocket Manhattan fire arms Co
N.Y. Wholes. pr. $9.75

This Manhattan Fire Arms Manufacturing Company Belt Pistol was listed as a potential infringement in Colt's notice to the public, dated 24 November 1859, due to the fact that the rear shoulders of the cylinder were drilled with holes to receive safety pins of the type protected by Colt's patent of 10 September 1850. Consequently, the notice contained the following warning extracted from Charles M. Keller's letter to Colt of 8 September 1859:

> If the persons who sell such direct the purchasers to put on the securing catch, and advise them to put on the catch, or cause it to be put on, such sellers as well as the purchasers who put on the catch, or cause it to be put on, become by such act infringers on letters patent granted to you, bearing the date the 10th day of Sept. 1850, and in suit against either, you can recover damages for the violation of the exclusive right secured to you by said patent.[1]

Note
1. Charles M. Keller to Samuel Colt, 8 September 1859. Connecticut State Library.

90

Marston Pocket Pistol

Serial number 584

Caliber .31 in., barrel length 4¾ in., overall length 9¼ in.

Date of Manufacture: 1858

Museum of Connecticut History, Hartford

Gift of the Pratt & Whitney Company Foundation, Inc., 326

Markings

Barrel: WM. W. MARSTON / PHENIX / NEW YORK CITY ARMORY

1861 Inventory of Colonel Colt's Large Office

Page I, line 8

1 Marston Revolver 4½" (pr 9.50)

1887 Museum Inventory Draft

236. .31 Cal., 5 shot, 4¼" oct, Wm. W. Marston Phenix Armory. N.Y. City. No. 584.3"/ $8.75 4" / 9.25 5" / 9.50 6" / 9.75

Although better known for his pepperboxes and three-barrel derringers, William Marston also manufactured a variety of revolvers at his Phenix Armory, located at the corner of 2nd Avenue and East 22nd Street in New York City. Introduced immediately after the expiration of Colt's 1848 patent extension in 1857, the Marston Pocket Pistol infringed on Colt's patent of 10 September 1850 protecting the use of shoulders between the cylinder's nipple recesses, as well as rectangular cylinder stops.

Despite Colt's warning that sellers and purchasers of these revolvers would be prosecuted, Marston continued to manufacture them, using a number of trade names, such as The Union Arms Company and the Western Arms Company, to disguise their true origin.[1]

Note

1. Frank M. Sellers and Samuel Smith, *American Percussion Revolvers* (Ottawa, Ont.: Museum Restoration Service, 1971), 89–90.

91

Savage & North Belt Pistol

Serial number 6

Caliber .36 in., barrel length 7½ in., overall length 14 in.

Date of Manufacture: 1859

Museum of Connecticut History, Hartford

Gift of the Pratt & Whitney Company Foundation, Inc., 1338 [originally 319]

Markings

Barrel: E. SAVAGE. MIDDLETOWN. CT. / H. S. NORTH. PATENTED. JUNE 17th, 1856

1861 Inventory of Colonel Colt's Large Office

Page I, line 5

1 Savage Revolver price marked $18.

1887 Museum Inventory Draft

319. 36 Cal., 6 shot, 7⅛" oct, d.a., H. S. North's Pat. 17/6.56, E. Savage, Midelltown, Conn.

Henry S. North's U.S. Patent Number 15,144, issued on 17 June 1856, described both the method of cocking and firing the pistol by means of the ring trigger and a geared system for rotating the cylinder.[1] The patent also described a method for moving the cylinder forward so that the chamber mouths came into contact with the mouth of the barrel's breech.[2]

Colt's patent attorney, Charles M. Keller, determined that the design of this revolver also incorporated features protected not only by E. K. Root's 25 December 1855 patent for a ring-trigger double-action revolver but also by the amended reissue of that patent granted on 1 November 1859. Consequently, it was deemed an infringement, and notice to that effect was published by Samuel Colt on 24 November 1859.[3]

Notes

1. U.S. Patent Office. Henry S. North, "Improvement in Fire-Arms," Number 15,144, issued 17 June 1856.

2. Ibid.

3. Samuel Colt, "CAUTION To Manufacturers, Merchants, and Purchasers of Rotating Breech Chambered Fire Arms," 24 November 1859. Connecticut State Library.

Overall left

92

Remington Beal's Patent Pocket Pistol
Serial number 150
Caliber .24 in., barrel length 3 1/16 in., overall length 6 1/2 in.
Museum of Connecticut History, Hartford
Gift of the Pratt & Whitney Company Foundation, Inc., 313

Markings
Barrel: F. BEALS' PATENT / JUNE 26.1856 / REMINGTON'S / ILION.N.Y.

1861 Inventory of Colonel Colt's Large Office
Page I, line 10
F. Beals, do [Revolver] *3 ($6.00)*

1887 Museum Inventory Draft
313. .31 Cal., 5 shot, Remington Pocket 3" oct. No C15, wholesale pr. $6

To evade Colt's reissued patent of 1848, Fordyce Beals designed a method for rotating the cylinder using a partially exposed pawl or hand linked to the hammer. The tip of this pawl engaged triangular recesses cut in the rear face of the cylinder. Beals was issued Patent Number 15,167 on 24 June 1856 for this design.[1]

Despite Beals's ingenuity, the resulting revolver was an infringement of another of the Hartford inventor's patents, that of 10 September 1850. In that patent Colt secured protection for a cylinder design wherein the percussion cap nipples were set into recesses along the rear periphery. This construction allowed the recesses to be separated from one another by a shoulder of solid metal. Since Beals's pistol had a cylinder of similar design, it infringed upon Colt's patent. Consequently, Remington redesigned the revolver to eliminate the cylinder shoulders. The replacement model also was fitted with a double-action lock, so that the cylinder was turned and the hammer cocked by pulling the pistol's trigger.

Note

1. U.S. Patent Office. Fordyce Beals, "Improvement in Fire-arms," Number 15,167, issued 24 June 1856.

93
Warner Pocket Pistol
Serial number 74
Caliber .27 in., barrel length 2⅝ in., overall length 6⁹/₁₆ in.
Museum of Connecticut History, Hartford
Gift of the Pratt & Whitney Company Foundation, Inc., 328

Markings
Barrel: SPRINGFIELD ARMS CO, WARNER'S PAT. JAN 1851
Cylinder: JAMES WARNER.SPRINGFIELD.MASS.

1861 Inventory of Colonel Colt's Small Office
Page 8, line 7
1 Small pistol by Jas Warner Springfield

The cylinder of this revolver was rotated by a spring-loaded gear connected to the hammer, as described in Warner's patent of 7 January 1851 (Number 7,894).[1] The hinged-barrel assembly was also designed by Warner and was protected by his U.S. Patent Number 8,229 of 15 July 1851.[2]

In common with the preceding revolvers, Warner's Pocket Pistol was an infringement of Colt's patent of 10 September 1850 due to the presence of shoulders between the nipple recesses.

Notes

1. U.S. Patent Office. James Warner, "Improved Means for Revolving the Breeches of Repeating Fire-Arms," Number 7,894, issued 7 January 1851.
2. U.S. Patent Office. James Warner, "Improvement in Revolving-Breech Fire-Arms," Number 8,229, issued 15 July 1851.

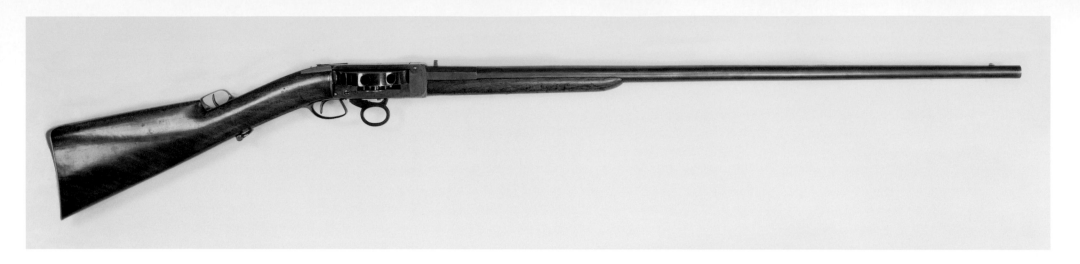

94
Cochran Patent Revolving Rifle
Serial number 7
Caliber .50 in., barrel length 32 13/16 in., overall length 52 1/2 in.
Date of Manufacture: ca. 1836
Museum of Connecticut History, Hartford
Gift of the Pratt & Whitney Company Foundation, Inc., 751

Markings
Cylinder Topstrap: COCHRAN / PATENT

1861 Inventory of Colonel Colt's Small Office
Page 1, lines 18 and 19
In Case / Cochran's Rifle & Pistol

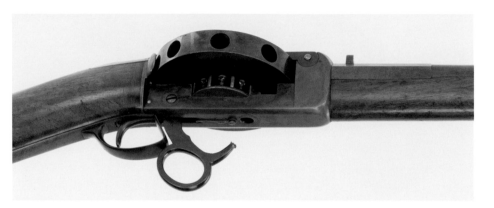

Detail of cylinder from below

One of the more interesting attempts to evade Colt's 1835 patent was conceived by John W. Cochran of New York City. Instead of using a round cylinder
having parallel chambers in line with the barrel, Cochran proposed using a flat
radial cylinder. The manually turned cylinder could be placed in or removed
from the arm's frame by raising a spring-loaded top strap that was hinged to
the upper rear surface of the barrel.[1] The horizontal positioning of the cylinder
immediately in front of the user's face must have given pause to those who
feared multiple discharges.

Note
1. U.S. Patent Office. John W. Cochran, "Improvement in Many-Chambered-Cylinder
Fire-Arms," Number 183, issued 29 April 1837.

95

Whittier Patent Revolving Rifle

Serial number 2

Caliber .70 in., barrel length 36 in., overall length 58 in.

Date of Manufacture: 1837–38

Wadsworth Atheneum Museum of Art

Bequest of Elizabeth Hart Jarvis Colt, 1905.1033

Markings

Barrel: WHITTIER'S / PATENT

Frame: PATENT [rear tang]

Although the construction of this rifle's cylinder is similar to those found on the Root prototype pocket pistols discussed earlier, it was rotated by an entirely different mechanism. In many respects, the lockwork used to turn the cylinder more closely resembles the works of a clock than those of a firearm. Nonetheless, to protect the designs he had developed in 1849, Elisha K. Root purchased Otis W. Whittier's U.S. Patent Number 216 of 30 May 1837 in 1850.[1] It is likely that this rifle was acquired by Samuel Colt at that time.

Note

1. U.S. Patent Office. Otis W. Whittier, "Improvement in Many-Chambered-Cylinder Fire-Arms," Number 216, issued 30 May 1837. The assignment of this patent to E. K. Root was in the collection of the late Alan S. Kelley; its present location is unknown.

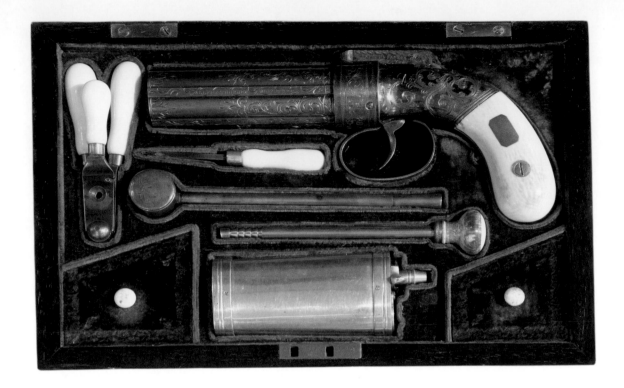

96

Allen & Thurber Pepperbox
Serial number 6
Caliber .31 in.
Date of Manufacture: ca. 1850
R. C. Romanella Collection

Markings

Barrel: ALLEN & THURBER WORCESTER / 1837 CAST STEEL
Hammer: ALLENS PATENT

Without question, Samuel Colt's primary competitor during the late 1840s and early 1850s was Allen & Thurber of Worcester, Massachusetts. Although the company did not make a cylinder revolver, it did produce four-, five-, and six-shot pepperboxes. Easily carried in either the belt or pocket, these arms also had the advantage of being relatively inexpensive in their plainest form.

Allen & Thurber's first pepperboxes had ring triggers and hammers with finger spurs. Later examples, such as the one illustrated here, had conventional triggers enclosed within a protective bow. In addition, the hammers were of bar form, which prevented them from catching on clothing when carried in the pocket. As with the original model patented by Ethan Allen on 16 April 1845 (U.S. Patent Number 3,998),[1] all Allen & Thurber arms were double-action

(pulling the trigger not only cocked the pistol but also rotated the barrel assembly).

Allen & Thurber pioneered the use of cast steel for pistols, and all of their pepperboxes were marked on the barrel assemblies with an inscription to that effect. Unfortunately cast steel barrels sometimes burst during firing; Colt kept an example of such a pistol in his factory's museum.[2]

By the time Samuel Colt launched his patent infringement suit against Allen & Thurber in 1852,[3] the firm's fortunes were beginning to fade. The weight of the firm's pepperboxes in comparison with Colt's revolvers had eroded their sales, and the double-action design prevented the pistols from being cocked by hand. Recognizing the declining popularity of the pepperbox, after 1855 Allen & Thurber increasingly focused on the production of inexpensive single-barrel percussion pocket pistols.[4]

As this pistol is cased, engraved, and silver-plated, it may have been used by its makers for exhibition purposes. Interestingly, the bullet mold differs from that normally seen in pepperboxes of this type, being of the same style as those used for the Paterson Patent Arms Manufacturing Company revolvers discussed previously.

Notes

1. U.S. Patent Office. Ethan Allen, "Improvement in Pistols and Other Fire-Arms," Number 3,998, issued 16 April 1845.
2. 1861 Inventory of Colonel Colt's Small Office, page 8, line 15: *Allen's pistol burst.*
3. Edward N. Dickerson, Printed Notice to the Arms Trade, 10 November 1852. Samuel Colt Papers, Box 7, Connecticut Historical Society.
4. Harold R. Mouillesseaux, *Ethan Allen, Gunmaker: His Partners, Patents & Firearms* (Ottawa, Ont.: Museum Restoration Service, 1973), 110–16.

97
Bacon Pepperbox
Serial number 68
Caliber .31 in., barrel length 4³⁄₈ in., overall length 8³⁄₄ in.
Date of Manufacture: 1850–52
Museum of Connecticut History, Hartford
Gift of the Pratt & Whitney Company Foundation, Inc., 217

Markings
Barrel group: BACON & CO. NORWICH C-T / CAST STEEL

1861 Inventory of Colonel Colt's Small Office
Page 8, line 11
Revolver Bacon & Co Norwich Conn

1887 Museum Inventory Draft
217. 31" Cal. 6 shot, pepperbox, bottom hammer, Bacon & Co Norwich

Fitted with an underhammer and an exposed trigger, Bacon pepperboxes never achieved great popularity despite their rather elegant lines.

98
Manhattan Fire Arms Manufacturing Company Belt Pistol
Serial number 18228
Caliber .36 in., barrel length 6¹⁄₂ in., overall length 11¹⁄₂ in.
Date of Manufacture: ca. 1860
Museum of Connecticut History, Hartford
Gift of the Pratt & Whitney Company Foundation, Inc., 321

Markings
Barrel: MANHATTAN FIRE ARMS MANUFACTURING COMPANY. NEWARK.
NEW JERSEY

When Colt's 1848 patent extension expired in 1857, numerous manufacturers began producing revolvers that closely resembled those made in Hartford. One of the more prolific copyists was the Manhattan Fire Arms Manufacturing Company of New York City and later Newark, New Jersey.[1]

Note
1. For a discussion of the Newark products, see Waldo E. Nutter, *Manhattan Firearms* (Harrisburg, Pa.: Stackpole Company, 1958), 143–80.

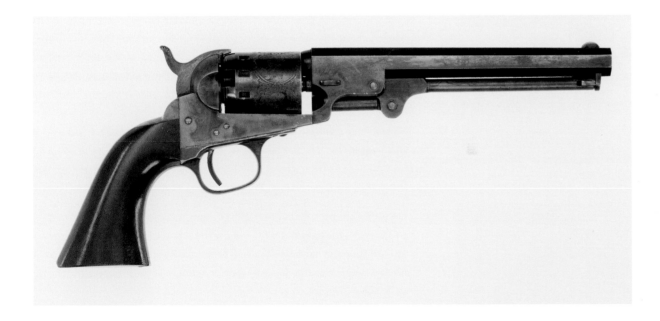

Overall right with primer door open

Cat. 99a. Illustration of a Massachusetts Arms Company Pocket Pistol with a Maynard patent primer mechanism, published in Silliman and Goodrich, *The World of Science, Art, and Industry* (New York, 1854).

99

Massachusetts Arms Company Pocket Pistol

Serial number 919

Caliber .28 in., barrel length 3 in., overall length 7¼ in.

Date of Manufacture: 1855–56

Museum of Connecticut History, Hartford

Gift of the Pratt & Whitney Company Foundation, Inc., 319

Markings

Frame Topstrap: MASS ARMS CO CHICOPEE FALLS

Primer Door: MAYNARD'S PATENT SEPT 22 1845

Backstrap: PATENT / JAN.2.1855

1861 Inventory of Colonel Colt's Small Office

Page 8, line 22

1 Revolver, Mass Arms Co. with primer

1887 Museum Inventory Draft

318. 27 Cal. 6 shot, 3" b Mass. Arms Co. Chicopee falls with Maynards percussion strip attachment

Despite its small size, this revolver had four separate patents encompassing its construction. The first of these, describing the ratchet and cog cylinder turning mechanism, was awarded to Edwin Wesson; the second, issued to Joshua Stevens, protects the hinged barrel design; and the third, also issued to Stevens, covers the cogged wheel that advances the percussion tape primer to the firing position.[1]

The fourth patent, for the tape primer, was awarded to Dr. Edward Maynard of Washington, D.C., on 22 September 1845.[2] Closely resembling the strips of paper caps used by youngsters in modern cap pistols, Maynard's invention was described in a contemporary publication:

One of these strips, containing fifty charges, is coiled up and placed in a magazine in the lock, and is fed out, by the action of the lock, one charge at each time the hammer is raised. When the hammer descends it cuts off and fires the charge fed out upon the vent or cone, thus igniting the cartridge within the barrel.

The detonating material of the "Maynard Primer" is in the form of little lozenges, each about one-sixth of an inch wide, and one-thirtieth of an inch thick. These lozenges are inclosed between two narrow strips of strong paper cemented together, and rendered water-proof and incombustible. The single strip thus formed is a little less than one-fourth of an inch wide, is very stiff and firm, and contains four of these lozenges (each of which is a charge) in every inch of its length [cat. 99a].[3]

The tape-priming system was adopted for use by the U.S. government in 1855, and as a result, Samuel Colt briefly entertained the possibility of equipping his New Model Rifles with Maynard tape-priming mechanisms. In June 1856 he instructed Elisha K. Root to make a sample rifle with a Maynard primer "to pleas the fances of our present Secretary of War & submit it with one of the others as soon as done for his inspection & tryal if he is inclined to favor it."[4]

Notes

1. U.S. Patent Office. Edwin Wesson (Edwin G. Ripley, Administrator), "Method of Connecting the Hammer with the Cylinder of a Revolving Fire-Arm," Number 6,669,

issued 28 August 1849; Joshua Stevens, "Improvement in the Locking Apparatus of Repeating Firearms," Number 7,802, issued 26 November 1850; Joshua Stevens, "Improvement in Repeating Fire-Arms," Number 9,929, issued 9 August 1853.

2. U.S. Patent Office. Edward Maynard, "Percussion-Primer and Gun-Lock Therefor," Number 4,208, issued 22 September 1845 (antedated 22 March 1845).

3. B. Silliman and C. R. Goodrich, *The World of Science, Art, and Industry Illustrated from Examples in The New-York Exhibition, 1853–54* (New York: G. P. Putnam & Company, 1854), 61.

4. Samuel Colt to Milton Joslin, 20 June 1856. Samuel Colt Papers, Box 7, Connecticut Historical Society.

100

Warner Pocket Pistol

Serial number 20

Caliber .31 in., barrel length 3½ in., overall length 9¼ in.

Date of Manufacture: 1851

Museum of Connecticut History, Hartford

Gift of the Pratt & Whitney Company Foundation, Inc., 318

Markings
None

1861 Inventory of Colonel Colt's Large Office
Page I, line 11
1 Pistol by James Warner Springfield – No 20

Despite the absence of maker's marks, the construction and mechanics of this pistol identify it as a product of James Warner's hand. Originally an employee of Eli Whitney, Jr., during the manufacture of the 1847 U.S. contract for Holster Pistols, Warner declined an offer to work for Colt in Hartford in 1848. Instead, he moved to Springfield, Massachusetts, where he became associated with what was to become the Springfield Arms Company. This revolver embodies features in Warner's U.S. Patent Number 7,894 of 7 January 1851: protecting the cylinder-turning mechanism and the design of the barrel-frame juncture described in a later patent.[1]

This revolver was purchased at Samuel Colt's request by his cousin Henry Sargeant in May 1851, so that its lockwork could be examined to determine whether it infringed upon Colt's patent of 1848.[2]

Notes

1. U.S. Patent Office. James Warner, "Improved Means for Revolving the Breeches of Repeating Fire-Arms," Number 7,894, issued 7 January 1851, and "Improvement in Revolving-Breech Fire-Arms," Number 8,229, issued 15 July 1851.

2. Samuel Colt to Henry Sargeant, 5 May 1851. Samuel Colt Papers, Box 6, Connecticut Historical Society.

Overall left

Whitney Pocket Pistol
Serial number DD4
Caliber .31 in., barrel length 5 in., overall length 9⅞ in.
Date of Manufacture: 1853
Museum of Connecticut History, Hartford
Gift of the Pratt & Whitney Company Foundation, Inc., 330

Markings
Barrel: E. WHITNEY, N. HAVEN, CT
Frame: PATENT APPLIED FOR

1887 Museum Inventory Draft
330. 31 Cal., 5 shot 5" oct, Eli Whitney. N.H. Conn.

For the first half of the nineteenth century Eli Whitney, Jr.'s armory in Whitneyville, Connecticut, was devoted solely to the manufacture of longarms. However, shortly after 1850, the firm began considering the production of revolving pistols.

In the firm's first major effort to design a revolver evading Samuel Colt's patents, a hand-revolved cylinder was used. It was released for rotation by pressing the vertical lever mounted forward of the trigger guard bow. Although Whitney attempted to patent the design (witness the frame marking), his application was denied because the cylinder construction, as well as other features, infringed upon Colt's reissued patent (Number 124) of 1848.

However, prior to this rejection, Whitney marketed the revolver with moderate success. He exhibited examples at the 1853 New York Crystal Palace Exhibition, where they received positive notices. In *The World of Science, Art, and Industry Illustrated From Examples In The New-York Exhibition, 1853–54*, by B. Silliman and C. R. Goodrich, a revolver of this type is shown with the following caption:

> From the first introduction of portable fire-arms numberless attempts have been made to increase their destructiveness by giving one instrument the power of many; but it was left to American ingenuity to carry out the idea with practical success.
>
> The latest of these novelties is exhibited by the inventor, Mr. E. WHITNEY, of New Haven. The chambered cylinder is detached for loading by removing the center-pin on which it revolves; when in place it is turned by the thumb or finger to the right or left, as may be desired. This repeater is discharged less rapidly than Colt's, but it is also much stronger and simpler in its construction, and therefore less liable to be injured by use, or if so, it may be easily repaired (cat. 101a).[1]

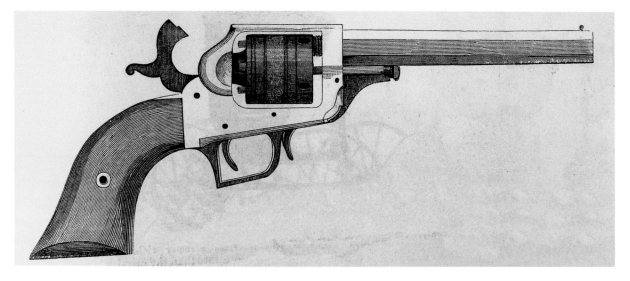

Cat. 101a. Illustration of a Whitney Pocket Pistol, published in Silliman and Goodrich, *The World of Science, Art, and Industry* (New York, 1854).

Note

1. B. Silliman and C. R. Goodrich, *The World of Science, Art, and Industry Illustrated From Examples In The New-York Exhibition, 1853–54* (New York: G. P. Putnam & Company, 1854), 63.

102

Whitney Pocket Pistol

Serial number 739

Caliber .31 in., barrel length 4 in., overall length 8⅞ in.

Date of Manufacture: 1854–55

Museum of Connecticut History, Hartford

Gift of the Pratt & Whitney Company Foundation, Inc., 331

Markings

None

1861 Inventory of Colonel Colt's Small Office

Page 8, line 24

1 Pistol supposed to be Whitney's

1887 Museum Inventory Draft

331. 31 Cal, 5 shot, 4 oct. Supposed to be Whitney's make

Dating from a slightly later period than the preceding revolver, this pistol was not marked by its maker for a very good reason: it is an infringement of Colt's 1848 and 1850 patents.

　　Following the expiration of Colt's patents in 1856, identical revolvers made by Whitney were fully marked as to their manufacture. Whitney's opposition to the extension of Colt's patents was long-standing. For example, in 1853 he had made it known that he would actively campaign against any efforts to secure congressional approval for the extension of Colt's reissued patent of 1848.[1] Consequently, it is quite likely that Whitney took some pleasure when that measure was defeated in 1854.

Note

1. Edward N. Dickerson to Samuel Colt, 20 July 1853. Samuel Colt Papers, Box 7, Connecticut State Library.

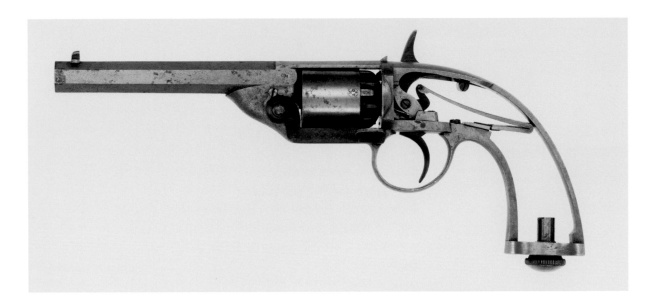

Overall disassembled

Devisme Belt Pistol

Serial number 1485

Caliber .28 in., barrel length 4⅛ in., overall length 9⅛ in.

Date of Manufacture: 1858–59

Museum of Connecticut History, Hartford

Gift of the Pratt & Whitney Company Foundation, Inc., 342

Markings

Barrel lug: DV beneath a crown and within a circular frame

1861 Inventory of Colonel Colt's Small Office

Page 4, line 20

Revolver by Devisme

1887 Museum Inventory Draft

342. 275 Cal., 6 shot, 4.15 oct 6, Devisme, bte. Liege. Belg. Unfinis.

Samuel Colt's acquisition of this pistol by Louis-François Devisme of Paris was no doubt because of its novel opening mechanism. To load the pistol, the lever on the left side of the frame is pressed downward, thereby releasing a transverse bolt from the cylinder arbor. The barrel can then be drawn forward free of the frame and cylinder arbor.

Like many other revolvers purchased in Europe by Colt or his agents, this pistol is unfinished, thereby avoiding the excise duties that would be payable upon being imported to the United States. As unfinished goods, they were exempt from customs fees.

Devisme was one of France's major gunmakers between 1840 and 1870.[1] He actively participated at all the French national industrial exhibitions and was awarded a *médaille de 1er classe* at the Exposition Universelle of 1855.[2]

Notes

1. Pierre Jarlier, *Répertoire d'arquebusiers et de fourbisseurs français* (St.-Julien-du-Sault: François-Pierre Lobies, 1976), 87.

2. *Exposition Universelle de 1855. Rapports du Jury Mixte Internationale* (Paris: Imprimerie Imperiale, 1856), I, 46.

Herbert G. Houze

104

Ghaye Belt Pistol

Serial number 311

Caliber .354 in., barrel length 5⅞ in., overall length 10⅜ in.

Date of Manufacture: 1857–58

Museum of Connecticut History, Hartford

Gift of the Pratt & Whitney Company Foundation, Inc., 338

Markings

Top Strap of Frame: L. GHAYE BREVETE

Cylinder: ACIER FONDU

1861 Inventory of Colonel Colt's Small Office

Page 4, line 22

1 Pistol French L Ghare

1887 Museum Inventory Draft

338. 354 6, 5¾, d.A., L. Chaye, Brevet, 311. Liege. Unf.

One of the most innovative revolver designs to be developed during the nineteenth century was that of Lt. Lambert Ghaye of the Belgian Army.[1] Its novelty lay in the fact that the trigger guard served three distinct functions. When it was lowered or pulled downward, it moved the barrel approximately one-quarter inch forward, disengaging it from the cylinder, rotated the cylinder, and cocked the hammer. When the trigger guard was returned to its normal position, the barrel was drawn back into contact with the cylinder's face.[2]

While the elimination of any gap between the barrel and the cylinder being fired substantially reduced any risk of flashover (that is, setting off an adjacent chamber), any fouling or accumulation of dirt on the lever arm moving the barrel rendered the pistol inoperable. Consequently, Ghaye revolvers never achieved any commercial success.

Notes

1. Pierre Jarlier, *Répertoire d'arquebusiers et de fourbisseurs français* (St.-Julien-du-Sault: François-Pierre Lobies, 1976), 120.

2. Claude Blair, *Pistols of the World* (London: B. T. Batsford Ltd., 1968), Nos. 678–79, 143.

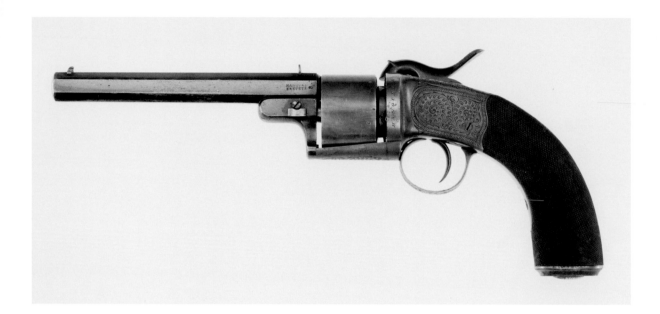

105

Hanquet Holster Pistol

Serial number 45

Caliber .41 in., barrel length 6³⁄₈ in., overall length 13 in.

Date of Manufacture: ca. 1850

Museum of Connecticut History, Hartford

Gift of the Pratt & Whitney Company Foundation, Inc., 332

Markings

Barrel: HANQUET / BREVETE

Recoil Shield: HANQUET'S BREVETE LIEGE

1861 Inventory of Colonel Colt's Small Office

Page 8, line 3

J. B. Hanquet's pistol Liege

1887 Museum Inventory Draft

332. .41 Cal, 6 shot, 6.35" oct. barrel J. E. Hanquet's Pat. Liege. Belgium

At least four members of the Hanquet family worked as gunmakers in Liège during the nineteenth century.[1] Georges Hanquet, who is believed to be the maker of this pistol, secured a Belgian patent for what is now known as a transitional revolver. Arms of this type essentially resembled pepperboxes that had separate barrels attached to them. They were immensely popular in Great Britain and Europe during the late 1840s and early 1850s.

Note

1. Pierre Jarlier, *Répertoire d'arquebusiers et de fourbisseurs français* (St.-Julien-du-Sault: François-Pierre Lobies, 1976), 135.

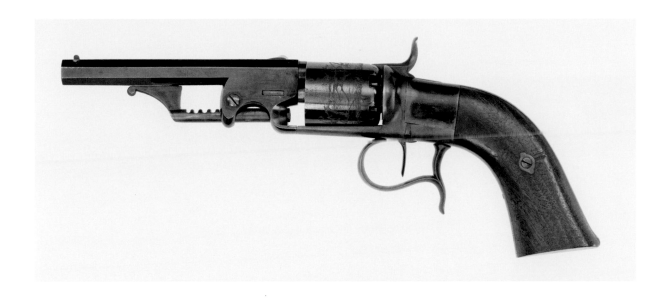

Overall right with loading lever lowered

106
Herman Belt Pistol
No serial number
Caliber .354 in., barrel length 5½ in., overall length 12⅜ in.
Museum of Connecticut History, Hartford
Gift of the Pratt & Whitney Company Foundation, Inc., 335

Markings
Barrel: J J Herman.Brevete.Liege.

1861 Inventory of Colonel Colt's Small Office
Page 8, line 4
1 Pistol Herman pat. France or Liege

1887 Museum Inventory Draft
335. 354 Cal, 6, 5½ oct. barrel, J. J. Herman. Brevete. Liege. Belgium

It is likely that the design of this revolver's loading lever was a source of some amusement to Samuel Colt. Although it was definitely an infringement of his rack-and-pinion arrangement patented in 1855, Herman's use of a side-mounted crank to operate the loading lever was novel to say the least.[1]

    In contrast to the usual idyllic scenes engraved on European revolver cylinders of the period, the Herman pistol is decorated with a tableau of mounted dragoons somewhat similar to that found on Colt's early Holster Pistols.

Note
1. Pierre Jarlier, *Répertoire d'arquebusiers et de fourbisseurs franais* (St.-Julien-du-Sault: François-Pierre Lobies, 1976), 138.

107

Lhoist Belt Pistol

No serial number

Caliber .354 in., barrel length 6 ¹³⁄₁₆ in., overall length 12 ⁵⁄₈ in.

Date of Manufacture: 1857–58

Museum of Connecticut History, Hartford

Gift of the Pratt & Whitney Company Foundation, Inc., 334

Markings

Barrel: LHOIST / BREVETE / A CHERATTE

1861 Inventory of Colonel Colt's Small Office

Page 7, line 25

C. L. Hoist France [Pistol]

1887 Museum Inventory Draft

334. 354 Cal., 6 shot, 6¾ oct. barrel, C. L. Hoist, Pat, A Cherratte France.

This transitional-style revolver made by Charles Lhoist[1] is fitted with a geared loading lever with a horizontally moving forward arm. While unusual in operation, it nevertheless was an infringement of Colt's patents covering the construction of vertically acting hinged loading levers, and a suit was filed against Lhoist in Brussels. A judgment in favor of Colt was handed down in July 1859, and Lhoist's revolver was withdrawn from the European market.[2]

Notes

1. Pierre Jarlier, *Répertoire d'arquebusiers et de fourbisseurs français* (St.-Julien-du-Sault: François-Pierre Lobies, 1976), 176.

2. Freidrich von Oppen to Samuel Colt, 5 July 1859. Records of the Colt's Patent Fire Arms Manufacturing Company, RG 103, Business File, Series III, Incoming Correspondence, Box 10, Connecticut State Library.

108

Renotte Belt Pistol

No serial number

Caliber .32 in., barrel length 4³⁄₈ in., overall length 8⁵⁄₈ in.

Date of Manufacture: 1855–56

Museum of Connecticut History, Hartford

Gift of the Pratt & Whitney Company Foundation, Inc., 341

Markings

Barrel Lug: D RENOTTE / BREVETE

1861 Inventory of Colonel Colt's Small Office

Page 4, line 16

A Renotte pistol with lever ramrod

1887 Museum Inventory Draft

341. 32 Cal. 5 shot 4½ oct. b., d.A. D. Renotte Brevete. Liege Belgium

Demonstrating that the makers in Liège produced infringements of designs other than those of Samuel Colt, this smooth-bore revolver is a copy of Lt. Frederick B. E. Beaumont's English patent allowing a double-action pistol to be safely cocked by hand by means of a secondary sear (that is, a hammer catch).[1] Although little is known about D. Renotte, he apparently was a rather prolific maker of revolvers based on other makers' patents.

Note

1. Frederick Blacket Edward Beaumont, "Improvements in Fire-Arms called Revolvers," Number 374, enrolled 20 February 1855 (H. M. Patent Office, *Abridgements of the Patent Specifications Relating to Firearms & Other Weapons, Ammunition & Accoutrements from 1588–1858* [London: George Eyre and William Spottiswoode, 1859], 204).

109

Tranter Pocket Pistol

Serial number 4721T

Caliber .38 in., barrel length 4½ in., overall length 9⁵/₁₆ in.

Date of Manufacture: 1856

Wadsworth Atheneum Museum of Art

Bequest of Elizabeth Hart Jarvis Colt, 1905.1006

Markings

Frame: No 4,721.T

Loading Lever: W. TRANTER'S / PATENT

1861 Inventory of Colonel Colt's Small Office

Page 8, line 17

Trantners Pistol (English)

Perhaps his attempts to design a double-action revolver during the 1840s led Samuel Colt to take a special interest in subsequent developments. During the early 1850s the Birmingham maker William Tranter manufactured the frame assemblies used by Deane, Adams & Deane of London for their double-action Adams patent revolvers. Drawing upon that experience, Tranter developed an improvement that allowed a revolver to be cocked and its cylinder turned by means of a lever extending below the trigger guard bow. Once the pistol was ready to be fired, it could be discharged by a conventional trigger set within the upper section of the lever.[1]

Though not specifically marked as a product of William Tranter's hand, the presence of the "T" at the end of the serial number identifies it as such.[2] The patent noted in the inscription on the loading lever refers to its specific design.[3]

Tranter patent revolvers were quite popular not only in Great Britain but also in the United States, where they were sold by such firms as Schuyler, Hartley & Graham of New York City.

Notes

1. William Tranter, "Certain Improvements in Fire-Arms," Number 212, enrolled 28 January 1853 (H. M. Patent Office. *Abridgements of the Patent Specifications Relating to Firearms & Other Weapons, Ammunition & Accoutrements from 1588–1858* [London: George Eyre and William Spottiswoode, 1859], 134).

2. W. H. J. Chamberlain and A. W. F. Taylerson, *Adams' Revolvers* (London: Barrie & Jenkins, 1976), 55–57.

3. William Tranter, "Improvements in Fire-Arms, and in Bullets and Waddings to be Used Therewith" (H. M. Patent Office, *Abridgements of the Patent Specifications*), 154–55.

Herbert G. Houze

The Memorial Collection Assembled by Elizabeth Hart Jarvis Colt

Surprisingly little is known about the memorial arms collection that Elizabeth Hart Jarvis Colt installed in Armsmear during the Civil War. Consisting entirely of firearms in production at the time of Samuel Colt's death, the collection definitely reflects the desire on Mrs. Colt's part to demonstrate her husband's posthumous contributions to the northern war effort. Yet no mention of the collection can be found in any records dating from that period.

Since the collection is composed primarily of revolving pistols and rifles whose origin and development have been previously described, the catalogue notes will be necessarily brief. In many instances the only references cited will list the date when a particular piece was withdrawn from the inventory stock of the Colt's Patent Fire Arms Manufacturing Company prior to its transfer to Armsmear. Based on these records, it appears that the collection was assembled shortly after 30 May 1863.[1]

Although the collection consists primarily of newly made pieces, some of the arms were drawn from returned inventories, and one, the New Model Holster Pistol, serial number 55794, was a revolver that had been rejected for government service. It is evident that Mrs. Colt wished to display only the models that were in production at the time of her husband's death, in that the Model 1861 Special Rifle Musket that entered production in late 1862 is not represented.[2]

Originally housed in four ornate walnut cabinets in Armsmear's library (fig. 1), the collection was later moved to the billiard room and then finally to a second-floor hallway (fig. 2). The cabinetry used in the library installation has corbels carved with portrait busts representing the arts and industry. Fittingly, the bust representing industry is a portrait of Samuel Colt (fig. 3). Although the case work is not signed, it undoubtedly is of American origin, as no similar items appear in the inventory of furniture sold to Samuel Colt when he first furnished Armsmear.[3] This attribution is circumstantially supported by a tradition in the Ulrich family that Conrad Ulrich the elder carved the allegorical corbel busts.[4]

Figure 1

The library at Armsmear, ca. 1900, showing the original casework built to house the arms collections assembled by Samuel Colt and his widow, Elizabeth Hart Jarvis Colt. Wadsworth Atheneum Museum of Art.

Figure 2 (below left)

The second-floor hallway at Armsmear showing the display cases that housed Elizabeth Hart Jarvis Colt's memorial arms collection after its removal from the library. Wadsworth Atheneum Museum of Art.

Figure 3 (above right)

Bust of Samuel Colt believed to have been carved by Conrad Ulrich, ca. 1863, installed on the left corbel of one of the original arms display cases at Armsmear. Wadsworth Atheneum Museum of Art.

Notes

1. Of the twenty pieces in the collection, six were listed in the Colt's Patent Fire Arms Manufacturing Company's Serial Number Ledger 4 under the date 30 May 1863. The remainder all have earlier entry dates ranging from 14 January 1861 (the New Model Rifle, serial number 1613, shipped to Joseph G. Grubb & Company in Philadelphia and later returned to the factory) to 29 May 1863 (the New Model Belt Pistol, serial number 13,039).

2. Herbert G. Houze, *Colt Rifles & Muskets from 1847 to 1870* (Iola, Wis.: Krause Publications, 1996), 101–11.

3. Ringuet-Leprince to Samuel Colt, 7 June 1856. Samuel Colt Papers, Box 11, File 1, Connecticut Historical Society.

4. Dorothy Ulrich Troubetzkoy (granddaughter of Conrad Ulrich), interview with the author, 28 September 1986. Conrad Ulrich (1815–1891) was employed as a pistol assembler and wood-carver at the Colt factory from 1855 through the mid-1870s.

110

Old Model Pocket Pistol
Serial number 233223
Caliber .31 in., barrel length 5 in., overall length 10 in.
Date of Manufacture: 1863
Wadsworth Atheneum Museum of Art
Bequest of Elizabeth Hart Jarvis Colt, 1905.1012

Markings
Barrel: ADDRESS COL. SAML COLT NEW-YORK U.S.AMERICA
Frame: COLTS / PATENT

Colt's Patent Fire Arms Manufacturing Company
Serial Number Ledger 4, page 236
26 May 1863

One of the most popular revolvers among infantrymen from the North and the South was Colt's .31 caliber Old Model Pocket Pistol because it provided some measure of protection in close combat where a musket or rifle would be useless.

The reason for identifying revolvers made after patterns produced prior to 1860 as "Old Models" was to differentiate them from the New Model series of pistols introduced that year.

111

Old Model Pocket Pistol

Serial number 232396

Caliber .31 in., barrel length 6 in., overall length 11 in.

Date of Manufacture: 1863

Wadsworth Atheneum Museum of Art

Bequest of Elizabeth Hart Jarvis Colt, 1905.1007

Markings

Barrel: ADDRESS COL. SAML COLT NEW-YORK U.S.AMERICA

Frame: COLTS / PATENT

Colt's Patent Fire Arms Manufacturing Company

Serial Number Ledger 4, page 213

30 May 1863

112

Old Model Belt Pistol with "Attachable Canteen Breech"

Serial number 128429 / S

Caliber .36 in., barrel length 7½ in., overall length of pistol 13 in., overall length with stock 25½ in.

Date of Manufacture: 1862

Wadsworth Atheneum Museum of Art

Bequest of Elizabeth Hart Jarvis Colt, 1905.984A,B

Markings

Barrel: -ADDRESS COL. SAML COLT NEW-YORK U.S.AMERICA-

Frame: COLTS / PATENT

Colt's Patent Fire Arms Manufacturing Company

Serial Number Ledger 4, page 157

30 September 1862

The Old Model Belt Pistol remained a mainstay of the Colt company's product line throughout the Civil War. However, examples such as this one with an "Attachable Canteen Breech" are rarities. Designed by Samuel Colt, this type of stock was made from two pieces of wood that had been hollowed out to hold a pewter canteen.[1] The halves were then glued together and the exterior given either an oil or varnished finish. The flask's mouth was located at the comb of the stock to prevent it from interfering with the pistol's use. It is not known what prompted Colt to design this stock, but it may have been the result of a suggestion made by his Arizona mine manager, N. King, as twenty-five canteen stocks were shipped to the Sonora Exploration & Mining Company in Tubac on 24 August 1858.[2]

In 1861 this pistol carbine would have cost twenty-eight dollars (eighteen dollars for the revolver plus ten dollars for the "canteen breech"). To put this amount into perspective, a skilled laborer of the period would have had to work over two hundred hours merely to cover its purchase price (cat. 112a).

Notes

1. U.S. Patent Office. Samuel Colt, "Canteen Gun-Stock," Number 22,627, issued 18 January 1859.

2. Herbert G. Houze, *Colt Presentations From the Factory Ledgers 1856–1869* (Lincoln, R.I.: Andrew Mowbray, 2003), 53.

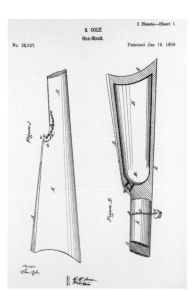

Cat. 112a. Drawing enrolled with Samuel Colt's U.S. Patent No. 22,627, issued 18 January 1859, protecting the design of the Canteen Breech. U.S. Patent and Trademark Office, Washington, D.C.

113

New Model Pocket Pistol

Serial number 6373

Caliber .31 in., barrel length 4½ in., overall length 9 in.

Date of Manufacture: 1863

Wadsworth Atheneum Museum of Art

Bequest of Elizabeth Hart Jarvis Colt, 1905.999

Markings

Barrel: ADDRESS COL. COLT / NEW-YORK U.S.A.

Cylinder: PATENTED SEPT. 10th 1850

Cylinder Pin: MAY.4th 1858

Frame: 31 CAL

Colt's Patent Fire Arms Manufacturing Company

Serial Number Ledger 4, page 29

30 May 1863

The .31 caliber New Model series of Pocket Pistols was introduced in 1860. Due to their weight and more complex design, they were never as popular as the Old Model Pistol. Consequently, fewer than 15,000 were manufactured before the model was discontinued in 1870.

114

New Model Pocket Pistol

Serial number 7162 L

Caliber .31 in., barrel length 3½ in., overall length 8 in.

Date of Manufacture: 1863

Wadsworth Atheneum Museum of Art

Bequest of Elizabeth Hart Jarvis Colt, 1905.997

Markings

Barrel: ADDRESS COL. COLT / NEW-YORK U.S.A.

Cylinder: PATENTED SEPT. 10th 1850

Cylinder Pin: MAY.4th 1858

Frame: 31 CAL

Colt's Patent Fire Arms Manufacturing Company

Serial Number Ledger 4, page 4

30 May 1863

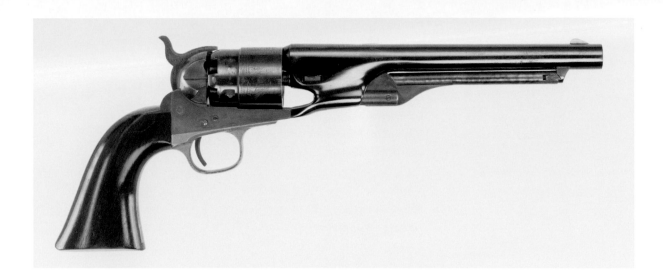

115

New Model Holster Pistol

Serial number 43821

Caliber .44 in., barrel length 8 in., overall length 14 in.

Date of Manufacture: 1862

Wadsworth Atheneum Museum of Art

Bequest of Elizabeth Hart Jarvis Colt, 1905.996

Markings

Barrel: -ADDRESS COL. SAML COLT NEW-YORK U.S.AMERICA-

Frame: COLTS / PATENT

Cylinder: PAT.SEPT.10th 1850

Trigger Guard: 44 CAL

In addition to manufacturing New Model Holster Pistols for the U.S. government during the Civil War, the Colt company continued to produce revolvers for the commercial market. These arms, of which this is an example, had highly polished metal surfaces, silver-plated back straps and trigger guards, and varnished grips. The majority of the New Model Holster Pistols finished in this manner were sold to Union officers by dealers in military goods, such as the firm of Schuyler, Hartley & Graham in New York City.

116

New Model Holster Pistol

Serial number 55794

Caliber .44 in., barrel length 8 in., overall length 14 in.

Date of Manufacture: 1862

Wadsworth Atheneum Museum of Art

Bequest of Elizabeth Hart Jarvis Colt, 1905.1010

Markings

Barrel: -ADDRESS COL. SAML COLT NEW-YORK U.S.AMERICA-

Frame: COLTS / PATENT

Cylinder: PAT.SEPT.10th 1850

Trigger Guard: 44 CAL

Colt's Patent Fire Arms Manufacturing Company

Serial Number Ledger 4, page 108

31 July 1862

In contrast to the preceding revolver, this Holster Pistol has a dull finish and plain brass furniture typical of the arms supplied to the U.S. government during the Civil War. During the course of that conflict, the Colt company delivered 128,157 New Model Holster Pistols to the Union Army.[1] Of that number, one thousand

Overall left

were fitted with "Attachable Breeches."[2] The cylinder of this revolver evidently failed to pass government inspection on two occasions, as it is stamped twice with the condemnation mark "C." It should also be noted that the revolver was partly assembled using civilian-finish, or high-gloss blue, screws.

Notes

1. Stuart C. Mowbray, ed., *Civil War Arms Purchases & Deliveries* (Lincoln, R.I.: Andrew Mowbray, 2000), 730–35.
2. Robert M. Reilly, *United States Military Small Arms 1816–1865* (Baton Rouge, La.: Eagle Press, 1970), 211.

117
New Model Belt Pistol with "Attachable Breech"
Serial number 11634 / S
Caliber .36 in., barrel length 7½ in., overall length of pistol 13 in., overall length with stock 25½ in.
Date of Manufacture: 1862
Wadsworth Atheneum Museum of Art
Bequest of Elizabeth Hart Jarvis Colt, 1905.987A,B

Markings
Barrel: -ADDRESS COL. SAML COLT NEW-YORK U.S.AMERICA-
Frame: COLTS / PATENT
Cylinder: PAT.SEPT.10th 1850
Trigger Guard: 36 CAL

Colt's Patent Fire Arms Manufacturing Company
Serial Number Ledger 4, page 337
31 December 1862

Of the approximately 38,000 New Model Belt Pistols made from 1860 to 1873, it is estimated that fewer than one hundred were equipped with shoulder stocks of the type illustrated here. In large part the lack of orders for such pistol-carbines was due to their cost. In 1861 the retail price for a plain "attachable breech" was eight dollars. Thus the total cost for a Belt Pistol and stock would have been twenty-eight dollars, or approximately five hundred dollars in today's money.

118

New Model Belt Pistol

Serial number 13039

Caliber .36 in., barrel length 7½ in., overall length 13 in.

Date of Manufacture: 1862

Wadsworth Atheneum Museum of Art

Bequest of Elizabeth Hart Jarvis Colt, 1905.990

Markings

Barrel: -ADDRESS COL. SAML COLT NEW-YORK U.S.AMERICA-

Frame: COLTS / PATENT

Cylinder: PAT.SEPT.10th 1850

Trigger Guard: 36 CAL

Colt's Patent Fire Arms Manufacturing Company

Serial Number Ledger 4, page 164

29 May 1863

Federal contract records indicate that the U.S. government purchased 2,056 New Model Belt Pistols of this type between 1861 and 1865. Most of these purchases were made from retail firms, such as Schuyler, Hartley & Graham of New York City, rather than directly from the Colt company.[1] The purchase of Colt revolvers on the open market was authorized by the government only when there was a need for immediate deliveries to satisfy armament deficiencies caused by battle losses or impending campaigns.

Note

1. Stuart C. Mowbray, ed., *Civil War Arms Purchases & Deliveries* (Lincoln, R.I.: Andrew Mowbray, 2000), 953–56.

119

New Model Police Pistol

Serial number 14617

Caliber .36 in., barrel length 6½ in., overall length 11½ in.

Date of Manufacture: 1862

Wadsworth Atheneum Museum of Art

Bequest of Elizabeth Hart Jarvis Colt, 1905.1004

Markings

Barrel: ADDRESS COL. SAML COLT NEW-YORK U.S.AMERICA.

Frame: COLTS / PATENT

Cylinder: PAT.SEPT.10th 1850

Trigger Guard: 36 CAL

Colt's Patent Fire Arms Manufacturing Company

Serial Number Ledger 4, page 45

29 November 1862

Introduced in December 1860, the New Model Police Pistol was made in three different barrel lengths. Of these, the 6½-inch barreled version was better suited for use with a belt holster, while its shorter counterparts were advertised as medium-caliber pocket pistols.

Although the serial number sequence for this model extends well into the 47,000 range, the number of percussion pistols probably did not exceed 24,000 units. This was due to the fact that approximately half the production was either altered or made up specifically for use with metallic cartridges beginning in 1871, when the Colt company ceased manufacturing percussion cap revolvers.

120

New Model Police Pistol

Serial number 18059

Caliber .36 in., barrel length 4½ in., overall length 9½ in.

Date of Manufacture: 1863

Wadsworth Atheneum Museum of Art

Bequest of Elizabeth Hart Jarvis Colt, 1905.998

Markings

Barrel: ADDRESS COL. SAML COLT NEW-YORK U.S.AMERICA.

Frame: COLTS / PATENT

Cylinder: PAT.SEPT.10th 1850

Trigger Guard: 36 CAL

Colt's Patent Fire Arms Manufacturing Company

Serial Number Ledger 4, page 65

30 May 1863

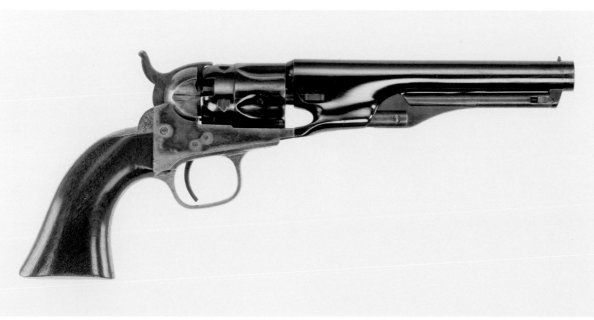

121

New Model Police Pistol

Serial number 19010

Caliber .36 in., barrel length 5½ in., overall length 10½ in.

Date of Manufacture: 1863

Wadsworth Atheneum Museum of Art

Bequest of Elizabeth Hart Jarvis Colt, 1905.1015

Markings

Barrel: ADDRESS COL. SAML COLT NEW-YORK U.S.AMERICA.

Frame: COLTS / PATENT

Cylinder: PAT.SEPT.10th 1850

Trigger Guard: 36 CAL

Colt's Patent Fire Arms Manufacturing Company

Serial Number Ledger 4, page 135

30 May 1863

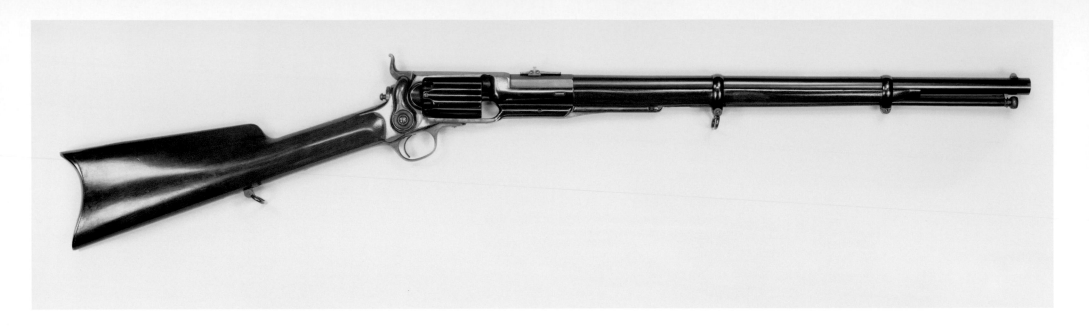

122

New Model Rifle

Serial number 1613

Caliber .44 in., barrel length 24 in., overall length 42½ in.

Date of Manufacture: 1860

Wadsworth Atheneum Museum of Art

Bequest of Elizabeth Hart Jarvis Colt, 1905.971

Markings

Frame: COLT'S PT. / 1856 / ADDRESS COL. COLT / HARTFORD CT. U.S.A. [top strap]

PATD. NOV. 24, 1857 [by cylinder pin aperture]

Cylinder: PATENTED SEPT. 10th 1850

Trigger Guard: 44 CAL.

Colt's Patent Fire Arms Manufacturing Company

Serial Number Ledger 1, page 24

14 January 1861 to Joseph G. Grubb & Company, Philadelphia

Due to the fact that the tactical applications of this short rifle could be duplicated by less expensive New Model Holster Pistols fitted with shoulder stocks, relatively few were made during the Civil War. However, some examples that had been purchased by state governments under the 1808 Militia Act actually did see service.

123

New Model Rifle

Serial number 2863

Caliber .56 in., barrel length 24 in., overall length 42½ in.

Date of Manufacture: 1860

Wadsworth Atheneum Museum of Art

Bequest of Elizabeth Hart Jarvis Colt, 1905.973

Markings

Frame: COL. COLT HARTFORD CT. U.S.A. [top strap]

COLT'S PATENT / Nov. 24th 1857 [left side]

PATD. NOV. 24, 1857 [by cylinder pin aperture]

Cylinder: PATENTED SEPT. 10th 1850

Cylinder Pin: PATENTED MAY 4th 1858

Trigger Guard: 56 CAL.

Colt's Patent Fire Arms Manufacturing Company

Serial Number Ledger 4, page 340

18 April 1863

As with the preceding rifle, the .56 caliber short rifle was not inexpensive.

Indeed, its price was fixed at $37.50 on 1 January 1861.

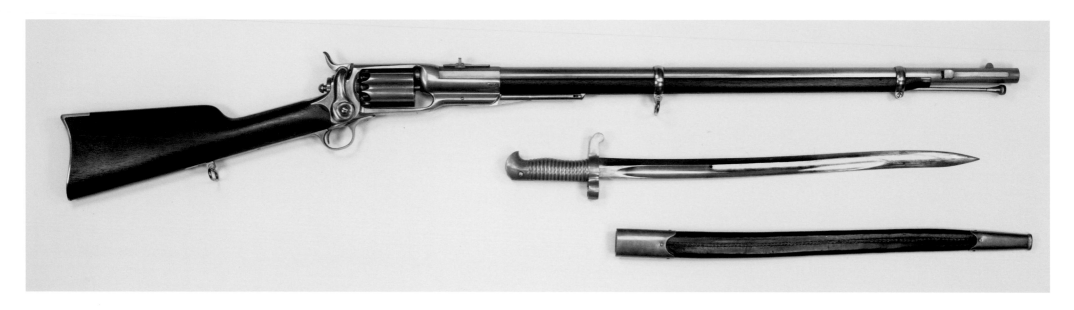

124

New Model Rifle Musket

Serial number 4775

Caliber .56 in., barrel length 31⁵/₁₆ in., overall length 49½ in.

Date of Manufacture: 1861

Wadsworth Atheneum Museum of Art

Bequest of Elizabeth Hart Jarvis Colt, 1905.974 (Bayonet 1905.1016 a–b)

Markings

Frame: COL. COLT HARTFORD CT. U.S.A. [top strap]

COLT'S PATENT / Nov. 24th 1857 [left side]

PATD. NOV. 24, 1857 [by cylinder pin aperture]

Cylinder: PATENTED SEPT. 10th 1850

Cylinder Pin: PATENTED MAY 4th 1858

Trigger Guard: 56 CAL.

This rifle is of the same pattern as those furnished by Samuel Colt to the regiment he raised in April 1861. Upon the amalgamation of the Colt Rifle Regiment with the 5th Regiment of Connecticut Infantry on 20 June 1861, the revolving rifles were returned to the Colt company. The general ledgers of the Colt's Patent Fire Arms Manufacturing Company indicate that a total of 222 New Model Rifles with 31 5/16-inch barrels were sold during the Civil War.

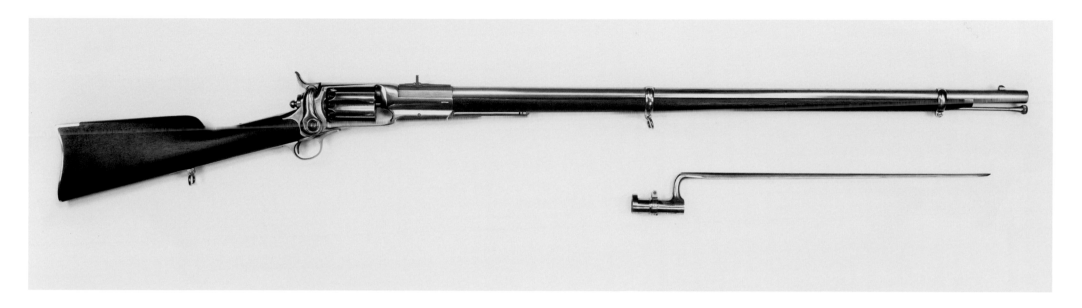

125

New Model Rifle Musket

Serial number 7391

Caliber .56 in., barrel length 37½ in., overall length 56 in.

Date of Manufacture: 1862

Wadsworth Atheneum Museum of Art

Bequest of Elizabeth Hart Jarvis Colt, 1905.975

Markings

Frame: COL. COLT HARTFORD CT. U.S.A. [top strap]

COLT'S PATENT / Nov. 24th 1857 [left side]

PATD. NOV. 24, 1857 [by cylinder pin aperture]

Cylinder: PATENTED SEPT. 10th 1850

Cylinder Pin: PATENTED MAY 4th 1858

Trigger Guard: 56 CAL.

Butt Stock: M.ST.J.

Colt's Patent Fire Arms Manufacturing Company

Serial Number Ledger 4, page 304

30 April 1862

A total of 6,827 rifle muskets of this pattern were made in 1862 and 1863. Of these, 3,725 were purchased by the U.S. government for issue to federal troops at an average cost of forty-eight dollars per rifle.[1]

As the New Model Rifle Musket had been designed solely for military use, few were sold after the Civil War ended. Despite a slight reduction in price to forty-two dollars in 1865, a total of 3,100 remained in the Colt company's inventory stock in 1870.

Note

1. John D. McAulay, *Rifles of the U.S. Army 1861–1906* (Lincoln, R.I.: Andrew Mowbray, 2003), 13–20.

126

New Model Shotgun

Serial number 91

Caliber .75 in., barrel length 27 in., overall length 46⅛ in.

Date of Manufacture: 1861

Wadsworth Atheneum Museum of Art

Bequest of Elizabeth Hart Jarvis Colt, 1905.980

Markings

Frame: COL. COLT HARTFORD CT. U.S.A. [top strap]

COLT'S PATENT / Nov. 24th 1857 [left side]

PATD. NOV. 24, 1857 [by cylinder pin aperture]

Cylinder: PATENTED SEPT. 10th 1850

Cylinder Pin: PATENTED MAY 4th 1858

Trigger Guard: 75 CAL.

Colt's Patent Fire Arms Manufacturing Company

Serial Number Ledger 1, page 102

27 March 1861 to the Colt company's New York City office

The .75 caliber New Model Shotgun entered the Colt company's product line in March 1861. Although approximately 1,100 were manufactured in 1861 and early 1862, this model has the distinction of being the least popular Colt revolver ever made. Due to its high retail cost ($47.25 to $51.75, depending upon barrel length) and weight, fewer than twenty were sold prior to 1870, when the New Model Shotgun was withdrawn from the Colt company's price lists.

Herbert G. Houze

Samuel Colt's South Meadows Armory

Figure 1

Colt's Patent Fire Arms Manufacturing Company's factory, engraving, ca. 1856. Wadsworth Atheneum Museum of Art.

At the time of Samuel Colt's death in January 1862, the South Meadows armory was arguably the most technologically advanced arms factory in the United States and, for that matter, the world. It boasted innumerable belt-driven machines, forges, and finishing departments that greatly reduced handwork. A model of efficiency, revolver and rifle components progressed along dedicated production lines, thereby minimizing unnecessary movement. Although period images of the factory (fig. 1) give some idea of its size, the following description provides an accurate account of the factory and the complex manufacturing processes involved in making Colt revolvers.

Colt's New Armory is located on the west side of the Connecticut River, about one hundred yards south of the mouth of Little River, immediately inside of a dyke which Col. Colt erected to exclude the overflow of the Connecticut River. This embankment is about two miles long, averaging over one hundred feet wide at the base, and from forty to sixty feet in width at the top, and from ten to thirty feet in height. It is built in the most substantial manner, the sides being covered with osier both for protection and ornament. The buildings are of Portland freestone and brick, and consist of four parallels, four stories high, each five hundred feet long, two of them sixty feet and three fifty feet wide, connected a fifth at right angles There are also two others of one story in height, five hundred feet long and fifty feet wide. The floors if extended in one line, would be a mile long by fifty feet wide, and contain an area of six and a half acres. Running through the center of the main buildings is a row of cast iron columns, sixty in number, to which is attached the shafting, which is fifteen inches in diameter, and arranged as a continuous pulley for driving the machines as close together as possible, only allowing sufficient space to get around and work them. The motive power is supplied by five different engines, having an aggregate of nine hundred horse power. One of them was built in Providence, Rhode Island—others by Woodruff & Beach of Hartford.

Within these buildings there are fifteen hundred machines, the majority of which were both invented and constructed on the premises. Every part of a Pistol or Rifle is made by machinery, and being made to a gauge, is an exact counterpart of every other piece for the same purpose. Even all the various parts of the lock are made by machinery, each having its relative initial point to work from, and on the correctness of which the perfection depends. Taking the lock frame for instance, they commence by fixing the center, and drilling and tapping the base for receiving the arbor or breech-pin, which has been previously prepared—the helical ground cut in it and the lower end screwed—once grasped is firmly fixed in its position, furnishing a definite point from which all the operations are performed and to which all the other parts bear relation. The facing and hollowing of the recoil shield and frame, the cutting and sinking of the central recesses, the cutting out all the grooves and orifices, planing the several flat surfaces and shaping the curved parts, prepare the frames for being introduced between hard steel clamps, through which all the holes are drilled, bored, and tapped, for the various screws; so that, after passing through thirty-three distinct operations, and the little hand finishing required in removing the

Figure 2

Vertical drop hammer designed and patented by Elisha K. Root (U.S. Patent No. 9,941, issued 16 August 1853). Drop hammers were used to forge iron and steel billets into rough forgings for barrels, cylinders, frames, and other revolver parts. Museum of Connecticut History (2000.494.03).

burr from the edges, the lock frame is ready for the inspector. The rotating chambered cylinder is turned out of cast-steel bars, manufactured expressly for the purpose. The machines, after getting them the desired length, drill center holes, square up ends, turn for ratchet, drill partitions, tap for nipples, cut pins for hammer-rest and ratchet, and screw in nipples. In all there are thirty-six separate operations before the cylinder is ready to follow the lock-frame to the inspector. In the same manner the barrel, forged solidly from a bar of cast steel, is bored and completed to caliber, and is then submitted to the various operations of planning, grooving the lower projection beneath the barrel, with which the base pin is ultimately connected, tapped, and then rifled. The barrel goes through forty-five separate operations on the machines. The other parts are subject to about the following number: lever, twenty-seven; rammer, nineteen; hammer, twenty-eight; hand, twenty; trigger, twenty-one; bolt, twenty-one; key, eighteen; lear spring, twelve; fourteen screws, seven each, ninety-eight; six cones, eight each, forty-eight; guard, eighteen; handle-strap, five; stock-five.

Besides the exactness and uniformity which are arrived at by the adaptation of machinery, there is additional security in the minuteness of inspection to which each weapon is subjected. As soon as completed and before being polished, the different parts are carried to the Inspectors or Assembling Department, and there undergo a rigid examination. The tools to inspect a cylinder, for example, are fifteen in number, each of which must gauge to a hair so great is the nicety observed, and on finishing his examination the inspector punches his initial letter on the piece inspected, thus pledging his reputation on its quality. Again, after the different parts have been finished, they are once more carried to the assembling room, and each chamber is loaded with the largest charge possible and practically tested by firing; after which they are wiped out by the prover and returned to the Inspection Department. The inspectors again take them apart, thoroughly oil and clean them, when they are for the last time put together and placed in a rack for the final inspection. The orders from the principals being perfection—the slightest blemish, a small scratch in the bluing or varnish,

Herbert G. Houze

Figure 3

Single spindle drill used for drilling a frame's recoil shield to receive the cylinder arbor or pin prior to its being placed in the frame jigging machine. Museum of Connecticut History (2002.431.09).

the immediate government, as prescribed by the code of rules laid down by the company. They number several hundred—some particular manufacturers requiring only their individual exertions, while others employ from one to forty assistants. Many of them are men of more than ordinary ability, some have been connected with the concern since it was first established, and have rendered themselves pecuniarily comfortable by their extertions.[1]

is sufficient to prevent the arm passing this final inspection. But if passed, it is to the store room and prepared, and then transferred to the wareroom and is now ready for the market. . . .

The Company at the present time [1863] are turning out about 250 rifled muskets and the same number of revolving pistols, besides a considerable number of revolving rifles and shotguns. They make forty-four different styles of pistols, six different patterns, eleven different lengths, and twenty-seven different finishes. Of rifles they make three different calibers and five different lengths. . . .

Besides Arms they also manufacture Bullet Moulds, Powder Flasks, and other accoutrements; and they have a separate factory for the production of Metallic Foil Cartridges, a contrivance invented by Col. Colt, that always insures "dry powder" to the possessor. They employ about 1500 persons, to whom they pay monthly over $80,000, or nearly a million dollars a year. Almost the entire manual labor of the establishment is performed by contract. The contractors are furnished room, power, material, heat, light—while they furnish muscle and skill—themselves and subordinates being all subject to

Although the author of this description, J. Leander Bishop, attributed a great deal of the factory's success to Elisha K. Root, whom he described as "one of the most accomplished mechanics of the age," he specifically mentions Root only for his drop hammer forges.[2] As the glass-plate images reproduced on the following pages demonstrate (figs. 2–16), Root's contributions to the development of specialized machinery were far broader. Indeed, had it not been for Root's inventive genius, Colt's dream of mass production would never have been realized.

Very little is known about the glass-plate negatives themselves. They were acquired by the Museum of Connecticut History from two different sources and are unmarked as to authorship and also undated. Nonetheless, the machinery depicted may allow the images to be dated to approximately 1857, or perhaps even earlier.[3]

Sadly, two years after the death of Samuel Colt, a substantial portion of his magnificent South Meadow armory was destroyed by fire on 4 February 1864 (figs. 17–19). Elizabeth Colt honored her husband's legacy and rebuilt the factory during the Civil War, completing the larger armory in 1867.

Figure 4

Revolver frame jigging machine designed and patented by Samuel Colt (English Patent No. 861, issued 12 April 1854). By using the various tool heads on this machine, all the exterior and interior surfaces of a frame could be cut in succession. The hub is engraved "Col. Saml. Colt Hartford, Ct." Museum of Connecticut History (2002.431.01).

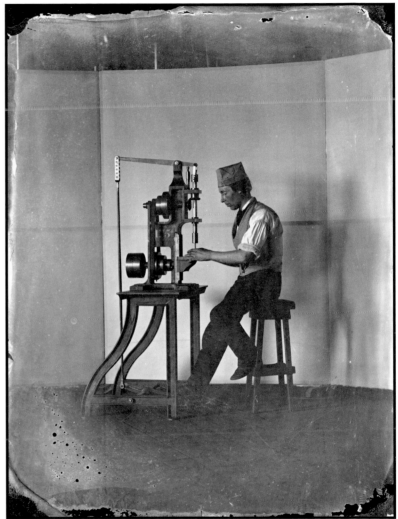

Figure 5 (left)
Milling machine believed to have been used to taper the sides of a revolver's frame. Museum of Connecticut History (2002.431.02).

Figure 6 (below)
Single spindle drill most likely used for drilling screw holes in a revolver's frame. Museum of Connecticut History (2000.494.04).

Figure 7
Cylinder shaping machine used to drill an arbor hole and to cut the ratchet teeth at the rear of the cylinder. Museum of Connecticut History (2002.431.03).

Figure 8

Cylinder boring machine designed and patented by Elisha K. Root (U.S. Patent No. 12,002, issued 28 November 1854). The arrangement of the drills allowed each chamber to be drilled in succession without moving the cylinder from its locking fixture. Museum of Connecticut History (2002.431.08).

Figure 9

Circular saw cutoff machine believed to have been used to cut barrel forgings to a desired length for further work. Museum of Connecticut History (2002.431.04).

Figure 10
Slide lathe used to cut the external flat planes of a barrel forging. Museum of Connecticut History (2000.494.05).

Figure 11 (far left)
Pistol barrel boring machine. Museum of Connecticut History (2002.431.06).

Figure 12 (left)
Deburring machines used to remove burrs and sharp edges from the components of various pistols prior to their being sent to the polishing shop. Museum of Connecticut History (2000.494.02).

Figure 13

Large slide lathe used to cut the external flats on rifle barrels. Museum of Connecticut History (2002.431.07).

Figure 14

Universal milling machine used for cutting and shaping small parts. Museum of Connecticut History (2000.494.06).

Figure 15

Large slotting machine made by the Lowell Machine Shop of Lowell, Mass. It is likely that this machine was used in making the specialized tools and fixtures needed to manufacture revolvers. Museum of Connecticut History (2000.494.01).

Figure 16

Vertical shaping machine possibly
used in cutting the ends of trigger
guards and backstraps. Museum of
Connecticut History (2002.431.05).

Figure 17 (above left)
Front exterior wall and corner office of the Colt factory following the fire of 4 February 1864. Wadsworth Atheneum Museum of Art.

Figure 18 (above right)
Interior view of the front gallery of the Colt factory following the fire of 4 February 1864. Wadsworth Atheneum Museum of Art.

Figure 19 (left)
Mass of fused revolver parts recovered from the Colt factory after the fire of 4 February 1864. Wadsworth Atheneum Museum of Art.

Notes

1. J. Leander Bishop, *A History of American Manufacture from 1608 to 1860 comprising annals of the industry of the United States in machinery, manufactures and useful arts, with a notice of the important inventions, tariffs, and the results of each decennial census* (Philadelphia and London: E. Young, 1864), II, 739–40. The introductory text of this description is drawn almost verbatim from "A Day at the Armory of 'Colt's Patent Fire-Arms Manufacturing Company,'" *United States Magazine* IV, no. 3 (March 1857): 233.

2. Bishop, *History of American Manufacture,* II, 741.

3. The cleanliness of the machinery suggests that the photographs were taken shortly after their installation. Furthermore, all of the tooling is of a type used to make percussion cap revolvers and rifles. Dean Nelson, director of the Museum of Connecticut History, has noted that one of the workmen shown bears a close resemblance to a worker illustrated in the line engravings used to illustrate "A Day at the Armory." Given Samuel Colt's avid interest in photography, it is a tempting possibility that he might have taken the photographs himself. Support for this attribution is to be found in the inventory of Samuel Colt's personal property that was drawn up for probate purposes in May 1862. Included among the material valued at the South Meadows armory is the following entry:

Photographic Apparatus—

1 Large New Camera consisting of tube box 2 plate holders, & 2 camera stands	125-
1 Quarter size Camera & fixtures as above	20-
1 Photographic Tent & fixtures	50-
1 Printing frame	3-
13 Sheets Albumen paper	1.30
59 Sheets common paper.	1.18
2 Rubber pans.	8-
4 Glass funnels.	1.50
1 Porcelian Bath 14 x 17 inches	4.50
1 Gutter Percha do. 18 x 20	6-
1 Small Scales & weights	75
1 Lot Chemicals & small articles	15-
2 China Platters	1-
3 Graduated Glasses	1.50 238.73

(W. N. H. Morgan, D. M. Seymour, and William B. Ely, "Inventory and Appraisement Of the Estate of the late Col. Samuel Colt Of Hartford Conn.," 20 May 1862, 24–25. Samuel Colt Papers, Box 11, File 5, Connecticut Historical Society.)

Samuel Colt and the World

It would not be an exaggeration to say that by 1860 Samuel Colt was the personification of an American in many parts of the world. Not only had he established wide and varied personal relationships, but also his incessant promotional efforts had indelibly linked his name to the revolvers he manufactured. Even if people did not know Colt the man, they knew of the Colt revolver.

The process of establishing name recognition for his arms began during the Paterson period. Through a series of carefully calculated presentations, Colt introduced his revolvers to parts of the world where they might find a viable market. The ethnicity, language, and religion of those regions were of little importance to Colt. What mattered were sales. Consequently, revolvers were given as freely to British and European officials as to those residing in the Arabian Peninsula, North Africa, the Ottoman Empire, Russia, and elsewhere. After Colt became successful, in 1848, this method of establishing relationships with individuals in positions of influence or power was intensified. While in most instances Colt did not disturb the status

quo, his republican principles did come to the fore on more than one occasion. He openly voiced his support for Louis Kossuth's efforts to establish an independent Hungarian state and later provided the arms Giuseppe Garibaldi needed in his campaigns to unify Italy. Colt did not, however, let his personal inclinations interfere with business decisions. At the same time that he was expressing support for Kossuth, he negotiated a manufacturing agreement with the Austro-Hungarian government. Similarly, during the Crimean War he sold arms to both Great Britain and Russia.

Colt's success as the world's first international arms dealer cannot be attributed solely to his own character. He recognized that as a foreigner his contacts in many countries would be limited. Consequently, where needed, he hired local men of finance or the law to act as his representatives. This network of agents was to prove indispensable to Colt in securing foreign contracts, as well as the patents he needed to protect his interests.

In many respects, the world's impression of Colt was reflected in the gifts, honors, and letters he received from abroad. Colt was immensely proud of these tokens of recognition and carefully preserved them. The arms he received were kept at his office in the South Meadows armory, and the more decorative items were displayed at his home, Armsmear, in a Cabinet of Presents in the music room. He apparently kept special correspondence separate from his general files, as these letters later formed part of Elizabeth Hart Jarvis Colt's bequest to the Wadsworth Atheneum Museum of Art.

To place these items in their proper context, they will be discussed by country of origin, accompanied by descriptions of Colt's activities in each region.

England

This country was the site of one of Samuel Colt's greatest triumphs and most embarrassing failures. The triumph was his selection in 1852 as the recipient of the Telford Premium Medal, awarded annually. The failure was his somewhat ill-conceived decision to establish an armory in London.

Following the successful debut of his revolvers at the Great Exhibition of the Works of Art & Industry of All Nations in 1851 (fig. 1),[1] Colt began an intense campaign to secure the adoption of his arms by Great Britain's land and sea forces. Using the techniques that had proved so successful in

Figure 1

Illustration of Samuel Colt's display at the Exhibition of the Works of Art & Industry of all Nations in London, published in the *Illustrated London News,* November 1851. Wadsworth Atheneum Museum of Art.

the United States, he distributed revolvers as presents and entertained anyone who might prove useful to his endeavors.[2] Initially these efforts appeared to hold considerable promise, and Colt decided to establish an arms factory in London to meet the anticipated demand. Opened in 1853, the new works produced Belt, Holster, and Pocket Pistols following the designs then made in Hartford.[3] The British government eventually purchased over 23,000 Belt Pistol revolvers from Colt, but those orders were not sufficient to sustain the London armory's operation.[4] As a result, the armory ceased operation in late 1856.[5]

Despite that setback, being awarded the Telford Premium Medal more than made up for the failure of the London armory. Then, as today, the Telford Medal was the highest accolade an engineer or inventor could receive, signifying recognition of the recipient's contributions to industry or design. Its value, therefore, was incalculable. It is no wonder that Samuel Colt prized this medal above all of the other awards he won between 1837 and 1861.

Reverse

Notes

1. *Official descriptive and illustrated Catalogue of the great Exhibition* (London: William Clowes & Sons, 1851), III, 1454.

2. Among those whose letters of appreciation are preserved in the Samuel Colt Correspondence at the Wadsworth Atheneum Museum of Art are the Earl of Granville, Viscount Palmerston, and Lord John Russell (24 December 1851, 6 January 1852, and 23 December 1851, respectively).

3. *New York Daily Times*, "COLT'S PISTOL MANUFACTORY IN LONDON," 2 December 1853, 8.

4. Joseph G. Rosa, *Colonel Colt, London: The History of Colt's London Firearms, 1851–1857* (London: Arms & Armour Press, 1976), 134.

5. Ibid., 101–3.

127

Institution of Civil Engineers Telford Premium Medal, 1852

"Colonel Samuel Colt, Assoc. Inst. C.E."

William Wyon

Silver

Diameter 2¼ in.

Wadsworth Atheneum Museum of Art

Bequest of Elizabeth Hart Jarvis Colt, 1905.1515

Named in honor of the Institution of Civil Engineers' founding president, Thomas Telford, this award was established in 1835. Among those who have received the medal are Sir Henry Bessemer, who developed an improved method for producing steel; Sir John Fowler, who designed the Firth of Forth Bridge; Sir Robert Harvey, the developer of a system to manufacture iodine; and Osborne Reynolds, who established the field of hydrodynamics. Colt's receipt of the award demonstrated that he had made material improvements not only to firearms but also to their production.

France

The surviving correspondence makes it difficult to gauge Colt's feelings toward France. Certainly he was interested in securing and protecting the patents he held there, but beyond that his involvement was minimal.

In early 1851 he tried to establish rapport with Louis Napoleon Bonaparte (later to become Napoleon III) through the usual method of presenting a cased set of revolvers. The gift was received with polite diffidence, and Colt did not pursue the matter.[1] Four years later, in 1855, when Colt displayed his arms at the Exposition Universelle, they elicited a mixed response. While his invention was described and praised in great detail in the exposition's official album published two years after the event,[2] he was awarded only the third-level prize, the silver *Médaille de 1er classe* (cat. 69).[3]

In general, it appears that the French regarded Colt's inventions with some antipathy, which is reflected in the views expressed in a report published in 1858 by that nation's official commission to the London exhibition of 1851.

> Fabrication des revolveurs.
>
> Cette industrie a pris naissance dans l'Etat du Connecticut. À l'Exposition de 1851, M. Samuel Colt avait envoyé de la ville de Hartford ses célèbres pistolets.... Ces pistolets, qu'on donné aux troupes légères des Etats-Unis, ont rendu de grands services dans les deux invasions du Texas at du Mexique. Les américains confectionnent aussi des carabines d'après le même principe. Comme on abuse de tout, les flibustiers, les voyageurs et les amis de la violence portent avec eux des revolveurs, même dans les villes paisibles; sous le plus léger prétexte, ils s'entretuent avec un acharnement incroyable. Les nouveaux Etats, le Texas, la Louisiane et surtout la Californie, se signalent par la fréquence et la férocité de ces attentats.

> The Manufacture of Revolvers
>
> This industry had its birth in the State of Connecticut. At the exposition of 1851, Mr. Samuel Colt sent his celebrated pistols from the city of Hartford.... These pistols, which are issued to the mounted troops of the United States, have done great service in the two invasions of Texas and Mexico. The Americans have also built carbines on the same principle. Since then they have been abused by all; filibusters, travelers, and friends of violence carry revolvers with them, the same in peaceful towns; under the slightest pretext they kill each other with an incredible fury. The new States, Texas, Louisiana, and above all, California, are signaled out by the frequency and ferocity of these assaults.[4]

Given this attitude, it is not surprising that Samuel Colt never pursued entering the French market, nor did he extend his usual largesse to French officials.[5]

Notes

1. Varedllior (?) to Samuel Colt, 1 February 1851. Samuel Colt Papers, Box 11, File 1, Connecticut Historical Society.

2. Baron Leon Brisse, *Album de L'Exposition Universelle dédié à S. A. I. Le Prince Napoleon* (Paris: Bureaux de l'Abeille Imperiale, 1857), II, 457–59.

3. *Exposition Universelle de 1855. Rapports du Jury Mixte Internationale* (Paris: Imprimerie Imperiale, 1856), I, 53. The order of awards at this exposition was as follows: *Grande médaille d'honneur* (gold), *Médaille d'honneur* (gold), *Médaille de 1er classe* (silver), *Médaille de 2ème classe* (bronze), and *Mention honorable*.

4. *Exposition Universelle de 1851. Travaux de la Commission Française sur l'Industrie des Nations publiés par Ordre de l'Empereur* (Paris: Imprimerie Imperiale, 1858), I, 493.

5. Aside from the pistols given to Louis Napoleon Bonaparte, during the 1850s Colt made a presentation to Field Marshal Pelletier, commander-in-chief of the French Army of the Orient in the Crimea (A. Deussin to Samuel Colt, 20 August 1855. Samuel Colt Correspondence, Wadsworth Atheneum Museum of Art, Bequest of Elizabeth Hart Jarvis Colt). Even then, the presentation was made through an intermediary, the Duke of Newcastle (Newcastle to Samuel Colt, 18 August 1855. Ibid.).

Hungary

Although Hungary existed as an independent state for only a few brief months in 1849, its president, Kossuth Lajos, known in the English-speaking world as Louis Kossuth, was lionized in the American press as both a liberator and a true republican. Kossuth's dreams for national self-determination were crushed when Russia sent troops to restore Hungary to Austria. Following the defeat of the republican forces at Vilagos in August 1849, Kossuth and other nationalists fled to the Ottoman Empire (present-day Turkey), where they were granted asylum. Austria and Russia were aware that the eloquent Kossuth remained a threat to the region's stability and immediately pressured the sultan to surrender him, as well as his compatriots.

In Europe Kossuth's predicament was viewed with mixed emotions.

Individuals praised him, while their governments maintained a discreet silence. A similar situation existed in the United States, at least within the State Department, prompting Samuel Colt and fourteen others to petition Dabney S. Carr, American minister to the Sublime Porte in Constantinople, to demand that he voice support for Kossuth's continued safety. The missive, dated 22 September 1849, was not softly worded, and Colt's signature on it indicates that he fervently supported the Hungarians' cause.

Dear Sir

Your fellow citizens Americans in Paris, are filled with indignation and amazement at the attempt now making by the Russian and Austrian governments to destroy in cold blood the heroes of the revolution in Hungary.

The persons of Kossuth, Been and Dembriski and their companions of all nations are sacred on the neutral ground of Turkey by every law human and divine. To surrender these patriots to the brutal demands of their persecutors would be a cowardly concession and lasting disgrace to any country—and we are rejoiced to see through the press that the Porte has adopted that honourable course which meets the applause of civilized countries and which will adorn the brightest pages of her history.

We just learn that the Sultan has replied in the negative to Russia as well as to Austria, although he had been threatened with hostilities in case of refusal—It is all important that this firm attitude of dignity and hospitality should be maintained, and the safety of the illustrious men in question should be placed out of doubt—that their protector should continue to be able and willing to preserve the rights belonging to neutral powers. . . .

The preservation of Kossuth and his friends who have been crushed in their struggle for republican independence is peculiarly the task of an American Minister—The chief of the proposed victims has emulated the example of our Washington by his deeds and character, and his companions in counsel and in arms are made by their sacrifices worthy of a place by the side of the heroes of our own revolution—Kossuth and many of the others had already lost their health in the great cause of human liberty, and if delivered up to the tyrants who have savaged their country and on the very hearths and alters perpetrated every cruelty and sacrilage [sic] they must die of imprisonment alone. It is not impossible that the cord would be ruthlessly applied to him without delay in order to insure his destruction—and that a similar fate or the worse terrors of a Siberian exile would overtake the rest. . . .

We feel it our duty to address you in advance of the government and masses at home, as the crisis admits of no delay—if you have acted we desire to sustain you, as we feel sure that you will have responded to the impulses of the great American heart by encouraging the Sultan with every possible assurance that the United States has the power, and will sustain him.[1]

Two years later Washington finally demonstrated its support in a tangible manner. President Millard Fillmore ordered the USS *Mississippi* to Constantinople to transport Kossuth and other Hungarian émigrés to England and the United States. After a brief stay in England, Kossuth traveled to the United States in December 1851, and for the next eight months he toured the country giving speeches.[2]

Samuel Colt's hope that Kossuth would visit Hartford was not realized. In 1853 Colt did meet Kossuth in London after presenting him with a pair of revolvers.[3] Colt had intended to have the pistols presented to Kossuth by a committee of his Hartford employees, but that not being possible, Colt delivered them with a note stating in part that he hoped "that even at this late day, they will not prove unacceptable and will be received with the same feelings of good will, with which they are sent."[4]

Kossuth's letter of thanks is of particular interest in that he viewed the present as being of "triple value," specifically, "that of your valuable sympathy, that of artistic-mechanical merit, and that of practical use."[5]

Notes

1. W. M. Corey, G. N. Landers, and S. Colt to Dabney S. Carr, 22 September 1849. Samuel Colt Papers, Box 6, Connecticut Historical Society.

2. Kossuth arrived at New York City on 4 December 1851 and returned to England on 14 July 1852.

3. These pistols—a Belt Pistol (serial no. 201) and a Pocket Pistol (serial no. 31059)—

Figure 2

A. Grepper, *Giuseppe Garibaldi*, lithograph, ca. 1859, published by E. Gambert & Company. Wadsworth Atheneum Museum of Art.

Italy

One of the lesser-known aspects of Samuel Colt's life involves his participation in the unification of Italy. Though he did not personally take part in those events, he was instrumental in their success.

Shortly after Victor Emmanuel II, king of Sardinia, commenced military operations to free northern Italy from Austrian domination in early 1859, Colt's London agent, Charles F. Dennett, began selling arms to the Sardinians. While these sales were modest in number,[1] they prompted the Italian Committee of New York to seek Samuel Colt's direct assistance. A delegation led by Giovanelli Albinola visited Hartford on 4 December 1859 to press the Italian cause. Realizing that support for Giuseppe Garibaldi's forces would be in his interest, given the positive press that would ensue, Colt gave the Italian Committee one hundred Colt revolvers, rifles, and carbines.[2] Aside from gaining publicity, he also hoped that the gift would prompt the kingdom of Sardinia to purchase a substantial number of percussion rifled muskets that he had originally made for the Russian government in 1854.[3] Following Garibaldi's conquest of Sicily in early 1860, this hope was fulfilled. In anticipation of an invasion of lower Italy, Garibaldi purchased 23,500 Colt Rifled Muskets at a cost of almost $160,000.[4] Colt's support for Garibaldi was to take a different form immediately following this sale, as he personally forgave $30,000 of the purchase price.[5]

Although the total unification of Italy was not achieved until 1870, Colt firearms played a significant role during the preliminary period. In recognition of the part he played, Colt received a personal letter of thanks from Garibaldi for the arms presented on 4 December 1859,[6] as well as a gold medal from Victor Emmanuel II. The latter was apparently given to Colt's aide, Maj. William H. B. Hartley, when he was in Italy with Giovanelli Albinola in August 1860. Upon Hartley's return to Hartford, he personally delivered the medal to Colt sometime between the 8 and 15 October 1860 (fig. 2).[7]

are preserved in the collections of the Hungarian National Museum (Ferenc Temesvary, *Pistolen Feuerwaffen des Ungarischen Nationalmuseums I* [Budapest: Akademai Kiado, 1988], no. 993, 470–71, pl. XCII). Both revolvers are engraved and have backstraps inscribed as follows: "*Govr Kossuth FROM Col. Colt*" (no. 301) and "*To Govr Kossuth from the Inventor*" (no. 31059). While the pistols were described by Colt as having been made in Hartford, the serial number and London proof marks found on the Belt Pistol indicate that it was assembled at the London factory from parts Colt had shipped to England.

4. Samuel Colt to Louis Kossuth, 20 March 1853. Samuel Colt Correspondence, Wadsworth Atheneum Museum of Art, Bequest of Elizabeth Hart Jarvis Colt.

5. Louis Kossuth to Samuel Colt, 27 March 1853. Samuel Colt Correspondence, Wadsworth Atheneum Museum of Art, Bequest of Elizabeth Hart Jarvis Colt.

Notes

1. Invoices for those sales, as well as others made from Fratelli Lollini of Bologna, reproduced by Enrico G. Arrigoni in *Le Colt di Garibaldi* (Milan: Il Grifo, 2000), 96–113, list approximately 450 Colt firearms.

2. The gift consisted of sixty Holster Pistols, thirty Belt Pistols, two Belt Pistols with shoulder stocks (one having a canteen), two Holster Pistols with shoulder stocks (one having a canteen), four carbines, and two rifles of .56 caliber ("Arms presented to the Italian Cause by Col Sam Colt–December, 1859-," Bill of Lading, n.d., reproduced in facsimile in Arrigoni, *Le Colt di Garibaldi,* 116).

3. Herbert G. Houze, *Colt Rifles & Muskets from 1847 to 1870* (Iola, Wis.: Krause Publications, 1996), 44–56. The Russian government had taken delivery of some rifled muskets, but further shipments were canceled at the end of the Crimean War.

4. Colt's Patent Firearms Depot, London, to the Sicilian government, Invoice, 30 July 1860 (reproduced in facsimile in Arrigoni, *Le Colt di Garibaldi,* 118). The price for the 23,500 Rifled Muskets is cited in this invoice as 31,960 pounds sterling. At the rate of exchange then in effect, this would equal $159,800.

5. The net deposit credited to the Colt company's account at Baring Brothers in London for the Rifled Muskets sold to Garibaldi was $127,992.08 (Colt's Patent Fire Arms Manufacturing Company, Account Ledger A, 466, D. Donnelly Collection).

6. Giuseppe Garibaldi to Samuel Colt, 15 January 1860. Samuel Colt Correspondence, Wadsworth Atheneum Museum of Art, Bequest of Elizabeth Hart Jarvis Colt.

7. Both the date of Hartley's return and the first mention of Colt's receiving the medal are noted in the Jarvis correspondence (William Jarvis to William Jarvis, Jr., 8 and 15 October 1860. William Jarvis Letters, MSS Coll. 70425, Connecticut Historical Society). During Hartley's visit to Italy he presented Victor Emmanuel with a cased pair of revolvers that Samuel Colt had specially prepared for the king (Samuel Colt to William B. Hartley, 15 July 1860. Records of the Colt's Patent Fire Arms Manufacturing Company, RG 103, Business Records, Series II, Outgoing Correspondence, Box 6, Connecticut State Library).

Reverse

128

Victor Emanuel Portrait Gold Medal, 1860

Italian

G. Galeazzi

Diameter 1⅞ in.

Wadsworth Atheneum Museum of Art

Bequest of Elizabeth Hart Jarvis Colt, 1905.1577

Prussia

In May 1856 Samuel Colt's agent in Berlin, C. F. Wappenhans, presented the king of Prussia, Friedrich Wilhelm IV, with a cased and engraved Belt Pistol.[1] He made similar presentations to the crown prince of Prussia, Friedrich Wilhelm, and to Prince Adalbert, commander-in-chief of the Prussian Navy.[2] The purpose of these gifts would seem to be related to Colt's attempts to secure the adoption of his Belt Pistol by the Prussian Navy, but in fact they were an overt attempt to influence the outcome of other events. Colt's primary aim was to secure the release of over three thousand Belt Pistols that had been seized by Prussian customs agents in August 1855.

Shortly after the outbreak of the Crimean War, involving Great Britain, France, Turkey, and Russia, the Prussian government closed its borders to arms shipments destined for any of the belligerents. While this closure had little effect on Britain or France, it had a profound impact upon Russia's ability to import arms from western Europe or the United States because the most economical and the fastest delivery route for goods from those sources was overland through Prussia.[3]

It was a particular annoyance to Colt, as he had just sold the Russians a large number of revolvers that needed to be speedily delivered. Whether at his order or someone else's (which seems more likely), the decision was made to ship these arms through Prussia hidden in bales of cotton.[4] The ruse unfortunately failed, and its discovery was a source of considerable public embarrassment for Colt, who at the same time was selling the British similar weapons.[5]

Colt's immediate concern was not about protecting his good name; he was more interested in protecting his substantial investment in the seized shipment. To secure the release of the impounded pistols, Wappenhans was instructed to begin a lobbying campaign stressing Colt's ignorance of the shipping details.[6] He was also to report any moves that the Prussian government might make concerning the arms' disposition.[7] When it became evident that the Prussians were in no hurry to settle the matter, Colt attempted to enlist the aid of Friedrich Wilhelm IV. His efforts resulted only in a gift from the king of some Prussian military weapons.[8]

Colt's long-term goals—the release of the 3,480 revolvers from customs impoundment and the adoption of his pistols for service by the Prussian Army or Navy—were ultimately realized, though not entirely in a manner he had hoped for. After over two years of administrative delays, the Prussian Bureau of Customs announced it would sell the arms at public auction, with the minimum acceptable bid set at the cost of the duty and fine that were due, plus interest and storage fees.[9] Neither the exact circumstances of this auction nor the identity of the successful bidder are presently known. The subsequent issuance of Colt Belt Pistols to officers and noncommissioned officers of the Prussian Navy suggests that the seized revolvers were purchased by the government.[10]

Notes

1. C. F. Wappenhans to Samuel Colt, 14 May 1856. Samuel Colt Papers, Box 7, Connecticut Historical Society.

2. Ibid.

3. The best alternate route by sea through the Baltic was somewhat problematic because of a blockade by an Anglo-French fleet.

4. It is believed that the decision to ship the 3,480 Belt Pistols in cotton bales was made by Colt's brother, James B. Colt, and that this was the cause of the subsequent enmity between the two men.

5. The first mention of the seizure appeared in the *Times* of London prior to 24 August 1855 (Col. Luther P. Sargeant to Samuel Colt, 24 August 1855 [attached clipping]. Records of the Colt's Patent Fire Arms Manufacturing Company, RG 103, Business File, Series III, Incoming Correspondence, Box 10, Connecticut State Library).

6. Typical of Colt's protestations of innocence are those contained in his letter of 22 May 1857 to C. F. Wappenhans: "can only hope the Prusion Government will at some future day in some way compensate me for this hevey loss for which I am in no ways to blame" (Samuel Colt to C. F. Wappenhans, 22 May 1857. Samuel Colt Papers, Box 7, Connecticut Historical Society).

7. Colt continued to press his European representatives regarding this matter well into 1857 (e.g., Samuel Colt to Charles Caesar, 19 September 1857. Samuel Colt Papers, Box 7, Connecticut Historical Society).

8. The suite consisted of a musket, the rifle described herein, a pistol, a heavy cavalry sword, light cavalry sword, and infantry cutlass (C. F. Wappenhans to Samuel Colt, 14 May 1856).

9. Col. Luther P. Sargeant to Samuel Colt, [?] December 1857. Samuel Colt Papers, Box 11, File 1, Connecticut Historical Society.

10. Colt Belt Pistols with "KM" markings have been the subject of considerable debate and speculation for the past forty years. Initially they were identified as having been issued to the Austrian Navy, then to the Prussian Navy. The marking itself can be read as either *Kaiserliche Marine* (Imperial Navy, as in Austria), *Koenigliche Marine* (Royal Navy, as in Prussia), or *Kriegsmarine* (war navy). Although the latter is the identification cited most often, it is the least likely because it was generally used at a later date. With respect to the sale, it may not have taken place until after Colt's death, as Colt revolvers were not introduced into Prussian service until 1863 (*Allgemeine Militar-Zeitung,* "Preussen," 38, no. 32 [1863], 255).

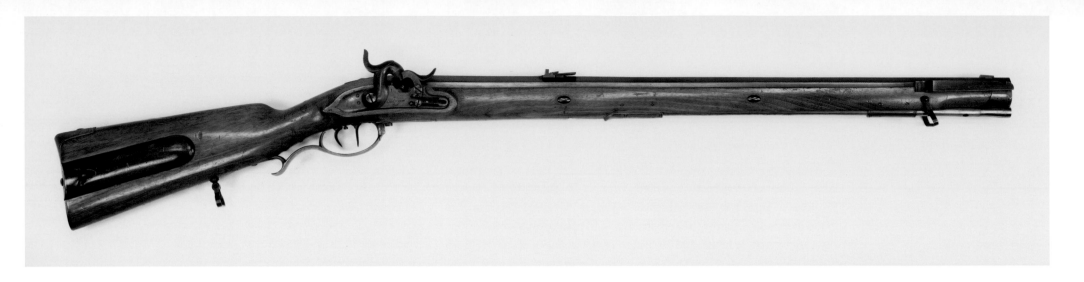

129

Prussian Model 1835 Jagerbusche

Potsdam

No serial number

Caliber .56 in., barrel length 28¾ in., overall length 44⅝ in.

Date of Manufacture: 1849/1855

Wadsworth Atheneum Museum of Art

Bequest of Elizabeth Hart Jarvis Colt, 1905.1020

Markings

Lockplate: Potsdam / G.S.

Sideplate: 1849

Barrel: 1855

1861 Inventory of Colonel Colt's Small Office

Page 4, line 22

English Rifle (1849) short & very heavy Brass mounted

This rifle, together with a percussion Model 1850 Cavalry Pistol, a needle-fire rifle, and a standard percussion infantry musket, was presented to Samuel Colt by Friedrich Wilhelm IV in May 1856.[1] The cavalry pistol and needle-fire rifle are now preserved in the Colt Collection of the Museum of Connecticut History (inv. nos. 208 and 3, respectively). The disposition of the infantry musket is unknown.

The Model 1835 Jagerbusche was considered one of the finest percussion military rifles issued to European troops between 1835 and 1860.[2] As a safety precaution, the lock is fitted with a pivoted guard that may be flipped rearward to prevent the hammer from coming into contact with the nipple when a percussion cap is in place. Originally the rifle was probably fitted with a saber bayonet.

Detail of lockplate area

Notes

1. C. F. Wappenhans to Samuel Colt, 16 May 1856. Samuel Colt Papers, Box 7, Connecticut Historical Society.

2. Hans-Dieter Gotz, *Militargewehre und Pistolen der deutschen Staaten 1800–1870* (Stuttgart: Motorbuch Verlag, 1978), 167.

Russia

The most opulent of the gifts Samuel Colt received from abroad were those presented to him by Czars Alexander II and Nicholas I. The same can be said about his presentations to the Russian court. The mutual largesse reflected the desire of both parties to establish a beneficial relationship between Russia and the United States. Russia needed to modernize its armed forces, and Colt realized that the country's vast territories presented untold opportunities.

Herbert G. Houze

Colt's first contacts with the Russian court took place in 1840 or 1841, at which time he was not able to fully exploit those opportunities.[1] By the early 1850s, however, he was in a position to be of use to the Russian government. Shortly after the Crimean War began, in 1853, Colt evidently approached the Russian legation to the United States in Washington regarding the purchase of his revolvers.[2] This resulted in an invitation to Colt to visit the country in 1854. Accompanied by his attorney, Edward N. Dickerson, Colt traveled to Russia to meet with officials of the czar's army. Following preliminary meetings, Colt and Dickerson were given a private audience with Czar Nicholas I on 11 November 1854 at the Winter Palace in Gatchina.[3] Following these meetings, Colt received an immediate order for 5,000 Belt Pistols, and the Russian government began negotiations with him for the potential purchase of 25,000 percussion rifled muskets. Subsequently, Colt and Dickerson were each given diamond rings inlaid with the czar's monogram.[4]

Although a substantial number of the 5,000 Belt Pistols purchased by Russia were impounded by the Prussian government in August 1855, Colt shipped additional arms from the United States to Russia and completely made up the deficiencies.[5] In doing so, he greatly strengthened the bonds of friendship that had been established in 1854.

In 1856 Colt again visited Russia, though this trip was not directly related to business interests. While on his honeymoon, Colt and his wife, Elizabeth, were invited to attend the coronation of Alexander II in Saint Petersburg.[6] To avoid any appearance of impropriety due to his involvement with the Russian government, Colt was appointed an acting attaché to the American legation by Ambassador Thomas H. Seymour, the former governor of Connecticut. In honor of the occasion, the imperial mint distributed commemorative medals to those who had been in attendance, and Colt received a medal of the second degree (struck in silver).

Samuel Colt's final visit to Russia took place in the late summer of 1858. During this trip he presented suites of engraved arms to Czar Alexander II, as well as to his brothers, the Grand Dukes Constantine Nikolayevich, Mikhail Nikolayevich, and Nikolay Nikolayevich.[7] In return, Colt was presented with a gold and diamond-mounted snuffbox bearing the czar's monogram.[8]

The sumptuousness of all these gifts indicates the importance of Colt's relationship with Russia. Although Soviet-era historians belittled Colt's contributions to the industrialization of the Russian arms industry,[9] there is little doubt that he was instrumental in bringing it about. Machinery, tooling, and fixtures that had been made in Hartford were purchased in quantity for installation at the Russian armories in Izhevsk, Sestroretsk, and Tula.[10] This equipment ensured that Russia would be able to produce arms of modern design without relying upon imports that might be compromised during periods of war (as had happened in 1855).

Notes

1. This date is based on the presence of a Patent Arms Manufacturing Company Number 5 Holster Pistol bearing the serial number 346 in the Hermitage Museum (inv. no. 3.0.No5283), which was recorded in the *Catalogue descriptif, raisonné et systematique de l'Arsenal de Tsarskoye-Selo*, drawn up in the 1860s under the entry G.143. Its original ownership by Czar Nicholas I is inferred by the reference to the "Emperor of Russia" having a Colt patent pistol, which was given in John Ehlers's 1845 advertisement, reproduced on page 66.

2. It is likely that the diplomat involved in these early discussions was Waldemar de Bodisco, the son of the Russian ambassador and an attaché in his own right, who was the recipient of a presentation Belt Pistol (R. L. Wilson, *Samuel Colt Presents* [Hartford, Conn.: Wadsworth Atheneum, 1961], 115).

3. Leonid Tarassuk, *The 'Russian' Colts* (North Hollywood, Calif.: Beinfeld Publishing, 1979), 6. It is believed that Colt presented Nicholas I with a suite of gold-inlaid and engraved revolvers during this audience.

4. The rings were evidently sent to Colt and Dickerson in January 1855 (Prince Dalgarovsky to Samuel Colt, 27 January 1855. Samuel Colt Correspondence, Wadsworth Atheneum Museum of Art, Bequest of Elizabeth Hart Jarvis Colt). Court documents cited by Tarassuk (*The 'Russian' Colts*, 10–11) indicated the presentations were authorized on 7 and 8 November 1854.

5. Samuel Colt to Milton Joslin, 20 June 1856. Samuel Colt Papers, Box 7, Connecticut Historical Society.

6. It is apparent from Colt's Saint Petersburg correspondence that he was trying to conduct business in between all the fetes and parties (Samuel Colt to Milton Joslin, 3 September 1856. Samuel Colt Papers, Box 7, Connecticut Historical Society).

7. These arms are fully described in Tarassuk, *The 'Russian' Colts,* 15, 18–26.

8. M. de Adlerburg to Samuel Colt, 4 March 1859. Samuel Colt Correspondence, Wadsworth Atheneum Museum of Art, Gift of Mrs. E. Sanderson Cushman, Acc. No. 1964.455.

9. In some instances they were simply ignored. For example, the source of the tooling sent to the Izhevsk factory was not cited in its official history (A. A. Aleksandrov, *Izhevskii zavod: Nauchno-populiarnyi ocherk istorii zavoda* [Izhevsk: 1957], 57–61).

10. Quite apart from the machinery sold to Russia to produce arms of his own design, Colt also supplied the tooling necessary to manufacture Eugene Lefaucheux's revolvers at Tula (see p. 66).

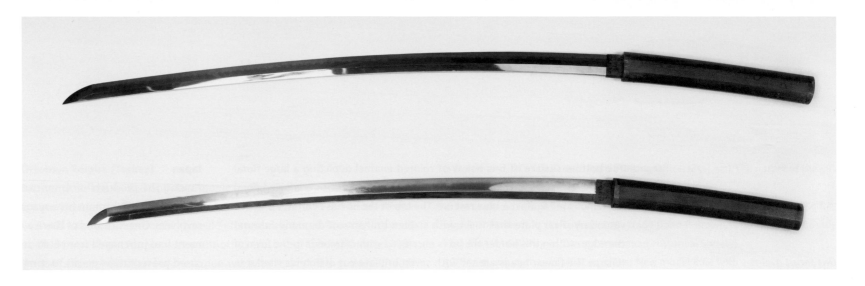

Notes

1. The requisitioned arms consisted of twenty-five Holster Pistols, fifty Belt Pistols, and twenty-five Pocket Pistols fitted with barrels of different lengths (Samuel Colt to C. Morris, 10 July 1852. Formerly in the James L. Mitchell Collection [Richard A. Bourne Co., Inc., *Antique Firearms and Related Items,* 17–18 March 1982, Lot 602]). The presentation pistols provided to Perry by Colt are mentioned in Perry's undated letter to Secretary of the Navy J. C. Dobbin (James Toucey to Samuel Colt [attachments], [?] May 1856. Records of the Colt's Patent Fire Arms Manufacturing Company, RG 103, Business File, Series III, Incoming Correspondence, Box 10, Connecticut State Library).

2. In his undated letter to Secretary of the Navy J. C. Dobbin, cited above, Perry states: "Mr. Colt placed in my hands for presentation to whomsoever I might elect, more than a thousand dollars worth of his patented pistols and each in a handsome case. Of these, besides other arms placed at my disposal by the Government, I presented a number to the Emperor and Princes of Japan."

3. John S. Cunningham to Samuel Colt, 7 March 1855. Samuel Colt Correspondence, Wadsworth Atheneum Museum of Art, Bequest of Elizabeth Hart Jarvis Colt, Acc. no. 1905.1491.

4. Ibid.

5. No evidence has yet been found as to who raised the questions or why the matter took so long to settle.

6. Samuel Colt to the Hon. James Toucey, 1 June 1856. Samuel Colt Papers, Box 7, Connecticut Historical Society.

7. A notice of Colt's meeting the Japanese embassy officials and presenting them with examples of his firearms was published in the *New York Times* ("From Washington . . . Our Japanese Visitors," 21 May 1860, 4).

8. W. N. H. Morgan, D. M. Seymour, and William B. Ely, "Inventory and Appraisement of the Estate of the late Col. Samuel Colt Of Hartford Conn.," 20 May 1862, 5. Samuel Colt Papers, Box 11, File 5, Connecticut Historical Society.

136 (above, top)
Katana Blade
Japanese
Ishido Unju Korekazu
Blade length 31³⁄₈ in., overall length 40¹⁄₂ in.
Date of Manufacture: August 1853
Wadsworth Atheneum Museum of Art
Bequest of Elizabeth Hart Jarvis Colt, 1905.1037

137 (above, bottom)
Katana Blade
Japanese
Takenaka Kunihiko
Blade length 29¹⁄₄ in., overall length 38 in.
Date of Manufacture: August 1853
Wadsworth Atheneum Museum of Art
Bequest of Elizabeth Hart Jarvis Colt, 1905.1042

1861 Inventory of Colonel Colt's Small Office
Page 10, line 22
2 Japanese 2 handed swords

For centuries Japanese sword blades have been highly valued for their strength, resilience, and beauty. Despite their severely plain form, these blades epitomize the art of the Japanese swordsmith during the mid-nineteenth century. The tang inscriptions identify them as the work of the Edo (Tokyo) artists Korekazu and Kunihiko. The secondary tang inscriptions (Kaei Rokunen Hachigatsu Hi) indicate that they were both made in August 1853. Ishido Unju Korekazu belonged to the seventh generation of the family who had founded

Details of tang markings for cats. 136 (left) and 137 (right)

the Ishido school of bladesmiths, and Takenaka Kunihiko of Bichu (presently the Okayama prefecture) studied under Inabanokami Toshi Yuki.

As noted in the preceding essay, both blades were given to Commodore Matthew Perry for presentation to Samuel Colt by the shogun, Tokugawa Yoshinobu, in 1854.

138 (below, top)
Matchlock Gun
Japanese
Caliber .75 in., barrel length 29⁷⁄₈ in., overall length 42³⁄₄ in.
Wadsworth Atheneum Museum of Art
Bequest of Elizabeth Hart Jarvis Colt, 1905.1018

139 (below, bottom)
Matchlock Gun
Japanese
Caliber .92 in., barrel length 29³⁄₈ in., overall length 42³⁄₄ in.
Wadsworth Atheneum Museum of Art
Bequest of Elizabeth Hart Jarvis Colt, 1905.1019

1861 Inventory of Colonel Colt's Small Office
Page 10, line 23
2 Japanese Guns -

Due to the isolationist policies adopted after 1639 by the Tokugawa shogunate, firearm design in Japan remained constant for more than two centuries. As a result, matchlock arms continued to be manufactured and used in the Japanese home islands. The two examples illustrated here, although made in 1854, are identical in form and construction to those produced during the late sixteenth century.[1] In contrast to Western-made arms, the barrels, locks, and other fittings are secured by pins instead of screws. Both pieces were presented to Colt by Tokugawa Yoshinobu in appreciation for the revolvers he and his court had received from Commodore Matthew C. Perry.

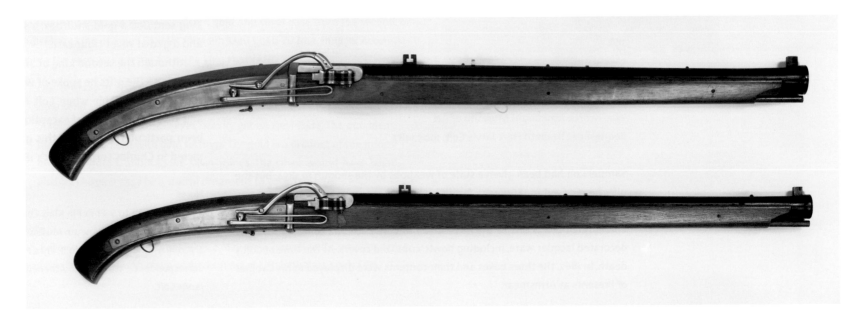

Epilogue: No New Thing Under the Sun

From the moment that Samuel Colt achieved some measure of success, detractors emerged to claim that he had stolen the idea for his revolver from them or someone else. During his lifetime the Darling Brothers of Massachusetts and Rhode Island, who had briefly made revolving pepperboxes, complained that the invention was theirs.[1] After Colt's death, John Pearson made the same claim, even though he did not become associated with Colt until well after the first prototypes had been made.[2]

Shortly before Samuel Colt's case against Hiram Terry and Edwin Leavitt was heard in New York City in October 1852, a Mr. Robb of Boston filed an affidavit in support of the defendants, swearing that Colt had surreptitiously removed a revolving matchlock gun from the Tower of London "to suppress it as evidence of the prior invention embodied in it."[3] Although Robb's allegations were easily quashed by Colt's attorney, Edward N. Dickerson, there was an element of truth in them.

Prior to presenting his lecture on revolving breech firearms to the Institution of Civil Engineers in 1851, Colt had visited the Tower of London to examine the early revolvers in its collection. During that visit he discovered that there was "no new thing under the sun."[4]

Made by an unknown Flemish or French gunmaker of the mid-seventeenth century, this flintlock fowling piece incorporated a cylinder turning mechanism that is remarkably similar to the one later refined by Colt. The flintlock cock is mounted on the inside of the lockplate so that its breast (the lower portion forward of the pivot point) could be fitted with a pawl. This pawl rose and fell in concert with the cock being drawn rearward or falling forward. In doing so, it successively engaged a cogwheel attached to the cylinder pin. As a result of this arrangement, the cylinder automatically turned a predetermined amount each time the cock was drawn back.

Although this created an effective revolver, the priming pans for each of the cylinder's chambers still needed to be charged with powder before the carbine could be fired. Nonetheless, the lock design was sufficiently similar to Colt's so that if its existence had become public knowledge, challenges to the inventor's 1835 English patent could have been filed and perhaps won. To prevent this from happening, Colt acquired the piece. Whether this was achieved by exchange or purchase is unknown; however, it most likely was not by theft, as Robb inferred.[5]

While Colt understandably did not discuss the piece in his 1851 lecture, he did not conceal its existence and origin. Consequently, when the inventory of his Large Office was drawn up in 1861, the compiler recorded that the piece had come from the Tower of London.[6]

Notes

1. Stuart C. Mowbray, *The Darling Pepperbox: The Story of Samuel Colt's Forgotten Competitors in Bellingham Mass. and Woonsocket, R.I.* (Lincoln, R.I.: Andrew Mowbray Inc., 2004), 89–92.
2. This claim was first put forward by Pearson in the 1880s.
3. "Colt's Revolvers," *New York Daily Times,* 13 October 1852, 6.
4. Ecclesiastes 1:9.
5. As the arms held at the Tower of London were Crown property, it is extremely unlikely that Colt would have stolen the piece, given the penalties and negative publicity that would have ensued. A more likely scenario involves his receiving it in exchange for samples of his own arms.
6. "In Col's Room," MSS Inventory [1861], VI, line 22. Records of the Colt's Patent Fire Arms Manufacturing Company, RG 103, Administrative File, Box 62, Connecticut State Library.

142

Flintlock Revolver
France or the Netherlands
Caliber .45 in., barrel length 31⅜ in., overall length 53 in.
Date of Manufacture: ca. 1640–50
Wadsworth Atheneum Museum of Art
Bequest of Elizabeth Hart Jarvis Colt, 1905.1031

1861 Inventory of Colonel Colt's Large Office
Page 6, line 22
1 Ancient Revolver Musket from Tower of London

Despite being exceptionally well made, this revolver is totally unmarked as to its place of manufacture or maker. Its construction, however, provides information that allows it to be attributed to a Flemish or French gunmaker of the 1640s.

The distinctive form of the butt stock, with its slab sides and swollen lower profile, is typical of longarms produced in northern France and the Low Countries

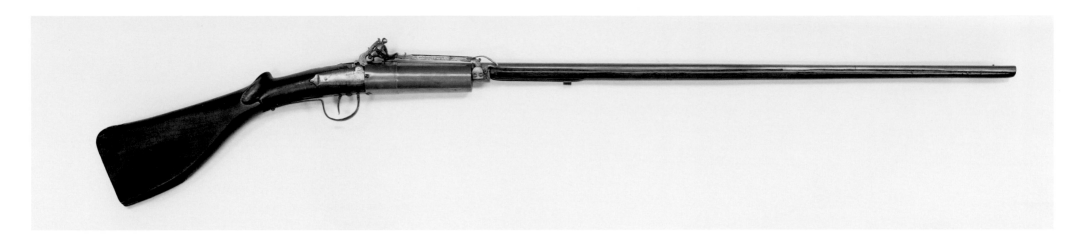

(present-day Belgium and Holland) during the 1640s.[1] Likewise, the projecting spur at the forward end of the stock's comb and the acanthus ornament carved at the butt's toe, as well as the heel, are seen on other firearms made in that region at approximately the same date.[2]

This date of manufacture is also supported by the construction of the lock's cock, which is of a particularly angular and robust form that was popular only during the 1640s.[3] In addition, the cock is secured to its pivot point by a pin. The latter feature is found only on early flintlocks because it proved to be unreliable.[4]

The cylinder is turned by a pawl or hand mounted on the cock's breast that engages a cogwheel sleeved onto the cylinder pin. When each chamber is brought into alignment with the barrel, the cylinder is held in place by a sliding pin catch located to the left of the cock. This pin catch has to be released each time the lock is cocked; otherwise the cylinder cannot rotate.

When originally made, this revolver had a far more striking appearance. In contrast to the polished brass cylinder cover, the butt and fore stocks were blackened. Traces of this ebonized or painted finish remain in the carved recesses of the acanthus ornament.

Notes

1. Four longarms with butt stocks similar in form that were made in France or the Low Countries during the 1640s are preserved in the Wrangel Armory at Skokloster, Sweden (Ake Meyerson and Lena Rangstrom, *Wrangel's Armoury: The Weapons Carl Gustaf Wrangel took from Wismar and Wlogast to Skokloster, in 1645 and 1653* [Stockholm: Royal Armoury Foundation Press, 1984], 221 [Nr. 148], 226 [Nr. 152], 236 [Nr. 164], and 261–62 [Nr. 194]).

2. Ibid., 221, and E. A. Yablonskaya, *Dutch Guns in Russia in the Moscow Kremlin Armoury, Moscow Historical Museum, Hermitage, St. Petersburg, Gatchina Palace Museum* (Amsterdam: Rijksmuseum, 1996), 88–101.

3. Torsten Lenk, *The Flintlock: Its Origin and Development*, trans. G. A. Urquhart (New York: Bramhall Press, 1965), 41–45 and pl. 23 (6).

4. Ibid., 21, and pl. 4 (3 and 5).

Interior view of cylinder turning mechanism

Interior view of lockplate

George Catlin and the Colt Firearms Series

Elizabeth Mankin Kornhauser

Samuel Colt commissioned a number of works of art over the course of his lifetime. But, unlike his wife, Elizabeth (see cat. 164), who would assemble one of the most ambitious and high-minded private picture galleries in America during the Civil War era, Samuel Colt sought to put artists in the service of his arms manufactury.[1] Most of the commissions that he engaged in were intended to further his determined efforts to promote sales and brand recognition, and several of these artworks were turned into prints for mass distribution. In addition, Colt patronized a number of Hartford artists, including Edward Sheffield Bartholomew (cats. 162–63), James Batterson, Joseph Ropes (cats. 154–57), and Matthew Wilson, who created portraits on canvas and in marble of Colt family members, as well as landscape views of his house and factory.[2] Many of the works were installed in the Colts' Hartford mansion, Armsmear (named for his profession and for the English word for a meadow), completed in 1856. A showplace for the Colts' enormous wealth, the Italianate villa overlooked the Colt armory (fig. 1). One of the earliest and most fascinating collaborations between the industrialist and an artist took place in the 1850s, when Colt commis-

sioned the renowned painter of Indians George Catlin (1796–1872) to create a series of works that would celebrate the novelty and effectiveness of Colt guns.

There is no better example of the alliance of art and commerce in mid-nineteenth-century America than the partnership of these two entrepreneurial showmen. By mid-century, both had attained international celebrity in their respective fields. However, while the early 1850s saw Colt's financial prospects on the ascent (as the *Illustrated London News* proclaimed on 30 April 1853, "Colonel Colt is rapidly becoming a millionaire, from the immense demand for his revolvers"), George Catlin faced debtor's prison, and he was in dire need of a generous patron when he sought Colt's help in securing financial support for his first trip to South America.[3] It was perhaps because of this vulnerable position that Catlin, in his role as celebrity artist, agreed to take on the promotion of Colt's latest guns. What makes the resulting images so extraordinary is the fact that Catlin placed himself in each scene, portraying himself using Colt guns in the wild. This group of paintings, and the lithographs and wood engravings that were made from them, are unique examples of a renowned artist providing a product endorsement. It is difficult to cite the occurrence of such a partnership for another century or more.

Colt and Catlin had much in common. Both came from patrician New England families with early roots in Hartford and both had fathers who held great aspirations for their families but failed in their business endeavors.[4] Their careers were shaped by historic events of the era, dominated by the claiming and settling of wilderness lands. The country's rapid territorial expansion and its embrace of the doctrine of Manifest Destiny provided, in different respects, the inspiration for their careers: Catlin's

Figure 1

Harry Fenn

Anglo-American, 1845–1911

View of "Armsmear," the Colt Residence, ca. 1870

Watercolor, gouache, and graphite on paper

Wadsworth Atheneum Museum of Art

Bequest of Elizabeth Hart Jarvis Colt, 1905.53

urgent mission to record the Indian tribes in the western territories before their ultimate demise, and Colt's recognition of the opportunity to be the first to mass-produce repeating firearms in the face of the inevitable conflicts that arose between white settlers and Indians. In the course of their careers, both men faced enormous financial hurdles and threats from their competitors. Fiercely ambitious, Catlin and Colt became talented showmen, successful entrepreneurs, and international celebrities.

Catlin's Indian Gallery

Eighteen years older than Colt, Catlin was born and raised in Wilkes-Barre, Pennsylvania, the fifth of fourteen children born to Putnam and Polly Catlin. Putnam was a country lawyer who never achieved great success but provided his children with a pleasant country upbringing. In 1817, at his father's request, George Catlin left for Litchfield, Connecticut (where a number of Catlin relatives resided), to attend his father's alma mater, the Litchfield Law School. He was admitted to the bar the following year but quickly expressed his displeasure with the profession, instead stating his desire to pursue a career as an artist. He first painted watercolor miniature portraits, then portraits in oil, before being elected a member of the Pennsylvania Academy of the Fine Arts in 1824 and the National Academy of Design in 1826. Catlin had larger ambitions, however, which were inspired by a sense of dissatisfaction with portrait painting (perhaps in light of the negative criticism he received for his portraits) and a desire to pursue the more elevated genre of history painting.[5] During visits to Philadelphia, Catlin was exposed to the city's pioneers of art, science, and natural history, including Charles Willson Peale and his museum, and in 1828 he saw a visiting delegation of western Indians, all of which helped to confirm his vocation.[6] In 1829 he wrote to General Peter B. Porter, secretary of war:

> Life is short, and I find that I have already traveled over half of it without stepping out of the beaten path in the unshackled pursuit of that Fame for which alone, the Art, to *me*, is valuable, and for the attainment of which I wish to devote the whole energies of my life.

Catlin proclaimed his ultimate desire to become a history painter "among the savage Indians," where he "could have the benefit of the finest school for an Historical painter now to be found in the world, where, among the naked savage [he] could select and study from the finest models in Nature, unmasked and moving in all their grace and beauty." He then proceeded to outline his plan to travel out west and to

> [r]eturn with such a collection of portraits of the principal chiefs of different nations and paintings representing all their different manners and customs, as would enable me to open such a gallery, first in this country and then in London, as would in all probability handsomely repay me for all my labours, and afford me the advantage of a successful introduction beyond the Atlantic.[7]

Catlin's mission was both altruistic and opportunistic. He is admired for his genuine concern for the fate of Native Americans and for his great achievement: helping to define the identity of the young nation by recording American Indian life—prime symbol of the New World—before it was obliterated by the country's western expansion. But he needed to make money from his art. Aware that his subjects would appeal to international audiences, he later resorted to exploitive displays of Indian troupes who traveled with him in an effort to attract attention to his Indian Gallery exhibitions.

Catlin undertook five journeys west from 1830 to 1836, enduring great hardships to paint the Plains Indians. His efforts resulted in the first representations of Indians in their native territories. In the first year he traveled to St. Louis to meet with William Clark, superintendent of the U.S. Department of Indian Affairs, learning as much as he could about the western lands and tribes he planned to visit. Catlin's mission became urgent upon the implementation of the Indian Removal Act of 1830, a twelve-year plan to remove Indians from their tribal lands east of the Mississippi. In the following years Catlin would witness the decimation of the Mandan tribe by smallpox. In the next decades he saw the near extinction of millions of buffalo and the transformation of the plains and high prairies from wilderness to cultivated fields, interrupted by rail lines. Catlin claimed to have visited fifty tribes living in territories west of the Mississippi River and made over five hundred portraits, landscapes, and scenes of Indian life, becoming one of the first artists to record the Plains Indians in their own natural world. To enhance the authenticity of his art, he gathered an impressive collection of Indian artifacts. He also depicted himself in a

Elizabeth Mankin Kornhauser

Figure 2
William Fisk
English, 1797–1873
George Catlin, 1849
Oil on canvas, 50 x 40 in.
National Portrait Gallery, Smithsonian Institution, Washington, D.C.
Gift of Miss May C. Kinney, Ernest C. Kinney, and Bradford Wikes, 1945

number of his paintings as a testament to his presence on the spot. In the introduction to his great treatise, *Letters and Notes on the Manners, Customs, and Conditions of the North American Indians* (1841), Catlin summed up his remarkable achievement: "I have, for many years past, contemplated the noble races of red men, who are now . . . melting away at the approach of civilization . . . and I have flown to their rescue–not of their lives or of their race (for they are *'doomed'* and must perish), but to the rescue of their looks . . . [so that] phoenix-like, they may rise from the 'stain on a painter's palette,' and live again upon the canvas, and stand forth for centuries yet to come, the living monuments of a noble race"[8] (fig. 2).

Catlin would spend the rest of his life attempting to find a home worthy of his life's work. To achieve that end, he courted prominent men, sought testimonials for the authenticity of his art, exhibited his collection in major American and European cities, lectured, wrote a series of books, and publicized his work in catalogues, broadsides, and newspaper advertisements. Failing to sell his impressive Indian Gallery, he resorted to increasingly commercial public displays, for which he was later criticized. Facing financial disaster, Catlin sought to create novelty for his Indian Gallery, sensationalizing Indians by touring tribal members abroad in an effort to attract greater numbers of paying visitors to his exhibitions. While he failed to achieve financial security, his exploits led to international fame. All along, Catlin believed that his life's work was deserving of government sponsorship and belonged in the nation's capital. His dream was not realized until 1879, seven years after his death, when the Indian Gallery was made a gift to the Smithsonian Institution by Mrs. Joseph Harrison following her husband's death.

Marketing Art and Firearms

As an artist-entrepreneur, Catlin, in an effort to promote his Indian Gallery, engaged in many of the same methods that Samuel Colt masterfully pursued for gun sales. Both men were natural showmen and shrewd marketers who were not above stretching the truth to make a point. They managed to enhance their public image by seeking official titles or adopting inflated ones. Colt was appointed a lieutenant colonel in 1850, known as Colonel Colt from that point onward, and Catlin was called "Governor" by his traveling companions during his travels in South America in the

1850s.[9] Both men dressed for their various roles as men of the world, show-men, or, in Catlin's case, as a frontiersman. They became impressive public speakers. Catlin gave evening lectures for the exhibitions of his Indian Gallery in New York, Washington, and London, while Colt addressed such distinguished bodies as the London Institution of Civil Engineers. In addition to newspaper advertisements and broadsides, they took full advantage of the many advances in printing to produce hand-colored lithographs and prints for promotional purposes. And both became expert at gathering testimonials from prominent men of the day.

Like Colt, Catlin was a master at entertaining dignitaries from the government, military, business world, and the press. One guest, the New York politician Philip Hone, recorded in his diary on 6 December 1837:

> I went this morning by invitation of the proprietor, Mr. Catlin, to see his great collection of paintings, consisting of portraits of Indian chiefs, landscapes, ceremonies, etc., of the Indian tribes, and implements of husbandry, and the chase, weapons of war, costumes, etc., which he collected in his travels … in the great West. … I have seldom witnessed so interesting an exhibition. Among the invited guests were Mr. [Daniel] Webster, some of the members of the Common Council, the mayor, and some newspaper editors. We had a collation of Buffaloes' tongues, and venison and the waters of the great spring, and smoked the calumet of peace under an Indian tent formed of buffalo skins.[10]

As they sought similar audiences in New York and Washington in the late 1830s, it is likely that the two men first met at this time. While Catlin exhibited his Indian Gallery in major cities in the Northeast, including Washington and New York, providing lectures for his audiences, Colt submitted his latest guns to the annual exhibitions of the American Institute in New York, where American mechanical innovations were promoted and where he frequently received awards.[11] Like Colt, who courted government contracts for his guns, Catlin had always viewed the federal government as the most suitable patron for the Indian Gallery, and he first approached Congress in May 1838. This would be the first of many government petitions, and Catlin and Colt both corresponded frequently with Secretary of War Joel R. Poinsett to promote their respective interests.

The two men responded to the most newsworthy events of the time to draw attention to their causes. During the Second Seminole War, Samuel Colt was relentless in seeking government endorsements for military contracts, and in February 1838 personally delivered his Paterson revolving rifles to the troops in Florida fighting the Seminoles.[12] The success of his guns gained him his first military testimonials (see "The Paterson Era, 1836–1841"). Catlin also attempted to capitalize on the notoriety of the war, particularly the capture, under a flag of truce, of the Seminole chief Osce-

CATLIN'S INDIAN GALLERY: In the Old Theatre, On Louisiana Avenue, and near the City Post Office.

MR. CATLIN,

Who has been for seven years traversing the Prairies of the "Far West," and procuring the Portraits of the most distinguished Indians of those uncivilized regions, together with Paintings of their VILLAGES, BUFFALO HUNTS, DANCES, LANDSCAPES OF THE COUNTRY &c. &c.

Will endeavor to entertain the Citizens of Washington, for a short time with an Exhibition of

THREE HUNDRED & THIRTY PORTRAITS & NUMEROUS OTHER PAINTINGS

Which he has collected from 38 different Tribes, speaking different languages, all of whom he has been among, and Painted his pictures from life.

Portraits of Black Hawk and nine of his Principal Warriors,

Are among the number, painted at Jefferson Barracks, while prisoners of war, in their war dress and war paint.

ALSO, FOUR PAINTINGS REPRESENTING THE

ANNUAL RELIGIOUS CEREMONY OF THE MANDANS,

Doing penance, by inflicting the most cruel tortures upon their own bodies—passing knives and splints through their flesh, and suspending their bodies by their wounds, &c.

A SERIES OF ONE HUNDRED LANDSCAPE VIEWS,

Descriptive of the picturesque Prairie Scenes of the Upper Missouri and other parts of the Western regions.

AND A SERIES OF TWELVE BUFFALO HUNTING SCENES,

Together with SPLENDID SPECIMENS OF COSTUME, will also be exhibited.

☞ The great interest of this collection consists in its being a representation of the wildest tribes of Indians in America, and entirely in their Native Habits and Costumes; consisting of Sioux, Puncahs, Konzas, Shiennes, Crows, Ojibbeways, Assinebonis, Mandans, Crees, Blackfeet, Snakes, Mahas, Ottoes, Ioways, Flatheads, Weahs, Peorias, Sacs, Fuxes, Winnebagoes, Menomonies, Minatarrees, Rickarees, Ouages, Camanches, Wicos, Pawnee-Picts, Kiowas, Seminoles, Euchees, and others.

☞ In order to render the Exhibition more instructive than it could otherwise be, the Paintings will be exhibited one at a time, and such explanations of their Dress, Customs, Traditions, &c. given by Mr. Catlin, as will enable the public to form a just idea of the Customs, Numbers, and Condition of the Savages yet in a state of nature in North America.

The Exhibition, with Explanations, will commence on Monday Evening, the 9th inst. in the old Theatre, and be repeated for several successive evenings, commencing at HALF PAST SEVEN O'CLOCK. Each Course will be limited to two evenings, Monday and Tuesday, Wednesday and Thursday, Friday and Saturday; and it his hoped that visiters will be in and seated as near the hour as possible, that they may see the whole collection. The portrait of OSEOLA will be shewn on each evening.

ADMITTANCE 50 CENTS.—CHILDREN HALF PRICE.

☞ These Lectures will be continued for one week only.

ola in October 1837. In January 1838 Catlin rushed to Charleston, South Carolina, where Osceola and the other Indian prisoners were being held, to paint their portraits and add them to his Indian Gallery. On 10 January 1838 Secretary Poinsett wrote to the commanding officer at Fort Moultrie that Catlin wished to paint the Indian prisoners and to please assist him.[13] While taking the portrait of Osceola, Catlin expressed concern for the chief's health. Osceola died the very next day, and Catlin rushed back with his prize, adding the portrait (see "A Connecticut Yankee Courts the World," fig. 1) to his Indian Gallery.[14] This timely addition was announced in a broadside of April 1838 advertising his latest exhibition in Washington and assuring his audience that "the portrait of OSCEOLA will be shown on each evening"[15] (fig. 3).

Like Colt, Catlin understood the power of personal endorsements, using them to verify the authenticity of his Indian portrayals "taken from life."

As an example, for his portraits of Osceola and the Seminole prisoners, Catlin obtained a certificate of authenticity signed by Capt. P. Morrison, 2nd Lieut. J. S. Hathaway, 2nd Lieut. H. Wharton, and Assistant Surgeon F. Weedon at Fort Moultrie on 26 January 1838, which reads: "We hereby certify that the portraits of Seminoles . . . named in this catalogue, were painted by George Catlin, from the life, at Fort Moultrie; that the Indians sat or stood in the costumes precisely in which they are painted, and that the likenesses are remarkably good."[16]

With no response from the U.S. government regarding the purchase of his Indian Gallery, Catlin made plans to take the collection to Europe. The artist became hopeful, however, when a letter from Congressman George Briggs informed him that on 11 February 1839 a resolution submitted by Briggs had passed in the House, authorizing the committee on Indian Affairs to inquire of Catlin the terms for acquiring the Indian Gallery collection. Concerned that they would not act during the current session, on 15 February 1839 Catlin wrote to Poinsett asking why the committee "have not, as yet, made any inquiry of me. . . . My paintings are nearly all finished and placed in neat and appropriate frames," and he threatened, "And ready for crossing the Atlantic."[17]

At the same time, Colt was busy petitioning Washington (see "The Paterson Era, 1836–1841"), using all manner of endorsements and incentives to induce the government to buy his revolvers. Colt also wrote to Poinsett on 6 March 1839, submitting to him "Recommendations for a Trial of Repeating Arms," a petition signed by thirty-two military officers and three civilians, one of whom was George Catlin.[18] This is the earliest-known direct contact between the two men.

During his extensive travels in the American West, Catlin had achieved notoriety as a frontiersman, proving to be an experienced marksman. Six months later, Catlin's name appeared again in a testimonial to the rapid-fire efficiency of Colt guns in one of the many promotional newspaper articles that Colt was able to garner in the years of his Paterson, New Jersey, factory. In an article published on 18 October 1839, a writer for the New York *Evening Post* noted that at the recent American Institute fair "[a] boastful case of Fire Arms, known as Colt's invention, attracts the eyes of almost every person who passed it. . . . They surpass in correctness and beauty of workmanship of the best arms of European manufacture, and

for simplicity of construction and power of execution, have no equal." After citing the testimonials of "officers of the army and navy" and a "General in the Mexican service" who had used the firearms, the writer concludes, "It was with one of Colt's pistols that Catlin, the artist of Indian manners, &c., recently shot three deer in succession while travelling through the state of Pennsylvania."[19] Catlin would later turn this scene into one of the paintings in the Colt Firearms series (cat. 145).

Catlin in Europe

By November 1839, having failed to interest the government in acquiring his Indian Gallery, Catlin sailed with his collection to Europe, where, with the exception of his journeys in the 1850s to South America, the American West, and beyond, he remained for most of his life. During the 1840s Catlin exhibited his Indian Gallery, along with troupes of Indians, in Egyptian Hall, where he became the toast of London. These live Indian shows were early precursors of the Wild West shows of P. T. Barnum and, later, Buffalo Bill Cody and Annie Oakley. The popularity of Catlin's shows gained him an audience with Queen Victoria and Prince Albert at Windsor Castle. He then went to Paris, where he exhibited at the Louvre, met King Louis Philippe, who received Catlin's entourage at the Tuileries, and later exhibited in Brussels. In 1848 the revolution in France forced Catlin to flee to England with his collections, which he undertook at great expense. Once settled, he found himself in serious debt. One of the ways Catlin attempted to relieve his financial woes was to create what he called "Albums Unique," which were handsomely bound sets of reduced line drawings based on subjects in his Indian Gallery, but as they were done in multiple sets, they were hardly unique.[20]

Colt in New York City

Meanwhile, Colt's Paterson factory closed in 1842, and he remained in New York, escaping creditors and planning his next ventures. He took rooms at New York University, where he met and befriended the artist-inventor Samuel F. B. Morse and the pioneering chemist and photographer John W. Draper. Inspired by his fellow inventors, Colt conducted his own experiments with submarine mines (see "Samuel Colt in New York, 1841–1846"). In 1842, in an effort to capture on canvas his great achievement, he

Figure 4

Antoine Placide Gibert

French, 1806–1875

The Last Experiment of Mr. Colt's Submarine Battery, 1844

Oil on canvas

Collection of Greg Martin

commissioned the French artist Antoine Placide Gibert (1806–1875), then working in New York, to paint *The Last Experiment of Mr. Colt's Submarine Battery,* 1844 (fig. 4), paying the artist sixty dollars upon its completion two years later.[21] That year, 1844, the painting was exhibited at the American Institute, while at the same time Colt won a gold medal at the institute for his improvement in ammunition.[22] By the end of the decade, Colt's fortunes were on the rise.

Catlin and Colt on the International Stage

Catlin and Colt met once again in London following Colt's trip to Europe in 1849 to seek an international clientele for his arms. Two years later both men were represented in the American section of the London Crystal Palace exhibition of 1851. Catlin presented two costumed figures from his Indian Gallery, which were placed near Hiram Powers's classical marble sculpture *The Greek Slave* (fig. 5). Colt's remarkable display of revolvers attracted favorable media attention (see "Samuel Colt and the World," fig. 1). As he had in the past, Colt gave presentation pistols to many dignitaries, including kings, officers, members of the press, artists, including Hiram Powers, museums, and also gave a pistol to Catlin's "Am. Indian Museum."[23]

By the following year, Colt's prospects were soaring. Plans for his new Hartford factory and one in London were under way. Catlin, on the other

hand, was desperately seeking money to save his Indian Gallery collection from being seized by numerous creditors and the likelihood of debtor's prison. To make matters worse, a Texas land company in which Catlin had invested substantial sums several years earlier collapsed in the 1850s. One acquaintance described Catlin's situation: "That celebrated tourist in Indian country, the poor fellow with all his enthusiasm & high souled temperament is manifestly, as often suffers to genius, no successful man, his whole collection is in the hands of judgment creditors."[24] By chance, the Philadelphia locomotive manufacturer Joseph Harrison stopped in London on a return trip from Russia and saved the Indian Gallery, acquiring it and shipping it to Philadelphia. Even though Catlin lost possession, his Indian Gallery was kept intact and returned to America. However, the artist clung to the hope that the collection would finally end up in the nation's capital. He managed to retrieve his sketchbooks, notebooks, and watercolors from his studio, which he would use in the future to make replicas of his Indian Gallery works. However, Catlin still had to deal with the many remaining unpaid creditors who had accepted an interest in his Indian Gallery as security on loans. He needed to escape his creditors and reinvent himself someplace other than England. To this end, and in the hope of renewing his career as an artist, Catlin developed a scheme to travel to South America in search of new native subjects for his art. In addition, he was inspired to search for lost gold mines in the Tumucumaque Mountains of Brazil.

Many American and European artists traveled to South America at mid-century. First and foremost was the Hartford native and the country's leading artist, Frederic Church (1826–1900), who, inspired by the scientific writings of the German naturalist-explorer Alexander von Humboldt, traveled to South America in 1853 and 1857.[25] Catlin had actually met von Humboldt during the exhibition of his Indian Gallery in 1845 in Paris and developed a correspondence with him during his South American trips. Catlin also made the acquaintance of a German botanist and a French naturalist who were scheduled to leave for South America on 19 March 1853 and were willing to assist him with part of the transit cost to accompany them.[26] He turned to past patrons and also sought new ones in order to finance his trip.

Catlin approached one of the few prospects to whom he was not already in debt, his English patron Sir Thomas Phillips, who had offered him fre-

Figure 5
United States Section of the Great Exhibition [London]
Lithograph by John Absolen for *Recollections of the Great Exhibition of 1851*
Lloyd Brothers & Co., London, 1851
University of Illinois Library, Urbana

Colt's Patronage of Catlin

It now seems clear that Samuel Colt supported, at least in part, Catlin's trips in the 1850s. While the details of the commission remain unclear, Catlin painted the Firearms series of seven oil paintings in 1854 and 1855, following the first journey; the works were then turned into a set of six lithographs that were distributed by Colt to promote his arms. Following his second trip in 1857, Catlin painted three additional oils that were added to Colt's Firearms series. The paintings and prints feature Catlin as artist-frontiersman and hunter in North and South America, expertly using Colt's latest guns.

Catlin's own accounts of his travels in the 1850s have proven to be unreliable at best, and the specific details of his itineraries remain to be established by future scholars. As Catlin historian Brian W. Dippie writes, "Catlin was never to be relied upon for dates. To him they were a matter of convenience, something to be used to excite an interest, create an impression, sell."[30] The artist chronicled his trips to South and Central America, Cuba, Mexico, the western coasts of the United States and Canada, and as far as Alaska (then held by Russia), in a series of books: *Life Amongst the Indians* (New York, 1857; London, 1861), *Last Rambles Amongst the Indians of the Rocky Mountains and the Andes* (New York, 1867; London, 1868), and *The Lifted and Subsided Rocks of America* (London, 1870). He painted on-the-spot scenes of his travels, quickly executed in thinly applied oil paint on Bristol board, measuring approximately 11 by 14 inches, and following his return to Europe painted South American subjects. He would later re-create his Indian Gallery, acquired by Harrison and eventually given to the Smithsonian, and combine them with his South American work to form what he called his Cartoon Collection, consisting of over six hundred paintings, now in the collection of the National Gallery of Art, Washington.[31] He also did a number of larger studio oils based on the Cartoon Collection paintings.

Catlin's First Trip to South America

While Catlin's accounts of his trips are inaccurate, contemporary newspaper reports of his travels, as well as his correspondence with Phillips and others during the mid-1850s, allow for a rough itinerary to be established.[32] Catlin claims that his first trip to South America took place in 1852,

quent support in the past. In 1851 the artist had secured a loan from Phillips by giving him twenty replicas, rendered in oil, of his Indian Gallery subjects, to be returned when the debt was repaid.[27] Now Catlin asked Phillips to assist him with "this second starting point of my life."[28] Despite several failed attempts to gain financial assistance from Phillips, and the subsequent departure in March of the German botanist and French naturalist, Catlin wrote Phillips on 3 May 1854, relating his final plans for the journey, "I wish you were free to take this splendid Tour with me. . . . I have procured a chain mail tunic to wear under a blanket capot [a long cloak], out of sight, and a perfect protection against knives, arrows or Tigers claws, & also Colt's rifle with six shots & pistol with 5. We are all armed & equipped alike, and form almost a match for a Rupian [Asian Indian] Regt."[29]

143
George Catlin
American, 1796–1872
Catlin the Artist and Sportsman
Relieving One of His Companions
from an Unpleasant Predicament
During His Travels in Brazil, 1854
Oil on canvas, 18¾ x 25½ in.
Wadsworth Atheneum
The Ella Gallup Sumner and Mary
Catlin Sumner Collection Fund,
2005.2.2

but it is now believed to have been two years later. Catlin's letter to Phillips on 3 May 1854, announcing his imminent departure for South America, likely signals the beginning of his first trip. According to Dippie, Catlin met up with the German botanist and possibly the French naturalist in Havana in May and boarded an American steamer bound for Georgetown, Guyana, where he was joined by an Englishman named Smyth, who traveled with him and on occasion sent letters to England reporting the details of their journey, excerpts of which were printed in the newspapers. In search of ancient gold mines, they either traveled up the Essequibo River or by mule over the Tumucumaque Mountains and down the Trombutas River to the Amazon. As Catlin recounted in his later writings, "Joined in Georgetown by an enterprising young man by the name of Smyth, an Englishman, a good shot, and carrying a first-rate Minié rifle, and armed myself with Colt's revolving carbine, we left the Essequibo."[33] Smyth's Minié rifle, named for the designer of the Minié ball, Captain Claude-Etienne Minié, was a muzzle-loading single-shot rifle. While traveling in Venezuela along the Orinoco River, Catlin first mentions his faithful gun, nicknamed "Sam." "Sam! Who's Sam? Why *Sam* Colt, a six-shot little rifle, always lying before me during the day and *in my* arms during the night, by which a tiger's or alligator's eye, at a hundred yards, was sure to drop a red tear."[34] Catlin further related that his faithful gun, "Sam Colt," was "made expressly for me by my old friend Colonel Colt, and which has answered to the nick-name 'Sam' in my former travels."[35] Catlin's first trip to South America was cut short when he learned of the possible purchase by the federal government of his Indian Gallery, then in the possession of Harrison. He returned, after six months, to Le Havre in mid-November, with plans to travel to Washington, but once again the deal was not consummated.

The Colt Firearms Series

Between November 1854 and late February or early March 1855, there were several opportunities for Catlin and Colt to meet in London. During this period Catlin also traveled to Berlin to consult with von Humboldt and report on his geological findings.[36] Meanwhile, Colt journeyed to Russia in late 1854 and then to London, when he likely met with Catlin, returning to the United States on 12 January 1855. Colt crossed the Atlantic twice more, landing in England in late May 1855 and traveling back to Hartford in August.

After consultation with Colt, Catlin painted the first seven of a total of ten oil paintings that made up the Firearms series. There has been debate among scholars as to the number of paintings in this series, with anywhere from nine to twelve being reported. Colt's probate inventory, taken shortly after his death in 1862, lists "9 Catlins Pictures" in the billiard room and "1 Catlin Picture" in "adjoining Rm-West (to North Blue Room)," which was his bedroom, next to that of his wife.[37] In addition, Colt's impressive library included "10 vols. Catlin's Indians," which likely represented a selection of Catlin's written works.[38] The ten paintings discussed in this essay all descended directly from Samuel Colt and, following his death in 1862, passed to his wife, Elizabeth. She gave the series to her sister, Hetty Hart Jarvis Beach, who died in 1898 and left them to her daughter Elizabeth Hart Jarvis Robinson, and so descended through the family until they were dispersed in the mid-twentieth century (see cats. 143–46).[39] In addition to nine Catlin paintings, Colt also displayed in his large billiard room a number of engravings and paintings, as well as animal heads, including buffalo and deer, Indian relics, and stuffed exotic birds.[40]

As he had in the past, Catlin produced the series of paintings for Colt intending that they tell a larger story. Initially, seven subjects were selected for the paintings—four depicting South America and three of North America—which were then turned into a set of six lithographs, produced for Colt in 1855. Catlin may have shared with Colt his series of on-the-spot studies from his recent travels in order to choose appropriate subjects that would serve to market Colt guns. The three South American subjects represent scenes in the Amazon region of Brazil and are dated 1854. Each painting features Catlin, dressed in the elaborate protective attire he described in his letter to Phillips, shown expertly using his new Colt revolving rifle (see cat. 26).

In *Catlin the Artist and Sportsman Relieving One of His Companions from an Unpleasant Predicament During His Travels in Brazil*, 1854 (cat. 143), Catlin rushes to the rescue of his companion Smyth, who, having spent his powder with a single shot from his Minié rifle has been treed by hundreds of wild peccaries or boar. Catlin saves his friend's life when he shoots the leaders of the charging animals with his faithful six-shot Colt rifle and watches the rest of the herd retreat. In the second painting, *Mid-Day Halt on the Rio Trumbutos*, 1854 (cat. 144), Catlin's meal of wild pig is interrupted

144

George Catlin

Mid-Day Halt on the Rio Trombutas, Brazil, 1854

Oil on canvas, 19 3/8 x 26 5/8 in.

Wadsworth Atheneum Museum of Art

The Ella Gallup Sumner and Mary Catlin Sumner Collection Fund, 2005.2.4

Figure 6

George Catlin

Catlin the Celebrated Indian Traveler and Artist Firing his Colt's Repeating Rifle Before a Tribe of Carib Indians in South America, 1855

Oil on canvas, 18²/₃ x 25½ in.

Max and Carolyn Williams Family Trust

by the arrival of two leopards, one of them toying with the legs of his sleeping guide. Catlin rushes to his boat to retrieve his Colt repeating rifle and proceeds to shoot the leopard between the eyes. These two paintings, filled with dramatic narrative detail, provide romantic images of the dangers found in exotic locales. Catlin, with his superior Colt rifle, serves as the hero in each scene, making the paintings excellent marketing tools for Colt.

In the third South American scene, which has no known earlier study, Catlin demonstrates his Colt rifle for a tribe of Carib Indians in Brazil. In *Catlin the Celebrated Indian Traveler and Artist Firing his Colt's Repeating Rifle Before a Tribe of Carib Indians in South America,* 1855 (fig. 6), the text below the lithograph after the painting (see cat. 149) relates, in Catlin's words: "It having been reported by one of my party that I had a Medicine Gun, which would fire all day without reloading, the men, Women & Children, assembled in front of the Chief's Lodge to get a sight of it,—when I found it necessary to make an exhibition—and arranged a target at a suitable distance where I took my position in front of the crowd rapidly discharging all the chambers, and cocked the piece for a continuation, but the chief advanced and assured me they were all satisfied, and I had better save my powder and balls, as I might want them, on a very long journey."

Catlin stands in the center of the composition, dressed in his elaborate attire, hardly suited for a tropical climate but serving to protect him, and has just fired a series of shots, as indicated by the six puffs of white smoke floating above the rifle. He carries his pistol in a shoulder holster. Catlin turns back toward the chief and three companions, one of whom is undoubtedly Smyth, his English traveling companion, seen holding his Minié rifle and wearing a derby hat. The other two men may represent the German botanist (holding a sheaf of grass in his right hand and a large portfolio under his arm) and the French naturalist standing behind him, whom

Catlin purportedly met up with on this trip. This is a complex composition filled with engaging narrative passages, including the two dogs in the foreground, running in fright from the rifle shots, and the Carib Indians shrinking back in fear as Catlin demonstrates the power of his Colt rifle.

Finally, the fourth South American subject, *Panther Shooting*, 1854 (fig. 7), shows Catlin in a boat with his Colt repeating rifle at the ready, as he and his guide approach two panthers on the shore. The painting is the same size as all the others and similar in subject, but it was not selected for the set of lithographs.[41]

The other three paintings, all reproduced for the set of six lithographs, represent scenes from Catlin's earlier travels in North America and show him hunting buffalo and deer. *Water Hunting for Deer, A Night Scene on the River Susquehanna, Penn.*, ca. 1854–55 (cat. 145), is a scene drawn from a trip the artist made to his family home in Pennsylvania, which had been reported in the New York *Evening Post*, in 1839, as an endorsement for the use of Colt's guns for sports hunting. In a night scene, lit only by a stationary torch on the boat, Catlin shoots his Colt rifle at the deer along the shore, which stand paralyzed by the light. The lithograph includes the following

Elizabeth Mankin Kornhauser

145

George Catlin

Water Hunting for Deer, A Night Scene on the River Susquehanna, Penn.,

ca. 1854–55

Oil on canvas, 19³/₈ x 26⁵/₈ in.

Wadsworth Atheneum Museum of Art

The Ella Gallup Sumner and Mary Catlin Sumner Collection Fund, 2005.2.3

146
George Catlin
Catlin the Artist Shooting Buffalos with Colt's Revolving Pistol, 1855
Oil on canvas, 19 x 26½ in.
Wadsworth Atheneum Museum of Art
The Ella Gallup Sumner and Mary Catlin Sumner Collection Fund, 2005.2.1

Cat. 146a. Detail of cat. 146

text: "Catlin writes, 'I was on the water all night with my Colt Revolving Rifle, and in the morning soon looked up seven of my victims, several others were wounded, but made their escape'" (see cat. 150).

The boldest, most original, and most overtly commercial image that Catlin painted for the Firearms series is *Catlin the Artist Shooting Buffalos with Colt's Revolving Pistol,* 1855 (cat. 146). The scene is a reminiscence of the artist's journey to the north fork of the Platte River in the early 1830s. Intriguingly, this is the only image in the series that shows Catlin using a Colt pistol rather than a rifle. Placed in the center foreground, Catlin and his pistol dominate the composition and are painted on a larger scale than that seen in the other works. Galloping alongside a herd of buffalo and dressed in fringed leather frontier attire, Catlin holds the reins of his horse in his left hand and the pistol in his right, as he fires successive shots, leaving five bloodied and dying buffalo in his wake.

In this painting Catlin is seen as a man of action, outdoing his Indian companions with their traditional weapons: having failed to fell a single buffalo, they are shown riding into the background, clearly symbolizing the yielding of old ways to the new. Catlin's horse rears up as he leans toward his prey, and his carefully delineated pistol (cat. 146a) gives off a

Elizabeth Mankin Kornhauser

Figure 8

George Catlin

Catlin the Artist and Hunter Shooting Buffalos with Colt's Revolving Rifle, 1854

Oil on canvas, 19 x 26½ in.

Location unknown; photo courtesy of Colt Family descendants

spray of flame and smoke as the hammer strikes and the bullet leaves the barrel. Large puffs of white smoke from each shot hang in the air. It is difficult not to think of Colt himself when looking at this image, which brings to mind a characterization of Colt that appeared in the *Hartford Daily Times* on 4 October 1854: "Col. Colt is himself a 'Patent Revolver'—is always

loaded and ready for action!"[42] This composition was used for the set of six lithographs and was also reproduced in the many media stories that Colt launched, using the Firearms series images. (Interestingly, Catlin is seated on a rearing horse, and Colt had by this time adopted the symbol of a rampant colt for himself and his firearms company, using it at every opportunity to define his business.)

Like the painting discussed above, *Catlin the Artist and Hunter Shooting Buffalos with Colt's Revolving Rifle,* 1854 (fig. 8), is thought to be based on the artist's actual experience on the Upper Missouri River in the early 1830s.[43] It is more typical of the smaller scale of figures seen in the other works in the Firearms series, with Catlin and two guides shown at the lower right.[44] This painting is likely drawn from an oil study, *Untitled [Catlin Shooting Buffalo],* ca. 1854, measuring 11¼ by 14¾ inches, in the collection of the Gilcrease Museum, Tulsa, Oklahoma. The painting was selected to be part of the set of six lithographs, and the text below the print describes the scene in Catlin's words: "[W]ith my two hired men Ba'tiste & Bogard, I took position where a numerous herd of Buffalo were crossing a deep ravine, and being unobserved I shot down eight or ten in succession leaving their carcasses / for the wolves to devour" (see cat. 152). Catlin identifies his guides, Baptiste and Abraham Bogard, from his earlier travels on the Missouri River.[45]

Taken as a whole, the series captures the effectiveness and efficiency of Colt guns, whether for hunting or self-defense. The wild animals represented in these scenes were thought to be unique to the regions of North and South America at that time and may have had special appeal for European and American sportsmen seeking new trophies for display in their own billiard or trophy rooms. In his paintings *Catlin the Artist Shooting Buffalos in the West with Colt's Revolving Pistol,* 1855, and *Catlin the Celebrated Indian Traveler and Artist, Firing his Colt's Repeating Rifle Before a Tribe of Carib Indians in South America,* 1855, the artist's inclusion of Native North and South Americans using ancient weapons to hunt buffalo, or standing in amazement as they witness for the first time the power of the white man's new weaponry, signals their demise in the face of white settlement. These two complex compositions, for which there are no known studies, stand out as the most original scenes and the most closely tied to Colt's marketing agenda.

Mass Production of the Firearms Series Images

Following Catlin's departure on his second trip to South America in late February or early March 1855, the English lithographic artist John McGahey drew Catlin's images on stone, and Day & Son, of London and Chester, the best-known British lithographic printers of the period, printed the plates (cats. 147–52). The lithographs were well under way that year. On 5 August 1855 McGahey wrote from Chester to Colt's associate in London, Col. Luther

P. Sargeant: "I am happy to inform you I have finished one of the drawings on wood (and which is in course of engraving) and am engaged upon a second which will be in a similar state in two or three days. I shall send you a proof of the first in the course of the week—also The reducing is progressing satisfactory for the Lithographs."[46] The letter indicates that McGahey not only drew Catlin's paintings on stone for the set of six lithographs but also "on wood" for engravings. This suggests that McGahey

150

George Catlin

Water Hunting for Deer, A Night Scene on the River Susquehanna, Penn., ca. 1855

Imprint: G. Catlin Pinxt / Day & Sons, Lithrs. to the Queen /

On Stone by J. M'Gahey City Walls Chester [England]

Tinted or hand-colored lithograph, 18 x 25 in.

Wadsworth Atheneum Museum of Art

The American Painting Purchase Fund, 2005.8.1

151

George Catlin

Catlin the Artist Shooting Buffalos with Colt's Revolving Pistol, ca. 1855

Imprint: G. Catlin Pinxt / Day & Sons, Lithrs. to the Queen /

On Stone by J. M'Gahey City Walls Chester [England]

Tinted or hand-colored lithograph on paper, 18 x 25 in.

Wadsworth Atheneum Museum of Art

The American Painting Purchase Fund, 2005.8.2

152

George Catlin

Catlin the Artist and Hunter Shooting Buffalos with Colt's Revolving Rifle, ca. 1855

Imprint: G. Catlin Pinxt / Day & Son Lithrs. to the Queen /

On Stone by J. M'Gahey Bold Sqre Chester [England]

Tinted or hand-colored lithograph on paper, 18 x 25 in.

Wadsworth Atheneum Museum of Art

The American Painting Purchase Fund, 2005.8.3

Figure 9

George Catlin

An Adventure in the Luxuriant Forests of Brazil, The Panthers of the Rio Trombutos,
ca. 1855

Wood engraving

From *Frank Leslie's Illustrated Newspaper,* 16 May 1857

Wadsworth Atheneum Museum of Art, 2005

Figure 10

George Catlin

Buffalo Hunting in the Far West. Colt's Revolving Pistol Vs. The Indian Arrow and Spear, ca. 1855

Wood engraving

From *Frank Leslie's Illustrated Newspaper,* 16 May 1857

Wadsworth Atheneum Museum of Art, 2005

McGahey was able to make some improvements in the compositions for the prints (see cats. 147–52), as he had done in the past for Catlin's Indian Portfolio.[47] In addition, an interesting update on the model of gun can be detected in the print version of *Catlin the Artist Shooting Buffalos with Colt's Revolving Pistol.* In the oil painting Catlin is using a Colt U.S. model 1847 with a nine-inch barrel. But in the lithograph McGahey shows a more current pistol made in the Hartford factory, dating from 1848 to 1850, with the newer, seven-and-a-half-inch shortened barrel (for examples of these pistols, see cats. 29 and 39).[48]

In selecting the images for his Firearms series, Colt was seeking to strengthen the international market for his latest guns by connecting his name with his product. In addition, he faced the prospect of being unable to secure extensions on his arms patents, so he needed to outmarket his competitors and imitators. For marketing purposes, he chose the themes of sports hunting and self-protection from wild animals to promote his guns, as these were more benign subjects than military conflict. His ability to secure the image of one of America's best-known artists, who was also a famous frontiersman and adventurer, portraying himself using the latest Colt guns in the wilds of North and South America, was more ambitious than any marketing scheme of the era.[49] By mass-producing the series in high-quality colored lithographs (at a time when nearly all advertising was in black-and-white) for a limited audience, he could distribute the images in an elegant and compelling manner.[50] The popularity of these prints was spread further when several of the images, likely executed by McGahey, began appearing in newspapers and magazines in 1855. Colt selected four of the lithographs to be used in print media: *Water Hunting for Deer, Catlin the Artist Shooting Buffalos with Colt's Revolving Pistol, Mid-day Halt on the Rio Trumbutos, Brazil,* and *Catlin the Celebrated Indian Traveller and Artist, Firing his Colt's Repeating Rifle Before a Tribe of Carib Indians in South America.* Accounts of Catlin's travels often accompanied with images after the Firearms series appeared in *The Crayon, London Morning Advertiser, Merry's Museum and Parley's Magazine,* New York, and *Saturday Evening Post.* In addition, articles on Samuel Colt and his guns make reference to the same scenes and stories, with accounts of Catlin's use of Colt guns, and appeared in the *Illustrated London News* (see cats. 144 and 145).

produced the wood engravings that were used in the mass marketing of these images in newspapers and magazines from 1855 to 1857. In the two engravings (figs. 9 and 10) that appeared in *Frank Leslie's Illustrated Newspaper,* 16 May 1857, for example, which may have been based on McGahey's work, the images are derived from the lithographs of 1855 but are further simplified and shown in black-and-white.

Catlin had previously worked with the firm of Day & Haghe (by the 1850s known as Day & Son) and with the artist McGahey, in the 1840s, for his Indian Portfolio. But the fact that Catlin was in South America at this time, and that McGahey was writing to Colt's London associate seeking his approval for the proofs, suggests that this commission was under the direction of Colt. A comparison of the oils and the lithographs reveals that

Figure 11

George Catlin

Ostrich Chase, Buenos Aires, 1857

Oil on canvas, 19¼ x 26¾ in.

Location unknown; photo courtesy of

Colt Family descendants

Catlin's Second Trip to South America

The artist's second trip to South America was announced in a number of newspapers, including the *Hartford Courant,* which noted on 6 March 1855: "Catlin the Indian portrait-painter . . . has gone to the head waters of the Amazon, determined to find for the subject of his pencil a race who have not yet been changed by the march of civilization from the state of nature."[51] On 7 March, the *New York Daily Times* made a similar announcement of Catlin's travels, revealing the artist's challenge to find ever more exotic locales for his art and citing letters "which have of late been received, [and] are from the head and tributary waters of the Amazon. . . . Mr. Catlin observes that, as civilization had not only reached, but overtaken and passed beyond his Pawnees, he was resolved to find some uncultured human beings, out of the reach of locomotives, on land or water." In a lengthy letter that Catlin wrote from Santarém, Rio Amazon, Brazil, published in the *Washington Intelligencer* on 28 May 1855 and in the New York *Evening Post* on 29 May 1855, he expressed his frustration with the government after learning of "the end of all my hopes in all my appli-

cations to Congress, and weighed down by pecuniary and domestic embarrassments which I had not the immediate power to rise above," and said that his response was " to throw myself again into the wilderness, into an untrodden field, and my further labors and further risks of my life, endeavoring to add new material . . . to my collection."[52]

The final three oils in the Firearms series, painted for Colt in 1856 and 1857, depict Catlin on hunting expeditions in South America. *Ostrich Chase, Buenos Aires,* 1857 (fig. 11), shows the artist in the center of the composition, galloping on a horse while shooting his rifle at rheas (flightless birds native to South America that are smaller than ostriches).[53] Catlin later wrote of the challenges he faced during this hunt, "I with 'Sam' in hand, and a six-shot revolver in my belt set out for the hunt. . . . I have joined in the buffalo chase in all its forms, but never before took part in a chase so difficult as this. After the brood was separated, they ran in all directions, darting in zig-zag and curved lines before and around us, leading our horses into angles difficult to turn."[54]

The final two paintings, *Reconnoitering Flamingoes in the Grand Saline,
Buenos Aires,* 1856 (unlocated; seen here in a version in the collection of
the Virginia Museum of Fine Arts; fig. 12), and *Shooting Flamingoes,* 1857
(fig. 13), function as a pair, with a humorous narrative that accompanies
the hunting theme. They portray an adventure during the artist's expedi-
tion south of Buenos Aires, in which the destination, according to Catlin's
Last Rambles, was the "Grand Saline," a "vast and interminable lake" near
the headwaters of the Salado River.[55] Catlin came upon an exotic scene,
where a seemingly endless number of flamingoes were tending to their
nests and their young. Catlin explained that the "incrustation of the muri-
ate of salt over much of the surface" of the saline and the "slimy mud associated with the salt" rendered it "so excessively difficult to travel on and so
nauseous that no animal whatever will venture into it, and none of the
feathered tribes except the stork species, of which are the flamingoes. They
build their nests and hatch their young in it, in perfect security from the
molestation by animals of the country."[56] The artist and his Indian guide
are seen in *Reconnoitering Flamingoes* at the lower left, hiding in a "bunch
of alder and willow bushes."[57] Catlin is dressed in the same protective
attire that he wears in the other South American scenes. In *Shooting
Flamingoes,* Catlin, with his rifle "Sam" in hand, watches one of the tallest
birds "with his mouth full of collected worms, seeming to be suspicious,
advanced . . . to take a look at us," causing the artist to "burst . . . into a loud

Elizabeth Mankin Kornhauser

Figure 13
George Catlin
Shooting Flamingoes, 1857
Oil on canvas, 19 x 26½ in.
Memorial Art Gallery of the
University of Rochester, N.Y.
Marion Stratton Gould Fund

laugh. He screamed, and I fired" repeatedly, causing his young guide to fall "backwards, entangled in the bushes."[58] As the flamingoes began to take flight, Catlin explained, "[O]f all the curious hunting or other scenes that I have seen on earth, that scene was the most curious."[59] The humorous narrative detail of the young guide, portrayed in caricature, sprawled out in the bushes, shrinking back in fear of Catlin's repeating rifle, and the enormous brilliantly colored birds falling from the sky as Catlin shot them, provide perhaps the most exotic images of the Colt Firearms series.[60] However, none of the 1857 paintings were mass-produced in print form. Colt did, however, use the earlier examples produced by John McGahey for newspaper and magazine articles that continued to appear in the media in 1857.

Final Years

Catlin would make a third and final trip to South America and beyond, leaving as early as 1858 and returning before September 1860.[61] On 1 March 1860 he wrote to his friend and patron Samuel Colt, again asking for financial assistance:

> I returned some months since from another long and laborious tour of South America, in which I have laboured very hard, and made valuable Collections & on my return voyage was attacked with an abcess [sic] in my right knee.... I know of no one whose good heart I can appeal to with the same Confidence as to yours ... to loan me that amount, for the security of which I will ... send you immediately as collateral security three Vols. of drawings by my own hand, Containing every painting in the N. Am. Collection with those gathered in my recent Tour of the Pacific side of the Rocky Mountains to the Russian Possessions and Kamskata ... about the size of the oil paintings I made for you & are the best works I have ever produced or ever shall produce. And there is not, nor can there be any duplicate of it on earth. And I know of no other man on earth in whose hands I would place it for keeping till my return.[62]

While a response from Colt has not been found, this letter is a testament to the long-standing friendship between the two men and to Colt's generous patronage of Catlin.

Both Catlin and Colt employed art in the service of their life's work. Art tended to soften the hard edges of the realities of their time, which included the often violent claiming of wilderness lands, the decimation of Indian tribes and their sustenance (the buffalo), slavery, world conflict, and the American Civil War. William Truettner writes of the conflict embedded in Catlin's art: "[H]e claimed preservation as the goal of his image-making, but one could argue that in doing so he was transferring the collective white guilt of destroying a race to the more benign process of recording it—a process that tended to soften and aestheticize the hard moral question of who was to blame."[63] Likewise, Colt commissioned compelling visual images in the form of paintings, colored lithographs, and black-and-white wood engravings to aestheticize and advertise his latest guns. While often presented as "peacemakers" or for use in hunting wild animals, and creatively designed to attract buyers, these were, in fact, lethal weapons that helped fuel world conflict. The Colt Firearms paintings and prints captured the power, novelty, and aesthetic qualities of Colt guns in a vivid and compelling narrative series and represent one of the most fascinating collaborations in the history of American art and industry.

Notes

I am grateful to Nancy Anderson and Bill Truettner for sharing with me information and insightful observations about Catlin, and thank them, as well as Ann Brandwein and Carol Troyen, for their thoughtful reading of my essay.

1. For information on Elizabeth Hart Jarvis Colt's picture gallery, see Elizabeth Mankin Kornhauser et al., *American Paintings before 1945 in the Wadsworth Atheneum* (London and New Haven: Yale University Press, 1996), 22–31, and cat. 163 in this book.
2. William Hosley, *Colt: The Making of a Legend* (Amherst: University of Massachusetts Press, 1996), 166–71.
3. *Illustrated London News,* 30 April 1853, 327; George Catlin Research Files, National Gallery of Art, Washington, D.C.; newspaper clipping courtesy of Merl M. Moore, Jr.
4. There was at least one Catlin descendant still living in Hartford in the nineteenth century during the period when Colt and George Catlin were acquainted. Julius Catlin (1798–1888) was born in Hartford and spent most of his life in the city, where he became one of the original subscribers to the Wadsworth Atheneum. A wealthy

Elizabeth Mankin Kornhauser

merchant, he joined Colt in providing funding to bring the contents of Edward Sheffield Bartholomew's studio in Rome (see cats. 162–63) back to the Wadsworth Atheneum. (See *Descendants of the Immigrant Thomas Catlin,* compiled by Spencer B. Reynolds [Harwinton, Conn.: unpublished, 1985], in the collection of the Litchfield Historical Society, Litchfield, Conn.)

5. For biographical information on George Catlin, see Brian W. Dippie, *Catlin and His Contemporaries: The Politics of Patronage* (Lincoln: University of Nebraska Press, 1990); William H. Truettner, *The Natural Man Observed: A Study of Catlin's Indian Gallery* (Washington, D.C.: Smithsonian Institution Press, 1979); George Gurney and Therese Thau Heyman, eds., *George Catlin and His Indian Gallery* (New York and London: W. W. Norton with the Smithsonian American Art Museum, 2002); and *George Catlin's Souvenir of the North American Indians: A Facsimile of the Original Album,* with an introduction by William H. Truettner (Tulsa, Okla.: Gilcrease Museum, 2003).

6. Truettner, *The Natural Man Observed,* 61–68.

7. Catlin to Gen. Peter B. Porter, 22 February 1829, Buffalo and Erie County Historical Society, Buffalo, N.Y., quoted in Truettner, *The Natural Man Observed,* 13.

8. Catlin, *Letters and Notes on the Manners, Customs, and Condition of the North American Indians,* 2 vols. (London, 1841; reprint, Edinburgh: John Grant, 1926), vol. I, 17.

9. Colt was appointed a lieutenant colonel in 1850 in Connecticut (see "Hartford and Success"). On Catlin's first South American trip, his English traveling companion Smyth gave him the title of "Governor."

10. Quoted in Truettner, *The Natural Man Observed,* 36; Allan Nevins, ed., *The Diary of Philip Hone 1828–1851* (New York, 1927), 290–91.

11. Hosley, *Colt: The Making of an American Legend,* 22.

12. Charles T. Haven and Frank A. Belden, *A History of the Colt Revolver* (New York: William Morrow, 1940), 33.

13. J. R. Poinsett to Commanding Officer, Fort Moultrie, Charleston, S.C., 10 January 1838; National Archives. Secretary of War, Letters Sent, Military Letter Book, No. 18, 217. My thanks to Nancy Anderson, curator of British and American Art, National Gallery of Art, Washington, D.C., for the latter citation.

14. Brian W. Dippie, "Green Fields and Red Men," in Gurney and Heyman, eds., *George Catlin and His Indian Gallery,* 54.

15. Gurney and Heyman, eds., *George Catlin and His Indian Gallery,* 53.

16. Thomas Donaldson, "The George Catlin Indian Gallery in the U.S. National Museum," in *Annual Report of the Board of Regent of the Smithsonian Institution, Showing the Operations, Expenditures, and Condition of the Institution to July 1885* (Washington, D.C.: U.S. Government Printing Office, 1886), 230. My thanks to Nancy Anderson for providing this reference.

17. Catlin to Joel R. Poinsett, New York, February 1839; J. R. Poinsett Papers, Historical Society of Pennsylvania, Philadelphia; Archives of American Art, roll 29, frame 202. My thanks to Nancy Anderson for making available a copy of this letter in the George Catlin Files, National Gallery of Art, Washington.

18. "Recommendations for a Trial of Repeating Arms," submitted by Colt to Joel R. Poinsett, secretary of war, 6 March 1839, Samuel Colt Papers, Box 2, Connecticut His-

torical Society, Hartford. I am grateful to Herb Houze for bringing this source to my attention.

19. "Fair at the American Institute," New York *Evening Post,* 18 October 1839.

20. For a discussion of Catlin's "Albums Unique," see Truettner, *George Catlin's Souvenir,* xvi–xix.

21. Receipt for the painting, "Saml Colt Esq. / to Mr. Gilbert—Dr. / For a picture representing the last / Experiment of Mr. Colt's Submarine battery / In Washington City . . . $60 / Received payement [*sic*] / New York. 15 octr. 1844." Samuel Colt Papers, Archives, Connecticut Historical Society, Hartford, reproduced in R. L. Wilson, *The Paterson Colt Book* (Palo Alto, Calif.: Sturtz-LeVett Publishing Company, 2002), 68.

22. George Groce and David H. Wallace, *Dictionary of Artists in America* (New Haven and London: Yale University Press, 1957), 256.

23. Colt's list of presentation pistols, dated 29 October 1851, is reproduced in Joseph G. Rosa, *The History of Colt's London Firearms 1851–1857* (London: Arms & Armour Press, 1976), 1951. The listing for Catlin's gun reads as follows: "1 Callen [*sic*] Am. Indian Museum," which is an erroneous transcription of "Catlin." For reference to the presentation pistol given to Hiram Powers, see Hiram Powers, Florence, Italy, to Samuel Colt, 10 September 1851, letter reproduced in Henry Barnard, ed., *Armsmear: the home, the arms, and the armory of Samuel Colt. A Memorial* (New York: Alvord Printer, 1866), 154.

24. Quoted in Therese Thau Heyman, "George Catlin and the Smithsonian," in *George Catlin and His Indian Gallery,* 256; John H. McIlvain to Spencer Baird, 31 January 1854, 52:8:64, Smithsonian Institution Archives, Washington, D.C.

25. Katherine Emma Manthorne, *Tropical Renaissance: North American Artists Exploring Latin America, 1839–1879* (Washington, D.C., and London: Smithsonian Institution Press, 1989), 67–84.

26. Brian W. Dippie, *Catlin and His Contemporaries: The Politics of Patronage* (London and Lincoln: University of Nebraska, 1990), 343.

27. Truettner, *The Natural Man Observed,* 132–33.

28. Dippie, *Catlin and His Contemporaries,* 344.

29. Quoted in Dippie, *Catlin and His Contemporaries,* 346; George Catlin to Thomas Phillips, 3 May 1854, Archives, Thomas Gilcrease Institute of American History and Art, Tulsa, Okla.

30. Ibid., 344.

31. Many of the cartoon sketches are illustrated in George Catlin, *EPISODES FROM Life Amongst the Indians and Last Rambles Amongst the Indians of the Rocky Mountains and the Andes,* ed. Marvin C. Ross (Norman: University of Oklahoma Press, 1959), 182–342. As part of the systematic cataloguing of the collections of the National Gallery of Art, the George Catlin collection at the gallery is being prepared under the direction of Nancy Anderson, Curator of British and American Painting.

32. In addition to the work of Brian Dippie, the following sources have been consulted to help define Catlin's travels: Edgardo Carlos Krebs, "George Catlin and South America: A Look at his 'Lost' Years and His Paintings of Northeastern Argentina," in *American Art Journal* 22, no. 4 (1990): 4–40; and Katherine Manthorne, *Tropical Renaissance,* 84–89.

illustrate a number of stories that appeared in newspapers and magazines in London and New York from 1855 to 1857 promoting the efficiency and effectiveness of Colt guns (see "George Catlin and the Colt Firearms Series," fig. 9). The scene in *A Mid-Day Halt on the Rio Trombutas* was explained in a letter from Catlin's traveling companion in South America, the young Englishman Smyth, written to the *London Morning Advertiser* and reproduced in a number of other papers, including *The Crayon*, 18 April 1855, which tells the story of Catlin, Smyth, and their party traveling down the Rio Trombutas in Brazil. While most of the group slept in the boat, Catlin and Smyth made a fire on shore and roasted a pig. Catlin suddenly exclaimed, "Now, I want you to keep perfectly cool, and don't spill your gravy—there is a splendid tiger behind you!" The tiger [actually a leopard] was playing with the legs of one of the men in their party, fast asleep. Catlin went to the boat to get his Colt rifle and, from the boat, took aim, whereupon "at the crack of the rifle the animal gave a piercing screech, and leaped about 15 feet straight into the air, and fell quite dead."[1]

In the painting Catlin places himself in the center foreground, surrounded by a luxuriant tropical forest. He stands with one leg on the boat and the other on shore, poised with his Colt rifle ready to take aim. The leopard, whose paw is on the leg of the sleeping Spaniard, stares back at Catlin with a look of awareness and alarm. Catlin's friend Smyth crouches by the fire, fearfully staring at the leopard. Catlin's hastily discarded hat lies nearby. All are seemingly unaware of the leopard's mate crouching in the foliage at left in the background.

Catlin, who was able to weave an entertaining tale around this adventure, also later wrote of this incident in *Life Amongst the Indians* (1857).[2] He made excellent use of the cupola boat seen in this painting, as he explained, "At Nauta I found a Portuguese, the owner of a cupola trading boat, with whom I made an arrangement to descend the Amazon with us to Obidos, a distance of one thousand miles, giving me every opportunity of stopping in front of various Indian villages and making my sketches. The cupola enabled us three to sleep comfortably, and was a good *atelier* in which to finish my sketches as we moved along."[3]

Among the numerous accounts of this story that appeared from 1855 to 1857 is an article that praised Colt's revolvers in the *Illustrated London News*, 11 April 1857, which was accompanied by an illustration of the work. Upon seeing the "panther" playing with the sleeping man's legs, "Catlin went cautiously down for his revolver rifle which had been left in the boat. . . . Catlin gave a whistle, the panther raised his head just the height he wanted, and immediately received a ball between the eyes." This image was also illustrated in *Frank Leslie's Illustrated Newspaper*, 16 May 1857, as "An Adventure in the Luxuriant Forests of Brazil, the Panthers of the Rio Trombutas."[4]

Notes

1. *London Morning Advertiser*, 5 March 1855; also in "Anecdotes of Catlin," *The Crayon*, 18 April 1855, 252; and "Anecdotes of Catlin," *Merry's Museum and Parley's Magazine*,

New York, 1 July 1855. The story appeared later in the *Illustrated London News*, 11 April 1857, 303, with an illustration after the lithograph (see "George Catlin and the Colt Firearms Series," fig. 9) and in the *Saturday Evening Post*, 16 May 1857, 5, with an illustration after the lithograph (see "George Catlin and the Colt Firearms Series," fig. 9).
2. George Catlin, EPISODES FROM *Life Amongst the Indians and Last Rambles Amongst the Indians of the Rocky Mountains and the Andes*, ed. Marvin C. Ross (Norman: University of Oklahoma Press, 1959), 43–45.
3. Ibid., 176–77.
4. *Illustrated London News*, 11 April 1857, 332, and *Frank Leslie's Illustrated Newspaper*, 16 May 1857, 364. The story also appears in *The Crayon*, 15 April 1855, 252. Catlin Research Files, National Gallery of Art, Washington, D.C., clippings courtesy of Merl M. Moore.

145

George Catlin
American, 1796–1872
Water Hunting for Deer, a Night Scene on the Susquehanna, Penn., ca. 1854–55
Oil on canvas, 19½ x 26¾ in. (49.5 x 68 cm)
Provenance: commissioned by Samuel Colt, Hartford, Conn.; by bequest to Elizabeth Hart Jarvis Colt, in 1862; to her sister Hetty Hart Jarvis, before 1898; to Hetty's daughter Elizabeth Hart Jarvis Robinson (Mrs. Charles L. F. Robinson), Newport, R.I.; to her son, Francis Robinson, Newport, R.I., about 1940; with Kennedy Galleries, New York, in 1961; collection of H. Britt Brown, Kansas, until 2005.
Wadsworth Atheneum Museum of Art
The Ella Gallup Sumner and Mary Catlin Sumner Collection Fund, 2005.2.3

Catlin's inspiration for this painting came from a trip he made to the region where he grew up. According to a report in the New York *Evening Post*, 18 October 1839, "It was with one of Colt's pistols that Catlin . . . recently shot three deer in succession while traveling [*sic*] through the state of Pennsylvania."[1] Catlin grew up near the banks of the Susquehanna River in Broome County, New York, where he "led an ideal rural existence, hunting, fishing, searching for Indian remains, and absorbing the colorful backwoods tales of the old settlers and trappers."[2]

In this night scene Catlin is shown in the bow of the boat, with his Colt repeating rifle aimed at the deer along the shore in front of him. His recent shots

Elizabeth Mankin Kornhauser

are indicated by puffs of white smoke above the gun. Two other figures are in the boat. A torch on a stationary pole illuminates the scene, and the sky above is moonlit, although the moon is concealed by foliage. Catlin uses earth red and raw umber to create the eerie reddish cast of light from the torch. He has hit four of the deer, which fall wounded and bloodied in the water. This subject was one of the six paintings in the Firearms series that was selected to be part of the series of lithographs for Samuel Colt (see cat. 150).

Catlin painted several other versions of this scene.[3] In addition, this painting was used to illustrate a number of articles promoting Colt's guns. In the *Illustrated London News,* 11 April 1857, the image appeared with the following account: "Another instance of the revolver principle applied to the rifle is in what is called 'water hunting' in that part of North America which Mr. Catlin describes himself as having been 'raised.' In the warm nights of summer the deer come down to the rivers to bathe and feed on the aquatic plants. The difficulty with the ordinary rifle was that only one shot could be got, as, from their rapidity and shyness, they are out of sight in a moment. Mr. Catlin, on one occasion, returning to the scenes of his boyhood on the shores of the Susquehanna, organized a party on a fair night, and seven deer were brought down by the revolver rifle, other deer having gone off bleeding."[4]

Notes

1. "Fair at the American Institute," New York *Evening Post,* 18 October 1839; courtesy of Merl M. Moore, The George Catlin Papers, National Gallery of Art, Washington, D.C.
2. William H. Truettner, *The Natural Man Observed: A Study of Catlin's Indian Gallery* (Washington, D.C.: Smithsonian Institution Press, 1979), 11.
3. Ibid., nos. 553 and 554, 301.
4. *Illustrated London News,* 11 April 1857, 332; George Catlin Files, National Gallery of Art, Washington, D.C; clipping courtesy of Merl M. Moore.

146

George Catlin

American, 1796–1872

Catlin the Artist Shooting Buffalos with Colt's Revolving Pistol, 1855

Oil on canvas, 19 x 26½ in. (48.3 x 67.3 cm)

Signed and dated lower left: Catlin. 55

Provenance: commissioned by Samuel Colt, Hartford, Conn.; by bequest to Elizabeth Hart Jarvis Colt, in 1862; to her sister Hetty Hart Jarvis, before 1898; to Hetty's daughter Elizabeth Hart Jarvis Robinson (Mrs. Charles L. F. Robinson), Newport, R.I.; to her daughter Elizabeth Robinson Cushman (Mrs. E. Sanderson Cushman), Port Washington, N.Y., and Newport, R.I., by 1940; with Kennedy Galleries, in 1961; collection of H. Britt Brown, Kansas, until 2005.

Wadsworth Atheneum Museum of Art

The Ella Gallup Sumner and Mary Catlin Sumner Collection Fund, 2005.2.1

This particular painting for the Colt Firearms series stands out from the others in a number of respects. While most of the paintings are based on specific incidents that took place during Catlin's North and South American travels, and were replicated by the artist, this painting is the only known version of this scene. In addition, it is the only painting of the group of ten that shows Catlin using a very recently made Colt pistol rather than the Paterson Colt repeating rifle seen in the other paintings. The scale of the main figure, Catlin himself, is placed more aggressively in the center foreground of the composition and appears larger than in the other works. Finally, the gun itself is the focus of the painting. This is the most powerful marketing image of the Firearms series.

Galloping at a fast pace in the midst of a herd of buffalo, Catlin is seen wearing frontiersman garb, inspired by Native American attire, including a cap with a visor and a fringed leather shirt and pants; a leather-fringed rifle holder, the butt of the rifle seen at the top, is slung across his left shoulder. Holding the reins in his left hand, he shoots at a buffalo with the heavy five-pound Colt pistol in his right hand. The viewer is drawn to the red flame and smoke at the striking point of the gun's hammer and emanating from the barrel. Puffs of white smoke from the repeated shots float in the air. Five bloodied and dying buffalo surround Catlin. The rest of the herd runs off toward the right side into the distance. At the left are two Indian hunters with their ancient weapons—bow and arrow and spear—chasing buffalo up a steep hillside toward the background, but unable to hit a single one. The message is clear. In this action-packed scene, which gains power from the artist's ability to compress the composition into a small space, Catlin conveys the superiority of the Colt repeating pistol and, at the same time, predicts the demise of the Indian and the buffalo.

The power of this image was not lost on Colt, and it appears numerous times, as one of a set of six lithographs (see cat. 151) and in the media. A reference to this scene first appears in the London press as early as February 1855 and continues to 1857.[1] In more recent times it was thought that the scene represented Catlin hunting buffalo in Texas. However, an article in the *Illustrated London News,* 11 April 1857, which promoted the use of Colt guns for sport, using Catlin's exploits as the example, described this scene as having taken place on the Platte River: "In a buffalo chase which took place on the north fork of the Platte River, out of five shots which Catlin fired right and left in immediate succession while at the full gallop, four were successful in bringing down unwieldy buffaloes. Hence the highest metaphor expressive of excellence was applied to Colt's Revolver by the Indians, and to this day it is called, in the language of that district, "the medicine gun."[2]

Notes

1. "A Traveller in South America—Colt and Catlin," *Court Journal,* London, 3 February 1855: "From a host of startling incidents we select one about Colt's pistols, because we remember some years since we think in 1851 talking with Catlin on this subject, and listening to his vivid accounts of hunting the buffalo on the prairie with this

weapon, riding parallel at full gallops with some great bull, and shooting him down with successive discharges." See Catlin Research Files, National Gallery of Art, Washington, D.C.

2. An illustration after the lithograph for this work (see cat. 151) appeared in the *Illustrated London News*, 11 April 1857, 332.

147

George Catlin

American, 1796–1872

Catlin The Artist and Sportsman Releiving [sic] One of His Companions from an Unpleasant Predicament During His Travels in Brazil, ca. 1855

Text: "This man strayed from the encampment and alone attacked a group of 200 or more Peccaries, when having extended his powder he was compelled to retreat into a fallen tree crying 'murder' Catlin ran to his rescue with his Colt's Revolver / when after knocking over three of the leaders of the besieging party suddenly, the rest took to their heels leaving only the dead upon the field."

Tinted or colored lithograph on paper, 18 x 25 in. (45.7 x 63.5 cm)

Wadsworth Atheneum Museum of Art

The American Painting Purchase Fund, 2005.8.5

148

George Catlin

American, 1796–1872

Mid-day Halt on the Rio Trumbutos, Brazil, ca. 1855

Text: "While the Artist Catlin and one of his attendants were preparing their meal the former discovered a large Leopard playing with the legs of another of his party, a Spaniard, who was fast asleep/under some small palms, Catlin crept to the boat and got his Colt's Revolver, when he shot the Leopard between the eyes producing instant death, and he adds, 'This was one of the most satisfactory shots I have ever had.'"

Tinted or colored lithograph on paper, 18 x 25 in. (45.7 x 63.5 cm)

Wadsworth Atheneum Museum of Art

The American Painting Purchase Fund, 2005.8.4

149

George Catlin

American, 1796–1872

Catlin The Celebrated Indian Traveller and Artist, Firing his Colt's Repeating Rifle Before a Tribe of Carib Indians in South America, ca. 1855

Text: "It having been reported by one of my party that I had a Medicine Gun, which would fire all day without reloading, the men, Women & Children, assembled in front of the Chief's Lodge to get a sight of it,—when I found it necessary to make an exhibition—and arranged a target at a suitable distance where I took my position / in front of the crowd rapidly discharging all the chambers, and cocked the piece for a continuation, but the chief advanced and assured me they were all satisfied, and I had better save my powder and balls, as I might want them, on a very long journey."

Tinted or colored lithograph on paper, 18 x 25 in. (45.7 x 63.5 cm)

Wadsworth Atheneum Museum of Art

The American Painting Purchase Fund, 2005.8.6

150

George Catlin

American, 1796–1872

Water Hunting for Deer, A Night Scene on the River Susquehanna, Penn., ca. 1855

Imprint: G. Catlin pinxt / Day & Son, Lithr. To the Queen / On stone by J. M'Gahey, Bold Sqre. Chester.

Text beneath: Catlin writes, "I was on the water all night with my Colt's Revolving Rifle, and in the morning soon looked up and seven of my victims, several others were wounded, but made their escape."

Tinted or colored lithograph on paper, 18 x 25 in. (45.7 x 63.5 cm)

Wadsworth Atheneum Museum of Art

The American Painting Purchase Fund, 2005.8.1

151

George Catlin

American, 1796–1872

Catlin the Artist Shooting Buffalos with Colt's Revolving Pistol, ca. 1855

Imprint: G.Catlin pinxt / Day & Son, Lithr. To the Queen / On stone by
J. M'Gahey, Dold Sqre. Chester.

Text: "He writes, 'I gave five shots to the right and left, four of which were fatal
to the heart, and all in less than half a minute.'"

Tinted or colored lithograph on paper, 18 x 25 in. (45.7 x 63.5 cm)

Wadsworth Atheneum Museum of Art

The American Painting Purchase Fund, 2005.8.2151

152

George Catlin

American, 1796–1872

Catlin the Artist and Hunter Shooting Buffalos with Colt's Revolving Rifle, ca. 1855

Text: "He says, '[W]ith my two hired men Ba'tiste & Bogard, I took position
where a numerous herd of Buffalo were crossing a deep ravine, and being
unobserved I shot down eight or ten in succession leaving their carcasses /
for the wolves to devour.'"

Tinted or colored lithograph on paper, 18 x 25 in. (45.7 x 63.5 cm)

Wadsworth Atheneum Museum of Art

The American Painting Purchase Fund, 2005.8.3

The six lithographs after paintings by George Catlin were part of the Colt
Firearms commission that was produced for Samuel Colt in 1855 to promote his
guns. The English lithographic artist John McGahey (b. 1817), who was based in
Chester by 1853, drew Catlin's images on stone and wood.[1] The best-known
British lithographic printers of the period, Day & Son of London and Chester,
printed the six plates in 1855 (see "George Catlin and the Colt Firearms Series,"
p. 218). It is not known how many sets were made. This set descended in the
Colt family to Samuel Colt's grandniece through marriage, Linda Colt Miller;
other sets are in the following collections: Connecticut State Library, Hartford;
Amon Carter Museum, Fort Worth; and Beinecke Rare Book Library, Yale University, New Haven.

An accomplished draftsman, McGahey made improvements in the compositions as he worked with Catlin's paintings and transferred them to stone. In
Water Hunting for Deer, for example, McGahey enhanced the effect of the
night scene by adding a moonlit sky above the torchlight seen in Catlin's
painting. He also took care to include such details, seen in Catlin's painting, as
the puffs of white smoke from the Colt rifle. In several of the lithographs,
McGahey presents the Indian guides in a slightly more dignified manner than
is found in Catlin's paintings. For example, in *Catlin the Artist & Sportsman
Releiving* [sic] *One of His Companions from an Unpleasant Predicament,* Catlin
portrays the Indian guide in near caricature, while in the lithograph McGahey
provides a more dignified likeness. In addition, improvements in perspective
and additions of foliage and vegetation in some of the South American scenes
are seen.

One of the most fascinating distinctions between Catlin's paintings and
McGahey's lithographs can found in *Catlin the Artist Shooting Buffalos with
Colt's Revolving Pistol.* In the painting, dated 1855, Catlin shows himself shooting a Colt U.S. Model 1847, produced in Colt's Whitneyville, Connecticut, factory.
This is likely the pistol Catlin took to South America. This model (cat. 29), which
weighs five pounds, has a long nine-inch barrel, which is clearly shown in
Catlin's painting. Samuel Colt had presented the artist with guns in 1839 and
again in 1851 (see "George Catlin and the Colt Firearms Series," notes 18, 23). But
in the lithograph drawn by McGahey, the gun has been updated to a more
recent model, the Hartford-made Holster Pistol of 1848 to 1850 (cat. 39), which
has a shorter seven-and-a-half-inch barrel. Colt was interested in using these
lithographs to sell his most recent guns and may have asked the lithographer
to update the gun in the print with a more recent model.[2]

This compelling image proved a powerful marketing tool for Colt, who
managed to have it placed in a number of newspaper and magazine articles
on the use of Colt guns.[3]

Notes

1. Little is known about the English lithographic artist John McGahey. The information here is drawn from the lithographs themselves and from *bwpics.co.uk/.html.*

2. My thanks to Herb Houze for providing this information.

3. *Illustrated London News,* 11 April 1857, 332, and *Frank Leslie's Illustrated Newspaper,*
16 May 1857; see "George Catlin and the Colt Firearms Series," fig. 10.

160

Gerald S. Hayward

English, 1845–1926

Samuel Colt, ca. 1856

Signed lower right:

Gerald S. Hayward

Watercolor on ivory in a gold locket

case with hair work on reverse

under a glass window, 3 x 3¼ in.

(7.6 x 8.3 cm)

Wadsworth Atheneum

Museum of Art

Bequest of Elizabeth Hart Jarvis

Colt, 1905.67

Gerald S. Hayward was a portrait miniature painter who was active in London and New York. He likely executed this miniature portrait of Samuel Colt to commemorate his wedding in June 1856.

161

Richard Morrell Staigg

Anglo-American, 1817–1881

Elizabeth Hart Jarvis, 1856

Signed at lower right: R.M.S.

Inscribed on verso: Lissie / EHJ June 1856

Watercolor on ivory in gold locket case with hair work on reverse under a

glass window, 2⅞ x 2⅜ in. (7.3 x 5.7 cm)

Wadsworth Atheneum Museum of Art

Bequest of Elizabeth Hart Jarvis Colt, 1905.65

Staigg was born in Leeds, England, and immigrated with his family to the United States in 1831, settling in Newport, Rhode Island. He was trained by the artist Jane Stuart in the rudiments of miniature portrait painting and was later influenced by Washington Allston and the celebrated Newport miniaturist Edward Greene Malbone.[1] He later lived in Boston and New York, from 1853 to 1864, when he executed this miniature portrait of Elizabeth Hart Jarvis Colt. It was painted at the time of her wedding to Samuel Colt, which took place on 5 June 1856.

Note

1. Dale T. Johnson, *American Portrait Miniatures in the Manney Collection* (New York: Metropolitan Museum of Art, 1991), 204–5.

Elizabeth Mankin Kornhauser

162

Edward Sheffield Bartholomew

American, 1822–1858

Colonel Samuel Colt, ca. 1857

Marble, height 38 in.

Wadsworth Atheneum Museum of Art

Bequest of Elizabeth Hart Jarvis Colt,

1905.980

163

Edward Sheffield Bartholomew

American, 1822–1858

Elizabeth Hart Jarvis Colt, ca. 1857

Marble, height 26 in.

Wadsworth Atheneum Museum of Art

Bequest of Elizabeth Hart Jarvis Colt, 1905.1122

The American sculptor Edward Sheffield Bartholomew was born in Colchester, Connecticut, and moved to Hartford when he was fifteen. Beginning in 1845, he worked for periods of time as "keeper of the gallery" at the newly opened Wadsworth Atheneum in Hartford. By December 1847, Bartholomew had moved to New York to attend classes at the National Academy of Design and lodged in the University Building where his Hartford friends Frederic Edwin Church and Samuel Colt also kept rooms. By 1851 Bartholomew had settled in Rome, where he produced notable neoclassical sculpture.[1]

In addition to his works drawn from biblical and classical sources, he also enjoyed popular success among the many Americans who, while visiting Rome, sat for their portraits in Bartholomew's studio. The artist's chief work, *Eve Repentant,* ca. 1855, was acquired by Joseph Harrison, Jr., the Philadelphia collector who had also purchased Catlin's Indian Gallery collection in London from creditors in 1852 (see "George Catlin and the Firearms Series"). The Wadsworth Atheneum acquired a replica of this work following Bartholomew's untimely death.

In November 1857, on one of Bartholomew's return trips to America, he and Frederic Church were honored at a testimonial dinner in Hartford. Samuel Colt attended and there commissioned portrait busts of himself and his wife, as well as a sculpture of their new son, Samuel Jarvis Colt, who died soon afterward, and Colt's sister-in-law, Hetty Jarvis.[2] Bartholomew returned to Rome in December with these and other important commissions. However, poor health, which had plagued him for much of his life, worsened, and he died shortly thereafter in Naples at the age of thirty-six. Colt, along with James Batterson, the Hartford architect, monument manufacturer, and art patron, and other civic leaders pledged money to purchase the contents of Bartholomew's studio, sending Batterson to Rome as their delegate.[3] As the lead sponsor, Colt pledged five hundred dollars and provided Batterson with a letter of introduction to the leading American sculptor in Rome, Hiram Powers.[4] The collection was retrieved for the Hartford community and put on display in the Wadsworth Atheneum in the summer of 1859.

The four Colt portraits were part of the studio works that returned to Hartford in the shipments containing the contents of Bartholomew's studio.[5] Samuel Colt's portrait bust shows him dressed in classical garb, while Elizabeth Colt wears a low cut Victorian dress with a rose at the bust for her portrait. The Colt portraits were based on photographs supplied by Elizabeth Colt for the artist to take to Rome, and were later returned.[6]

Notes

1. For biographical information on Bartholomew, see Thayer Tolles, ed., *American Sculpture in the Metropolitan Museum of Art,* vol. I (New York: Metropolitan Museum of Art, 1999–2001), 96; H. Nichols B. Clark, *A Marble Quarry: The James H. Ricau Collection of Sculpture at the Chrysler Museum of Art* (New York: Hudson Hills Press, 1997), 178–80; William G. Wendell, "Edward Sheffield Bartholomew, Sculptor," *Wadsworth Atheneum Bulletin* (Winter 1962): 1–18.

2. Henry Deming, "Oration," *Hartford Daily Times,* 20 November 1857, and William Hosley, *Colt: The Making of a Legend* (Amherst: University of Massachusetts Press, 1996), 168.

3. James Batterson also founded the Travelers Insurance Company in 1864 and served as a trustee of the Wadsworth Atheneum from 1861 until his death in 1901.

4. *Historical Documents and Notes* (Hartford: Connecticut Historical Society, 1889), 46.

5. "Miscellaneous," *New York Times,* 26 October 1859: "Another consignment of the Bartholomew Marbles was received by Mr. Battison [*sic*], of Hartford. . . . The marbles for Col. Colt's family including portrait busts of Mr. and Mrs. Colt, Miss Jarvis, and the statue of the little boy who died so suddenly after the models were made by Mr. Bartholomew, are embraced in the consignment . . . they will be put on exhibition, for the benefit of Mr. Bartholomew's mother. The statue of "Eve," for the Hartford Atheneum, is not expected to arrive before April."

6. Edward Bartholomew to Frederic Church, Rome, 29 May 1856, Archives, Wadsworth Atheneum. This letter indicates that Bartholomew sent the Colt photographs back, but had not heard from the Colts regarding their safe return.

165a–b. South (left) and northeast (right) views of Elizabeth Colt's Picture Gallery on the second floor of Armsmear, ca. 1880. Wadsworth Atheneum Museum of Art.

Horsley's *Portrait Group of Queen Victoria with Her Children* (ca. 1854, Forbes Magazine Collection, New York City). On her right hand, Elizabeth wears the enormous diamond ring given to her by her husband. Known as the "stone of fire," it was a gift to Colonel Colt from Charles Albert, king of Sardinia. In contrast, as a religious woman, Colt holds a book of Scripture in her hand. Her son leans toward his mother and holds the string of a miniature cannon, a memento of Colonel Colt's from the Mexican War. The subjects are surrounded by the elaborate furnishings of Armsmear.

The portraits were installed on the two end walls of the picture gallery on its completion in 1867 (see cats. 165a–b). Elizabeth Colt's vision for her deceased husband's portrait was fulfilled: the massive image of Sam Colt allowed his powerful presence to live on after his death. The portraits dominated the space, which became a major focal point for civic and social events in Hartford until the end of the century. In 1866 Elliott also painted Colt's friend and neigh-

bor, Joseph Church (1793–1876), a wealthy Hartford insurance adjuster, who was the father of Frederic Church. Elliott would paint his fellow artist Church in the following year.

Notes

1. Henry T. Tuckerman, *Book of the Artists* (New York: Putnam, 1867), 302.
2. Elizabeth Hart Jarvis Colt to Frederic Church, 18 December 1863, Olana State Historic Site, Hudson, N.Y.
3. Rev. William Jarvis to his nephew William Jarvis, 10 March 1865, Jarvis Family Papers, Connecticut Historical Society, Hartford.
4. Ibid., 29 March 1865

Elizabeth Mankin Kornhauser

166

J. Massey Rhind

American, 1860–1936

Samuel Colt as a Boy, 1902

Inscribed on the base: Copyright 1902 / J. Massey Rhind / sculpt.

Roman Bronze Works, New York

Bronze, height 10 in.

Wadsworth Atheneum Museum of Art

Bequest of Elizabeth Hart Jarvis Colt, 1905.1554

167

J. Massey Rhind

American, 1860–1936

Colonel Samuel Colt, 1902

Inscribed on base: 1902 by / J. Massey Rhind / Fecit

Roman Bronze Works, New York

Bronze, height 10½ in.

Wadsworth Atheneum Museum of Art

Bequest of Elizabeth Hart Jarvis Colt, 1905.1120

John Massey Rhind was a third-generation sculptor when he left Scotland for America in 1889. With a background in decorative architectural sculpture, Rhind arrived in the United States at a propitious time for his specialty and quickly became one of the country's leading sculptors of large public monuments and architectural designs. He received commissions for major works in many East Coast cities, including Hartford, where he created the monumental Corning Fountain for Bushnell Park.[1]

Elizabeth Hart Jarvis Colt commissioned Rhind to undertake the final memorial to her husband, the massive twenty-by-eighteen-foot Colt Memorial Statue, 1905. Located at the entrance to Colt Park (originally on the grounds of Armsmear), it was dedicated on 26 April 1906. The artist completed two small bronze maquettes in 1902, which were used as models for the monumental statue, which was cast at the Gorham Manufacturing Company Foundry in Providence, Rhode Island. *Samuel Colt as a Boy* served as the maquette for the bronze sculpture of Colt as a young man, positioned on the granite steps of the monument at the left, showing the seated boy "genius" as a young sailor holding a wooden revolver that he had whittled. The memorial's granite steps lead to an exedra (outdoor seat) topped by a bronze full-length standing portrait of Samuel Colt, based on the maquette *Colonel Samuel Colt,* holding a large document under his right arm and wearing a heavy overcoat. The wings of the exedra contain two relief panels depicting high points in Colt's life, showing him presenting sample guns to the czar of Russia, inscribed: "Royal presentation Saint Peters 8VRC 1853," and Colt's presentation to the British House of Commons on the use of machines in the manufacture of firearms, inscribed: "Demonstration before House of Commons 1854." An inscription on the front, devised by Elizabeth, reads: "Samuel Colt / 1814–1862 / On the Grounds on Which / This Memorial Stands / To Speak of His Genius / His Enterprise and His / Success and of His/ Great and Loyal Heart / His Wife in Faithful Affection / Dedicates this Memorial."[2]

Notes

1. For biographical information, see Wayne Craven, *Sculpture in America* (Newark: University of Delaware Press and New York and London: Cornwall Books, 1968; reprint, 1984), 486–89.

2. Save Outdoor Sculpture, Connecticut Survey, 1993, Library, Wadsworth Atheneum, and Hosley, *Colt,* 223–24.

Colt Family Tree

Benjamin Colt
(1698–1754)
m.
Miriam Harris
(1702–?)

| John Colt (1725–1784) m. Mary Lord | Joseph Colt (1727–?) m. Desire Pratt | Mary Colt (1728–1810) m. Thomas Giddings | Harris Colt (1731–1797) m. Elizabeth Turner | Sarah Colt (c. 1733–1799) | Temperance Colt (1736–1799) m. Abner Lord |

| Benjamin Colt (1762–1848) m. Polly Hopkins | Lucretia Colt (1763–1767) | Daniel Colt (1767–1816) | Lucretia Colt (1769–1771) | Ethelinda Colt (1771–1864) | Amy Colt (1773–1843) m. Moses Parker | Betsy Colt (1774–?) m. Ebenezer Foot |

Ethelinda Colt
(1792–1845)
m.
Joseph Dudley Selden

Dudley Selden
(1794–1855)

| Margaret Collier Colt (1806–1825) | Sarah Ann Colt (1808–1829) | John Caldwell Colt (1810–1842) m. Caroline Henshaw | Christopher Colt (1812–1855) | Samuel Colt (1814–1862) m. Elizabeth Hart Jarvis |

Samuel Caldwell Colt
(1841–1915)

| | | Samuel Jarvis Colt (1857) | Caldwell Hart Colt (1858–1894) | Elizabeth Jarvis Colt (1860) |

Benjamin Colt
(1738–1781)
m.
Lucretia Ely

James Danielson Colt
(1740–1809)
m.
Phebe Ely

Jabez Colt
(1742–?)

Peter Colt
(1744–1824)
m.
Sarah Lyman

Roswell Lyman Colt
(1779–1856)
m.

Lucretia Colt
(1776–?)
m.
[?] Prince

Elisha Colt
(1778–1827)
m.
Rebecca Cooke

m.
Lucretia Ann Davis

Christopher Colt
(1780–1850)
m.
Sarah Caldwell

Margaret Oliver
m.
Olivia Sargeant
(sister of Luther P. Sargeant)

Catherine Warriner

Julia Colt
(1835–?)
m.
Friedrich von Oppen

Elisha Colt
(1804–1874)
m.
Elizabeth Selden Spencer

Matilda Colt
(1820–?)
m.
Elisha King Root
(1808–1865)

James Benjamin Colt
(1816–1878)

Norman Knox Colt
(1821–?)

William Upson Colt
(1824–1848)

Mary Lucretia Colt
(1826–1828)

Olivia Payne Colt
(1828–1838)

Henrietta Selden Colt
(1861–1862)

[daughter]
(1862)

Patents, Patent Reissues, and Caveats Issued to Samuel Colt and Elisha K. Root

Patents awarded in the United States for new, novel, or useful inventions protected such designs for fourteen years. If during that period another individual copied or used elements of a patented design without the express approval of the patentee, monetary damages could be sought through court actions.

The life of a patent could be extended beyond the fourteen years allowed by law if the patentee applied to the patent commissioner for an extension or a reissue. Both provided the patentee with an additional seven years of protection. Extensions were granted to patentees upon the presentation of evidence that they had yet to fully realize the profit potential of their inventions (for example, if they had spent a protracted amount of time developing a product before it could be brought to market or had been prevented from doing so by other circumstances). During Samuel Colt's lifetime the process of securing an extension went through three changes. Initially, approval could be granted by a committee composed of the secretary of state, the commissioner of patents, and the solicitor of the Treasury. In 1848 this committee was abolished, and thereafter approval was solely at the discretion of the patent commissioner. Subsequently the process was again changed, and extensions became subject to congressional action. A much simpler method of extending a patent's life involved its reissue. Reissues were granted to patentees if they could demonstrate that they had accidentally omitted key descriptions in the specifications filed with their patents. If this could be proved, the original patent was surrendered and a new one awarded. Reissues were generally sought near the end of the original patent's validity.

Samuel Colt used both of the above methods to extend the life of his patents. His efforts met with varying degrees of success. In 1848 he was successful in receiving a reissue for his patent of 1836. However, when he tried to extend the life of that reissue in 1854, Congress defeated the measure.

Prior to the submission of a patent application, the U.S. Patent Office provided inventors with a mechanism to protect their designs. For a nominal fee a description of an invention with drawings illustrating its design could be submitted as a caveat. Caveats were used to protect designs under development and to establish primacy, as well as authorship, should questions arise as to who had first invented a design. Due to their sensitive content, they were kept in the secret files of the Patent Office. As patents were commercial documents, they could be traded or sold by their owners. When that occurred, assignments were attached to patents and the details recorded in the Patent Office files.

Patents issued in England also had a life of fourteen years. They could be extended by the rather novel method of applying for a separate Scottish patent at any time during that period. While Her Majesty's Patent Office did not accept caveats, designs could be registered. Continental patents offered the same protection as those issued in England and the United States. They differed, however, in that the patent had to be proved or verified within a set period of time after its issuance. Verification involved the construction of a model demonstrating the features and function of the design that had been patented.

U.S. Patents Issued to Samuel Colt

25 February 1836—Number 138, "Improvement in Fire-Arms" (designs for pistols and rifles having revolving cylinders)

29 August 1839—Number 1,304, "Improvement in Fire-Arms and in the Apparatus Used Therewith"

5 August 1853—disclaimer issued concerning claim number 3 (concerning the construction of percussion cap nipples in above patent)

24 October 1848—Reissue Number 124 for Patent Number 138 of 25 February 1836

3 September 1850—Number 7,613, "Improvement in Repeating Fire-Arms" (hinged barrel design)

10 September 1850—Number 7,629, "Improvement in Revolving Chambered Fire-Arms" (designs for cylinder stops and safety pins)

20 May 1856—Number 14,905, "Improvement in Fire-Arms" (slide and groove turning design)

24 February 1857—Number 16,683, "Improvement in Many-Chambered Rotating-Breech Fire-Arms" (construction of cylinder with turning grooves on rear face)

3 March 1857—Number 16,717, "Improvement in the Mode of Lubricating Fire-Arms" (design for syringe-style lubricator used on New Model Rifles)

24 November 1857—Number 18,678, "Improvement in Many-Chambered Rotating-Breech Fire-Arms" (cylinder pin design)

4 May 1858—Number 20,144, "Improvement in Revolving Fire-Arms" (redesigned cylinder pin)

18 January 1859—Number 22,626, "Improved Mode of Coupling Gun-Stocks with Pistols" (shoulder stock attachment design)

18 January 1859—Number 22,627, "Canteen Gun-Stock"

15 March 1859—Number 22,230, "Packing Cartridges" (use of string, wire, etc., to open cartridge packets)

U.S. Patent Applications Filed by Samuel Colt

7 June 1844—for tinfoil cartridges (withdrawn 8 June 1844)

8 June 1844—for Submarine Battery (withdrawn 9 June 1844)

29 March 1850—for powder flasks having plunger chargers (rejected 20 May 1850)

28 March 1851—for tinfoil cartridges (rejected 6 May 1851)

29 March 1856—for powder flasks having plunger chargers (rejected 17 April 1856)

Caveat Applications Filed by Samuel Colt with the U.S. Patent Office

28 March 1837—chamfering mouths of cylinder chambers

[October 1838]—design of hand and pawl to effect cylinder rotation

8 March 1839—construction of tinfoil cartridges suitable for use in pistols or rifles

28 August 1848—cylinder stop design

1 September 1848—cylinder stop design

16 September 1848—construction of revolving pistol and rifle, as well as loading lever improvements including smoke escape grooves, chamfered lead into cylinder stops

21 January 1851—loading lever designs

21 January 1851—loading lever plunger cut with ratchet teeth

English Patents Issued or Assigned to Samuel Colt

22 October 1835—Number 6,909, "Improvements in Firearms" (designs for pistols and rifles having revolving cylinders)

20 June 1849—Number 12,668, "Improvements in Firearms" (for the hand and pawl cylinder turning mechanism, cylinder stop design, loading lever catch, and the chamfered mouths of both the cylinder chambers, as well as the barrel breech)

22 November 1851—Number 13,823, "Certain Improvements in fire-arms" (letters patent voided due to Colt's failure to enroll the specifications)

3 March 1853—Number 535, "Improvements in Firearms" (for a slide and groove cylinder turning mechanism)

3 March 1853—Number 536, "Improvements in Blowers" (letters patent voided due to Colt's failure to enroll the specifications)

3 March 1853—Number 537, "Improvements in Forging Metals" (letters patent voided due to Colt's failure to enroll the specifications)

3 March 1853—Number 538, "Improvements in Firearms" (for a short cylinder pin, rack-and-pinion loading lever, as well as a hinged barrel design)

16 March 1853—Number 654, "Improvements in Annealing Metals"

3 September 1853—Number 2,039, "Improvements in Blowers" issued to Gage Stickney (assigned to Colt)

3 September 1853—Number 2,040, "Improvements in Forging Metals" issued to Gage Stickney (assigned to Colt)

22 February 1854—Number 429, "Improvements in Rifling Firearms" (for a machine capable of rifling multiple barrels at the same time)

12 April 1854—Number 861, "Improvements in Cutting Metals" (for milling and screw cutting machines used for shaping the frame, as well as other parts, of firearms)

9 June 1855—Number 1,323, "Improvements in Firearms" (for the design of a nipple bolster used to alter flintlock arms to the percussion ignition system)

16 April 1856—Number 908, "Improvements in Firearms" (issued to A. V. Newton on behalf of Samuel Colt for an adjustable rear sight and the lubricating device later protected by Colt's U.S. Patent Number 16,716, issued on 3 March 1857)

4 September 1858—Number 2,009, "Improvements in Firearms" (issued to A. V. Newton on behalf of Samuel Colt for a shoulder stock attachment device later protected by Colt's U.S. Patent Number 22,626, issued on 18 January 1859)

Austrian Patents Issued to Samuel Colt

22 April 1857—Improvements in Firearms

22 April 1857—Improvements in Powder Flasks

Belgian Patents Issued to Samuel Colt

16 October 1858—Improvements in Firearms

Selected Bibliography

Unpublished Materials

Christopher Colt Papers, Special Collections, University of Rhode Island Libraries, Providence, Rhode Island.

Colt Family Papers, Private Collection.

Colt Papers, Archives and Collection Files, Wadsworth Atheneum Museum of Art, Hartford, Connecticut.

Colt Papers, Connecticut Historical Society, Hartford, Connecticut.

Records of the Colt's Patent Fire Arms Manufacturing Company, Connecticut State Library, Hartford, Connecticut.

Published Materials

Arrigoni, Enrico G. *Le Colt di Garibaldi*. Milan: Il Grifo, 2000.

Bishop, J. Leander. *A History of American manufacture from 1608 to 1860 comprising annals of the industry of the United States in machinery, manufactures and useful arts, with a notice of the important inventions, tariffs, and the results of each decennial census*. 2 vols. Philadelphia and London: Edward Young & Co., 1864.

Blackmore, Howard L. *Gunmakers of London 1350–1850*. York, Pa.: George Shumway, 1986.

Catlin, George. EPISODES FROM *Life Amongst the Indians and Last Rambles Amongst the Indians of the Rocky Mountains and the Andes, with 152 Scenes and Portraits by the Artist*. Marvin C. Ross, ed. Norman: University of Oklahoma Press, 1959.

———. *Letters and Notes on the Manners, Customs, and Condition of the North American Indians*. 2 vols. London, 1841. Reprint, New York: Dover Publications, Inc., 1973.

Colt, Col. Samuel. "On the application of Machinery to the manufacture of Rotating Chambered-Breech Fire-Arms, and the peculiarities of those Arms." *Minutes of Proceedings of the Institution of Civil Engineers, with Abstracts of the Discussions*. Vol. XI, session 1851–52. London: Institution of Civil Engineers, 1852.

Dickens, Charles, ed. "Revolvers." *Household Words: A Weekly Journal* 9, no. 218 (27 May 1854): 352–56.

Dippie, Brian W. *Catlin and His Contemporaries: The Politics of Patronage*. Lincoln: University of Nebraska Press, 1990.

Grant, Ellsworth S. *The Colt Legacy: The Story of the Colt Armoury in Hartford, 1855–1980*. Providence, R.I.: Andrew Mowbray Inc., Publishers, 1974.

Gurney, George, and Therese Thau Heyman, eds. *George Catlin and His Indian Gallery*. New York and London: W. W. Norton & Co. with the Smithsonian American Art Museum, 2002.

Haven, Charles T., and Frank A. Belden. *A History of the Colt Revolver*. New York: William Morrow & Co., 1940.

Hosley, William. *Colt: The Making of an American Legend*. Amherst: University of Massachusetts Press, 1996.

Houze, Herbert G. *Colt Presentations from the Factory Ledgers 1856–1869*. Lincoln, R.I.: Andrew Mowbray Inc., Publishers, 2003.

———. *Colt Rifles and Muskets from 1847 to 1870*. Iola, Wis.: Krause Publications, 1996.

———. "Further Notes on the Forsyth Material in the Arms Collection of Colonel Colt." *Armax* 1, no. 1 (Spring/Summer 1987).

———. "The 1861 Inventory of the Arms and Miscellaneous Material in the Museum Room of the Colt Factory." *Armax* 1, no. 1 (Fall/Winter 1987).

———. "The 1861 Inventory of the Arms and Miscellaneous Material in the Office of Colonel Samuel Colt." *Armax* 1, no. 1 (Spring/Summer 1987).

Jarlier, Pierre. *Répertoire d'arquebusiers et de fourbisseurs français*. St.-Julien-du-Sault: François-Pierre Lobies, 1976.

Kornhauser, Elizabeth Mankin, et al. *American Paintings Before 1945 in the Wadsworth Atheneum*. 2 vols. New Haven and London: Yale University Press and the Wadsworth Atheneum, 1996.

Lamar, Howard R. *The Far Southwest 1846–1912: A Territorial History*. New York: W. W. Norton & Co., 1970.

Manthorne, Katherine Emma. *Tropical Renaissance: North American Artists Exploring Latin America, 1839–1879*. Washington D.C.: Smithsonian Institution Press, ca. 1989.

Mitchell, James L. *Colt: A Collection of Letters and Photographs about the Man, the Arms, the Company*. Harrisburg, Pa.: Stackpole Company, 1959.

Mowbray, Stuart C. *The Darling Pepperbox: The Story of Samuel Colt's Forgotten Competitors in Bellingham, Mass., and Woonsocket, R.I.* Lincoln, R.I.: Andrew Mowbray Inc., Publishers, 2004.

Parsons, John E., ed. *Sam'l Colt's Own Record*. Hartford: Connecticut Historical Society, 1949.

Patterson, Robert M. *In the Circuit Court of the United States, District of Massachusetts. Samuel Colt vs. The Mass. Arms Company. Report on the Trial of the*

Above-Entitled Cause, At Boston, on the Thirtieth Day of June, A.D. 1851, Before His Honor, Levi Woodbury, Associate Justice of the Supreme Court of the United States. Boston: White & Potter, 1851.

Phillips, Philip R., and R. L. Wilson. *Paterson Colt Pistol Variations*. Dallas: Jackson Arms, 1979.

Rosa, Joseph G. *Colonel Colt, London: The History of Colt's London Firearms, 1851–1857*. London: Arms & Armour Press, 1976.

Rosenberg, Nathan. *The American System of Manufactures*. Edinburgh: Edinburgh University Press, 1969.

Schreier, Philip. "Walker's Walkers: The Colt Walker Revolvers of Captain Samuel H. Walker, Texas Ranger." *Man at Arms* 20, no. 3 (May/June 1998).

Sellers, Frank M., and Samuel Smith. *American Percussion Revolvers*. Ottawa, Ontario: Museum Restoration Service, 1971.

Smith, Merritt Roe. *Harpers Ferry Armory and the New Technology*. Ithaca, N.Y.: Cornell University Press, 1977.

Sutherland, Robert Q., and R. L. Wilson. *The Book of Colt Firearms*. Kansas City, Mo.: R. Q. Sutherland, 1971.

Truettner, William H. Introduction to *George Catlin's Souvenir of the North American Indians: A Facsimile of the Original Album*. Tulsa, Okla.: Gilcrease Museum, 2003.

————. *The Natural Man Observed: A Study of Catlin's Indian Gallery*. Washington, D.C.: Smithsonian Institution Press, 1979.

Wilson, R. L. *The Paterson Colt Book: The Early Evolution of Samuel Colt's Repeating Arms*. Palo Alto, Calif.: Strutz-LeVett Publishing Co., 2002.

Collier, Elisha Hayden (continued)
  cat. 4, *29*, 30
  Collier's Patent Flintlock Revolving
    Rifle, cat. 5, *30*, 31
Colt, Caldwell, son of Samuel, 13
  Mrs. Elizabeth Hart Jarvis Colt and
    Son Caldwell, by Charles Loring
    Elliott, cat. 164, *242*, 243–44
Colt, Caroline Henshaw, 69n.14
Colt, Christopher, father of Samuel,
  37–38, 40, 42–43, 57nn. 1–2, 68
Colt, Elisha, 57n.2, 83n.23, 110, 111n.3, 112
Colt, Elizabeth Hart Jarvis, wife of
  Samuel, 9–10, 13, 80, 84n.36, 191,
  242
  and Colt Memorial Statue, 38, 245
  memorial collection of firearms, 13,
    21, *157*, 158
  private picture gallery, 203, 242, *244*
  Wadsworth Atheneum bequest, 13,
    183, 238
  Bartholomew, *Elizabeth Hart Jarvis*
    Colt, cat. 163, *241*
  Elliott, *Mrs. Elizabeth Hart Jarvis*
    Colt and Son Caldwell, cat. 164,
    242, 243–44
  Staigg, *Elizabeth Hart Jarvis*, cat.
    161, *240*
Colt, James B., brother of Samuel, 75
Colt, John, brother of Samuel, 2, 66,
  69n.14
Colt, Olivia Sargeant, stepmother of
  Samuel, 37–38
Colt, Samuel:
  childhood and education of, 37
  Congressional bribery, charges of,
    80
  correspondence of, 19
  death of, 13, 82
  demonstrating nitrous oxide, 1, 40
  as lieutenant colonel, *79*, 205
  marriage of, 80, 191
  medals and gifts awarded to,
    110–14, 184, 188–99

at sea, 1, 37–38
on slavery, 81
Bartholomew, *Colonel Samuel Colt*,
  cat. 162, *241*
Elliott, *Colonel Samuel Colt*, cat. 165,
  198, 242, *243*
Hayward, *Samuel Colt*, cat. 160, *240*
Lithopane Portrait of Samuel Colt,
  cat. 153, *232*
Rhind, *Colonel Samuel Colt*, cat. 167,
  245
Rhind, Colt Memorial Statue, 38,
  245
Rhind, *Samuel Colt as a Boy*, cat.
  166, *245*
Ulrich, bust of Samuel Colt, 157
Colt, Samuel Caldwell, nephew of
  Samuel, 69n.14
Colt, Samuel Jarvis, son of Samuel, 241
Colt, Sarah Caldwell, mother of
  Samuel, 37
Colt's Patent Fire Arms Manufacturing
  Company, Hartford (Coltsville), 4, 7,
  8, 11, 13, 78–84, 157, 171–82, 239, 243
  fire of, 13, 109, 173, *181*
  glass plate negatives, factory
    machinery, 172–80, *173*
  Grove Lane location, *4*, 79, 92
  and Hartford flood, 236–37
  Pearl St. location, 4, 78–79, 85
  unknown artist, *View of the Colt*
    Factory from Dutch Point or Little
    River, cat. 158, *239*
  unknown artist, *View of the Colt*
    Works with Steamboat from the
    South, Colt Meadows, cat. 159, *239*
  See also Armsmear
Coltsville, 8
Comblain, Hubert-Joseph, 122
  Comblain Pepperbox, cat. 77, *121*, 122
Connecticut State Agricultural
  Society Gold Medal, 1855, cat. 68,
  113
counterfeits, 123–24

Crimean War, 8–10
  Colt firearms provided for, 1, 9, 183,
    188–89, 191
  Gibb, *The Thin Red Line*, 9

Dafte, John, 27–28
Darling Brothers, 200
Day & Son (Day & Haghe), 218, 220, 231
Delvigne, Gustave, 119
Dennett, Charles F., 124, 187
Devisme, Louis-François, 93, 134
  Devisme Belt Pistol, cat. 103, *150*
Dickerson, Edward N., 80, 83n.33,
  123–25, 191, 200
Dickinson, Edward, 37
Dippie, Brian W., 209
Dorr, Thomas W., 64
Dorr rebellion, Rhode Island, 64
  Colt firearms provided for, 64
Douglas, Stephen A., 81
Dreyse, Nikolaus von, 115
  Colt-Dreyse Belt Pistol, cat. 78, 116,
    122

Egg, Joseph, 24
Ehlers, John, 57, 64–67, 72, 112
  sale of Colt patent rights, 65, *66*,
    68n.3
Elliott, Charles Loring, 242, 244
  Colonel Samuel Colt, cat. 165, 198,
    242, *243*
  Mrs. Elizabeth Hart Jarvis Colt and
    Son Caldwell, cat. 164, *242*,
    243–44
Elliott, E. G., Captain, 75–76
Ellsworth, Henry L., 41, 54
Enfield, rifles of, 10
England:
  Beaumont-Adams revolver, 9
  and Colt, 183–84, 189
  Colt patents filed in, 41, 100n.1
  Escopeta carbine, *76*
  Pimlico factory, London, 1, *6*, 8, 11,
    100, 134, 183–84

Royal Small Arms Factory, Enfield,
  8, 9
Tower of London, flintlock revolver
  from, cat. 142, 200, *201*
Worshipful Company of London
  Gunmakers, 33
  See also Crimean War; Great
    Exhibition, London; Institution
    of Civil Engineers, London; Sepoy
    Mutiny
Exhibition of the Industry of All
  Nations, New York, 1853
  Colt exhibition, *110*
  Exhibition Medal, 1853, cat. 67, *113*
exhibitions. *See* American Institute,
  New York, exhibitions
Exhibition of the Industry of All
  Nations, New York, 1853
Exposition Universelle, Paris, 1855
Great Exhibition of the Works of Art
  and Industry of All Nations,
  London, 1851
Exposition Universelle, Paris, 1855:
  Colt exhibition, 185
  Lefaucheux exhibition, 118
  Silver Medal, 1855, cat. 69, *114*, 185

factories, Colt. *See* Colt's Patent Fire
  Arms Manufacturing Company,
  Hartford (Coltsville)
  Kaiserliche Konigliche
    Privilegierten Machinen Fabrik,
    Innsbruck
  Patent Arms Manufacturing
    Company, Paterson
  Pimlico factory, London
Faxon, William, 107
Fenn, Harry, *View of "Armsmear,"* 203
Fillmore, Millard, president, 186, 195
Fisk, William, *George Catlin*, 205
flintlock firearms, 23, *24*
  Collier's Patent Flintlock Revolver,
    · cat. 4, *29*, 30
  Collier's Patent Flintlock Revolving

Rifle, cat. 5, *30*, *31*
Flintlock Revolver, cat. 142, 200, *201*
Forsyth, Reverend Alexander James,
    24, 31–33, 115, 116–17n.2
Forsyth and Co., 24, 31–33, 96
    Forsyth's Patent Exhibition Roller
        Primer Gunlock, cat. 6, *31*, 32
    Forsyth's Patent Exhibition Sliding
        Primer Gunlock, cat. 7, *32*
    Forsyth Patent Sliding Primer Pistol,
        cat. 8, *33*
France:
    and Colt, 184–86
    Colt patents filed in, 41, 93
Friedrich Wilhelm IV, king of Prussia,
    188–90

Gadsden Purchase, 11, *12*
Garibaldi, Giuseppe, 183, 187
    Grepper, *Giuseppe Garibaldi*, 185
Gehrmann, Theodor, 97, 115, 122
Ghaye, Lambert, Lieutenant, 151
Gibb, Robert, *The Thin Red Line*, *9*
Gibert, Antoine Placide, *The Last
    Experiment of Mr. Colt's
    Submarine Battery*, *208*
gifts to Colt, 183–85, 187–99
    Alexander II Portrait Silver Medal,
        cat. 131, *192*
    Katana Blade, cat. 136, 195, *196*, 197
    Katana Blade, cat. 137, 195, *196*, 197
    Lacquer Box, cat. 140, *198*
    Matchlock Gun, cat. 138, 25n.14, 195,
        197, 198
    Matchlock Gun, cat. 139, 25n.14, 195,
        197, 198
    Order of Mejidie, cat. 135, *194*, *195*
    Presentation Diamond Ring, 1854,
        cat. 130, *192*, 244
    Presentation Diamond Ring, 1856 or
        1858, cat. 132, *192*
    Presentation Snuffbox, cat. 133, *193*
    Prussian Model 1835 Jagerbusche,
        cat. 129, *190*

Snuffbox (gift of Sultan Abd-al-
    Majid), cat. 134, *194*, *195*
Two-Stage Vase, cat. 141, 198, *199*,
    243
Victor Emanuel Portrait Gold
    Medal, cat. 128, 110, 187, *188*
See also medals and awards to Colt
Gilon, N., 131–32
Great Exhibition of the Works of Art
    and Industry of All Nations,
    London, 1851, 1, 4–6, 96, 115
    Absolen, *United States Section of
        the Great Exhibition*, *209*
    Bibby, *North Transept, Great
        Exhibition of 1851*, *5*
    Bronze Exhibitor's Medal, 1851, cat.
        66, *113*
    Catlin Presentation, 208
    Colt exhibition, 4–5, *6*, 8, *80*, *183*,
        185, 208
    Crystal Palace, *5*, 6
    Forsyth & Co. exhibition, 31, 96
Grepper, A., *Giuseppe Garibaldi*, 185
Grubb, Joseph C., 117n.18
gunlocks:
    flintlock ignition, 23, *24*
    Forsyth's Patent Exhibition Roller
        Primer Gunlock, cat. 6, *31*, 32
    Forsyth's Patent Exhibition Sliding
        Primer Gunlock, cat. 7, *32*
    fulminate of mercury ignition, 24,
        116–17n.2
    pellet primers, 35
    percussion cap, *24*, 36, 115–16, 164
    revolver cylinder, Colt's, *37–38*,
        56–57
    wheel locks, *23*, 117n.3

Hanquet, Georges, 152
    Hanquet Holster Pistol, cat. 105, *152*
Harney, William S., Colonel, 2, 55,
    57n.13, 60, 75
Harrison, Joseph, Jr., 208–9, 241
Harrison, Mrs. Joseph, Jr., 205

Hartford County Agricultural Society
    Gold Medal, 1856, cat. 70, *114*
Hartley, William H. B., Major, 81, 187
Hayes, John Coffee, Captain, 74–76
Hayward, Gerald S., *Samuel Colt*, cat.
    160, *240*, 243
Henry VIII, king of England, 117n.3
Henshaw, Richard B., 46–47, 50
Herman, J. J., 153
    Herman Belt Pistol, cat. 106, *153*
holster pistols:
    Hanquet Holster Pistol, cat. 105, *152*
    Wesson & Leavitt Holster Pistol,
        cat. 87, 124, *135*, 136
holster pistols, Colt:
    Colt-Lefaucheux Holster Pistol,
        cat. 76, 116, *121*
    Experimental Holster Pistol, cat. 32,
        86–87
    Experimental "Reduced Weight"
        Holster Pistol, cat. 50, *103*, 104
    Hartford Holster Pistol, 78, 85
    Holster Pistol, cat. 39, *94*, 220, 229,
        231
    New Model Holster Pistol, 105–6,
        108–9
    New Model Holster Pistol, cat. 115,
        161
    New Model Holster Pistol, cat. 116,
        157, *161*, 162
    New Model Holster Pistol with
        "Attachable Breech," cat. 55, *106*,
        162, 166
    Number 5 Holster Pistol, cat. 25, 60,
        63, 64, 73–74
    Prototype Holster Pistol, cat. 28, 4,
        68, 72–73
    Prototype Revolving Holster Pistol,
        cat. 18, *51*, 52
    Prototype New Model Holster
        Pistol, cat. 54, *105*, 106
    U.S. 1847 Holster Pistol, cat. 29, 4,
        60, 68, 73, *74–75*, 76–79, 220, 229,
        231

Hone, Philip, 206
Hoppin, Augustus, *Apache Indians
    Attacking the Train and Party*, 11
Horsley, John Calcott, *Portrait Group
    of Queen Victoria with Her
    Children*, 244
Humboldt, Alexander von, 208
Hunter, Charles G. Alvarado, Captain,
    75, 78
hunting as sport, 11
    and Colt firearms, 60, 98, 102

Institution of Civil Engineers, London:
    Colt lecture to, 6, 20, 26–28, 30–31,
        38, 57, 59, 80, 200
    Colt membership in, 241
    Telford Premium Medal, cat. 127, 110,
        183, *184*
interchangeability and uniformity, 1,
    6
Italy, unification of, and Colt, 110,
    187–88

Jackson, Andrew, president, 2
Japan, and Colt, 25n.14, 195–98
Jarvis, Reverend William, 84n.36,
    242–43
Jarvis, Richard W. H., 81, 127n.32
Jesup, Thomas S., Major General, 2,
    54, 60
Joslin, Milton, 81
    letter from Colt, *19*
J. R. Cooper & Co., 96n.1

Kaiserliche Konigliche Privilegierten
    Machinen Fabrik, Innsbruck, 79,
    83n.25, 124, 134–35
Keller, Charles M., 116, 137, 139
King, Samuel Ward, 64
Korekazu, Ishido Unju
    Katana Blade, cat. 136, 195, *196*, 197
Kossuth, Louis, 183, 185–86
Kunihiko, Takenaka
    Katana Blade, cat. 137, 195, *196*, 197

Landers, George, 194
Lawrence, Samuel, 37–38
Lawton, Pliny, 20, 54, 59, 61–62, 71
Leavitt, Daniel, 124
    Wesson & Leavitt Holster Pistol,
        cat. 87, 124, *135*, 136
Leavitt, Edwin, 125, 200
Lefaucheux, Casimir, 115, 118
Lefaucheux, Eugene, 115–16, 118
    Colt-Lefaucheux Holster Pistol,
        cat. 76, 116, *121*
    Lefaucheux Cartridge Revolver,
        cat. 73, *118*
Lhoist, Charles, 154
    Lhoist Belt Pistol, cat. 107, *154*
Lialen, Alexander, Alexander II Portrait
    Silver Medal, cat. 131, 110, 191, *192*
lithopanes, 232
    Lithopane Portrait of Samuel Colt,
        cat. 153, *232*
    windows at Armsmear with hang-
        ing lithopanes, *232*

Manhattan Fire Arms Manufacturing
    Company, 127n.29
    Manhattan Fire Arms
        Manufacturing Company Belt
        Pistol, cat. 89, *137*
    Manhattan Fire Arms
        Manufacturing Company Belt
        Pistol, cat. 98, *145*
Manton, Thomas, flintlock by, *24*
Marcy, William L., Secretary of War,
    68, 73, 79
Marin le Bourgeoys, 23
Marston, William M., 127n.29
    Marston Pocket Pistol, cat. 90, *138*
Mason, John, 42
Mason, John, Jr., 78
Massachusetts Arms Company, 125–26
    and Colt patent case, 35, 38, 124–25,
        135–36
    Massachusetts Arms Company
        Pocket Pistol, cat. 99, *146*, 147

matchlock firearms:
    cannons, 22–23
    Matchlock Gun, cat. 138, 25n.14, 195,
        197, 198
    Matchlock Gun, cat. 139, 25n.14, 195,
        197, 198
    Matchlock Revolver, cat. 2, *26*, 27
Mathieu, Louis, 115
Maynard, Edward, 146–47
McDonald, Lt. Bedney F., 75–76, 77n.13
    letter to Colt, *75*
McGahey, John:
    and Catlin's Indian Portfolio, 220
    lithographs of Catlin paintings,
        218–20, 224, 231
    See also cats. 147–52
Mecham, Clifford Henry, *Lying in Wait*,
    10
medals and awards to Colt, 110–14,
    183–85, 187–99
    Buehl Box, display case, cat. 59, 110,
        111
    See also cats. 60–71 and 127 *and*
        under exhibitions and societies
Mexican War, 1, 3–4, 68, 185, 244
    See also Texas, Republic of
Milemete, Walter de, 22
Miller, J. D., 65, 68n.3
Miller, James and John, 35
    Miller Patent Percussion Ignition
        Revolving Rifle, cat. 10, *35*
Miller, Linda Colt, 231
mines, electrically detonated, 2–3,
    65–66, 207
    demonstrations of, 3, 67, 70n.27
    Sub-Marine Battery Company, 66
Minié, Claude-Etienne, Captain, 211
    Minié rifle, 211, 227
mining companies, 12
Moore & Baker, 75
Morse, Samuel F. B., 2, 4, 67–68, 79,
    194, 207
Mowry, Sylvester, 12, 14n.45

Navy, U.S.:
    Colt firearms provided for, 43,
        63–64
    tinfoil cartridges provided for, 67
    trials of early Colt revolvers, 42–43,
        51–52
Newbold, Herman LeRoy, 65
New Haven Arms Company, 120
    Henry Rifle, 120
Newton, William E., 93, 123, 131
Nicholas I, czar of Russia, 8–9, 190–92
    Presentation Diamond Ring, 1854,
        cat. 130, *192*, 244
Nicoll, Edward A., 65, 68n.3
North, Henry S., 139
North & Savage, 127n.29
    Savage & North Belt Pistol, cat. 91,
        139

O'Brian, Charles C. C., 48
Olney, James N., 64
Ormsby, Waterman L., 74, 85
Osceola, 2, 14n.4, 206
    Catlin, *Os-ce-ol-à*, *2*, 206–7
Ottoman Empire, and Colt, 79, 81, 183,
    194–95
    See also Crimean War

Pan, J., 46
Parker, William, 41, 48
Patent Arms Manufacturing
    Company, Paterson, 1–2, 42–43,
        53–58
    arms made by, 59–64
    and counterfeiting, 123
    dissolution of, 65–67, 72, 207
    sale of patent rights, 65, *66*, 68n.2
patent infringements, 123–25
    and Massachusetts Arms Company,
        35, 38, 124–25, 135, 146–47
patents, Colt's, 1
    See also Appendix Two
Paterson, N.J., 1–2, 54
Pauley, Samuel Johannes, 115

Pearson, John, 41–43, 46, 48, 50–53, 59,
    200
pepperbox pistols, 38, 96n.1, 200
    Allen & Thurber Pepperbox, cat. 96,
        144
    Bacon Pepperbox, cat. 97, *145*
    Comblain Pepperbox, cat. 77, *121*, 122
pepperbox revolving pistol, Colt,
    38–39, 200
    drawings for, 38, *39*
    wooden model for, *38*
percussion cap firearms, *24*, 36, 115–16,
    164
    Miller Patent Percussion Ignition
        Revolving Rifle, cat. 10, *35*
    Porter Percussion Cap Revolving
        Rifle, cat. 9, *34*
    Richardson Four-Barrel Percussion
        Cap Pistol, cat. 11, *36*
Perry, Matthew C., Commodore, 195,
    197–98
Phenix Armory. *See* Marston,
    William M.
Phillips, Sir Thomas, 208–11, 227
Pimlico factory, London, 1, *6*, 8, 11, 100,
    134, 183–84
pistols, Colt:
    New Model series of pistols, 20, 96,
        105–9
    Sample Patent Verification Pistol,
        cat. 42, *97*
    See also belt pistols, Colt; holster
        pistols, Colt; police pistols, Colt;
        pocket pistols, Colt
Pliers, A., 127n.29, 130
Plomdeur, Nicolas Vivario, 119
Plunger Powder Flask, cat. 45, *99*,
    100
pocket pistols:
    Allen & Wheelock Pocket Pistol, cat.
        88, *136*
    Marston Pocket Pistol, cat. 90, *138*
    Massachusetts Arms Company
        Pocket Pistol, cat. 99, *146*, 147

Remington Beal's Patent Pocket
Pistol, cat. 92, *140*
Tranter Pocket Pistol, cat. 109, *156*
Warner Pocket Pistol, cat. 93, *141*
Warner Pocket Pistol, cat. 100, 124,
147
Whitney Pocket Pistol, cat. 101, *148,*
149
Whitney Pocket Pistol, cat. 102, *149*
pocket pistols, Colt:
Counterfeit Colt Pocket Pistol, cat.
80, *129*
Experimental Pocket Pistol, cat. 33,
88, 89
Experimental Pocket Pistol, cat. 35,
90–91, 94
Experimental "Reduced Weight"
Pocket Pistol, cat. 51, *104*
New Model Pocket Pistol, cat. 41, *96*
New Model Pocket Pistol, cat. 113,
160
New Model Pocket Pistol, cat. 114,
160
Number 1 Pocket Pistol, cat. 23, 54,
61, 62
Old Model Pocket Pistol, cat. 110, *158*
Old Model Pocket Pistol, cat. 111, *159*
Pocket Pistol, cat. 30, 79, *85*
Pocket Pistol, cat. 36, *92,* 96
Prototype Revolving Pocket Pistol,
cat. 17, *50*
Poinsett, Joel R., Secretary of War, 56,
206–7
police pistols, Colt:
New Model Police Pistol, cat. 58, *109*
New Model Police Pistol, cat. 119, *164*
New Model Police Pistol, cat. 120, *165*
New Model Police Pistol, cat. 121, *165*
Prototype New Model Police Pistol,
cat. 57, *108*
Polk, James K., president, 3, 68
Porter, Rufus, 34
Porter Percussion Cap Revolving
Rifle, cat. 9, *34*

Porter, Solomon, 78–80
Powers, Hiram, 40, 241
The Greek Slave, 5, *6,* 208
Pratt and Whitney, 7
Prosser, John, 25n.18
Prussia:
and Colt, 188–90
Colt patents filed in, 1, 97
Prussian Model 1835 Jagerbusche,
cat. 129, *190*

Remington, E., 126, 127n.29
Renotte, D., 120
Renotte Belt Pistol, cat. 108, *155*
revolvers. *See under individual*
firearm types
Rhind, John Massey, 245
Colonel Samuel Colt, cat. 167, *245*
Colt Memorial Statue, 38, 245
Samuel Colt as a Boy, cat. 166,
245
Richardson, James, 36
Richardson Four-Barrel Percussion
Cap Pistol, cat. 11, *36*
rifle, cartridge:
Henry Rifle, 120
rifle muskets, Colt:
Model 1861 Special Rifle Musket, 13,
157
New Model Rifle Musket, cat. 124,
168
New Model Rifle Musket, cat. 125,
169
rifles, revolving:
Cochran Patent Revolving Rifle, cat.
94, *142*
Collier's Patent Flintlock Revolving
Rifle, cat. 5, *30,* 31
Miller Patent Percussion Ignition
Revolving Rifle, cat. 10, *35*
Porter Percussion Cap Revolving
Rifle, cat. 9, *34*
Whittier Patent Revolving Rifle, cat.
95, *143*

rifles, revolving, Colt, 39–40
Experimental Rifle, cat. 34, *89*
New Model Rifle, cat. 43, *98*
New Model Rifle, cat. 44, *99*
New Model Rifle, cat. 122, *166*
New Model Rifle, cat. 123, *167*
Number 1 Rifle, cat. 22, 2, 53–54, *60,*
61
Number 2 Rifle, 54
Number 1 Ring Lever Rifle, 55
Prototype Revolving Rifle, cat. 12,
39–40, *45*
Prototype Revolving Rifle, cat. 13, *46*
Prototype Revolving Rifle, cat. 14, *47*
Prototype Revolving Rifle, cat. 16,
49, 50
Prototype Revolving Rifle, cat. 19, *52*
Prototype Revolving Rifle, cat. 20, *53*
Robb, Mr., 200
Robinson, Elizabeth Hart Jarvis, 211
Robinson, William, 68
Root, Elisha K., 4, 7, 20, 79, 173
and Coltsville factory, 4, 82, 83n.22,
127n.32
death of, 82, 84n.54
and machines for Coltsville factory,
7, 20, 172, 173, 176
patents of, 81, 88, 139, 143 (*see also*
Appendix Two)
Plunger Powder Flask, cat. 45, *99,*
100
pocket pistol design, 88, 95–96, 98
See also cats. 33, 40, 41, 43
Root, Matilda Colt, cousin of Samuel,
79, 83n.23
Ropes, Joseph, 203, 233–39
daguerreotype, showing Colt's
factory, *238*
The Flood of 1854 in Hartford
(drawing and lithog.), 237
View of Hartford to the East, cat.
157, *236,* 238
View of Hartford to the North, cat.
155, *234,* 237–38

View of Hartford to the South, cat.
154, *4, 233,* 237
View of Hartford to the West, cat.
156, *235,* 238
Russia:
and Colt, 189–93
Colt arms provided to, 9, 189, 191
Tula Arsenal, 80, 116, 124, 126n.12, 191
See also Alexander II; Nicholas I

Sainthill, John, 124
Santa Anna, Antonio López de,
General, 3
Sargeant, Henry, 124, 135, 147
Sargeant, Luther P., 97, 122, 218
Schreier, Philip, 75–76
Schuyler, Hartley & Graham, 156, 161,
163
Selden, Dudley, 42–43, 54–57, 66,
68n.2
Seminole Indian War, Second, 1–3
Colt firearms provided for, 2, 54–55,
60, 206
Sepoy Mutiny, 10
Colt firearms provided for, 1, 10, *13*
Seymour, Thomas H., governor of
Connecticut, 79, 191
shotguns, Colt:
New Model Shotgun, cat. 49, *102*
New Model Shotgun, cat. 126, *170*
Prototype Revolving Shotgun, cat.
15, *48,* 49
Siam, and Colt, 198–99
Smith & Wesson, 120
Smyth (companion of Catlin), 211,
227–28
snaphaunce gunlock, 23, 27–28
Snaphaunce Revolving Carbine,
cat. 3, 27, 28–29
Springfield Armory, 1, 4
Staigg, Richard Morrell, *Elizabeth Hart*
Jarvis, cat. 161, *240*
Stevens, Joshua, *146*

Taylor, Zachary, General, president, 3, 75–76
telegraph cable, underwater, 2, 67, 69n.13
  Colt & Robinson Telegraph Company, 68
Telford, Thomas, 184
Terry, Hiram, 125, 200
Texas, Republic of, 3
  Colt firearms provided for, 2–3, 42, 60, 63–65, 68n.1, 185
Tokugawa Yoshinobu, shogun, Japan, 25n.14, 195–98
  See also cats. 136–40
Tranter, William, 156
  Tranter Pocket Pistol, cat. 109, *156*
Truettner, William, 224
Tubac, Ariz., 12
Tuckerman, Henry, 242
Twain, Mark, 7

Ulrich, Conrad, 158n.4
  bust of Samuel Colt, *157*
Universal Society for the Encouragement of Arts and Industry Bronze Medal, 1856, cat. 71, *114*
unknown artist, *View of the Colt Factory from Dutch Point or Little River*, cat. 158, *239*
unknown artist, *View of the Colt Works with Steamboat from the South, Colt Meadows*, cat. 159, *239*
Upshur, Abel P., Secretary of the Navy, 66, 70n.29

Victor Emmanuel II, king of Italy, 187, 188n.7
  Victor Emanuel Portrait Gold Medal, cat. 128, 110, 187, *188*

Wadsworth Atheneum, Hartford, Conn.:
  Elizabeth Colt bequest, 13, 183, 238
  and E. S. Bartholomew, 225n.4, 241
Walker, Jonathon Thomas, 76
Walker, Samuel H., Captain, 3–4, 68, 73–76, 79
Wappenhans, C. F., 97, 122, 188, 232
Warner, James, 127n.29, 147
  Warner Pocket Pistol, cat. 93, *141*
  Warner Pocket Pistol, cat. 100, 124, *147*
Warner, Thomas, 4
Wesson, Daniel B., 124
  Wesson & Leavitt Holster Pistol, cat. 87, 124, *135*, 136
Wesson, Edwin, *146*
Wesson, Stevens & Miller, 135
White, Rollin, 116
Whiting, Samuel, Major, 42–43, 60
Whitney, Eli, 1, 4
Whitney, Eli, Jr., 4, 68, 74–75, 85, 126, 148–49
  Whitney Pocket Pistol, cat. 101, *148*, 149
  Whitney Pocket Pistol, cat. 102, *149*
Whittier, Otis W., 143
  Whittier Patent Revolving Rifle, cat. 95, *143*
willow goods factory, South Meadows, 8, 81
Wilson, Matthew, 203